Linguistic Variation in the Minimalist Framework

Linguistic Variation in the Minimalist Framework

Edited by
M. CARME PICALLO

OXFORD
UNIVERSITY PRESS

OXFORD
UNIVERSITY PRESS

Great Clarendon Street, Oxford, OX2 6DP,
United Kingdom

Oxford University Press is a department of the University of Oxford.
It furthers the University's objective of excellence in research, scholarship,
and education by publishing worldwide. Oxford is a registered trade mark of
Oxford University Press in the UK and in certain other countries

First Edition published in 2014
Impression: 1

Published in the United States of America by Oxford University Press
198 Madison Avenue, New York, NY 10016, United States of America

British Library Cataloguing in Publication Data
Data available

Library of Congress Control Number: 2013953487

ISBN 978-0-19-870289-4

As printed and bound by
CPI Group (UK) Ltd, Croydon, CR0 4YY

Contents

Foreword

With the exception of Chapters 1 and 11, this volume contains a set of essays corresponding to the papers presented by the speakers invited to the workshop *Linguistic Variation in the Minimalist Framework*, held in Barcelona on January 14–15, 2010. At this event, the speakers were asked to present a contribution in response to the following call:

Over the past years, the question of how a hypothesis on optimal design can be harmonized with a theory of parameters has been posed in the generative literature, either implicitly or explicitly. The traditional GB-Principles and Parameters model assumed a highly structured UG architecture, with respect to both principles of grammar as well as the presumable interaction of their parametric setting, with a hypothetical cascade of subsequent effects. The Minimalist Program has changed this perspective, the point at issue being not how much, but how little can be attributed to UG. In fact, our conjecture about the design of what we call narrow syntax naturally leads to the conclusion that UG may have an extraordinarily reduced number of principles. Moreover, one could consider several arguments to the effect that, if design is optimal, then parametric variation in the computational system is practically impossible: it should either belong to the Lexicon (whatever its properties are), or to the (morpho-)phonological component.

The aim of the workshop is to consider the phenomenon of variation under Minimalist premises, both empirically and theoretically. The issue is of paramount importance given the current predicament in the Minimalist framework, which does not offer many conceptual reasons to account for variation, for, although it undoubtedly exists, it does not fit with 'third factor'-like desiderata. In order to do so, the workshop will pay special attention to discussing: (i) the nature of 'principles' and 'parameters' (e.g. What is their format? How can we tease them apart? What is the status of the so-called micro-/macrodistinction?), (ii) the connection between variation, morphology, and the Lexicon, (iii) the impact of parameters in a Minimalist architecture, and (iv) the role played by the interfaces and other principles not specific to the faculty of language.

Thanks to all contributors, and to Julia Steer, commissioning editor at OUP, for their interest in this project from its inception, and for their patience at the various stages of the publication process. Thanks also to two anonymous referees for Oxford University Press for their comments and suggestions. Regretfully, three of the papers read at the conference could not be included in this volume.

For the support provided for this project, many thanks to the linguists at the Centre de Lingüística Teòrica/UAB, in particular O. Borik, J. M. Brucart, A. Fasanella-Seligrat, Á. Gallego, Y. M. Gutiérrez, J. Fernández Sánchez, J. Fortuny, Y. Jeong, A. S. Markova, S. Martínez-Ferreiro, J. McDonald, G. Rigau, and C. Rubio Alcalá. All those who attended the workshop have our gratitude for their interest in participating and for so actively contributing to the discussions.

Funding by the projects HUM2006-13295-C02(-01/-02), FFI2011-29440-C03-03, and 2009 SGR/1079 (Ministerio de Ciencia e Innovación and Generalitat de Catalunya) is also acknowledged.

Notes on contributors

DAVID ADGER is Professor of Linguistics at Queen Mary, University of London. He is author of *Core Syntax* (OUP, 2003), *A Syntax of Substance* (MIT Press, 2013), and *Mirrors and Microparameters,* with D. Harbour and L. Watkins, (CUP, 2009), as well as co-editor of the journal *Syntax* (2007–2013). His publications on syntax and its interfaces with other components of the grammar include articles in journals such as *Linguistic Analysis, Journal of Linguistics, Language, Linguistic Inquiry, Natural Language and Linguistic Theory,* and *International Journal of American Linguistics,* among others. He is also the author of many book chapters in refereed collective volumes.

MARK BAKER is Professor of Linguistics at Rutgers, the State University of New Jersey. He received his PhD in 1985 from MIT, and has also taught at McGill University. He specializes in the syntax and morphology of less-studied languages, seeking to bring together generative-style theorizing and data from fieldwork and typology in a way that deepens and illuminates both. He is the author of four research monographs and one book addressed to a general audience—*The Atoms of Language* (Basic Books, 2001).

SJEF BARBIERS is senior researcher at the Meertens Institute (Amsterdam) and Professor of Variation Linguistics at Utrecht University. His research concentrates on the theory of syntactic variation, in particular syntactic doubling phenomena, and is based on large-scale comparison of the syntax of closely related language varieties. He was the leader of the project Syntactic Atlas of the Dutch Dialects (SAND; 2000–2005) and the project European Dialect Syntax (Edisyn; 2005–2012). He is currently the leader of the project Maps and Grammar on the relation between geographic distribution of linguistic features and the cognitive representation of grammars.

CEDRIC BOECKX is Research Professor at the Catalan Institute for Advanced Studies (ICREA), and a member of the Department of Linguistics at the Universitat de Barcelona. Before coming to Barcelona, he was Associate Professor of Linguistics at Harvard University. He is the author of several books including, among others, *Islands and Chains* (John Benjamins, 2003), *Linguistic Minimalism* (OUP, 2006), *Understanding Minimalist Syntax* (Wiley-Blackwell, 2007), *Bare Syntax* (OUP, 2008), *Language in Cognition* (Wiley-Blackwell, 2009), and *Syntactic Islands* (CUP, 2012). He is also the editor of numerous volumes, the founding co-editor, with Kleanthes K. Grohmann, of the Open Access journal *Biolinguistics,* and the founding editor of the Oxford University Press monograph series 'Oxford Studies in Biolinguistics'.

ANNA CARDINALETTI is Professor of Linguistics at the Ca' Foscari University of Venice. Her research interests include comparative syntax (Italian, Italian dialects, Germanic languages, Italian sign language), language acquisition, the syntactic analysis of translations, and the applications of linguistic theory to language teaching. Her recent publications include, among many others: 'On a (wh-)moved Topic in Italian, compared to Germanic' in *Advances in Comparative Germanic Syntax* (John Benjamins, 2009), 'German and Italian Modal Particles and Clause

Structure' (*Linguistic Review* 2011), and 'On clitic omission and the acquisition of subject clitic pronouns' in *Pronouns and Clitics in Early Language* (2012).

RICARDO ETXEPARE is researcher at the CNRS (France) and head of the lab IKER (UMR5478). His main areas of specialization are semantics, and Basque morphosyntax. His publications include, among many others, 'Root Infinitives: A Comparative Perspective', with K. Grohmann (*Probus* 2003), 'From hearsay evidentiality to samesaying relations' (*Lingua* 2010), and several chapters in the collective volume *A Grammar of Basque* (Mouton de Gruyter, 2003). With U. Etxeberria and M. Uribe-Etxeberria, he has edited *Nouns and Nominalizations in Basque* (John Benjamins, 2012), and he is the co-editor, with Beatriz Fernandez, of the volume *Variation in Datives: A Micro-Comparative Perspective* (OUP, 2013).

ANDERS HOLMBERG is Professor in Theoretical Linguistics at Newcastle University. His research interests are syntactic theory and comparative syntax. He is the author of many papers in peer-reviewed international publications including, among others, 'Is there a little *pro*? Evidence from Finnish' (*Linguistic Inquiry* 2005), 'Parameters in minimalist theory: The case of Scandinavian' (*Theoretical Linguistics* 2010), 'The syntax-morphology relation' (with I. Roberts, *Lingua* 2013), and 'The syntax of answers to negative yes/no questions in English and Swedish (*Lingua* 2013). With T. Biberauer, I. Roberts, and M. Sheehan, he has co-authored the volume *Parametric Variation: Null Subjects in Minimalist Theory* (CUP, 2010).

M. CARME PICALLO is Professor at the Universitat Autònoma de Barcelona and member of the *Centre de Lingüística Teòrica*. Her research interests focus on syntactic theory and syntactic variation.

LUIGI RIZZI is Professor of General Linguistics at the University of Siena. He has been on the faculty of Departments of Linguistics in European and American Universities: in particular, he was Full Professor at the University of Geneva, Associate Professor at MIT (Cambridge, Massachusetts), and Visiting Professor at the École Normale Supérieure (Paris). His research interests include syntactic theory and comparative syntax; in particular, he contributed to the development of the parametric approach to syntactic comparison, to the theory of locality, and to the cartography of syntactic structures. He also works on language acquisition, with particular reference to the development of morphosyntax in the child.

IAN ROBERTS is Professor of Linguistics at the University of Cambridge and a fellow of Downing College, Cambridge. He has worked on historical and comparative syntax in Celtic, Germanic, and Romance languages. He has written several books including, among others, *Syntactic Change: A Minimalist Approach to Grammaticalization*, with A. Roussou (CUP, 2003), *Diachronic Syntax* (OUP, 2007), *Agreement and Head Movement: Clitics, Incorporation, and Defective Goals* (MIT Press, 2010), and *Parametric Variation: Null Subjects in Minimalist Theory*, with T. Biberauer, A. Holmberg, and M. Sheehan (CUP, 2010). He has also edited many volumes, among them, *Syntactic Variation: The Dialects of Italy*, with R. D'Alessandro and A. Ledgeway (CUP, 2010).

MICHAL STARKE is the originator of Nanosyntax, a theory of language which seeks to unify the results of modern syntax, semantics, and morphology into one coherent and minimal whole, deriving many effects from regular syntax and semantics happening *inside* single morphemes. He has developed this approach while at NYU and continued at the University of Tromsø. Starke is also the creator of LingBuzz, the standard archive of linguistic research, and of the EGG summer school which has introduced generations of students to modern linguistics. His publications include, among others, *The Typology of Structural Deficiency: On the Three Grammatical Classes* (with Anna Cardinaletti, 1999), *On the Inexistence of Specifiers and the Nature of Heads* (2004), and 'Nanosyntax: A short primer to a new approach to Language', (2009).

List of abbreviations

1	first person
2	second person
3	third person
a	functional adjective
ABL	ablative
ABS	absolutive
ACC	accusative
Adj	adjective
AFF	affirmative
AGNOML	agentive nominalizer
ALL	allative
AOR	aorist
A-P	articulatory-phonological interface
Appl	applicative
ASP/Asp	aspect
AspP	Aspect Phrase
AUX	auxiliary
AxP	axial part
BN	bounding node
C	complementizer
CDAP	Case Dependence Agreement Parameter
C-I	conceptual-intensional interface
CL	classifier
Cl	clitic
CN	connector
COM	comitative
CP	complementizer phrase
D/Det	determiner
DaD	Doubling and Deletion Hypothesis
DAT	dative
Dem	demonstrative

DITR	ditransitive
DOM	differential object marking
DP	determiner phrase
ECP	Empty Category Principle
EF	edge feature
EPP	Extended Projection Principle
ERG	Ergative
EST	Extended Standard Theory
EXT	aspect extension
F	feature
Fem/FEM	feminine
Fin	finiteness
FL	Faculty of Language
Foc/FOC	focus
FUT	future
FV	final vowel
GB	Government and Binding
GEN	genitive
GER	gerund
HAB	habitual
HPSG	Head-Driven Phrase Structure Grammar
IE	Indo-European
IG	Input Generalization
IMPF	imperfective
INE	inessive
INEL	inellesive
INSTR	instrumental
IO	indirect object
IP	inflectional phrase
K	case
KP	Case Phrase
LF	Logical Form
LFG	Lexical Functional Grammar
LIs	lexical items
LK	linker

LOC	locative
LU	Linguistic Universal
MASC	masculine
Mod	modal
n	functional noun
N	noun
NEG	negation/negative
NIDs	Northern Italian Dialects
NOM	nominative
NOMLZ	nominalized clause
NOMLZ-DAT	dative nominalized clause
NOMLZ-INE	inessive nominalized clause
NP	noun phrase
Num	number
O	object
OBL	oblique
OSV	Object Verb Subject
OV	Object Verb
p	functional preposition
P	preposition
PASS	passive
PAST	past tense
PERF	perfective
PF	Phonological Form
PL/pl	plural
PLD	Primary Linguistic Data
PN	proper noun
Pol/POL	polarity
POSS	possessive
PP	prepositional phrase
P&P/PP	Principles and Parameters
PRES	present
PROG	progressive
PTPL	participle
Q	quantifier

REL	relative
SG/s	singular
SOV	Subject Object Verb
Spec	specifier
Subj	subject
SUBJ	subjunctive
SVO	Subject Verb Object
T	tense
Top	topic
TP	tense phrase
TR	transitive
UG	Universal Grammar
UL	Universal Lexicon
v	functional verb
V	verb
V2	verb second
VO	Verb Object
VP	verb phrase
VSO	Verb Subject Object

1

Introduction: Syntactic variation and Minimalist inquiries

M. CARME PICALLO

1.1 The framework

Among the inquiries that have been at the forefront of the generative research agenda, questions about the limits and possible range of linguistic variation have always been prominent. The Principles and Parameters (PP) theory of the late 1970s proposed a model—known as the Government and Binding (GB) model—to address these issues, making it conceivable that a comprehensive account of such variation might be within reach. The PP (GB) model allowed researchers to set aside earlier accounts of linguistic diversity that took the form of specific rules to characterize syntactic relations between constructions. In the decades that preceded the PP hypothesis, evidence had been accumulating that human languages were subject to a great number of regularities. It also became increasingly clear that the path of language learning had to be directed by general principles of computation, which were identical for all humans. Conditions on rule application were showing slightly different points of variation across languages, a limited diversity that could be expressed by assuming that such conditions could be parameterized (see Rizzi (1978) for one of the earliest attempts). The range and depth of cross-linguistic uniformity that, within the observable variation, had already been unravelled since the 1960s made it finally possible to abandon the idea that sets of ordered grammatical rules, subject to general conditions on their application, could account not only for the intricacy and wealth of linguistic diversity but also for the conditions in which language acquisition could take place. Specific rules on constructions were shown to be decomposable into a structured set of interacting basic operations that obeyed abstract principles. The complexity of former theoretical constructs was sharply diminished while different types of apparently unrelated phenomena could be related—and appeared to be accountable for—under the general scope of this new over-arching theory. The model also allowed researchers to conceive a plausible theory of language acquisition, because the model allows one to disregard the unlikely assumption that children have to undertake the task of making computational decisions based on the format and structure of entire grammars.

The initial PP framework posited a richly structured Universal Grammar (UG)[1] based on a number of fundamental principles open to limited variability (i.e. parameterized principles). The articulated system of principles took the format of a modular 'language organ' and had the goal of sharply restricting the class of attainable grammars while narrowly constraining their form (Chomsky 1981: 4). Linguistic diversity could be framed within the limited choices of values allowed by the principles. Thus, a particular grammar was conceived of as UG with parameters set in specific values, and language acquisition as an operation of parameter setting on the basis of the child's linguistic experience and environmental stimuli.

The PP (GB) model of the general architecture of the language faculty has had an extraordinary impact on synchronic and diachronic comparative syntax and has been able to increase and sharpen our understanding of cross-linguistic uniformity, while allowing finely grained characterizations of variation and change that have achieved significant levels of descriptive and explanatory power. It is more than fair to say that the application of its postulates has deepened the study of grammar in an unprecedented way by unravelling a considerable variety of relations among grammatical constructs that go far beyond the linguistic generalizations that can be arrived at by inductive observation. As the PP hypothesis has been developed and research has progressed, it has been noted that its implementation, as originally conceived of, revealed a number of new methodological and empirical problems, showing that some assumptions that were being adopted did not appear to provide as neat a level of explanation as initially thought. The set of assumed devices of the early PP (GB) model appeared to be too rich in language-tailored theoretical assumptions, which made difficult the task of reaching a comprehensive understanding of how language is organized, learned, and instantiated in the mind/brain (see Boeckx 2006, this volume; Chomsky 1986b; Rizzi this volume; Starke this volume, among many others).

A shift in the conception of a model for UG was proposed in the early 1990s under the expectation that its descriptive and explanatory force would be enhanced if some of the earlier theoretical apparatus was lightened and some of its assumptions subjected

---

[1] *Universal Grammar* (UG) is a technical term to refer to the genetically determined, innate state of the language faculty. This nativist stance has always been assumed in the Generative tradition, driven by epistemological inquiries about, for example, what knowledge of language consists of, or the extent to which this human trait can be comprehended in relation to current lines of research in the biological sciences. Non-nativist approaches claim that languages functionally adapt to communication and cognition and do not address the question of which basic property (or properties) human beings may innately have that could result in those kinds of purported adaptations. UG should not be confused with Linguistic Universals (LUs), a term generally used to refer to cross-linguistic generalizations arrived at by examining a number of languages. LUs are based on a range of typological characteristics expressing tendencies, apparently absolute or merely statistical (see Dryer 1998; Greenberg 1963).

to critical scrutiny (Chomsky 1993b, 1995). The Minimalist conjecture, as this conceptual shift is known, constitutes a programmatic attempt to reformulate some of the foundations of the initial Principles and Parameters approach by exploring whether or not the complexity of the earlier model can be reduced to more elementary yet all-encompassing principles. A more underspecified UG system has been posited, devoid of dispensable empirical or conceptual constructs, and unburdened of much of its previous language-specific premises. Included in the equation of the mechanisms that may comprise the I-language of speakers[2] is the possible role of peripheral devices, general conditions or cognitive functions that, not being specific to the faculty of language, can nevertheless constrain its form and expression (see Berwick et al. 2013; Chomsky 2005; Hauser et al. 2002, among many others).

Clear boundaries between what may correspond to genetic endowment and what corresponds to language-independent general constraints in shaping the properties of language are not easy to come by and, so far, have not been clearly established. A step in this direction has been to consider that the grammatical model itself should only postulate the unavoidable machinery that would allow the language faculty to interact with other systems, the ultimate goal being to better understand the nature of human cognition and how language is integrated in the natural world. Such an approach to language has the consequence that particular grammars can be conceived as variants of one and the same system, while regarding linguistic expressions as grounded on specific and simple computational mechanisms, which are able to provide an infinite array of structured expressions. Each expression is assigned an interpretation at two interfaces: a sensory motor interface connecting the internal syntactic constructs formed by syntactic operations to the physical world, via perception and production—the so-called Phonetic Form/PF—and a conceptual interface—labelled Logical Form/LF—relating such internal constructs to other mental activities (reasoning, presupposing, planning, etc.).[3] The format of computations is assumed to be tight, consisting of two basic devices: (i) a process of Merge that takes two syntactic units to form larger complex units, and (ii) a Search operation that may trigger movement (i.e. a 're-merge' process) of complexes already formed by Merge, under certain strict conditions. Search may also create dependencies among linguistic expressions without

---

[2] The technical notion of *I-language* (where 'I-' stands for individual, internal, and intensional) refers to the state of the language faculty in the mind/brain of any human being, within a theory of UG that proposes a hypothesis of the initial state. This notion is in contraposition to that of *E-language*, the external manifestations of the internal state, studied independently of the properties of the mind/brain (see Chomsky 1986a for discussion on these issues).

[3] Chomsky (2008) points to a necessary asymmetry between the two interface levels. While practically no variation appears to be likely at the conceptual (LF) level, variation is ubiquitous at PF. Pushing the asymmetry much further, Hinzen (2006, 2009) has claimed that the syntactic computational system cannot be distinguished from the system that generates abstract thought.

necessarily involving displacement.[4] Such a lean model for the language faculty dispenses with many grammatical assumptions that were formerly part of the theory.

As noted, the programmatic shift towards assuming an enfeebled UG component contemplates the incidence on the language faculty of constraints of various natures: a very limited number of highly general computational devices (arguably unique to humans and required for syntax) as well as the possible effects of domain-general conditions or mechanisms of a non-linguistic nature that may have a varied origin, some of them shared with other species (Gallistel 2009). This conjecture fits a body of research in language acquisition and development that suggests that at least two complementary sets of mechanisms appear to be at play in the learning process. Some aspects must be acquired through language-specific abilities, while other aspects may result from the incidence of general resources not inherent to the faculty of language but rather recruited or 'recycled' for the task, such as the maturation of neural signals to execute memory, sensory-motor skills, categorial perception, or the ability to perform statistical computations.[5] Questions still to be elucidated in this domain are many, such as what role do developmental constraints play in rendering linguistic calculations efficient and short-timed, or how children are able to 'filter' the avalanche of data they are exposed to in order to implement very selective computations, a task that may be further complicated when the language learner is in a multilingual environment, a common situation in many parts of the world.

The interaction of all these factors, both language-specific and language-external, suggests that the grammatical system is highly malleable and offers ample space for variation, a system therefore now more complex and intricate than what was imagined in the early 1980s. Yet the elasticity allowed by the interaction of the many components that may enter the picture is not limitless, and should be neither unpredictable nor impossible to account for—given that abstract general principles are assumed to be at play. Nonetheless, the role of architectural constraints of very different natures appears to be now more difficult to evaluate, characterize, or empirically verify. Alternative points of view on the role of syntactic computation in shaping the limits of variation are explored in the following chapters. Very broadly speaking, one can say that Part I and Part II of the present volume correspond to contributions following two different research strategies that are being pursued within Minimalist premises. They mostly differ on the issue of whether variation should be strongly or weakly determined by syntactic factors, which amounts to taking a stance on whether or not the theoretical notion of *parameter* can be maintained as has generally been understood under the traditional Principles and Parameters approach. Within these general views,

---

[4] Actually, whether some types of dependencies, such as anaphora resolution or variable binding, may or may not involve movement is a topic under active discussion. For different views on this subject see Boeckx et al. (2010); Hornstein (1999); Kayne (2002); Landau (2000); Reuland (2011), among others.

[5] For a general overview of this body of research see Gervain and Mehler (2010). A specific case study in this domain is also discussed in Rizzi (this volume).

researchers adopt different perspectives on the possible nature or origin of constraints, on their incidence in the linguistic system, and on the assumptions that can be—or should be—adopted to include them within a workable and explanatory model.

1.2 An overview of the volume

1.2.1 *Part I. The parametric approach: The PP revisited view*

The rigour and scope of the syntactic analyses that have emerged under the 'classi-cal' PP (i.e. GB) model have lead a number of researchers to pursue a reformulated approach to this general hypothesis by retaining its insights while trying to overcome the problems we have noted. Within the limits imposed by universal and presum-ably invariant grammatical constraints, proponents of a reformulated PP hypothesis maintain the theoretical notion of *parameter*, while switching the earlier perspective on modular principles to consider variation a phenomenon conducted, and licensed, mainly by properties of the features of functional categories. The rationale within this view is that the characterization of syntactic principles will not offer significant results unless the study of parameters is taken to deeper levels. Several contributions in this section of the volume exemplify the various lines that are being pursued under this (reformulated) parametric approach.

In his contribution, Luigi Rizzi suggests a possible typology of parameters, set up around the basic operations of Merge, Move (i.e. re-merge), and Spell-Out.[6] He claims that the problems observed under the early implementation of the PP hypothesis mainly stemmed from not maintaining a strict conceptual separation between what should be a very restricted *parametric format* and the possible *parameter loci*, which offer ample space for variation. The format of parametric paths is severely limited by binary options instructing whether or not a syntactic head has a feature that directs the system to either apply or not apply any of the basic Merge, Move, or Spell-Out operations. Loci, on the other hand, can be multiple as they manifest specifications of a possibly large functional lexicon such as the one that cartographic models of syntactic structures have proposed.[7] Rizzi's proposal suggests that parameters can be predicted to abound, and it is unlikely that a single one can fully control complex sets of properties, given the number of possible interactions between them. Note that the multiplicity of possibilities is reduced if parametric variation is associated with

---

[6] As noted, *Merge* is an iterative operation that takes two elements and combines them into a set to create a new expression. *Move* is the operation of re-merging a previously merged element in a structure previously formed by Merge. *Spell-Out* can be defined as a cyclic operation that transfers a substructure already formed by Merge to the PF/LF interfaces (see Chomsky 2000, 2004, 2008).

[7] Cartographic approaches to syntactic structures, whose aim is to define a map as complete as possible of architectural configurations, have advanced the conjecture that languages may be strongly uniform in this respect. See Cinque (1999); Cinque and Rizzi (2008); Rizzi (2013a), and references cited therein, for an overview of the aims and goals of this research topic.

unvalued features exclusively, as suggested in Kayne (2008). Many clusters of constructions related by the effects of a single parameter choice defined by a high-level property, as assumed in the earlier PP model, may likely dissolve into descriptive artefacts
under Rizzi's approach. A reticular view of variation emerges in that setting, leading
to the conjecture that every possible parameter is a micro-parameter (Kayne 2005a,
2005b). Apparent macro-parametric differences may turn out to be better accounted
for as arrays of interacting binary choices allowed by the feature properties of syntactic
units, mainly of the functional types.

The focus on the study of micro-parameters is not the only research strategy being
pursued within the general lines of the Principles and Parameters hypothesis. Macro-
parametric, or typological, approaches to language variation have also been proposed.
A macro-parameter can be defined as a single characteristic affecting a large number
of syntactic categories, which result in a clearly salient non-composite property distinguishing clusters of grammars (right/left headedness, topic prominence, or null argument licensing, among other possible ones). Such defining characteristics of groups of
languages may then expand in a cascade-like downward fashion into arrays of options
that are allowed by, and dependent on, a given high-level property. Baker (1996, 2001,
2008a,b) has defended this strategy, offering methodological reasons to pursue this
line of inquiry. In his view, the assessment of properties that appear to define clusters of languages should offer a window for the study of principles of grammar that
delimit possible language types. In his contribution to this volume, Mark Baker does
not address general macro-parametric concerns but focuses on the formalization of
case assignment patterns and on case-licensing variation. He proposes two possible
parametric alternatives on case marking, which depend on whether or not the operation Agree applies and is related to the assignment of case.[8] In some language types,
case appears to be sensitive to a feature relation between a case-bearing item and
a functional head whereas some evidence Baker discusses suggests to him that, in
other grammatical systems, case may be dependent on the characteristics of the Noun
Phrases involved in a single local domain and, possibly, on the tense-aspect of the
clause as well. He notes that mixed procedures to assign case may also be at work in
some languages.

Parametric approaches to account for variation have also been argued for by Anders
Holmberg and Ian Roberts who, with other researchers, have proposed a 'mixed'
model where points of variation may form not unstructured sets, but rather schemata
relative to formal and categorial feature sets and their interactions with general
principles of data analysis (see Biberauer et al. 2013). They consider that a UG-restricted
account for variability, as in the traditional PP (GB) model, can no longer be adopted,

---

[8] *Agree* is a syntactic operation that relates two sets of features in an asymmetric configuration. It assigns
values to the features in one of the sets while deleting those that are uninterpretable for LF purposes
(see, for discussion, Chomsky 1995, 2000, 2001, 2004).

given Minimalist premises. They have suggested, instead, that parametric options or variables, which are made possible by the absence of UG specifications, can form hierarchical clusters of (micro- or macro-)parametric distinctions that define linguistic typologies along a number of dimensions. The proposed schemata give rise to embedded downward expansions (or sub-parameters) guided by markedness considerations (see Biberauer, Roberts, and Sheehan 2013a; Holmberg 2010a; Roberts and Holmberg 2010; Roberts and Roussou 2003). Such a model adapts Chomsky's (1981: 8) suggestion—coached then in terms of parameterized principles—that markedness imposes a preference structure where the value of one parameter is the default one, and—assuming parameters to be binary—the other value is chosen if the evidence leads to that choice. This approach is argued to characterize variation and learning paths by assuming that language learners start at the highest position of the hierarchy and keep testing down if the primary linguistic data is incompatible with a given option. The suggested format is claimed to offer a restricted array of choices, under the claim that the parametric space is reduced if conceived of as organized into descents forming highly structured systems. In their contribution, Anders Holmberg and Ian Roberts pursue that line while arguing against the tenet that all variation is a matter of externalization (Berwick and Chomsky 2011; Boeckx 2010a, 2011, this volume; Sigurðsson 2011b, among others). As variation and parameter hierarchies cannot directly be determined by a minimal UG component, they are claimed to be the result of the combined effects of the language-specific genetic endowment, the nature of the linguistic environment (the triggering experience of the learner), and general cognitive strategies of computation and optimization; that is, a combination of the so-called 'three factors of language design' (Chomsky 2005). Holmberg and Roberts illustrate their claims by offering a case study on yes-no questions in several languages, which shows how the basic operations of Merge and Agree are subject to variation due to the feature content of functional projections.

The considerations discussed raise questions about the extent to which conditions external to the faculty of language could be recycled (or co-opted) by the grammatical system and become part of narrow syntax, as inquired in Kayne (2011).[9] A related question concerns the degree to which the pressure of external conditions of various kinds that are not part of narrow syntax may trigger variation. Such external conditions may feed or bleed the expression of possible variants, and conduct (or block)

---

[9] Kayne (2011) expands the scope of his antisymmetry hypothesis (Kayne 1994) by focusing on restrictions applying to head-initial/head-final order patterns, a readily observable fact of linguistic variation. He entertains a derivational approach to antisymmetry by suggesting that universally left upward derivations may be the result of having incorporated into the syntactic computation the time-sequence factor. Noting that precedence reflects the directionality of the probe-to-goal relation under Search, he suggests that they may interact and that precedence might have been built into the competence system, incorporated into the computation as part of narrow syntax.

possible paths of change in a given grammar. The empirically detailed contributions of Cardinaletti and Etxepare in this volume assess, in part, effects of that sort.

While assuming that parameters are limited by the feature values of the functional lexicon, Anna Cardinaletti discusses two cases of variation involving the syntax of subjects that exemplifies instances of micro-parametric variation between Standard Italian and several Northern Italian dialects. The first case studied by Cardinaletti focuses on verb placement and the relative position of the subject in interrogative sentences. She proposes that verb raising can be associated with different heads in the clausal structure, an operation that, in turn, affects the placement of subjects—of the nominal or pronominal types—in two possible positions. The second case involves subtle differences observed between Standard Italian and Northern Italian dialects with respect to the possibility of licensing a phonologically null subject (i.e. *pro*-drop). Her study shows that the relation between richness of inflection, verbal syncretism in some forms, and the possibility of having null subjects is more complex than initially thought (see also Holmberg 2005, 2010a). The evidence allows Cardinaletti to suggest that the distribution of *pro*-drop in closely related varieties cannot be entirely attributed to syntactic factors or the properties of the Complementizer-Tense field but rather that, in addition to them, syntax-independent principles regulating data processing and computational efficiency appear to interact with the particularities of Italian morphosyntax.

The possible effects of language independent pressures are also addressed in Ricardo Etxepare's contribution. He directs his attention to diachronic changes affecting the distribution and agreement properties of dative arguments in some northern varieties of Basque. He suggests that the changes have been driven by a combination of at least two causes: interface optimization strategies and the reanalysis that some borrowings may trigger for syntactic computation. In the cases he discusses, an environmental condition (language contact between French and North-Eastern Basque) appears to have favoured an adapted reconversion of the properties of some French prepositional elements in the variety of Basque he focuses on. The combination of this external factor and a change involving overt agreement between a dative argument and the verb appears to have triggered the further consequence of having driven the selection of another option: the changes are shown to have word order repercussions, a typical typological parameter.

The characterization and properties of syntactic features, the atoms of computation, is a research line being actively pursued under some of the studies alluded to in this chapter, together with feature bundling, or feature organization, in processes of lexicalization. The nanosyntactic proposal put forward by Michal Starke (2009, this volume) takes a cartographic approach to feature organization (see note 7). He argues that each feature heads a syntactic node that takes a feature-complement, forming a rosary of cross-linguistically invariant binary branching projections of sub-morphemic elements. Starke's goal is to provide a theory of the lexicon able to account for variation, arguing against proposals suggesting that sources of variation can reside in the instruction-providing properties of individual features. The only possible instruction that features should have in the system he proposes is the edge property, which makes them able to merge. In his account, variation can simply be reduced to the complexity of the cartographic territory (i.e. the tree size) that individual lexical units express. There is no need for a morphological post-syntactic component feeding phonology to be posited under this account, since lexical differences are rooted in the spelling out of different zones (i.e. sub-trees) of the featural hierarchy, their syntax mapping directly to phonology.

1.2.2 Part II. Variation without parameters

The combination of internal and external constraints places the questions about why variation exists, where it is located, and how much of it is possible, in large part on considerations about whether variation is considered to be strongly or weakly determined by syntactic factors. If narrow syntax is strongly feature-driven, variation is mainly a property of the syntactic component, as reformulated PP approaches presented in the last section—in any of their specific implementations—maintain. The approach offered in this section's contributions attribute to syntax a much less determinant role in shaping the range of variation, relegating much of it to external conditions.

In his contribution, Cedric Boeckx offers a perspective that differs in important respects from the one adopted by research paths pursuing a PP reformulated approach. He considers that variation is not unrestricted, but it is not parametric either, and explicitly claims that the notion of parameter should be reserved for use as a descriptive label and not used as a theoretical concept.[10] The quest for a biologically sound model of UG must be disconnected from individual languages, which leads Boeckx to conclude that the core properties of the language faculty should be more abstract and farther away from observable grammatical systems than parametric approaches propose. A more restricted hypothesis on the input to syntactic derivations should be entertained that aims to characterize what the minimal toolkit—the basic blocks of computation—could consist of such that iterated Merge may ultimately result in cross-linguistically different lexicalization processes. In other words, one should aim to provide not a theory of the observed variation but rather a theory of its limits, as the question of why variation exists would be akin to asking, say, why there are so many species of arthropods. Variability is simply inevitable when the relation between combinations of abstract linguistic units and the different realizations of their lexical exponents is underspecified.

Factors like frequency or conventionalization in the use of forms probably have an impact on lexical access during production. The role of frequency and

---

[10] See also for discussion on this issue Lohndal and Uriagereka (2010).

conventionalization are specifically addressed in the contributions by Adger (this volume) and Barbiers (this volume). Both studies suggest that the effect of optionality at Spell-Out may play a crucial role in some accounts of linguistic diversity.

David Adger focuses on case studies in which these components appear to affect the choice of a morphological variant, suggesting that parameterization may largely be determined by factors that are not necessarily in the syntax itself. The existence of functionally equivalent exponents for given grammatical items together with the rate at which such items are used may affect the probability that one variant will emerge over another. Under this perspective, it is easy to imagine that probability and frequency, together with the favoured use of certain forms in certain registers, can induce the emergence of parameter settings. For a variety of (sociocultural or other) reasons, children may alter the ratio in which they use a particular variable in a particular context, as compared to the ratio in which it is used by their caretakers. Such frequency ratios may be passed on to the next generation until a point is reached where a distinction between variants may emerge, one being attributed a particular nuance or 'flavour', with the result that acquirers may raise this variable difference to a categorial property.

Sjef Barbiers focuses on the observed variability in the manifestation of doubling phenomena. The case studies he discusses involve instances of particle doubling and cases of predication where two formally identical elements are phonologically realized. Cases of doubling could appear to be a redundancy in the grammatical system and could be said to constitute a violation of good language design. On the contrary, Barbiers claims that doubling phenomena constitute a core property of the syntactic component, which may be necessary to achieve full interpretation. In interaction with deletion, this core property is a source of cross- and inter- linguistic variation because features—or bundles of them—may allow various syntactically and semantically equivalent options for doubled elements at Spell-Out. Externalization may generate multiple morphological choices, which compete not for grammaticality but for use. The observation that some apparently equivalent constructions tend to be more subject to variation than others suggests to Barbiers that frequency in the use of some constructions over others may play a role in the range of dialectal variation. He further suggests that perhaps certain frequency thresholds must be reached in order for a particular variant to be exploitable by sociolinguistic effects or geographical distribution.

Part I

The Parametric Approach: The PP Revisited View

2

On the elements of syntactic variation

LUIGI RIZZI

2.1 Introduction

How to properly characterize syntactic invariance and variation is the core question of theoretical and comparative syntax. The parametric approach introduced a novel technical language to address this issue, which inspired much descriptive and theoretical work in syntax, as well as a new way to study language acquisition. The approach also raised questions and controversy, both within generative grammar and in the larger setting of the study of language as a cognitive capacity. This chapter offers a personal view on the debate raised by the theory of parameters, based on my own research experience and current work, and with no ambition of a systematic coverage of the relevant issues.* In the first part of the chapter, I will briefly describe the origins of the parametric approach, the context in which it was introduced and the impact that the idea had on syntactic and acquisition studies. In the second part, I will discuss the way in which parameters can be integrated in a minimalist grammar, and nourished by the results of cartographic studies. I will address some critical appraisals which question the restrictiveness and deductive richness of the approach, and will try to respond to such critiques. In the third part, I will broaden the picture to the larger debate between 'language faculty' and 'cultural' approaches to language diversity and language acquisition: I will address the question of how the study of acquisition could bear on this conceptual divide, and review some experimental results which are naturally expected within an approach based on a biologically determined language faculty consisting of principles and parameters.

* A preliminary version of this chapter was presented at the Workshop *Linguistic Variation in the Minimalist Framework*. January 14–15, 2010 UAB. Casa de Convalescència. Hospital de Sant Pau. Barcelona, and appeared in STiL—*Studies in Linguistics*, CISCL Working Papers, 4, 2011, University of Siena.

2.2 Origins of the parametric approach

The problem of syntactic variation was explicitly addressed in the early 1970s in the context of the discussion on 'explanatory adequacy'. This is the level of empirical adequacy that is attained by an analysis which comes with a reasonable account of how the property under investigation is acquired by the language learner (Chomsky 1964). The crucial model at the time was the Extended Standard Theory (EST), based on the following notions:

(1) EST Model (i.e. Chomsky 1973, 1976, 1977):
   - Particular grammar: a system of language-specific, construction-specific rules, expressing the adult speaker's linguistic competence.
   - Universal grammar: a grammatical metatheory specifying a broad format for rules and some general principles on rule application.
   - Acquisition: rule induction

Much as in earlier formulations of generative grammar, the theory was really focused on the notion of particular grammars as systems of formal rules specific to a particular language, and construction-specific: language-specific phrase structure rules were assumed for major phrases, as well as construction-related transformational rules like passive, question formation, relative clause formation, etc. Such a rule system would constitute the grammar of English, and similar systems were postulated for Italian, Chinese, etc. Universal Grammar (UG) was thought of as a kind of general metatheory of grammatical properties specifying the format for rules and expressing certain general constraints on rule application such as the A over A principle and, after Ross' (1967) thesis, the island constraints. This system presupposed a particular conception of language acquisition. Acquisition would be rule induction: the child would act like a 'small linguist', unconsciously formulating and testing hypotheses in order to figure out what the rules of her particular grammar were on the basis of the format provided by Universal Grammar and of the empirical evidence presented to her.

There were some obvious problems with this way of looking at things. One critical problem was that a system based on language specific rules was not suitable for comparing languages: one would build a rule system for language A, and then start from scratch and build another rule system for language B, etc. Such rule systems would obviously bear some kind of family resemblance, but the architecture of the model would not favour a clear identification of the primitive properties that remained uniform and of those that varied, a rather frustrating state of affairs. Comparative syntax was not really feasible on that basis because the fundamental invariant and variable elements could not be isolated in a sufficiently transparent manner.[1]

---

[1] Part of the problem was related to the construction-dependent definition of grammatical rules (relative clause formation, passive, etc.). The problem is that constructions are molecular entities, organized structures made of finer atomic ingredients: while variation is overwhelming at the construction level, it is

Another serious problem was that this system could not successfully address the problem of acquisition because ideas were not precise enough about how rule induction could work so that the analyses did not attain the level of 'explanatory adequacy' in the technical sense defined by Chomsky (1964). It was clear at that time that one could hope to successfully address this problem only by radically restricting the options offered by UG, i.e. by making the rule systems among which the child was assumed to choose more and more constrained, in order to make the selection of the 'right' rule system feasible within the limits of time and access to the data that characterize language acquisition. Constraining the expressive power of UG was a major success of EST around the mid 1970s, thus making the goal of reaching explanatory adequacy more feasible. Still, the theory needed an appropriate technical language to address linguistic variation, and a suitable mechanism for the acquisition of language-specific properties.

Things changed around the second half of the 1970s. Recently, I came across the passage in (2) in Chomsky's 'Conditions on Rules of Grammar'; which contains, as far as I can tell, the first mention of the term 'parameter':

(2)   'Even if conditions are language- or rule-particular, there are limits to the possible diversity of grammar. Thus, such conditions can be regarded as parameters that have to be fixed (for the language, or for particular rules, in the worst case), in language learning. . . . It has often been supposed that conditions on application of rules must be quite general, even universal, to be significant, but that need not be the case if establishing a "parametric" condition permits us to reduce substantially the class of possible rules.'

N. Chomsky (1976). 'Conditions on Rules of Grammar', republished in Chomsky (1977: 175).

The passage considers the possibility that certain principles or rules could be parameterized and that could account for certain aspects of variation. The idea was purely abstract at that time but the first concrete instantiation came up a few years later through the study of extraction from wh-islands. It turned out that in some languages it is possible to extract an element from an indirect question as in (3) in Italian, while in other languages this option is marginal or absent (Rizzi 1978, reprinted in Rizzi 1982, chapter 2):

(3)   Ecco un incarico [$_{CP}$ che [$_{IP}$ non so proprio [$_{CP}$a chi [$_{IP}$ potremmo affidare ___]]]]
'Here is a task that I really don't know to whom we could entrust'

only at a finer level of granularity that invariant properties fully emerge. Constructions can be looked at, in current models, as structural molecules consisting of elementary operations such as merge and move, and the featural specifications in the functional lexicon triggering them, the latter specifications being the natural locus of variation in an otherwise invariant system (see section 4 for discussion). An important antecedent to a 'compositional' approach to constructions providing a basis for comparative syntax is to be found in Bach (1965).

If we take the word by word equivalent in other languages, e.g. German (modulo word order and other properties), we obtain a deviant structure (on complexity and variation in English, the language originally compared to Italian, see the discussion in Grimshaw 1986):

(4) *Das ist eine Aufgabe, [$_{CP}$ die [$_{IP}$ ich wirklich nicht weiss [$_{CP}$ wem [$_{IP}$ wir ___ anvertrauen koennten]]]].
     'Here is a task that I really don't know to whom we could entrust'

It seemed too radical to assume that the relevant locality principle deemed to be responsible for (4), Subjacency, would not be operative at all in languages like Italian: somewhat more complex examples showed that Italian is sensitive to locality effects reasonably amenable to Subjacency. For instance, while extraction from an indirect question is normally possible, extraction from an indirect question which in turn is embedded under another indirect question (a double wh-island) is clearly degraded:

(5) *Ecco un incarico [$_{CP}$ che [$_{IP}$ non so proprio [$_{CP}$ a chi [$_{IP}$ si domandino [$_{CP}$ se [$_{IP}$ potremmo affidare ___]]]]]]
     'Here is a task that I really don't know to whom they wonder if we could entrust'

So, the idea was proposed that Subjacency is operative in both language types, banning movement across two bounding nodes; but the set of bounding nodes could be parameterized in a way that would yield the difference: i.e. by taking CP as the clausal bounding node for Italian, and IP for more restrictive languages (in fact, S' and S in the original notation). So that two BN (two occurrences of IP) would be crossed in (4), but only one BN (CP) would be crossed in (3); two CPs would be crossed in the double wh-island (5), thus accounting for the deviance of the structure in Italian.[2]

In retrospect, this turned out to be a rather peripheral kind of variation. Judgements are complex, graded, affected by many factors, difficult to compare across languages,[3] and in fact this kind of variation is not easily amenable to the general format of parameters to be discussed later on. Nevertheless, it was soon realized that this kind of mechanism could be successfully employed to express major, crystal-clear

---

[2] Certain varieties of German are very restrictive on wh-extraction, banning extraction even from embedded declaratives and permitting the expression of questions like 'Who do you think we should meet?' through other techniques, such as 'partial movement' (Felser 2004). The strong restrictions on extraction in such varieties have sometimes been treated in terms of the parametrization of bounding nodes, e.g. in Freidin and Quicoli (1989). Other varieties, spoken e.g. in Southern Germany and Austria, straightforwardly permit extraction from declaratives. More liberal varieties may also marginally permit certain kinds of extractions from wh-islands, showing the asymmetries referred to in the following footnote (Grewendorf 2012).

[3] Relevant factors involve structural and interpretive properties of the extracted element, such as Discourse-linking. In fact, a very stable cross-linguistic pattern emerged from this line of research: the existence of asymmetries between elements at least marginally extractable from indirect questions, and elements which strongly resist extraction. This led to the discovery of weak islands and to much theoretical work to capture the asymmetries. See Szabolcsi (2005) for a general overview.

cross-linguistic differences, and one could entertain the ambitious programme of dealing with the core of cross-linguistic variation in terms of a system of parametric choices; the postulation of a set of language specific rules could thus be disposed with entirely.

Parametric theory introduced a powerful technical language for doing comparative syntax, one which permitted a transparent identification of invariant and variable properties. So it is not surprising that comparative syntax flourished as soon as the new 'principles and parameters' approach was introduced (Chomsky 1981). I believe it would not be difficult for a historian of our field to gather massive evidence in scholarly journals, proceedings of conferences, and book series documenting a rather dramatic shift: in very few years, comparative generative grammar grew from very sparse attempts to a substantial body of scholarly work on dozens or hundreds of languages analysed in a comparative perspective in terms of the parametric model. Moreover, the theory of principles and parameters provided a promising model of the acquisition of syntax *qua* parameter setting, a much more appealing conception than one based on an obscure notion of rule induction (see Hyams (1986) for a proposal which inspired much acquisition research, and Rizzi (2000), Introduction, for a general assessment). Reaching the level of explanatory adequacy thus became a feasible enterprise, even if by no means an obvious one, due to the ambiguity that the primary data may leave open about distinct arrays of parametric values (Gibson and Wexler 1994).

2.3 Some problems with the initial parametric model

A theory of parameters should address the questions of the **format** (what is a possible parameter?) and of the **locus** (where are parameters expressed?) of such entities. Initially, not much theoretical reflection was devoted to the format of parameters, but one clear idea on the locus was explored. As the first concrete proposal on parametrization looked like an option specified on a principle, perhaps that was the locus of parameters in general. So the hypothesis was entertained that parameters would be expressed in the set of UG principles:

(6) Parameters expressed in principles: each UG principle specifies one (or a small number of) parameter(s), a choice point to be fixed on a certain value for the principle to become operative.

This had certain consequences. For instance, it gave a rough estimate of the size of the set of parameters: as there were few principles in the modular structure assumed by the government-binding approach (X-bar theory, Case theory, Theta theory, the theory of binding, the ECP, Subjacency, and a few others), one would expect relatively few parameters. The approach also gave rise to the so-called switchboard metaphor (an image originally due to James Higginbotham): the child is confronted with a little switchboard with principles specifying parameters, and the acquisition process consists essentially in setting the switches on the basis of experience; once this is done, the syntax of the language is acquired.

Not much attention was paid initially to the format of parameters, that is to say, to what a possible parameter is. So that virtually every property was proposed as a potential target of parametrization. In (7), I give a little list of parameters that were identified around the late 1970s or in the early or mid-1980s:

(7)   - the bounding nodes are . . . (Rizzi 1978, Sportiche 1981, . . .)
      - null subjects are licit, (Taraldsen 1978, Rizzi 1982, . . .)
      - *believe* type verbs select an IP (English vs. Romance: Chomsky 1981)
      - P assigns structural/inherent Case (P-stranding, . . . Kayne 1983a)
      - the head precedes/follows the complement
      - V moves to I (Emonds 1978, Pollock 1989)
      - V moves to C (V-2 Germanic: den Besten 1977/1983)
      - N incorporates into V (Baker 1988a)
      - Nominative is assigned under agreement (SVO) or under government (VSO) (Koopman and Sportiche 1991)
      - there are long-distance anaphors (English vs. Icelandic, etc.: Manzini and Wexler 1987)
      - wh-movement is overt or covert . . . (English vs. Chinese, etc.: Huang 1982)
      - the language is non-configurational (Hale 1983)

The list thus includes properties of locality, the licensing of empty elements, selectional properties of special verb classes like *believe*-type epistemic verbs, movement properties of various sorts, linear order, and also very general statements about global properties of a language like Ken Hale's proposal that there is a configurationality parameter. Some languages are configurational, based on hierarchically organized structures, others are non-configurational, involving flat (or flatter) structures, and that affects in a very deep way the whole structure of the language; first and foremost this property is responsible for the freedom in word order.

It became clear pretty soon, already in the early 80s, that this approach had to face serious problems. One was the unnatural character of the list in (7), and then, there were other problems, some of which are indicated in (8):

(8)   Some problems with the model of 'parameters as specifications on principles':
      a. the arbitrary-looking character of the list of the first parameters;
      b. some principles don't seem to require/allow any parametrization;
      c. some parameters do not express global properties of the particular language, but appear to be directly keyed to the presence of particular items in the lexicon of the language;
      d. certain global parameters like non-configurationality can be advantageously reanalysed as conglomerates of more elementary parameters.

Point a. is self-evident on inspection of list (7). As for point b., one can consider, for instance, the hierarchical properties of X-bar theory—always the same across languages, presumably: structures are built by heads projecting and taking complements and specifiers, following a binary branching organization (Kayne 1983a); the core of the Theta Criterion also seems to be exceptionless; e.g. no known language seems to admit structures like '*My friends seem that John likes Mary', '*Bill happens that John left early', leaving a DP in argument position not integrated into a thematic nucleus; certain aspects of the Binding theory, such as the core case of Principle C, appear to be exceptionless: whenever a pronoun c-commands a DP, a referential dependency is uniformly banned, as in 'He thinks that John will win' and its equivalent across languages, modulo linear order and other language-specific peculiarities.

Point c., perhaps more important, is that some parameters appeared to be directly related to the presence of a particular lexical item in the language. Take for instance long-distance anaphora. It is very clear that we cannot say that long-distance anaphora is a global parameter concerning the binding theory in one language because it depends on the presence in the lexicon of that language of a particular item that functions as a long-distance anaphor, like *sig* in Icelandic for instance, which has such type of binding properties. So, clearly, long-distance anaphora is not a global property of binding in a particular language, it is a property of a particular lexical item, and cross-linguistic variation depends on the presence or absence of that particular item in the lexicon of the language.

As for point d., it turned out that certain global parameters like non-configurationality could be advantageously reanalysed as conglomerates of smaller parameters. On the one hand, detailed work on extreme cases of 'non-configurationality' led to the observation of many manifestations of a strictly configurational hierarchical structure: c-command effects, positive response to constituency tests, strict orders in special environments, etc. (see the discussion in section 7). On the other hand, it became progressively clear that languages manifest distinct degrees of 'non-configurational' properties such as freedom of word order, a gradation that is not expected under the view of a single 'all or nothing' configurationality parameter. For instance, it is clear that null subject languages are, in an intuitive sense, less configurational than non-null subject languages because they manifest a higher level of freedom in the position of the overt subject (with subject inversion, subject dislocation, and the like). Scrambling languages are also more non-configurational than non-scrambling languages as they admit a number of alternative orderings (but if the analysis is refined, one particular order generally emerges as the fundamental one, as shown in much detailed work on scrambling in German and Japanese over the years: see Grewendorf and Sternefeld (1991) and references quoted there). There are more surface ordering options in languages in which it is possible to split the DP than in languages which necessarily preserve the DP integrity, a property plausibly related to the nature of the D system (Bošković 2009), etc. So, one observes a gradation of non-configurationality, not a continuum in the technical sense of course, but a number of discrete degrees that are better accounted for in terms of smaller parameters. The extreme cases of this spectrum (say, English and Warlpiri) look like radically different systems, but many intermediate cases are attested, which again suggests the necessity of breaking up a very radical macroparameter into a set of parameters independent from one another and more restricted in scope.

2.4 From 'parameters expressed in principles' to 'parameters in the functional lexicon'

A significant shift with respect to the initial assumption on the locus of parameters, directly suggested by problem (8)c, can be expressed as follows:

(9)   Parameters are specified in the functional lexicon of particular grammars.

This hypothesis was in fact formulated very early on, and is clearly expressed in the following quote taken from Hagit Borer's work:

(10)   'The inventory of inflectional rules and of grammatical formatives in any given
       language is idiosyncratic and learned on the basis of input data. If all interlan-
       guage variation is attributable to that system, the burden of learning is placed
       exactly on that component of grammar for which there is strong evidence of
       learning: the vocabulary and its idiosyncratic properties.'

                                                                    Borer (1984: 29)

This view was widely accepted from its initial formulation, but, in much work in comparative syntax, it coexisted for a long time with the view of 'parameters expressed in principles', and only more recently (9) started being quite generally assumed as the exclusive characterization of the locus of parameters.

I will basically adhere to this conception in the rest of this chapter, but a preliminary caveat is in order. The idea of restricting the expression of parameters to the functional lexicon is clearly motivated by the desire of constraining the parametric space as much as possible. But it is not entirely obvious that all the properties that we want to consider parametric are exclusively associated to functional elements, at least if we assume a simple-minded, traditional view of the functional-contentive divide. Take, for instance, the familiar, sharp difference in syntactic behaviour between the infinitival complements of epistemic verbs like *believe* in English and Romance as in (11) and (12):

(11)   English:
       a. I believe [John to know the answer]
       b. *I believe [PRO to know the answer]
       c. John was believed [___ to know the answer]

(12)   Italian (Romance):
     a. *Credo [(di) [Gianni sapere la risposta]]
     b. Credo [di [PRO sapere la risposta]]
     c. *Gianni era creduto [(di) [___ sapere la risposta]]

In English, *believe* type verbs take infinitival complements which manifest exceptional Case marking, no control, and the possibility of licensing subject to subject raising with the passive voice, as in (11). In Romance, one observes the mirror image of
these properties: no exceptional Case marking, control, and impossibility of raising, as
in (12). Now, these properties seem somehow to be keyed to the selectional properties
of *believe* vs. the equivalent in Romance languages: in classical GB terms, we have a lexical parameter differentiating the categorial selectional properties of epistemic verbs
in Romance (which uniformly select a CP as a clausal complement, with non-finite
C overtly realized as Italian *di*, or null, as in French) and English (which apparently
directly selects an infinitival IP, with the whole CP layer truncated); these seem to
be parametric properties associated to (classes of) lexical verbs, at least if the divide
between lexical and functional verbs is maintained in a traditional form. The fact that
these systematic properties affect whole classes of verbs, rather than single items, suggests a possible analysis consistent with the assumption that the parametrization is
limited to the functional lexicon, as Frédérique Berthelot (p.c.) points out. Thinking
of the decomposition of verbs into v and root components (Harley 2011; Marantz 2013;
Ramchand 2008, and references quoted there), the class could be characterized by
the presence of a specially 'flavoured' v, say v_{epist}, a functional element whose featural specification could be responsible for the c-selectional properties of the complex
v_{epist} + root.[4]

Other problematic cases come to mind, e.g. the cross-linguistically (and language
internally) variable c-selection of DP vs. PP complements (*écouter la radio* vs. *listen to
the radio*; *entrer dans la chamber* vs. *enter the room*), etc., and all the item-particular
cases in which categorial selection seems to depart from the Canonical Structural
Realization of semantic selection (Grimshaw 1979; Pesetsky 1982) in language-specific,
and item-specific ways. A possible solution here may be provided if 'selected' prepo-
sitions are reanalysed as being part of the functional structure associated to the verb
(again, to specially flavoured v items), much as in Kayne (2000a).

In the remainder I will continue to make the assumption that the locus for the
expression of parameters is the functional lexicon, but it is important to bear in mind
the problems just mentioned, which may require a rethinking of the traditional divide
between functional and substantive lexicon (on this issue see Kayne 2005b, Cinque
and Rizzi 2010 for discussion).

---

[4] Things are further complicated by the fact that the class does not behave in a fully homogeneous manner (Postal 1974: *allege* differs somewhat from *believe*, etc.), which may require further refinements of the
decomposition v + root.

2.5 The theory of parameters in current models

What does a parameter look like in current syntactic theorizing? The drastic simpli-fication of the structure of UG assumed by Minimalism makes hypothesis (9) on the locus of parameters particularly congenial to minimalist thinking. Capitalizing on the emphasis put by Minimalism on the elementary ingredients of linguistic computations (Chomsky 1995, 2000), and building on some suggestions in Rizzi (2009a), I would like to propose the following informal characterization:

(13)   A parameter is an **instruction to perform a certain syntactic action** expressed as a feature on an item of the functional lexicon, and made operative when the item enters syntax as a head.

So, when an item is selected from the functional lexicon and enters syntax, it will contain certain formal featural specifications which will instruct syntax by triggering certain syntactic actions, first and foremost Merge itself.

More precisely, I would like to propose the following extremely simple format for parameters, which is accompanied by the specification of the locus:

(14)   **Format:** H has F {yes, no}
        Locus: parameters are specified in the functional lexicon

Where H is an item of the functional lexicon, and F is a morphosyntactic feature. In order to make the system properly restrictive, we must now specify the range of F more precisely. Features express properties of various kinds: of sounds, of meanings, of morphological characteristics, etc. Most of such properties do not affect syntax in any way, so that they are not relevant here. I will make the rather standard assumption that in the set of possible linguistic features there is a well-defined subset of morphosyntac-tic features which are capable of triggering the basic syntactic actions.[5] If we assume

---

[5] Boeckx (this volume) underscores the importance of a proper understanding of how morphosyntactic features are assigned to heads. This is indeed an important issue, not only for the proposed approach to linguistic variation, but for the study of morphosyntax in general. A proper account should provide a char-acterization 1) of what a possible morphosyntactic feature is; 2) of what a possible functional head is; 3) of how a morphosyntactic feature can be associated to a functional head. As for the first question, see Cinque's (2013) discussion on the fact that only a small subset of cognitively relevant features are 'grammaticalized' and used by natural language syntax: here a fruitful integration is possible of much work on grammati-calization pursued within the typological tradition (e.g. Heine and Kuteva 2002), Cinque points out. As for the second question, one guideline of cartographic studies is the assumption that each (interpretable) morphosyntactic feature defines a functional head, both in the inflectional space and in the left periph-ery (Cinque and Rizzi 2010); complex conglomerates of features could thus only be derived syntactically, through head movement; if this guideline is on the right track, the third question on feature assignment to heads becomes trivial. Whether this strong position can be fully upheld (see also much work in Nanosyn-tax, Starke 2009), or it must be weakened in some form, the problem of the assignment of morphosyntactic features to functional heads is clearly and narrowly defined: there is no risk of combinatorial explosion or uncontrolled complexity, and the restrictiveness of the proposed approach to parametrization is ensured by the highly restrictive character of minimalist syntax (see section 6).

a highly restrictive theory of possible syntactic actions, as in minimalist syntax, parametric features will be restricted to the features triggering the elementary operations of Merge, Move, and Spell-out. So, in a nutshell, we have the following basic typology of parameters:

(15)   A typology of parameters:
      1. Merge parameters;
      2. Movement parameters;
      3. Spell-out parameters.

Merge parameters may primarily express cases in which the head's categorial selection (c-selection) does not immediately reflect principles of canonical structural realization (Grimshaw 1979; Pesetsky 1982): e.g. the cases of 'truncated' clausal selection of English epistemic verbs referred to in the previous section. Other cases may involve the permissible cross-linguistic variation in functional hierarchies: a Negative Phrase which can be very high (in the CP zone), or in the high, intermediate, or low IP zone (Zanuttini 1997; Cinque 1999; Moscati 2007); types of Agreement (or agreement-bearing) heads, which can vary significantly from language to language (Haegeman 1992; Cinque 1999; Belletti 2001); single or recursive Topic in the left periphery, presence or absence of a Top position in the lower left periphery (Rizzi 1997; Bianchi and Frascarelli 2010; Haegeman 2012), presence or absence of Focus projections in the CP and/or in the vP periphery specialized to new information or contrast (Rizzi 1997, 2004a; Belletti 2004a, 2009; Cruschina 2006), etc.

Move parameters express the ability that a head has of attracting another head (incorporation), or a phrase to its specifier position (the latter case being uncontroversial and subsuming the former in some approaches). Parametric properties involving the movement of the verb to an inflectional head (Emonds 1978; Pollock 1989; Cinque 1999; Holmberg and Platzack 1995; Roberts and Holmberg 2005; Holmberg and Roberts 2013), and of the inflected verb to the C-system are expressed here, as well as all the parametric variation involved in movement to a Spec position (wh-movement languages vs. wh-*in-situ* languages, etc.); I omit here the further refinements required by the assumption that movement is search + (internal) merge (as in Chomsky 2000), which could lead to distinct possible parametrizations on the search operation, and on internal merge.

The head-complement ordering parameters may be seen as merge parameters in more traditional approaches (merge the complement to the left/right of the head), or as movement parameters in antisymmetric approaches (Kayne 1994: move the complement to a higher Spec position); or else as a spell-out parameter if ordering is a property confined to externalization (Berwick and Chomsky 2008: spell out the complement before/after the head). Whatever the exact nature of this property, the ordering parameters can be seen as particular instances of format (14), with the crucial feature specified on the functional categories assigning the categorial status to lexical roots (i.e. v, n, a, p, etc.), and with the greenbergean tendency to uniformity across categories (Greenberg 1963) expressed grammatically (Biberauer et al. 2008) or extra-grammatically (Newmeyer 2005).

A straightforward spell-out parameter has to do with whether or not a given functional head is pronounced: so, a Top head is pronounced in Gungbe (Aboh 2004), but not in English; and with the licensing of a null specifier: Top has this property in Topic Drop languages (perhaps derivatively from the capacity that a given node may have to constitute the 'root' of the structure: Rizzi 2006a); and some inflectional heads have the capacity to license a null pronominal subject and/or a null pronominal object in some languages (Rizzi 1982, 1986), etc. Various kinds of ellipsis may also be head-driven (Merchant 2001), and functional nouns may have null variants in particular structural environments (Kayne 2000a).

In a sense, this view leads us back to a version of the switchboard model, except that the switches are now expressed in the lexical items: each item of the functional lexicon has a small number of switches, corresponding to the typology in (15); acquiring the syntactic properties of the lexical item amounts to setting its switches on the basis of the linguistic data the learner is confronted with. So, a given head may c-select a particular category (departing from the canonical structural realization of its s-selectional properties), attract another head or a specifier, be spelled out or not, and govern the spell-out properties of its dependents.

2.6 On the numerosity of parameters

The view that the functional lexicon is the locus of parameters affects the expectations on the number of parameters. We will have many more parameters than it was initially assumed if the size of the set of parameters is related to the size of the functional lexicon: clearly, there are many more opportunities for parametric specifications than in the assumption that the locus is the small set of UG principles. Moreover, if cartographic studies are on the right track (Cinque 2002; Belletti 2004b; Rizzi 2004b; Cinque and Rizzi 2010), the functional lexicon is much richer than in more traditional approaches, so the number of potential parametric specifications is even greater.

Such assumptions on the numerosity of parameters, a natural, and in fact virtually inescapable consequence of the conceptual shift reported in section 3 and of the view on the format in (14), are sometimes taken as a kind of *reductio ad absurdum* of the core idea of parametric syntax, the idea that syntactic diversity is amenable to a finite set of binary options open to all languages. If the options offered by the system are so numerous, why continue to call them parameters? Doesn't the term improperly suggest a highly restrictive space of variation? So, the current conception is sometimes seen as an undeclared retreat to the EST conception of grammar as a system of language-specific rules (see, e.g., Newmeyer 2004, 2005): if there are so many possible parameters, how is this conception different from one treating variation through language specific rules?

This argument does not take into account the fundamental distinction between the locus and the format of parameters. Under the current conception, the loci of parameters are quite numerous and diverse, but the format is extremely restrictive, as determined by the restrictiveness of minimalist syntax and its mechanisms. The syntactic actions that a featural specification on a head can trigger are very few, restricted to the very basic and general operations of merge, move, and spell-out: the parametric space is thus radically more restricted than the space of possible language-specific rules of arbitrary complexity in EST models.

We are thus very far from the explosion of possibilities determined by an unconstrained notion of language specific rule system. Therefore, the problem of restrictiveness which hampered the explanatory capacity of pre-parametric models does not arise here. Assimilating current views on variation to EST models thus overlooks the genuine and substantial progress in the identification of the basic ingredients of linguistic computations over more than thirty years of syntactic research.[6]

The assumption we are now making on the size of the set of parameters has other consequences. If the system had only few parameters, sparse and relatively isolated in their consequences, one could expect that a single parameter could control a complex set of properties varying across languages: this was a natural expectation in a system based on few parameters expressed on principles (consider, e.g., Chomsky 1981, Rizzi 1982 on the Null Subject Parameter, which I go back to shortly). On the other hand, many parameters imply many intricate interactions: if parameters are so numerous, and ubiquitously expressed in the functional lexicon, it is very unlikely that a single parameter may fully control complex sets of properties. Again, this is sometimes taken as a major drawback of current parametric models, as evidence that parameters in the current view only have local consequences and a parameter-based system with many parameters has no deductive depth, hence, ultimately it is not a particularly revealing model of language variation. Quite the contrary is true, in my opinion. Parameters undoubtedly express local properties, encoding how a particular item interacts with

---

[6] Of course, the choice of a particular terminology is largely an arbitrary decision. So, one may decide not to use the term 'parameters' for the devices referred to by (14), (15) and call them 'language-particular rules', or the like, without changing in any way the structure of the approach. Nevertheless, using the term 'rule' in connection to such theoretical entities would be misleading. First, because the term 'rule' evokes the complex phrase structure and transformational rules of pre-parametric models, which are quite different from the highly restrictive devices expressed in (14), (15). Second, because the shift of the locus for parameters from UG principles to the functional lexicon took place already around the mid-1980s, is a development largely (if not unanimously) accepted by the scientific community of comparative syntacticians, and major work in comparative syntax over the last quarter of a century has consistently used the parametric terminology to refer to such concepts and tools both in the pre-minimalist and minimalist era (see, e.g., Kayne 2000a, and many contributions in Cinque and Kayne 2005). In the absence of a new conceptual or formal shift, I think it would be misleading to introduce a new terminology, or go back to a highly connotated old terminology.

its immediate structural environment; but the deductive structure of the system is tight and rich, so that even a small difference at a particular point may well have systemic consequences, through the interaction with principles, computational mechanisms, and other parametric choices.

Consider an analogy with the structure of DNA and its role in determining the development, shape, and functioning of the organism. The action of a single gene may be local—perhaps limited to turning on or off another gene, but this local action may have cascading effects with pervasive consequences for the structure of the phenotype. At the same time, it is very unlikely that a single gene may autonomously control a complex isolable component of the body, say the shape and organization of a complex organ: this will be typically done by many interacting genes. This state of affairs could hardly be advocated as pointing to inadequacies of DNA-based models of the shape and growth of the body.

The action of parameters is very local, particularly if the format is something like (14). But then some of these local actions may happen to be performed in structural positions close to certain crucial ganglia or crossroads of the system, hence give rise to systemic repercussions through interactions with other subsystems. For instance, the licensing of a null subject pronoun tightly interacts with various special properties of subjects: the obligatoriness of the subject position in the clausal structure (or the 'EPP' in traditional GB terms), the constraints on subject extraction and ECP effects (two properties that may well be closely related: Rizzi 2006b; Rizzi and Shlonsky 2007), properties of the Case-agreement system, interpretive properties associated with the subject position, etc. So we observe that null subject languages may have automatic and systematic access to null expletives permitting the formal satisfaction of the EPP property, hence endowing the system with more freedom on the surface distribution of the subject, with the options of subject inversion and free subject extraction (no manifestation of that-trace effects).[7] Should we then expect a perfect correlation between such properties? In a system with few sparse parameters, this was a reasonable expectation, but in a system based on (14) we cannot expect such correlations to hold perfectly in general, simply because some other microparametric property of the language may affect the general pattern. For instance, the language might disallow extraction from a tensed clause altogether, hence make the presence of a potential 'skipping' device irrelevant. Analogously, we cannot expect non-Null Subject Languages to systematically manifest that-trace effects because other parametric options (such as a morphologically null version of the French *que→qui* rule) might create an independent skipping device, as presumably happens in the varieties of English not sensitive to that-trace,

---

[7] In the terms of Rizzi and Shlonsky (2007), the null expletive offers a free skipping device from the freezing effects of the Subject Criterion: the expletive formally satisfies the criterion, and the thematic subject can be extracted from a lower position, thus skipping the freezing position). On the null subject parameter as a minimalist system see the discussion in Biberauer et al. (2010a).

Sobin (2002), in Norwegian, Taraldsen (1986), etc. Along similar lines, 'free subject inversion' in Romance null subject languages has been reanalysed as a device permitting focalization of the subject in a low, clause final position (Belletti 2004a). This property capitalizes on the availability of null subjects, but also requires an independent parametric option, the activation of the low focal position. So, certain Bantu null subject languages (Lingala etc.) do not have this option, hence they do not manifest the 'subject inversion' characteristic of Romance null subject languages.

In conclusion, there are very intricate cross-linguistic patterns of interactions which parametric theory can capture and elucidate, but, under current assumptions on the numerosity of parameters, there is no reason to expect that a single parameter could autonomously determine a complex cluster of properties. Of course, complex interactions are harder to fully spell out in a system with many parameters, but the deductive structure and its explanatory potential is intact, it only requires accuracy and ingenuity to be charted.

Fully elucidating the deductive consequences of a system of parametric values may be a difficult enterprise in general, but there are two kinds of privileged situations from which the endeavour is more immediately feasible. One is the case of very close grammatical systems. Consider the abstract situation in which, literally, 'all other things are equal', i.e. in the case of two systems differing for only one parameter, thus avoiding a priori the potential interfering effects of other parametric differences. Of course, such an extreme case never arises in practice; but reasonable approximations may be found through the microcomparison of historically very close grammatical systems, i.e. in the cases provided by dialectological studies. This is the microcomparative perspective, the closest approximation to a controlled experiment in comparative syntax, as Richard Kayne pointed out (see Kayne 2000a, 2013 for discussion).[8]

Another possible way to chart deep deductive consequences of parametric values is to identify a domain which, because of its very nature and properties, is relatively insulated from too many parametric interactions. Consider for instance Cinque's (2005) revisitation of Greenberg's (1963) Universal 20: roughly, when N is final, the only attested order of demonstrative, numeral, and adjective is the one illustrated by English—*These three nice books*—, while when N is in non-final position many orders are possible, some very frequent and some rare. Cinque is able to explain this non-trivial pattern of variation in terms of general properties of syntactic computations interacting with a handful of possible parametric choices: the basic order, determined by selection and scope properties, is Dem Num Adj N; it may be altered by stepwise N movement (as a head, or as a nominal projection) with or without pied-piping, determining different possible orders (with the relative frequency of the order correlated to the complexity of the required pied-piping operation); but if N does not move and

---

[8] An extremely minimal case is the comparison of two registers of the same language, which may also be amenable to a parametric analysis: Haegeman (2013).

remains in final position, there is no other possible source of movement to reshuffle the elements, and the basic order always surfaces. The basic ingredients of Cinque's explanation thus are External Merge (determining the uniform basic ordering) and Internal Merge, or movement, of N. The parametrization on movement (if it takes place, if it involves pied-piping, what kind of pied-piping is involved) determines the observed cross-linguistic variation in the derived order. The unattested orders are simply underivable by such restrictive mechanisms.

Why is it that clear cross-linguistic patterns emerge in the nominal domain, while things are more opaque in the verbal or clausal domain? Presumably, this is due to the fact that the nominal system is relatively insulated, in the sense that major movement processes determining word order in clauses, e.g. movement to express scope-discourse properties of operator scope, focus, topicality, etc., pervasive at the clausal level, typically do not apply (or apply in a reduced form) in the nominal domain, thus excluding important interacting factors which blur the word order picture (but see Cinque 2013 for an attempt to adopt the same logic for the clausal domain).

In conclusion, parametric choices give rise to deep deductive chains with systemic effects. In order to fully capture this deductive structure, blurred in other cases by the numerous interactions with other parametric values, one may conduct microparametric analyses of very close systems, which are differentiated by relatively few parameters (as in much current Romance and Germanic dialectology), or macroparametric analyses of relatively insulated subsystems, like the nominal system. In general, both micro- and macro-comparative dimensions are needed: microparametric studies offer optimal conditions for identifying the irreducible parameters of the system; macroparametric studies (on which see Baker 2001, 2013) allow us not to lose track of the grand picture of language variation.

2.7 Broadening the picture: Language faculty vs. language as culture

The critiques addressed in the previous section target specific aspects of the parametric models, but do not question the general view that cross-linguistic variation is tightly constrained by a dedicated language faculty, part of the biological endowment of our species. This view, though, is not uncontroversial. More radical critical appraisals focusing on language diversity have questioned the existence of a prevailing cross-linguistic invariance: in the words of a contribution which recently attracted much attention (Evans and Levinson 2009), linguistic universals are a 'myth' which does not withstand empirical scrutiny, a view which echoes a dominant analytic tradition in American structuralism (Joos 1957 etc.), later marginalized under the impact of the ideas and discoveries of generative grammar. In this view, language is a cultural product, and virtually no aspect of the structure of language is immune from variability.

I will not address such radical critiques of the programme of generative grammar here (see many short responses to Evans and Levinson 2009 in the same issue of *Brain and Behavioral Sciences*; I have expressed my own view in more detail in Rizzi 2010, and many other responses are available in the current literature). I will simply hint at aspects of this debate which are directly related to the previous discussion of parameters, and, in the final part, I will discuss some acquisition research which bears on the general issue.

Granting the importance of carefully studying language diversity, I believe that there are serious reasons to doubt the validity of the conclusion that, in Joos' (1957) words 'languages can vary without assignable limits . . .'. It simply is not the case that 'anything goes' in cross-linguistic variation. The general architecture of language is constant, there is a structured system of strict language universals (e.g. the ubiquitous role of hierarchical structure illustrated by the pervasive c-command effects that are observed in language after language), and also in domains in which variation seems to be the dominant factor, precise patterns of exclusion emerge (as in the Greenberg-Cinque discussion of word order properties already referred to). Clearly, though, abstract properties may take very different superficial forms because of the complex interactions between parametric choices, as we have seen, so that the underlying uniformity may need a lot of detailed analytical work to be detected. Consider, for instance, the issue of non-configurationality, already hinted at in section 3. Languages with very free word order (literary Latin, Australian Aboriginal languages, etc.) seem to defy configurational laws, not respect hierarchical constituent structure, and, in short, use representations different from Merge-based hierarchical structures. In fact, for some time the hypothesis was seriously entertained and explored, also within mainstream generative grammar, that such languages may differ from configurational languages in substantive ways. Later, careful analytic work stemming from the same tradition on extreme cases of 'free word order' languages, such as the Australian language Warlpiri, showed the pervasive presence of configurational effects such as the role of c-command, symptoms of hierarchically articulated constituent structure, rigid word order in certain environments, and various exclusion patterns: we are far from an 'anything goes' situation in the syntax of such languages and we find clear signs of a configurational organization, blurred in part on the surface by certain language specific properties (Legate 2002, 2008). Analogously, properties of classical free word order languages turned out to be analysable with revealing results through the configurational tools developed for unquestionably configurational languages (e.g. Salvi 2005, Dankaert 2012 on Latin using the tools introduced for the study of Romance left periphery in Rizzi 1997 etc.). In conclusion, assessing the configurational (or other architectural) properties of language requires much detailed analytical work on individual languages: the simple scrutiny of superficial properties will not allow us to reach firm comparative conclusions, such as the proper assessment of hypotheses on the universal structure of language. As soon as a detailed analytical work is undertaken, much as in the cases just quoted, a rich invariant structure always emerges from the variability of surface arrangements. This is true for configurationality and other word order properties, for properties of binding and case-agreement systems, for movement and locality, etc. (see many contributions in Rizzi 2013b for relevant discussion of these points).

2.8 On the early acquisition of abstract grammatical properties

Very different kinds of evidence can be brought to bear on the broad divide between 'language faculty' and 'language as culture' approaches. In this final part, I would like to briefly review some evidence coming from the study of language acquisition. The timing of the acquisition process matters here. The 'language faculty' approach naturally leads to the expectation of a fast acquisition of cross-linguistically variable properties. In this approach, the problem that the language learner is confronted with is very well defined and narrowly circumscribed: as far as syntax is concerned, it is a matter of fixing the parameters of (the functional lexicon of) the language, and the learner is guided by task-specific cognitive resources which allow her to quickly converge to the correct parametric values. The 'language as culture' approach, all other things being equal, leads to the expectation of a slower acquisition process, basically in line with other aspects of the development of general problem-solving capacities and the acquisition of cultural skills. So, one would expect a certain degree of correspondence between the acquisition of variable properties of language and the acquisition of culturally-driven technical abilities of various sorts.

Let us address the question of the time course in connection with the acquisition of a fundamental cross-linguistically variable property: word order, and in particular the VO vs. OV order of the language. How early is this property acquired by the language learner? Corpus studies are unambiguous on this point: already in the first syntactically relevant productions, in the two-word stage, the child conforms to the target order: so the two-year-old learning English will typically say 'eat cake', and the two-year-old learning Japanese will say 'cake eat' (modulo morphophonological and lexical choices).

This is acknowledged by everyone, but the interpretations given by the two camps are very different. The language faculty approach typically assumes that the child has from very early on the abstract grammatical knowledge 'my language is VO', 'my language is OV', as a consequence of the early fixation of an ordering parameter (whether this is a merge, move, or spell-out parameter, as per our previous discussion, is not crucial here).

On the contrary, the 'language as culture' approach, represented here by the 'constructivist' or 'item-based' acquisition hypothesis proposed by Michael Tomasello and his associates in a number of papers (Tomasello 2000, 2003; Akhtar and Tomasello 1997; Tomasello et al. 1997), assumes that the child initially memorizes fragments she hears, and stores in memory individual items with the associated syntactic environments. There is no abstract generalization initially, there is only memorization of fragments, individual items with the syntactic structures in which they are found. The hypothesis is that for a while the child stores this item-based knowledge and retrieves and reproduces it in her early productions; only much later on does the child generalize the item-based knowledge to abstract and general grammatical statements like 'my language is OV (or VO)' through a domain-general capacity for analogical generalization.

So, both approaches are consistent with the corpus data; but they lead to clearly different expectations about the child's early capacity to generalize her knowledge to new items and structures: the parametric approach leads one to expect that there should be an immediate generalization to a novel item because the relevant knowledge is abstract from early on; on the contrary, the 'constructivist' approach expects that the young child should not be able to generalize because her initial knowledge is concrete, item-based (she hears and memorizes 'eat apples', and obediently reproduces 'eat apples'), hence initially she has no basis to generalize to new items.[9]

2.9 Some experimental evidence

Franck et al. (2013) recently provided experimental evidence bearing on this question. In order to test the abstract grammatical knowledge of 19-month-old infants exposed to French, these authors combined three ingredients:

1. The preferential looking paradigm: the infant sits on her caretaker's lap in front of two computer screens, and hears a sentence. The two screens reproduce short videos with two distinct actions, one matching and the other not matching the uttered sentence. The child looks preferentially (for a longer time) at the screen with the matching video (see Naigles 1990; Gertner et al. 2006; Hirsh-Pasek and Golinkoff 1996 for detailed discussion of this method).
2. The 'weird word order' paradigm: the uttered sentence is sometimes an NP V NP sequence (grammatical in French), and sometimes an ungrammatical NP NP V sequence (this method is borrowed from production experiments reported in Abbot-Smith et al. 2001; Akhtar and Tomasello 1997; Matthews et al. 2005, 2007, and adapted to comprehension).

---

[9] To be fair, neither approach is structured enough to make a very precise prediction on the time course of the acquisition of such abstract properties; nevertheless, within the parametric approach the straightforward interpretation of the target-consistent ordering in the two-word stage (hence before the second birthday) is that the relevant parameter has already been correctly fixed at this point (much as in Wexler's 'very early parameter setting', see Wexler 1998), while constructivist approaches seem to assume that abstract knowledge will arise through analogical generalization only well after the third birthday (consider, e.g., the fact that Matthews et al., on which see later in the chapter, compare a younger group around age 2.9 and an older group around age 4 in view of showing the abstract character of linguistic knowledge in the second group). So, even though the two approaches do not generate sharp predictions about the exact time course of the acquisition of abstract knowledge, they clearly lead to quite distinct expectations about the earlier or later character of such acquisition.

3. Pseudo-verbs are used, morphophonologically possible items which are not listed in the French lexicon, so that we can be sure that the child has never heard them in her previous experience.

Concretely, there are two conditions: grammatical (NP V NP) and ungrammatical (NP NP V) sentence. In the grammatical condition the infant hears a sentence like *Le lion dase le chien* 'the lion dases the dog', *daser* a possible but non-existent French verb. One of the videos reproduces a transitive action (for instance, the lion puts a crown on the dog's head), and the other video a reflexive action (each one of the characters puts a crown on his own head). In the ungrammatical condition the infant hears an ungrammatical sentence like *L' âne le chat poune* 'the donkey the cat pounes', a sentence violating the SVO order of French, with *pouner* a possible but non-existent French verb. Attention is paid to assign a natural-sounding prosody to the ungrammatical sentence, so that no obvious prosodic cue will mark it as deviant. As before, one of the videos reproduces a transitive action (for instance, the donkey puts a crown on the cat's head), and the other video a reflexive action (each one of the characters puts a crown on his own head).

The two approaches make clearly distinct predictions here. The parametric approach predicts a preference for the transitive video in the grammatical NP V NP condition, and no preference in the ungrammatical condition: in this approach it is natural to expect that at 19 months, or 1.7 years, around or right before the onset of the two-word stage, the infant will already have the abstract knowledge 'my language is SVO'. So, as soon as she hears a sentence like *Le lion dase le chien*, even if she has never heard that particular verb, she will immediately recognize a transitive NP V NP, or 'agent – action – patient' sentence scheme and will look preferentially at the transitive video. On the other hand, the ungrammatical sentence *L' âne le chat poune* will not evoke any abstract grammatical scheme in French, so the sentence will not offer any guidance to the child to preferentially look at one or at the other video.

An item-based approach assuming no abstract grammatical knowledge in young children, on the other hand, does not predict any preference in either case. As in this approach the infant does not have any general grammatical scheme to build on, but only item-specific knowledge, she would have no good reason to prefer the transitive action only with the grammatical NP V NP order: both in the grammatical and ungrammatical order she has not previously heard the occurring verb, hence in neither case does she have previous item-based knowledge to build on. So, no preference for a particular video specifically linked to the grammatical word order is expected in either case.[10]

---

[10] More precisely, the item-based approach would lead us to expect no preference *specifically linked to the grammatical word order*: it would be consistent with a grammatically unselective preference that children might have, e.g. a general preference for transitive videos over reflexive videos, irrespective of the grammatical or ungrammatical character of the sentence which is uttered. So, crucial evidence to disentangle the two approaches can be provided by the existence of a contrast (or lack thereof) between the grammatical and ungrammatical condition.

The experimental evidence clearly is in line with the expectations of the 'abstract grammar' approach: it is reported in Franck et al. (2013) that infants look at the transitive video significantly more than at the reflexive video in the grammatical NP V NP condition, while they show no preference between the two videos in the ungrammatical NP NP V condition (hence one cannot say that they prefer to look at transitive actions in general, regardless of the sentence they hear). So, the child acquiring French at 19 months appears to have abstract knowledge of the type 'my language is SVO'.[11]

There is an apparent contradiction between these results and the conclusion reached, e.g. by Matthews et al. (2005, 2007) on the basis of production experiments. They elicited the repetition of sentences with pseudo-verbs which had been presented both in grammatical and weird word order; their claim is that older children (at 4 years) correct more weird word order sentences than younger children (at 2 years 9 months), who reproduce sentences in the weird word order more frequently than the older group. These authors thus claim that their production study supports the constructivist position: younger children at age 2.9 only have an item-based knowledge, which does not allow them to correct ungrammatical orders on the basis of an abstract grammatical scheme. This result clearly conflicts with our result in comprehension, which shows abstract grammatical knowledge already at age of 1.7. Should one postulate a major divide between production and comprehension systems with respect to the availability of abstract grammatical properties?

Franck et al. (2011) have redone the Matthews et al. (2005, 2007) experiments by introducing certain modifications in the methodology, in particular by improving the communicative situation; they found that younger children acquiring French at 2.11 were not distinguishable from older children at 3.11 in the repetition of grammatical and weird word order sentences, showing as much abstract grammatical knowledge as the older group: both groups were found to match the grammatical word order significantly more often than ungrammatical word orders, also with pseudo-verbs they had not heard before. Moreover, both younger and older children's productions gave clear indications of morphosyntactic productivity in the grammatical NP V NP order, sometimes modifying the input to produce sentences like *La vache, elle a dasé le chien* 'the cow, it has dased the dog' with pronominalization, dislocation, the introduction of compound tenses, etc. In contrast, children in both groups failed to manifest any sign of productivity in the rare ungrammatical NP NP V sentences they produced: no compound tenses, no special inflectional properties on the verb, no pronouns, dislocations, or other manipulations in their ungrammatical NP NP V sentences, which were systematically produced with full NPs and verbs in the present tense exactly as they appeared in the input. Both groups of children therefore used their productive grammatical knowledge when they produced sentences in the grammatical order, while

---

[11] On the possible prosodic cues or statistical analysis which may guide the child to fix this fundamental word order property very early on, see Christophe et al. (2003); Gervain et al. (2008).

they just repeated the input string in the (rare) occasions in which they reproduced the ungrammatical NP NP V order. These authors therefore conclude that the younger group also shows grammatical knowledge of abstract word order properties: there is no basis for assuming an asymmetry between the two groups, nor between production and comprehension (except that, of course, production could not be tested in a reliable manner with children as young as 1.7, as they are just entering, or about to enter, the two-word stage). Franck et al. (2011) then conclude that when production is tested in plausible communicative conditions, children of the younger group show no less abstract knowledge than children of the older group. This is in line with the result of the comprehension experiment, and is what the language faculty approach would lead us to expect.[12]

2.10 Conclusions

Parameters of syntactic variation can be thought of as morphosyntactic features expressed on the items of the functional lexicon and acting as instructions for the basic syntactic actions: Merge, Move, Spell-out. Parameters are numerous because their locus of expression, the functional lexicon, is rich; nevertheless, the space of variation is severely constrained because the possible syntactic actions in a minimalist model are so limited. Combining the central idea of the principles and parameters approach with minimalist syntax thus yields a coherent, restrictive system for the study of language variation. The numerosity of parameters makes it unlikely that a single parameter may be able to fully control a complex cluster of properties, because there will inevitably be too many interactions with other parametric values (with the possible exception of Kayne's 'controlled experiments' in comparative syntax, the privileged cases arising from the micro-comparative analysis of very close varieties, and approximating the ideal of two systems differing for a single parametric value; and of the macro-comparative study of structural systems which are sufficiently insulated to limit parametric interactions). The complexity of the interactions does not mean that the system has a limited deductive structure and that each parameter only has local consequences. Quite the contrary is true: each parameter will enter into complex deductive interactions with principles and other parametric values, and disentangling and reassembling the elementary components of such interactions will continue to shed light on the observed, complex patterns of variation.

In the last part of the chapter, I have broadened the perspective to the general issue of the nature of cross-linguistic variation, and the plausibility of assuming dedicated

---

[12] See also Franck and Lassotta's (2012) detailed critical discussion of the methods, results, and argumentation of papers using the Weird Word Order paradigm in production (Akhtar 1999; Matthews et al. 2005, 2007, etc.). Under Franck and Lassotta's reanalysis, the data presented in these papers actually support the hypothesis that children have abstract grammatical knowledge of word order from early on.

cognitive resources constraining linguistic variability. Relevant evidence here can be gathered from comparative syntax, but also from the study of the timing and characteristics of language acquisition (and, in principle, from many other sources: pathology, brain imaging, etc.). I have focused on one particular case study: the rapidity of the acquisition of language-particular word order properties in the form of abstract and general grammatical knowledge is unexpected under views looking at language as a cultural object, with the acquisition of variable properties solely guided by general intelligence and general problem-solving skills, much as the acquisition of a simple technology of some kind; the evidence just reviewed is more readily consistent with a view in which the child is guided very early on to have certain expectations about structural properties of the language, and to quickly make well-defined choices of a rather abstract character, as in parametric models.

3

Types of cross-linguistic variation in case assignment

MARK BAKER

3.1 Introduction

In this chapter, I do not address in direct top-down fashion issues about what range of hypotheses concerning cross-linguistic variation are or aren't Minimalist, or questions about micro- vs. macro-parameters, or about the role of the lexicon versus syntactic principles in cross-linguistic variation.[1] It is not that I'm above talking about such things or that I don't have opinions about them; they are simply not what I want to focus on here. Rather I want to offer something more along the lines of addressing what Cedric Boeckx calls Greenberg's problem. I agree with him that Greenberg's problem is quite distinct from Plato's problem, but I think that it's also interesting, and we should be trying to come up with solutions for it—although not perhaps in exactly the way Greenberg might have foreseen.

In particular, I focus on a specific issue in syntactic variation, namely the theory of morphological case, especially overt structural case. I imagine that if there is such a thing as abstract Case (i.e. NP licensing), then that is systematically related, but that topic is not my focus here. In presenting this research, I also want to illustrate a style of relating to the material that I want to recommend, what I've been calling Formal Generative Typology (Baker 2010). This involves committing to two kinds of ideas which I think are both attractive. The first is the generativist vision of accepting a degree of abstractness in our descriptions of languages, and looking at how insight into empirical details can emerge from a precise formalization of the patterns. The second is the idea from Greenbergian typology that it can be valuable to compare radically

---

[1] This work was first presented in January 2010 at a workshop in Barcelona, and has been only lightly revised since. The exposition retains to some extent an informal oral style. Furthermore, in my work since then some of these ideas have been (not abandoned, but) developed further in ways that I cannot do justice to here. See Baker (in progress) for some more recent developments.

different linguistic systems. Here I try to combine these two threads within case theory, to see what kinds of phenomena might be out there, and to pose in a preliminary way the question of what might be the most interesting proposals to make about the variations that we find. Once that spadework has been done, we can speculate about whether the results are truly Minimalist or not.

This chapter breaks down into two large parts. In the first part (sections 3.2 and 3.3), I review two studies of mine that have bearing on how one might think about cross-linguistic variation in morphological case. In the second part (sections 3.4–3.6), I give some first thoughts about what might emerge if we use those studies as wedges into the more general issue of cross-linguistic variation in this area. The second part is somewhat preliminary, but hopefully we will feel like we have learned something by approaching the topic in this way.

3.2 Implications of a typology of agreement for case assignment

One seed of a new approach to case comes from my formal generative typology of agreement systems in Baker (2008a). It emerged as a result of that study that languages differ significantly in how agreement and case relate to each other. In Chomsky's (2000, 2001) vision, agreement and case are two sides of the same coin (he credits precedents to this idea, notably George and Kornfilt 1981). And indeed, there is a tight relationship between subject agreement and nominative case in many Indo-European (IE) languages, where the two track each other reasonably closely. It is reasonable, then, to conclude that these are two morphological realizations of a single abstract agreement relationship (Agree). One result of my (2008a) study was that this holds true for a large class of languages, but it is parameterized in some sense; it is a point of cross-linguistic variation. Indeed, I argued that this was a macroparameter: it is variation in the syntactic operation of Agree, not in the feature content of individual functional heads involved in agreement.

The kind of data that first led me to think along these lines involved differences between Niger-Congo languages and IE languages. Languages from both families have subject agreement. When one says something like 'the women chopped wood with an axe', the finite verb 'chop' agrees with the subject 'women' in both a Bantu language like Kinande (see (1)) and an IE language like Catalan.[2]

---

[2] Glosses used in the abbreviations include: ABS, absolutive; ACC, accusative; AFF, affirmative; AGNOML, agentive nominalizer; AOR, aorist; ASP, aspect; AUX, auxiliary; CN, connector; COM, comitative; DAT, dative; ERG, ergative; EXT, aspect extension; F, feminine; FUT, future; FV, final vowel; GEN, genitive; IMPF, imperfective; INEL, inellesive; INSTR, instrumental; LK, linker; LOC, locative; M, masculine; NEG, negative; NOM, nominative; OBL, oblique; PASS, passive; PAST, past tense; PERF, perfective; PL, plural; PN, proper noun; PRES, present; PTPL, participle; SG, singular; T, tense. Agreement affixes are glossed with a triple symbol, starting with a number indicating the person (1, 2, or 3), a lower-case letter indicating number (s or p), and an upper-case letter expressing the grammatical function/case (S, O, A, E, P) of the agreed-with nominal. Other numbers in the glosses of Kinande examples indicate noun classes (gender-number combinations).

(1) Abakali   mo-ba-seny-ire   olukwi (lw'-omo-mbasa).
     women.2 AFF-2S/T-chop-EXT wood.11 LK11-LOC.18-axe.9
     'The woman chopped wood (with an axe).'   (Kinande)

However, when one looks more closely one finds that there are two senses of the term 'subject' in play here. In one set of languages, the crucial notion of subject is Spec,TP. That seems to be what the finite verb agrees with in most Bantu languages. In contrast, in IE languages what we call subject agreement is really agreement with the thematic subject, or (better) the NP that gets the nominative case. One is a case-oriented principle, the other is a position-oriented principle. One can see the difference in inversion constructions, like those in (2) and (3):

(2) Oko-mesa   kw-a-hir-aw-a   ehilanga.   (Locative Inversion)
     LOC.17-table 17S-T-put-PASS-FV peanuts.19   (Kinande)
     'On the table were put peanuts.'

(3) a. Olukwi si-lu-li-seny-a   bakali   (omo-mbasa).   (Kinande)
        wood.11 NEG-11S-PRES-chop-FV women.2 LOC.18-axe.9
        'WOMEN do not chop wood (with an axe).'   (Object fronting)

     b. (I believe that) no good things does/*do he withhold from those who walk uprightly.

(2) is a locative inversion sentence. Here you didn't put the highest argument, or the thing with nominative case, in the Spec,TP position, so the two senses of subject come apart. In English and in most other IE languages, the verb agrees with 'peanuts' in the inversion sentence. 'Peanuts' is in nominative case, it's arguably the highest argument, and that's what you agree with. In contrast, in the Bantu languages the verb agrees with the fronted element 'on the table' (see also Bresnan and Kanerva 1989). You also see something similar in languages which allow you to move the object to Spec,TP position. This is less common in both language families, but it happens in some. In Kinande, you can put the thematic object 'wood' in the Spec,TP position to get 3a. In this situation, the finite verb in Kinande agrees with 'wood', not with 'women'. There are arguably some IE languages in which a similar kind of object fronting happens, such as Yiddish and Icelandic, as well as negative inversion in English. The exact details of these fronting processes may not be identical in the various languages. But the crucial thing is that in any such inversion structures in IE the verb still agrees with the nominative subject, as in 3b: 'No good things' is plural, but 'does' is singular, matching the postverbal NP 'he' instead. So there is a different agreement pattern in IE as opposed to Bantu. This led me to propose (4) as a statement of the relevant parameter:

(4) *The Case Dependence of Agreement Parameter (CDAP):* (Baker 2008a)
     F agrees with DP/NP only if F values the case feature of DP/NP (or vice versa).
     (No: most Niger Congo languages; Yes: most IE languages)

Saying that a functional head F agrees with a noun phrase only if F values the case feature of that noun phrase is a statement that comes out of Chomsky's Agree theory. I concur that it is a property of grammar, but claim it is a parameterized property, not a universal one. It holds of some linguistic systems and not others.

I went on to claim that the CDAP in (4) is a macroparameter in two senses. First, it seems to hold of all functional heads in the relevant languages, not just one particular functional head (see Baker 2008a: ch. 5).[3] If this is right, then it is properly thought of as a grammatical property of the grammar as a whole, not to be reduced to the feature specifications assigned to particular functional items in the lexicon. As such, it goes beyond the most widespread and constrained way of thinking about parametric variation within the Minimalist Program. (See Baker (2008b) for more general discussion of this issue.) Second, (4) is macroparametric in that it has other kinds of grammatical consequences that you might not have noticed at first. Another consequence concerns how agreement happens in constructions consisting of a main verb together with one or more auxiliary verb. Here too there is difference between Niger-Congo languages and IE languages, shown in (5) versus (6):

(5) a. Abakali *ba*-bya *ba*-ka-gul-a   amatunda.   (Kinande)
        women.2 2S-were 2S-PTPL-buy-FV fruits.6
        'The women were buying fruits.'

     b. *Tú*-lwé   *tú*-ká-ly-a.
        1pS-leave 1pS-PTPL-eat-FV
        'We were eating.'

(6) a. *John is comes.   (English)

     b. <u>Nosotros</u> <u>estamos</u> <u>leyendo</u> el   libro. (*leyendemos)   (Spanish)
        we   are(1pP) reading the book (reading-1pS)

Bantu languages often allow more than one verb to agree fully with the same NP in these constructions. For example, in (5a) you have the same number-gender agreement *ba*- on both 'were' and 'buy'. This happens even with person agreement, as shown in (5b), where the first person plural prefix *tu*- appears on both verbs. You don't find this kind of full multiple agreement in IE, as shown in (6). Typically in IE you have agreement on the auxiliary, but not on the main verb. Depending on the language, you

---

[3] Luigi Rizzi points out that person agreement in Italian is related to (nominative) case assignment, but number-gender agreement on adjectives or participles is not. He suggests then that the CDAP might have different values for different heads in the same language. In Baker (2008a), I suggested a different interpretation: I claimed that agreement is always contingent on there being a case relationship in IE languages, but the necessary case relationship can be one of case concord as well as one of case assignment. Indeed, in richly-inflected Icelandic it is clear that an adjective that agrees with an NP in case also agrees with it in number and gender, whereas an adjective that cannot agree with an NP in case (because the NP has quirky case) does not agree with it in number and gender either. This is my reason for including the phrase 'or vice versa' in (4). A fully-developed theory of case concord remains to be worked out, however.

might also have a reduced adjectival-like agreement on the main verb under some circumstances, but not full person agreement. I claimed that this was another effect of the CDAP. Suppose that the CDAP is set 'yes'. Then the fact that you can't have multiple agreement with the same NP follows from the fact that you can't have multiple case marking of that NP. Imagine that the first head agrees with the NP. That presupposes that it assigns case to that NP. An NP can only be case-marked once (I assume). Then if another head tries to agree with the NP, it can't because the NP has already been case-marked. Therefore multiple agreement with the same argument can't arise. However, this result follows crucially because we assumed that there's a relationship between case-marking and agreement in the language in question. If there is no such relationship, as in Bantu languages, then the conclusion doesn't hold and nothing rules out two distinct items agreeing with the same NP. That's the source of the difference between (5) and (6), I claim.

Any claim about case in Bantu languages is a bit abstract because case is not morphologically realized in these languages. I assumed that the fronted object in (3a) is accusative, but that could be debated. Fortunately, you see the same parametric difference in languages that have overt case marking. In this domain too one finds two classes of languages: languages where morphological case marking is closely correlated with the agreement, and languages where it isn't. Hindi is a language in which there is a close connection, as seen in familiar examples like those in (7) (Mohanan, 1995:83):

(7)   a. <u>Anil</u>   kitaabē   <u>becegaa.</u>
         Anil.M(NOM) book-F.PL sell-FUT.M.SG
         'Anil will sell (the) books.'

      b. Anil-ne   <u>kitaabē</u>   <u>becīī.</u>
         Anil-ERG   book-F.PL   sell-PERF-F.PL
         'Anil sold (the) books.'

      c. Anil-ne   kitaabō-ko   becaa.
         Anil-ERG   book-F.PL-ACC   sell-PERF-M.SG
         'Anil sold the books.'

Hindi is a split ergative language. In (7a) the subject is in nominative case, but in (7b), in a different tense-aspect, the subject is in ergative case. This difference impacts the agreement. When the subject is in nominative case, as in (7a), the verb agrees with the subject. When the subject is in ergative case in (7b), the verb doesn't agree with it; rather it agrees with a nominative case object. In (7c) where neither the subject nor the object is nominative, the verb has a default third person singular form. Case and agreement are closely interrelated here. But there are also languages like Burushaski, a language spoken in the Himalayas, where you find just the opposite (data from Lorimer 1935). Burushaski has case marking similar to Hindi, but the T of the finite verb consistently agrees with the subject, regardless of its case. (8a) has a nominative case subject, and the verbs agree with it. (8b) has an ergative case subject and the verbs still agree with it. There's no relevant morphological difference on the verbs:

(8)   a. J<u>ɛ</u>   uːɳɛ xidmʌt ɛč-<u>a</u>   b-<u>a</u>.
          I.NOM your service do-1sS(IMPF) be-1sS
          '(For these many years) I have been at your service.'

       b. J<u>a</u>   be.ʌdʌpi.ɛn ɛt-<u>a</u>   b-<u>a</u>.
          I.ERG discourtesy do-1sS(PERF) be-1sS
          'I have committed a discourtesy.'

Something very similar is true of object agreement as well. According to standard Chomskyan theory, object agreement should be related to accusative case assignment. (9a) shows object agreement on the verb with the object 'you' in absolutive case. (9b) shows that you have the same morpheme *gu* agreeing with an object bearing dative case:

(9)   a. (Uːɳ)   <u>gu</u>-yɛtsʌ-m.
          you.ABS 2sO-see-1sS
          'I saw you.'

       b. Uːɳ-ər   hik trʌɳ <u>gu</u>-čičʌ-m.
          you-DAT one half 2sS-give-1sS
          'I shall give a half to you.'

Hindi then is a CDAP=yes language, Burushaski a CDAP=no language. Notice also that the Burushaski examples in (8) have multiple person agreement: the main verb 'do' is first person singular, and the auxiliary verb 'be' is also first person singular, both agreeing with the subject. In this respect also Burushaski is like Kinande, whereas Hindi is like other IE languages.

When I carried out this research, I was studying agreement, not case. Nevertheless, we can follow up by asking what this parameterization in the relationship between agreement and case tells us about case. What are the sources of case marking across languages? Having the CDAP set 'yes' implies that case comes from the agreement-bearing functional categories in those languages. But what about languages like Burushaski or Kinande where case is not related to agreement? Does case come from some different kind of source in such languages? Does my agreement parameter imply that case theory is also more parameterized than we have realized?

3.3 Modalities of case assignment in Sakha (Turkic)

With these questions in mind, I next review the highlights of a language-particular study I did with Nadya Vinokurova on case assignment in Sakha, a Turkic language spoken in Siberia (Baker and Vinokurova 2010). The hope here is that if you take knowledge about how case assignment works in one language and combine it with a picture of how agreement works across languages, you might be able to project this into some new ideas about how case works across languages. In particular, I compare nominative case in Sakha to accusative case in the same language. I show that nominative case is related to agreement on T in the familiar way. But accusative case is not related to agreement with a functional head. Instead I claim that the rule for accusative case assignment is quite different in nature from the rule of nominative assignment.

Consider first nominative case and its relationship to agreement. I claim that Sakha is a CDAP=yes language, like IE, so this aspect of the language looks familiar. More specifically, the two heads that agree overtly in Sakha, finite T and possessive D, both respect the CDAP. I only discuss finite T here, in the interest of space. Examples (10) and (11) show that finite verbs in this language cannot agree with an NP that has case other than nominative. (10) is a minimal pair from the passive construction (Vinokurova, 2005:336):

(10)   a. Sonun-nar aaq-ylyn-ny-lar.
          news-PL   read-PASS-PAST-3pS
          'The news was read.'

       b. Sonun-nar-y   aaq-ylyn-na.   (*aaq-ylyn-ny-lar)
          news-PL-ACC read-PASS-PAST.3sS   read-PASS-PAST-3pS
          'The news was read.'

In the Sakha passive, the theme argument can be nominative, as in (10a). But it can also be accusative, as it is in (10b). (I return to this later.) Note that the agreement on the verb is also different in the two examples: in (10a), it agrees with 'news'; in (10b) it does not, but has to be a default, third person singular form. Example (11) presents data from a dative subject construction. This shows that you can't have plural agreement with a dative subject—just as you cannot in Icelandic, for example:

(11)   Oqo-lor-go   üüt   naada-(*lar).
       child-PL-DAT milk need-(*3pS)
       'The children need milk.'

So we see that in Sakha the finite verb agrees with nominative NPs, but not NPs with any other kind of case, like Hindi but unlike Burushaski. Sakha is a language with case-sensitive agreement.

Example (12) shows another consequence of this parameter setting, involving agreement in auxiliary verb constructions. If we are right to treat Sakha as a CDAP=yes language, then we expect that there should not be multiple agreement with the same subject in such constructions. (12) shows that that's correct. (12a) shows that you can put person agreement on the auxiliary verb. (12b) shows that you can put person agreement on the main verb instead—an option that IE doesn't allow. But (12c) shows that, unlike Kinande or Burushaski, you can't have agreement on both verbs. So the cluster of properties associated with the 'yes' setting of the CDAP holds together nicely in Sakha:

(12)   a. En   süüj-büt   e-bik-**kin**.
         you   win-PTPL   AUX-PTPL-2sS
         '(The result is that) you won.'

     b. En   süüj-**bük-kün**   e-bit.
         you   win-PTPL-2sS   AUX-PTPL

     c. *En   süüj-**bük-kün**   e-bik-**kin**.
         you   win-PTPL-2sS   AUX-PTPL-2sS

    Based on data like this, Baker and Vinokurova (2010) end up with (13) as the rule of nominative case assignment in Sakha. This is just all the fine print from Chomsky's (2000, 2001) theory of Agree brought together in a single statement:

(13)   If a functional head F ∈ {T, D} has unvalued phi-features and an NP X has an unvalued case feature [and certain locality conditions hold], then agreement happens between F and X, resulting in the phi-features of X being assigned to F and the case associated with F (nominative or genitive) being assigned to X.

    Now let's shift attention to accusative case. Where does that come from? The standard Minimalist view has been to generalize the story of where nominative case comes from to accusative. We say that there's another functional head, small *v* or something similar, that agrees with an NP lower down in the structure, the object. That relationship is spelled out as accusative on the object, and as agreement on the functional head. However, this relationship need not be spelled out; maybe postsyntactic vocabulary insertion happens not to put in forms for this agreement, even though it happened in the syntax in the normal way. But I claim that that's not the right approach to the assignment of accusative case in Sakha. It's not a coincidence that we do not see object agreement overtly here; this is telling us something grammatically significant in this particular language. I argue instead for the formulation in (14), based on Marantz (1991). Marantz introduced the notion of what's called dependent case assignment. His view was that case doesn't necessarily come from a functional head; rather you look at certain domains, and if you have two NPs in a particular local domain you assign accusative case to the lower one. What's distinctive about this is it's a relationship between two noun phrases, without functional heads coming into it per se (except perhaps to help define the relevant domains). (14) is a concrete version of this leading idea:[4]

---

[4] Andrea Moro asks whether (14) would apply to predicate nominal constructions, assigning accusative to the predicate NP. That would be wrong for most languages, including Sakha, where the predicate nominal

(14)   If there are two distinct argumental NPs in the same phase such that NP1 c-commands NP2, then value the case feature of NP2 as accusative unless NP1 has already been marked for case.

In defence of (14), I briefly go through three bits of evidence in Sakha, all of which support arguments of approximately the same form: whether you have accusative case depends on whether a subject is around and doesn't depend on the nature of the functional heads that are nearby.

First, (15) shows again that in a Sakha passive the theme argument can be nominative or accusative. What is the grammatical difference between these two possibilities? There is no morphological difference on the verb that we can see; both verbs bear the same passive suffix. But there is an interpretative difference, pointed out by Vinokurova (2005). There's a sense in which the agent is syntactically present in (15b) that it isn't in (15a). This becomes evident if you include adverbs that presuppose an agent—adverbs like 'intentionally', or instrumental expressions like 'with a hammer'. If such elements are included, then the thematic object 'the cup' can only be accusative:

(15)   a. Caakky (*sorujan)   (*ötüje-nen)   aldjat-ylyn-na.
           cup   intentionally hammer-INSTR break-PASS-PAST.3sS
           'The cup was broken (intentionally) (with a hammer).'

        b. Caakky-ny sorujan   ötüje-nen   aldjat-ylyn-na.
           cup-ACC intentionally hammer-INSTR break-PASS-PAST.3sS
           'The cup was broken intentionally with a hammer.'

I assume this means that (15b) has some kind of empty category subject in the syntax, and (15a) doesn't, and the empty category is involved in licensing these adverbs in some way. Now if (15b) has a null subject in the syntax, then there's a second NP in the local domain that triggers accusative case on the theme by the dependent case rule in (14). In contrast, (15a) has no independent evidence for a covert agent NP in the syntactic representation. Therefore, there's nothing to trigger dependent case assignment on the theme argument and that argument shows up as nominative in (15a). So there's no detectable difference in the functional categories associated with the verb in these two sentences. There is a detectable difference in whether an agent is present or not, however. And whether the agent is present or not determines whether accusative is assigned or not. That's a success for the Marantzian view of dependent

is nominative/unmarked. But in fact (14) does not apply if the predicate nominal does not count as 'argumental'. We originally included this qualification to prevent null expletive NPs from triggering accusative in examples like (20), and to prevent bare NP adverbs like 'here' and 'now' from being accusative in Sakha, but it could cover this situation too. We do, however, have to be alert to this issue when it comes to cross-linguistic variation, since how borderline NPs count for (14) may be a point of variation. (Expletives may trigger accusative on other nominals in Amharic, for example (Amberber 2005), and NP adverbs are marked accusative in ways that suggest (14) in Quechua (Lefebvre and Muysken 1988). And indeed a predicate nominal is accusative in Classical Arabic, if there is an overt copula.)

case assignment, as contrasted with the conventional view that accusative case comes from a particular functional category.[5]

Another structure where you can see this is agentive nominalizations like (16):

(16)   Terilte-ni   salaj-aaccy   kel-le.
        company-ACC manage-AGNOML come-PAST.3sS
        'The manager of the company came.'

Here we have a deverbal nominal 'manager', and its theme argument 'company' has accusative case on it. This is clearly different from languages like English, which do not allow an object in accusative case in comparable structures. The question then is: Where does this accusative case come from? Why is it possible in Sakha, but not in familiar Indo-European languages? My claim is that it's the rule of accusative case assignment that is different, not the structure of the agentive nominalizations. So, in these kinds of nominalizations in Sakha, there is no evidence that any verbal functional heads are present. You can't have any voice marker on the nominalized verb, you can't have any aspect markers, you can't have negation, and you can't have adverbs, just as you can't in English. This is shown in part in (17) (see Baker and Vinokurova 2009 for more data):

(17)   a. (*Ücügejdik) terilte-ni   (*ücügejdik) salaj-aaccy   kel-le.
           (*well)   company-ACC (*well)   manage-AGNOML come-3sS
           'The one who manages the company well came.'   (no adverb)

        b. *tal-yll-aaccy   (no voice morphology)
           choose-PASS-AGNOML
           'the one who is chosen, the be-chosen-er'

So there's no sign of any clausal structure in these constructions, except the verb and its complement. That's a real problem if you think accusative case comes by agreement with a clausal functional head; then there would be no source for accusative here. That is arguably a good result for English, but it is a bad one for Sakha. There is however a syntactic expression of the verb's agent in (16), namely the agentive nominalizer itself. So, if you take the dependent case view where it's having two nominal elements in the same domain that's crucial for the assignment of case, then you can generalize that rule to this structure with relatively few difficulties. (The main issue is that one has

---

[5] Richard Kayne points out that the difference between (15a) and (15b) in Sakha might be syntactically analogous to the difference between a true passive and a (reflexive) impersonal construction in Italian, constructions that have distinct morphological marking. If so, the similarity in verbal morphology might be semi-accidental. I accept that this is a possibility, but do not think it detracts much from the point at hand: even if the voice marker is technically different in (15a) and (15b), the examples still point toward there being a relationship between having a syntactic subject (possibly covert) and having an accusative object.

to define 'argumental NP' in (14) in such a way that the nominalizing suffix –*aaccy* counts as one.)

Perhaps the strongest argument for (14) comes from the examples in (18)–(20). These illustrate an interesting kind of raising to object that is found in Sakha. Similar to Turkish (Moore, 1998), but not identical to Turkish, there is a kind of exceptional case marking even with finite clauses in this language. (18a) shows a simple embedded clause, and the embedded subject 'you' has nominative case, as you would expect. But, if you raise 'you' to the edge of this clause, putting it before all the material properly belonging to the lower clause, then it can be marked accusative, as in (18b):

(18) a. Min   [sarsyn   ehigi-(*ni)   kel-iex-xit   dien] ihit-ti-m.
          I(NOM) tomorrow you-(*ACC) come-FUT-2pS that   hear-PAST-1sS
          'I heard that tomorrow you will come.'

      b. Min [ehigi-ni [bügün kyaj-yax-xyt   dien]] ihit-ti-m.
          I   you-ACC today   win-FUT-2pS that   hear-PAST-1sS
          'I heard that you will win today.'

This fact by itself doesn't distinguish between the two kinds of case assignment. You can get this result by dependent case assignment, or by case coming from a functional head in the matrix clause. It would be pretty much the same story either way: when you raise the NP up, it comes to be in the domain of the main clause, so it can get accusative case in the matrix clause, either by agreement with the matrix v, or by (14). What's more revealing is the other conditions on this case assignment. What happens when the matrix verb is intransitive rather than transitive? In (19), the matrix verbs 'become sad' and 'return' are unaccusative verbs that do not have a transitive v. These verbs cannot license accusative case in a simple one-clause sentence. They're the kind of verbs that we would say don't have the functional head that assigns accusative case. But, if you raise the embedded subject from the complement of this sort of verb, it still gets accusative case:

(19) a. Keskil Aisen-y   [t kel-be-t   dien] xomoj-do.
          Keskil Aisen-ACC   come-NEG-AOR that   become.sad-PAST.3sS
          'Keskil became sad that Aisen is not coming.' (p. 366)

      b. Masha Misha-ny   [t yaldj-ya   dien] tönün-ne.
          Masha Misha-ACC   fall.sick-FUT that   return-PAST.3sS
          'Masha returned (for fear) that Misha would fall sick.'

'Become sad' doesn't have the right kind of functional head to assign accusative, but there is an NP in the matrix clause domain, the matrix subject. When we raise the subject from the embedded clause to the matrix clause, now there are two NPs in the matrix domain. Accusative is assigned to the lower one, according to the rule in (14).

Further evidence comes from an example like (20), where there isn't an argumental NP in the matrix clause, because the matrix clause contains an impersonal verb 'it became certain'. (20) shows that if you raise the embedded subject into this kind of matrix clause, it does not get accusative case:

(20)   Bügün munnjax-xa   [Masha-(*ny)   [ehiil   Moskva-qa
        today   meeting-DAT   [Masha-(*ACC)   [next.year Moscow-DAT
        bar-ya   dien]] cuolkajdan-na.
        go-FUT.3sS that]   become.certain-PAST.3sS
        'It became clear today at the meeting that Masha will go to Moscow next year.'

The contrast between (19) and (20) shows that whether or not there's a thematic subject in the matrix clause is crucial to accusative case assignment. At the same time, the lack of contrast between (18) and (19) shows that the nature of the matrix verb and the functional categories associated with it is not crucial to whether one gets accusative case in Sakha.

On the basis of evidence like this, I conclude that Sakha is a language where accusative case comes from a rule of dependent case assignment, not one where accusative case is a manifestation of an agreement relationship with some dedicated functional category. When you control the structure to eliminate the functional category, accusative case is still there.

This was a very language specific study. But it is typologically significant because it gives us good reason to believe that there's a richer range of different kinds of case assignment available in the languages of the world than most of us have thought.

Suppose then that we try to project this forward into a more general theory of how case can vary across languages. Section 3.2 (based on Baker 2008a) showed that case comes from functional heads in some languages (CDAP=yes languages) but not others (CDAP=no languages). Section 3.3 (based on Baker and Vinokurova 2010) showed that even in one language (Sakha), two kinds of case assignment are at work: case assignment by agreement with a functional head (nominative), and case assignment by dependent case marking—a calculation involving two NPs in the same domain. Maybe then the language-particular study helps us to answer the question of where case comes from in CDAP=no languages like Burushaski, or in languages with little or no sign of agreement on functional heads, like Chinese and Japanese. Maybe it comes from Marantzian dependent case assignment rules. If so, case in agreement-rich languages would come from a partially different source than case in agreement-poor languages. I want to begin considering whether that's true or not.

More specifically, I have begun to do sketches of about 25 non-IE languages with overt case marking, to see how these matters play out in that sample. I'm going for 25 languages, not two, in the hope of achieving a fair degree of generality. But I'm going for 25 languages, not three hundred or a thousand, so as to be able to apply a touch of generative sophistication in the analysis of each of them. With this methodology in mind, the rest of this chapter presents some preliminary conclusions along these lines.

3.4 On ergative case marking and its distribution

I start with the observation that it's always been a bit tricky to know where ergative case systems fit in with a Chomskyan approach to case assignment. In a morphologically ergative language you have the subject in the SpecTP position (maybe) but that doesn't determine its case. Even if the subject doesn't raise to SpecTP, it is probably the closest NP to T, but that doesn't necessarily determine its case either. Thus in Burushaski the subject is sometimes absolutive (21a,b), sometimes ergative (21c), even though structural tests suggest that it is always in the same position. Sometimes the absolutive NP agrees with T (21a,b), but sometimes it shows object agreement (21c). There's no tight correlation between case and either position or agreement in this language. That's a problem for the standard Chomskyan approach. There have been plenty of clever suggestions about what to do about this, but some kind of patch seems needed:

(21) a. Acaanák <u>hilés</u>   i-ír-<u>imi</u>   (Willson, 1996:19)
         suddenly boy.ABS 3m-die-PAST.MsS
         'Suddenly the boy died.'

      b. <u>Dasín</u>   há-e   le hurúT-<u>umo</u>   (Willson 1996:3)
         girl.ABS house-OBL in sit-PAST.FsS
         'The girl sat in the house.'

      c. <u>Hilés-e</u>   *dasin*   *mu*-yeéts-<u>imi</u>.   (Willson 1996:17)
         boy-ERG girl.ABS FsO-see-PAST.MsS
         'The boy saw the girl.'

In contrast, it's very easy to fit ergative case systems into the dependent case approach. Indeed, part of Marantz's original motivation for this view was that you can account for accusative and ergative in the same way. (22a) repeats the accusative case rule from (14) (with a slight change; see note 7). You get an ergative pattern out of the same rule if you simply say that when you have two NPs in the same phase, you mark the higher one with overt case, rather than the lower one, as stated in (22b). For Marantz, that's all there is to morphological ergativity:

(22) a. If there are two distinct argumental NPs in the same spell out domain such that NP1 c-commands NP2, then value the case feature of *NP2* as *accusative*.

      b. If there are two distinct argumental NPs in the same spell out domain such that NP1 c-commands NP2, then value the case feature of *NP1* as *ergative*.

Another virtue of the Marantzian approach (not mentioned by Marantz himself) is that it generalizes easily to so-called tripartite systems like Nez Perce, illustrated in (23). (23a) has an intransitive verb, and 'man' has no explicit case marking. (23b) is a transitive; the subject has ergative case *and* the object has accusative case. So in this language you have a three-way contrast: an NP can be plain (nominative/absolutive) or ergative or accusative:

(23) a. Hi-páay-na   háama.   (Rude, 1986:126)
          3S-arrive-ASP man
          'The man arrived.'

      b. <u>Háama-nm</u> <u>hi</u>-néec-'wi-ye   wewúkiye-ne.   (Rude 1986:127)
          man-ERG   3S-pO-shoot-ASP elk-ACC
          'The man shot the elk(pl).'

So we get a simple sort of typology from the Marantz picture, in which you either mark the higher of two NPs in the same domain ergative (Burushaski), or you mark the lower one accusative (Sakha), or you mark both (Nez Perce), or you mark neither (Mohawk, Swahili, etc.). One might say, then, that languages are parameterized to make use of (22a), or (22b), or both, or neither.

Now, what might this imply if we say that some languages do case assignment by the Chomskyan way, and others do it by the Marantzian way? What would that suggest about the distribution of ergativity? We know that ergativity is not evenly distributed across the languages of the world: for example, ergativity is rare in Europe (apart from Basque) and Africa but common in New Guinea and Australia. So this suggests the following conjecture: In CDAP=yes languages, including most of IE, case is related to agreement. But you can't get ergative patterns out of normal theories of agreement. Therefore, you should not have ergative case marking in languages with that kind of system. In contrast, in languages where you either have no agreement or where agreement is independent of case marking, like Burushaski, then case does not come from agreement. Instead, it comes from Marantzian dependent case rules. And in those kinds of languages you can equally well have ergative and accusative. So the conjecture would be that CDAP=yes languages will always be nominative-accusative (if they have overt case marking at all), whereas CDAP=no languages and languages in which agreement is not active in the syntax will be nominative-accusative half the time and ergative-absolutive half the time.

The table in (24) is my preliminary attempt to test this conjecture. Here I cross my CDAP, taken from Baker (2008a), with whether the language is ergative or accusative or has no case marking at all, according to *The World Atlas of Language Structures* (Comrie 2005) (counting tripartite languages as ergative):

(24)   (n = 102)

	Agreement is Case-Sensitive (CDAP=yes) (41)	Agreement is not Case-sensitive (CDAP=no) (32)	Languages with no Agreement (29)
Ergative-Absolutive (18)	**2? (expected: 7.4) Hindi, Greenlandic**	12 (expected: 5.8) Georgian, Warlpiri, Basque, Burushaki…	4 (expected 5.2) Lezgian, Ngiyambaa
Nominative-Accusative (29)	12 (expected: 11.9) Hebrew, Greek, Sakha, Kannada…	7 (expected: 9.3) Persian, Guarani, I. Quechua, Maricopa,	10 (expected 8.4) Malagasy, Japanese, Marthathunira, Hiaki
No case marking (55)	26 (expected: 22.6) English, Mapudungun, Yimas, Hausa…	14 (expected: 17.6) Kinande, Slave, Arapesh, Ojibwa…	15 (expected 16) Yoruba, Mandarin, Mixtec, …

There are two suggestive features of this table to point out. The first is that you have very few ergative-absolutive languages with case sensitive agreement in the top left corner of the table: only Hindi and Greenlandic. It seems to be true, then, that languages where case is sensitive to agreement are almost all nominative-accusative (a 6:1 ratio), as predicted. In contrast, in the other two columns, you have quite a few ergative-absolutive languages. Indeed, if you sum up the other two columns, you have sixteen ergative-absolutive languages and 17 nominative-accusative languages: a 50-50 split, as predicted. This roughly supports my conjecture. It is admittedly quite crude so far. One would like to dive into all of these languages with more care, and especially the potentially anomalous languages Hindi and Greenlandic (both of which have nontrivial generative literatures that would be significant).[6] But even these very preliminary results look quite promising.

3.5 Specificity of the object and dependent case marking

This proposal about ergativity makes a novel typological prediction—one that at first glance seems troubling, but turns out to be true. The characteristic feature of dependent case assignment is that it assigns accusative or ergative case if and only if there are two NPs *in the same local domain*. It does not apply if, for example, you have one noun phrase way up in the matrix clause, and a second one far below it, in a triply embedded clause. In the current theoretical climate, it makes sense to say that the crucial local environment is the phase or spell out domain in Chomsky's (2000, 2001) sense. So we expect the rule of dependent case assignment to be of the form 'If there are two noun phrases in the same spell out domain then mark one of them accusative or ergative.'

---

[6] For example, Hindi is known to have inherent/quirky ergative case, which is present on subjects of some monadic unergative verbs and missing on subjects of some dyadic verbs, based on lexical factors (cf. Woolford 2006). Greenlandic is tricky because both subject and object agree with a single head, T, according to Bok-Bennema (1991).

For nominative-accusative languages, this looks like it has straightforwardly positive results, accounting for a particular kind of 'differential object marking' (DOM).
Indeed, Sakha itself is a DOM language: it's a language in which the object may or may
not be accusative, depending on its position and its specificity. Thus, the direct object
'book' in (25) is marked accusative only if it is specific or definite:

(25) a. Erel kinige-ni   atyylas-ta.
         Erel book-ACC buy-PAST.3sS
         'Erel bought the/a certain book.'

      b. Erel kinige   atyylas-ta.
         Erel book-Ø buy-PAST.3sS
         'Erel bought a book/books.'

There's also an interaction between case and word order in Sakha, as shown in (26).
The accusative object most naturally appears in front of adverbs and other VP-internal
elements, as in (26a), whereas the bare object must be after adverbs and other VP-
internal elements, as in (26b):

(26) a. Masha salamaat-*(y) türgennik sie-te.
         Masha porridge-ACC quickly   eat-PAST.3sS
         'Masha ate the porridge quickly.' (ACC is required)

      b. Masha türgennik salamaat-(#y) sie-te.
         Masha quickly   porridge-ACC   eat-PAST.3sS
         'Masha ate porridge quickly.' (ACC is marked, only with focus on 'porridge')

What we seem to have here is a classic case of object-shift. The object is first generated inside VP. It can, however, move out of VP. This affects its word order with respect
to adverbs. It also affects its interpretation, assuming that Diesing's (1992) Mapping
Hypothesis, or something like it, is correct in saying that the scope of a certain type of
nonspecific interpretation is the VP. The new point is that given the dependent case
theory it makes sense that object shift affects the case marking of the object as well.
The VP is a distinct spell out domain from the clause as a whole.[7] When the object
NP moves out of the VP, it will be spelled out in the same domain as the subject and
therefore is marked accusative. When the object stays in VP, it gets a different kind
of interpretation and it is not in the same domain as the subject. Then (22a) does not
apply, and the NP remains unmarked for case, showing up in bare-nominative form.
This is diagrammed in (27):

---

[7] See Baker and Vinokurova (2010) for discussion of technical issues of whether vP or VP is the smaller
phase in Sakha. Their assumptions are significantly revised in Baker (in progress), where I say that dependent case marking applies when a domain (e.g. VP, complement of the phase head v, or TP, complement of
the phase head C) is spelled out. Thus, I changed 'phase' in (14) to 'spell out domain' in (22) to reflect my
more recent understanding. It is crucial here that VP, not vP is the first domain of dependent case assignment, but the details of how that result emerges from a theory of phases are not.

(27) a.   b.

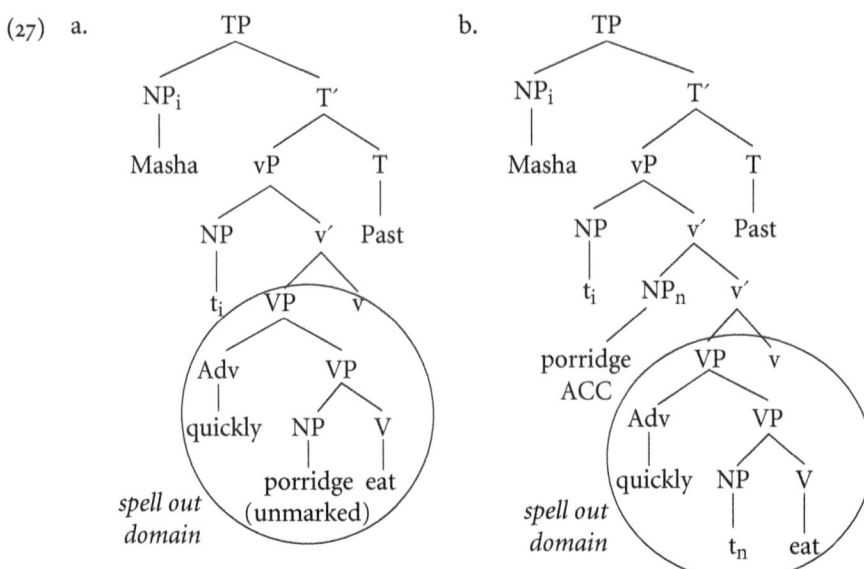

This leads to a prediction. If the Marantzian rules of dependent case assignment hold in languages in which the CDAP is not set 'yes', and if those rules can be sensitive to phase boundaries, then it follows that ergative case marking on the subject should also depend on object shift in some languages. At the empirical level, whether the subject is marked ergative or not should be related to where the object is in the word order of the clause, and whether it is interpreted as specific or not. And that is a somewhat surprising prediction. It is perhaps not surprising that features of the object, such as whether it's specific or not, would influence the case marking of the object itself; that's a very local sort of effect. But if what is really at work is object shift plus dependent case marking, then whether the object shifts or not should also influence whether the subject is ergative or not—a nonlocal, intrinsically relational effect. This seems a bit counterintuitive and is not known from classical typological descriptions of case systems (e.g. Hopper and Thompson 1980; Blake 1994; Dixon 1994).

But it turns out not to be so hard to find languages that have the predicted properties. One is Ika, a Chibcan language of Columbia. Ika is an SOV language. In (28a), the direct object 'jaguar' is indefinite and inside VP, adjacent to the verb. In this example, there's no ergative case marking on the subject. But in (28b) the object is 'his pig', a definite object, and now the subject is marked ergative. The interpretation of the object determines the marking of the subject, as predicted. (28c) shows an object 'puma' that's explicitly moved out of the verb phrase into the higher domain, to give OSV word order; here too the subject is marked ergative. So, the case marking of the subject depends on the position and interpretation of the object in Ika, exactly as predicted:

(28) a. GsΛriwieri tigri   aʔwasa-na.   (Frank 1990:115)
         Gabriel   jaguar chase-DIST
         'Gabriel went after a jaguar.'

      b. Tigri-seʔ   tšinu kΛ-ga-na.   (Frank 1990:9)
         Jaguar-ERG pig   PERI-eat-DIST
         'A jaguar ate his pig.'

      c. Guiadžina zΛ-gΛmmɨ perɨ-seʔ an-aʔkuss-i   guak-akí nuʔ-na
         puma   GEN-child dog-ERG   REF-bite-while kill-PRF AUX-DIST
         'The dog had killed the puma's cub, biting it.'   (Frank 1990:116)

(29) shows a similar paradigm from Eastern Ostyak, a Finno-Ugric language spoken in Siberia. (29a) has an indefinite object next to the verb, and the subject is not marked ergative; (29b) has a definite object shifted over a PP, and the subject is marked ergative (Gulya 1966):

(29) a. Mä   t'əkäjəɣ lämnä   ula   mənɣäləm.
         We.dual(nom) younger.sister-COM berry pick-PAST-1pS
         'I went to pick berries with my younger sister.'

      b. Mə-ŋən ləɣə əllə juɣ kanŋa aməɣaloɣ.
         We-ERG them large tree beside put-PAST-3pO/1pS
         'We put them (pots of berries) beside a big tree.'

Kanuri (Nilo-Saharan, spoken in Africa) is a third language that meets this description, with ergative suffix *–ye* appearing on the subject only in OSV order, or sometimes if the object is definite (Hutchison 1981).

Nez Perce, the language with a tripartite case system, is also relevant to this prediction. In this language, the case of *both* the subject and the object depend on the definiteness of the object, because both (22a) and (22b) are in force. In (30a), the object is indefinite, and neither the subject nor the object is marked for case. In (30b), the object is definite, and both are marked for case: the subject ergative and the object accusative. One finds either both ergative and accusative in a Nez Perce sentence, or one finds neither. The two are conditioned by the same factor—the position/interpretation of the object—just as this system expects:

(30) a. Háama   hi-'wí-ye   wewúkiye.   (Rude 1988:552)
         man.NOM 3S-shoot-ASP elk.NOM
         'The man shot an elk.'

      b. Háama-nm hi-néec-'wi-ye   wewúkiye-ne.   (Rude 1986:127)
         man-ERG   3S-pO-shoot-ASP elk-ACC
         'The man shot the elk(pl).'

Moralizing on this just briefly, I think we have here an instructive example of the weakness of a purely bottom-up, data-driven methodology, such as characterizes most functionalist-typological research on topics like this. That research has noticed the dependence of object marking on object interpretation, because that is a relatively direct, obvious dependency. But it has not (as far as I know) noticed the dependence of subject marking on object interpretation, even though it is out there, because that is a less obvious dependency. People apparently did not think to look for it—and to a significant degree you only find what you know to look for. That is why it is important to also operate in a top-down, deductive manner: theoretical reflection can give you valuable new ideas of what we should be looking for.[8]

3.6 Tense-Aspect splits and dependent case marking

This approach also makes a converse prediction, which I discuss in a brief and tentative manner. We know from the typological literature that some of the so-called ergative languages are really split ergative languages: whether the subject is marked ergative or not depends on the tense-aspect of the clause. Hindi is a familiar example of this (see (7)); it is also true in Burushaski (see (8), also Willson 1996:17): the subject of a past/perfective sentence is marked ergative, but the subject of a future/imperfective sentence is not. Within a theory of ergative case marking built around (22b), it is tempting to analyse this phenomenon also in terms of phases and spell out domains. We might say that the future tense morpheme in Burushaski is an extra phase head, marking its complement (vP?) as being an extra spell out domain, in addition to the normal spell out domains TP and VP. As a result, the subject in SpecTP is in a different phase from the object, even if the object shifts out of VP and into vP to get a definite interpretation. Given this, (22b) would not apply. In contrast, the complement of past T/perfective aspect is not a spell out domain, so ergative case assignment could apply in this tense.

Whatever the exact details might be, if it is right to account for tense-aspect conditioned split ergativity in something like these terms, then I predict that accusative case marking should also be sensitive to the tense-aspect of the clause in some languages. Again, this follows directly from the symmetry of the rules for ergative case marking

---

[8] It is intriguing to wonder if there might be an even deeper relationship between object shift and ergative case marking. Richard Kayne points out that people have observed that there are no strictly SVO languages with ergative case marking (e.g. Bittner and Hale 1996)—an observation supported by the *World Atlas of Language Structures,* which lists 17 ergative languages with SOV order but 0 with SVO order (Dryer 2005 plus Comrie 2005). It is tempting to incorporate this by combining my ideas about case assignment with Kayne's (1994) claim, rooted in antisymmetry, that SOV is always a derived order, created by leftward movement of the object or something that contains it. So unlike SVO languages, SOV languages always have a kind of object shift, which could feed ergative case marking. But there are issues to face along this line too. First, one would have to distinguish two kinds of object movement, one that feeds ergative marking and one that does not, to account for the languages mentioned in this section. More seriously, one would also expect overt accusative case only in SOV languages given the symmetry built into (22). It is true that overt accusative is more common in SOV languages than in SVO languages (28 languages versus 9), but there clearly are SVO languages with overt accusative. This is an interesting area for further research.

and accusative case marking in (22). If this conception is right, then what one is sensitive to, the other should also be sensitive to. But again, the sensitivity of accusative case assignment to tense-aspect is not familiar from typological research.

In fact, my preliminary sample of 25 languages does not contain many examples of even ergative case marking being conditioned by tense-aspect. I begin to wonder if this kind of split ergativity is really an areal phenomenon, characteristic of languages in South and Southwestern Asia. Other than Burushaski, the one language in my sample with split ergativity is Coast Tsimshian, an Amerindian language of British Columbia. The case system of this language is summarized in (31). Note that the case markers associated with common nouns show an ergative-absolutive pattern, with the special marker *da* used for transitive subjects, whereas those associated with proper nouns display a tripartite system, with distinct markers for intransitive subject, transitive subject, and object, similar to Nez Perce:

(31)   Coast Tsimshian Case: absolutive ergative accusative
       Common: (a)   da   (a)
       Proper: (a)s   dit   (a)t

(32) gives sentences with common nouns, ergative case appearing on the subject of the transitive verb in (32b). (Note that the case particle associated with the following NP actually encliticizes to the preceding word at PF; compare Anderson (2005) on Kwakwala.):

(32)   a. Yagwa baa-[*a*]   wan.   (Dunn 1995:60)
          PRES   run-ABS deer
          'The deer is running.'

       b. Yagwa-t   niis-*da*   ts'uu'ts-*a*   laalt
          PRES-3sE see-ERG   bird-ACC   worm
          'The bird sees the worm.'

(33) is an example with a different tense, past instead of present, and in (33b) the subject is not marked as ergative, but rather absolutive, just like the object:

(33)   a. Nah   siipg-*a*   hana'a   (Dunn 1995:60)
          PAST be.sick-ABS woman
          'The woman was sick.'

       b. Nah   t'uus-*a*   'yuuta   hana'k̲
          PAST push-ABS man-(ABS)   woman
          'The man pushed the woman.'

So this qualifies as an instance of tense-aspect based split ergativity. We might then say that the complement of *nah* (but not *yagwa*) is an extra spell out domain, as diagrammed in (34). (Alternatively, we might say that vP is a spell out in both tenses, but *nah* has an EPP feature that causes the subject to move out of the vP prior to case assignment, whereas *yagwa* does not.)

(34)

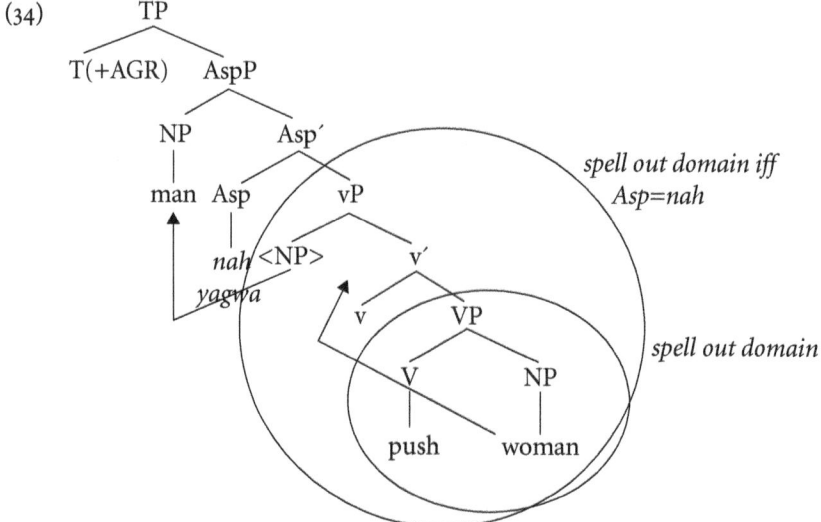

If the object is highly indefinite, it doesn't undergo object shift out of VP, but 'incorporates' into the verb. Then the subject is not marked ergative even with present tense *yagwa*:

(35) a. Yagwa łee-m-la̱k-*s*   nagwaat.
          PRES   haul-CN-firewood-ABS.PN   his.father
          'His father is hauling firewood.'   (Dunn 1995:61)

      b. Yagwa sa-a̓asg-*as*   noo-yu.
          PRES   make-seaweed-ABS.PN   mother.my
          'My mother is picking seaweed.'   (Mulder 1994)

On the other hand, if the object is a pronoun, then it raises all the way out of vP as well as VP to cliticize to (the verb in) T. Then the subject is marked ergative even with past tense *nah*:

(36) a. Na-t   ʻniidz-n-*t*   Dzon.
          past-3sE see-2Obj-ERG.PN   John
          'John saw you.'   (Dunn 1995:63)

      b. Na-t   luʻniis-d-*it*   nagwaadu.
          Past-3sE stare.at-3Obj-ERG.PN my.father
          'My father was staring at them.'   (Mulder 1994:87)

These examples confirm that it is inadequate simply to say that *yagwa* assigns ergative case to the subject, but *nah* assigns absolutive across the board. In both tenses, the transitive subject can be ergative or absolutive, depending on exactly where the object is. There is a difference between the two tenses when it comes to case marking, but where the NPs are in the structure of the clause is an equally important factor. This is expected within the dependent case theory.

The question now is whether accusative case assignment is ever sensitive to tense-aspect in the same way that ergative assignment is. We can answer this within Coast Tsimshian by considering the proper nouns, where there is an accusative case distinct from absolutive. And the answer turns out to be yes, as shown in (37). (37a) is a present tense sentence, with ergative marking for the subject and accusative marking for the object. (37b) is the corresponding past tense sentence. It has absolutive marking on the subject, as expected. But it also has absolutive marking, not accusative marking, on the object:

(37) a. Yagwa-t t'uus-***dit***   Dzon-***it***   Meli.   (Dunn 1995:67)
          Pres-3sE push-ERG.PN John-ACC.PN Mary.
          'John is pushing Mary.'

      b. Nah t'uus-***as***   Dzon-*s*   Meli.
          past push-ABS.PN John-ABS.PN Mary
          'John pushed Mary.'

So the tense-aspect split in Coast Tsimshian affects ergative case marking and accusative case marking equally, just as the definiteness of the object affects ergative and accusative equally in Nez Perce. This supports the logic of rules like (22). I don't yet know of a language that is purely nominative-accusative in which accusative case varies with tense-aspect in this way. But that might just be an accidental gap, since tense-aspect conditioning doesn't seem to be all that widespread anyway.

3.7 Variable case-marking languages versus consistent case-marking languages

While the symmetries presented in the last two sections support my neo-Marantzian approach to morphological case in languages where the CDAP is not set 'yes', they also raise one additional question about cross-linguistic variation in case assignment. Some languages are DOM languages, in which object shift affects the case marking of the subject and/or the object. But other languages are not: they have uniform case marking regardless of properties of the object. What kind of cross-linguistic variation is this?

Perhaps the most obvious thing to say would be that in some languages object shift is only triggered by definiteness, whereas in others all objects undergo object shift. This would be a plausible sort of minimalist analysis, in that one can build it into the features of the *v* node in a familiar way. In some languages, v has an unspecified EPP feature that can attract any kind of nominal. In other languages v bears a specific feature that only attracts +definite phrases. That would be a fairly straightforward sort of theory.

The problem is that word order doesn't seem to bear it out. If this approach were correct, one might expect Subject-Object-PP/Adverb-Verb order to be normal in languages with consistent case marking. The object being regularly separated from the verb would be evidence that objects of all sorts shift out of VP. In contrast, Subject-Adverb/PP-Object-Verb order would be normal for indefinite objects in DOM languages, because the indefinite object does not shift out of VP in this kind of language. But this seems to be false. Burushaski and Lezgian are languages that have ergative case on the transitive subject regardless of the definiteness of the object, but still S-X-O-V order is perfectly possible, perhaps even preferred in these languages when the object is indefinite (38a,b). Imbabura Quechua is a language in which objects in matrix clauses are always marked accusative, but it favours S-X-O-V order when the object is indefinite (38c), just as Sakha does:

(38) a. Hilés-e   dasín-mo-r   toofá-muts píish   o-t-imi.
         Boy-ERG girl-OBL.F-to gift-PL   present 3pO-do-PAST.3sS
         'The boy presented gifts to the girl.'   (Burushaski, Willson 1996)

      b. Gada.di wiči-n   žibin.da-j   c'akul aqud-na.
         Boy.ERG self-GEN pocket-INEL feather take.out-AOR
         'The boy took a feather out of his pocket.'   (Lezgian, Haspelmath 1993)

      c. Juzi Marya-man muti-ta   kara-rka.
         José María-to   mote-ACC give-PAST.3sS
         'José gave/served mote María.'   (Quechua, Cole 1985:70–71)

It is conceivable that a more careful study of word order, which controlled closely for discourse functions and information status, might reveal some sort of difference between languages with DOM and languages without. But we do not have much reason to hope so, given the data at hand.[9]

---

[9] Another alternative might be to parameterize whether VP counts as a spell out domain or not. In a DOM language like Sakha, VP would count as a domain, as already considered, but in a non-DOM language like Quechua, VP would not count as a spell out domain, so the subject and object would always automatically be in the same domain for (22). This might work for some languages, but not in general. Baker and Vinokurova (2010) claim that in some languages (Sakha) dative case is also a dependent case, assigned to the higher of two NPs in a VP-phase. The proposal under consideration would then predict that no language could have dative as a dependent case without also having differential object marking. That seems seems unlikely, since Burushaski, Lezgian, and Quechua all have rather normal dative cases (although I don't know their properties for sure). See Baker (in progress) for more thorough discussion of this issue.

Languages in which dative case is assigned structurally to the higher of two NPs in a VP-like domain could give us a way to investigate a question raised by an anonymous reviewer: whether an applicative head (Appl) is a phase head for case purposes (cf. McGinnis 2001). I assume that the more common situation is that Appl is not a phase head. If not, then the whole ApplP complement of v will be the smallest spell out domain, the applied object will be in the same domain as a direct object, and dative case will show up

The most promising proposal from an empirical viewpoint that I am aware of sounds distinctly unminimalist. It would be to say that in some languages, you calculate case for the VP, you throw the VP material away, and then you calculate the case for the rest of the clause. That is the standard view of how phases work, and it gives you a DOM language. To get a language without DOM, you calculate case on the VP domain (perhaps assigning dative; see note 9), then you extend to the larger domain, *but you don't throw the VP-internal material away.* You keep that material, and it is included in the calculation of how to assign case on the CP domain. Then when the subject comes into view, you always have the object as well, regardless of where it is. As a result, in this sort of language you get ergative or accusative case marking across the board, not depending on object shift or definiteness. This would admittedly be a surprising kind of parameter. Some have been so rash as to say that what counts as a phase might vary across languages (e.g. Fox and Pesetsky 2004), but no one has said that how phases function in the derivation can vary across languages. But I do not think that we should rule out such possibilities a priori, as being fundamentally not minimalist, given whatever notion of minimalism we have at the time. If such radical-sounding kinds of parameterization give us the best and most principled overall explanation of the facts, then we should not be afraid to propose them . . . at least until a better proposal comes to light.

3.8 Conclusions

I have argued that there are (at least) two ways of assigning morphological case in natural languages: case can be assigned by a functional head to a nearby NP under agreement (Chomskyan case assignment), and case can be assigned to one NP if there is another NP in the same local domain (Marantzian case assignment). Languages in which the Case Dependence of Agreement Parameter of Baker (2008a) is set 'yes' have (at least some) Chomskyan case assignment; in contrast, languages in which the CDAP is set 'no' may have only Marantzian case assignment. Languages can also have a mixture of the two modes of case assignment, Sakha being a case in point. I then went on to conjecture that structural ergative case is always a Marantzian dependent case, hence it is only found in CDAP=no languages or languages without agreement, and I presented preliminary typological evidence that this might be true. This approach makes

on the applied argument, just as it does on the goal argument of a simple ditransitive verbs. If there are also languages in which Appl is a phase head, then the VP complement of Appl will be a distinct spell out domain, it will contain only the direct object and not the applied object, and dative case will not be realized on the applied object, although it is (by hypothesis) on the goal argument of a simple ditransitive (or maybe the applied object is dative if and only if the direct object is definite, so that it shifts out of VP). I don't think I know any languages offhand that have this second profile—but I have never looked for them either, and the matter is worth more careful investigation. (Similar issues might be raised by causative heads as well.)

the seemingly radical prediction that, since ergative case and accusative case are sensitive to the same local domains (phases), the definiteness/position of the object can affect both, and the tense-aspect of the clause can affect both. However, there is supporting evidence for these predictions from Ika, Ostyak, and Coast Tsimshian. Finally, and perhaps most radically, I suggested that languages differ as to whether NPs in the lower case domain (VP) are automatically included in the higher case domain (TP) or not. The latter sort of language is prone to differential object marking and split ergativity; the former has uniform case assignment across virtually all clause types. This then is a survey of some types of variation and parameterization that we seem to find in systems of morphological case, within current generative (minimalist) terms.

4

Parameters and the three factors of language design

ANDERS HOLMBERG AND IAN ROBERTS

4.1 Introduction

In this chapter[1] we will argue for an 'emergentist' view of parametric variation (see Biberauer 2011, 2012; Biberauer and Branigan 2012; Roberts 2012). Our thesis is that parametric variation, like many other linguistically significant phenomena, is an emergent property of the three factors of language design. Following Chomsky (2005:6), we take the three factors to be as in (1).

(1) F1: the genetic endowment, Universal Grammar.
 F2: the environment: Primary Linguistic Data for language acquisition.
 F3: General principles of computation and cognition (more details later).

As we shall see, UG creates the space for parametric variation by leaving certain options underspecified. These options appear to involve a rather small subset of the formal features manipulated by the computational system of narrow syntax, a feature triggering movement and those associated with the phase heads (C, D and v), along with morphophonological options of realization (including selective spell-out, null realization, impoverishment, etc). For empirical and theoretical reasons to be

[1] This work is funded by the European Research Council Advanced Grant No. 269752 'Rethinking Comparative Syntax' (ReCoS) and a Major Fellowship from the Leverhulme Trust for Anders Holmberg. Many thanks to the other members of the ReCoS project group: Andras Barány, Tim Bazalgette, Theresa Biberauer, Alison Biggs, Jessica Brown, Georg Hoehn, Michelle Sheehan, and Jenneke van der Wal for comments, critique, and much more. Much of what is reported here touches on joint work with various subsets of the overall group; the nature of ongoing collaborations is such that it is not always possible to properly cite every contribution in every case without overburdening the presentation. However, we are solely responsible for the overall content and for any errors. We would also like to thank the audiences in Barcelona and Durham, where this work was presented.

addressed in section 4.6, we see no reason to limit variation to the 'externalization' component of the system, although of course we do not deny that variation exists there.

Before developing our view of parametric variation, however, we want to address the partly terminological issue of justifying the postulation of parameters in the first place.

4.2 On the existence of parameters

It has recently been claimed, notably by Newmeyer (2005) and by Boeckx (2011a, this volume), that the principles-and-parameters approach to comparative syntax has proven a failure (Newmeyer) or is radically incompatible with a minimalist approach to linguistic theory (Boeckx); either way, these authors suggest that linguistic theory would benefit from its abandonment. The issue is partly terminological, in that both authors recognize that a very weak notion of parametric variation may exist, but that this would more accurately be simply termed a 'difference' between languages or grammars. Both authors, however, correctly point out that the original conception of parameter was much stronger than this, in that it entailed the idea of clustering of phenomena: a single parameter was thought to have complex effects across a range of surface phenomena.

Newmeyer raises empirical problems for the formulation of the null-subject parameter in Rizzi (1982), largely based on Gilligan (1987), and concludes from this that the programme as a whole has failed. He advocates replacing the notion of parameter with language-specific rules. As we have pointed out elsewhere (Roberts and Holmberg 2010), it is not at all clear that this notion of rule, if equivalent to a weak notion of parameter, is not subject to exactly the same empirical and theoretical difficulties as those ascribed by Newmeyer to the notion of parameter. Moreover, as it stands the approach seems to be little more than a return to the *status quo ante* Chomsky (1981), and as such essentially gives up the attempt at explanatory adequacy that the original postulation of principles and parameters represented, in favour of a largely typologically driven notion of descriptive adequacy. For this reason, we do not believe Newmeyer's alternative offers anything to linguistic theory to the extent that linguistic theory should continue to pursue the basic Chomskyan goals of attaining or exceeding explanatory adequacy.

Boeckx raises no empirical issues, although he alludes to Newmeyer's position, which he seems to take to be correct. Instead, he insists on the logical point that if there are no principles of syntax, as the Minimalist Program can be thought to entail, then there can be no parametrized principles. This is of course true. However, it does not follow from this that syntax should necessarily be invariant: since languages at least appear to vary in their syntactic properties, the possibility that syntax varies remains open. Indeed, the burden of proof surely falls on those who claim that it does not vary. No such proof is to be found in Boeckx (2011a, this volume). On the contrary, we submit that the simplest, arguably the most 'minimalist', view of syntactic variation is that small parts of UG are underspecified and that the inherent computational conservatism of the learner interacts with the Primary Linguistic Data (PLD) in such a way as to impose a structure on the space of variation that this underspecification creates. The structural units in this variation can be called 'parameters' (although, if we were starting from scratch, we would probably call them something else).

More precisely, we take the following view. There are universal features of natural language which are plausibly not learned (or learnable, if we take learnable to mean instantiated in the PLD in the form of some obvious trigger or cue): these include the nature of Merge, categorial features, the architecture of the system, and numerous aspects of the syntax-semantics interface (many aspects of word meaning, as pointed out by Chomsky (1993a and elsewhere), negation, reference, quantification, etc). These properties derive either from the first or the third factor, and are overtly instantiated (or not) in the PLD. Call this set of universal, unlearned properties U (this is not a theoretical claim, merely the definition of a set). On the other hand, every language instantiates a very large number of obviously non-universal properties, e.g. in the case of English, the fact that 'dog' means something like $\lambda x[dog(x)]$, the nature of '*do*-support', the vowel and consonant inventory, the fact that there is wh-movement, no nominal case-marking, etc. Call this set of properties L. L must be learned from the PLD, although perhaps the other factors somehow interact with the PLD in this. The PLD must therefore instantiate L.

U is defined as listing universal and unlearnable properties of language; L as listing non-universal and learnable properties. Must universality and (non-)learnability go together? Certainly not as a matter of logical necessity. Perhaps there are learnable universal properties of language, although we will not speculate further on this as this is not our major concern. More interestingly (for us), perhaps there are unlearnable, non-universal properties (where unlearnable means 'not instantiated in the PLD'). The interest of the (residual) notion of parameter is that it may instantiate this last logical possibility. Consider the following definition:

(2)   A grammatical property *P* in a given language is diagnostic of a parameter if *P* is
   a. non-universal;
   b. plausibly unlearnable from PLD.

A property meeting the definition in (2) shows that variation must be partly a matter for F1 and/or F3; F2 is not enough, by definition. The 'traditional' view in the era of government-binding theory, as clearly stated in Chomsky (1981, 1986a), was that only F1 was implicated, and that therefore UG was heavily prespecified for all cross-linguistic options.

A good example of a grammatical property characterized by (2a) and (b) is the existence of 'that-trace effects' in English as opposed to Italian, first described in Perlmutter (1971) and analysed in terms of the wider null-subject parameter by Rizzi

(1982). The central observation is that Italian allows a subordinate-clause subject to be wh-moved 'over' a complementizer, while English does not, although it nonetheless allows agent-extraction, e.g. in passives. The examples below illustrate:

(3) a. Chi hai detto che <chi>ha scritto queste lettere?   [Italian]
        Who you said that (who) has written these letters?
        'Who did you say has written these letters?'

    b. Da chi hai detto che sono state scritte queste lettere <da chi>?
        by who you said that are been written these letters (by who)?
        'By whom did you say these letters have been written?'

(4) a. *Who did you say that <who> wrote these letters?
    b. Who did you say that these letters were written by <who>?

(3a) and (4a) contrast minimally in English and Italian. Since this kind of example can hardly be thought to be frequent in the PLD, and indeed may be of a complexity that goes beyond the capacities of young children to parse (note that the examples involve 'degree-1' embedding and hence do not conform to Lightfoot's (1991) 'degree-0' constraint), and since the judgements are robust and consistent in both groups of native speakers, we have here a case of a parameter—or the reflex of a parameter—in the sense defined in (2). In fact, of course, this contrast between English and Italian follows from the null-subject parameter as formulated by Rizzi (1982); moreover, the correlation between 'free subject inversion' and toleration of that-trace effects, first observed by Perlmutter, survives Gilligan's cross-linguistic investigation and critique. This is very significant: the one property in the cluster identified by Rizzi which arguably is not directly instantiated in the PLD is the one which correlates most clearly with something which is readily instantiated, namely free subject inversion. This is exactly the kind of phenomenon the original notion of parameter was designed to explain. Boeckx and Newmeyer are silent on alternative explanations for this kind of case, and we therefore retain the view that a notion of parameter retains explanatory utility.

Assuming the contrast in (3) vs. (4) is not acquired directly from PLD, the innate endowment must play a role in the Italian/English contrast. In other words, F2 is inoperative, and so F1 and/or F3 must somehow specify the difference. This leads us to the view that the internal properties of the organism, either in the form of UG or in the form of F3, lead to *differences* as well as *similarities* among languages. This idea, first articulated clearly in Chomsky (1981), has proven extremely fruitful for comparative work, if only as a heuristic. As Chomsky (2002:95) pointed out, we have probably learned more about comparative syntax in the decades since 1980 than in the preceding millennia. To put it another way, the notion of parameter lies at the interface of language typology and biolinguistics. As Kayne has repeatedly stressed (see for example Kayne 2005a), one profitable way to study language universals is to study language variation. To dismiss variation as 'Greenberg's problem' (never defined), as in Boeckx (2011a), is to miss a central question for biolinguistics: to paraphrase Longobardi (2003) and Longobardi and Roberts (2010), why is it meaningful, as a first approximation, to speak of 'Chinese word order', 'Japanese interrogatives', etc., but not of 'Russian vision', 'Spanish memory', etc?

The traditional GB view, again aptly illustrated by Rizzi (1982), stated the difference between English and Italian illustrated in (3) and (4) in terms of the UG-internal null-subject parameter, which had to do with rather specific properties of the I(nfl) head. In this case, it is quite easy to see the role of F1, but relatively rather hard to see role of F3. However, in this connection Newmeyer makes one extremely telling remark:

we are not yet at the point of being able to 'prove' that the child is not equipped with 7,846 . . . parameters, each of whose settings is fixed by some relevant triggering experience. I would put my money, however, on the fact that evolution has not endowed human beings in such an exuberant fashion   (Newmeyer 2005: 83)

On this we can only concur. However, closer investigation of Rizzi's proposal in this particular connection reveals that he saw the null-subject parameter in terms of variation in what we would now see as a formal feature of I, which we could without anachrony refer to as 'D' (see Rizzi 1982:143). We are therefore free to regard this feature as underspecified: at the UG level I may or may not have a D-feature. This is the role of F1. Acquirers 'fill in the gap' according to the PLD to which they are exposed (F2), perhaps with a bias in one direction or the other (markedness, which arises from F3). There is no pre-equipped parameter, merely an optional feature which occurs in numerous parts of the system.

4.3 The three factors in linguistic phenomena

It is quite easy to find other examples of significant linguistic phenomena which arise as a result of the interaction of the three factors. Consider for example wh-movement in English. Here the contribution of UG consists in the [wh] feature marking a class of Ds and Cs, the nature of 'A'-movement' and/or 'A'-positions', the nature of (internal) Merge and properties of the copies which result from movement/Internal Merge and determine reconstruction and possibly some kinds of crossover phenomena. F2 provides the cues for the range of typological variation which has emerged in recent years. Roughly, this consists in whether wh-movement is restricted to just one wh-phrase in a given domain, as in English, or whether all wh-phrases must front, giving the equivalent of *Who what saw?* It is well known that this restriction does not hold of the Slavonic languages and other languages; furthermore, those languages which allow 'multiple fronting' differ in more subtle ways (see Rudin 1988; McDaniel 1989; Bošković 2002, etc.). Moreover, (adult) English does not allow 'partial movement' (as in *What did you say who left?*, found in various German dialects), but requires ('full') movement of exactly one wh-phrase, unlike Chinese and other 'in-situ' languages, which instead allow the equivalents of *You met which boy?* etc. All of this variation is arguably directly determined by PLD.

F3, on the other hand, determines universal features of 'A'-movement' which are probably deducible from more general cognitive principles than UG itself. These include locality, which we take to consist in relativized minimality and Phase Impenetrability (the former a natural expression of 'minimal search', the latter a natural consequence of 'derivation by phase'). A further element is linearization of a hierarchically 'upward' dependency as 'leftward', deriving from general linearization conditions, which arguably cannot be exhaustively determined by UG (see Biberauer et al. 2010b; Biberauer, Roberts, and Sheehan 2013b). Further, there is the bijective nature of quantifier-variable relation (not a logical necessity, but a natural simplifying constraint), and perhaps the nature of quantification itself, which if it just involves relations among sets as assumed in generalized-quantification theory (Barwise and Cooper 1981), is presumably not language-specific, but rather reflects a domain-general aspect of human cognition.

We can extend this line of reasoning in an obvious way. Many other linguistic phenomena are probably best seen as emergent properties of the interaction of the three factors. Passives, for example, arguably involve Agree, and the nature of 'A-movement' and/or 'A-positions' (F1); language-specific variant properties triggered by PLD (e.g. whether the language allows impersonal passives, *by*-phrases, passives of ditransitives, passives of causatives, etc.), all attributable to F2; and θ-roles, which arguably derive from domain-general—or at least not language-specific—aspects of cognition concerning the mental representation of events, causes, intentions, etc.

Or consider the notion of 'subject'. This clearly involves F1 considerations—essentially whatever the theory of grammatical functions amounts to or derives from. But again PLD must be relevant as subject properties are notoriously variable across languages, especially once ergative languages are considered. Finally, θ-theory is again relevant to the extent that the notion of subject implies or subsumes agentivity.

Moving beyond syntax, consider the familiar notion of a consonant. Here again all three factors are relevant. UG must determine the nature of phonetically complex and syllable-dependent notions such as rhotics and glides. Again F2 determines what counts as a consonant in a given language, not simply the consonant inventory (e.g. whether /θ/ is a phoneme or not), but also for example whether /ɹ/ is a consonant (English) or a vowel (Mandarin). Finally, articulatory and perceptual phonetics clearly involve anatomical, neurological and cognitive capacities which are not specific to language, and of course are highly relevant to any understanding of what a consonant is.

We can go a step further, perhaps. Consider the concept 'English' (or obviously the name of any language as a sociocultural entity). F1 is relevant since whatever is common to all native speakers includes first what is common to all humans with a language faculty and furthermore some subset of UG options which is common to all varieties of English. F2 is the PLD English-speakers were exposed to when small, and which makes them speakers of English and not some other 'language'. Finally, F3 consists of the rather complex set of cognitive abilities which allow an English-speaker to recognize a 'linguistic con-specific'; this involves theory of mind as well as a number of aspects of communicative competence (Hymes 1971) and sociolinguistic accommodation theory (Giles 1994).

All of this is just to say that our view of parametric variation is nothing special. Cross-linguistic variation arises from the interaction of the three factors in language design, just as the vast majority of the superficial phenomena of language that are of interest to linguists do. The key thing for linguistic theory is to understand the role and interaction of the three factors.

4.4 Three factors in language variation

In this connection, we should be a little more precise about how the three factors create parametric variation. The first factor stems directly from the language-specific genetic endowment. Following the general line of thinking in recent linguistic theory (notably Chomsky 1995), we take this to mean variation in the formal features of functional heads. More precisely, there is reason to think that only a narrow subset of formal features of a subset of functional heads varies: probably only movement-triggering features (following Biberauer, Holmberg, and Roberts (in press) we take this to be the diacritic $^\wedge$) and unvalued (hence underspecified) features associated with D, C and v. This very small 'window of variation' is left open by UG: to paraphrase the very apt formulation of Biberauer and Richards (2006), this is where UG 'doesn't mind'. So we are adding nothing to UG here; in fact, we are taking something away (see Biberauer 2011, 2012 for an extension of this approach).

F2 is the 'trigger experience' or 'cues' in Lightfoot's (1991) terminology, for parameters. Here we take the notion of 'parameter-expression' of Clark and Roberts (1993), Roberts and Roussou (2003) to be central, and we define it as follows:

(5) a. Parameter expression:
     A substring of the input text S expresses a parameter p_i just in case a grammar must have p_i set to a definite value in order to assign a well-formed representation to S.

   b. Trigger: A substring of the input text S is a trigger for parameter p_i if S expresses p_i.

This is neither a postulate of UG nor a characterization of a third factor. It is a definition of a causal relation between experience and an internal property of the learner.

The term was deliberately modelled on the concept of 'gene expression' in genetics. The relation between a given gap in UG and the linguistic phenomenon which expresses it may be just as indirect as the relation between a missing or extra amino acid in a gene and its expression in some observable property of the organism (blue eyes, compound eyes, no eyes, etc.).

F3 is perhaps most important here as it is least familiar. In this context, the third factor relates to general strategies of L1 acquisition based on computational conservatism. We are aware of three of these. The first is Input Generalization (IG), which we define as follows:

(6)   For a given set of features F and a given set of functional heads H, given a trigger for feature f∈F of a functional head h∈H, the learning device generalizes f to all other functional heads $h_1 \ldots h_n \in H$.

This represents a simple 'shortcut' mechanism on the part of the learner: if you see one white swan, assume all swans are white until further notice (purple or black swans, or swans without colour properties). In grammatical terms, if you parse one phrase as head-final, assume they are all head-final, until an exception is encountered. IG may run rather deep: it is fundamentally connected to the notion of category itself, which Pinker (2011:323) has argued is essential to intelligence ('categorization is indispensable to intelligence. Categories allow us to make inferences from a few observed qualities to a larger number of unobserved ones'). Biberauer (2011, 2012) and Biberauer and Branigan (2012) develop the connection between IG and the emergence of syntactic categories in language acquisition in a very interesting way. IG is an instance of Piercean abduction, which we could state with maximum simplicity, at the same time making clear its fallacy as a deduction as $\exists x[F(x)] \rightarrow \forall x[F(x)]$. And it is defeasible: the first black swan encountered ensures that the generalization to white swans is abandoned. In historical linguistics, IG has long been familiar in the guise of analogy of various kinds.

Another aspect of computational conservativity is simple feature economy. This can be thought of along the general lines of Chomsky and Halle (1968): the fewer the formal features postulated in a given parse the more highly valued that parse. Again, the strategy is defeasible: if n features are required then n features will be postulated. But the learner always favours the smallest number of formal features it can 'get away with'. This has been documented as a force in language change: Roberts and Roussou (2003) argue that essentially this constraint (construed in a particular way) underlies the diachronically ubiquitous phenomenon of grammaticalization. Clark and Roberts (1993) argued that it played a causal role in certain major changes in the history of French.

Third, there is—or may be—the Subset Principle of Berwick (1995). We state the Subset Principle in (7):

(7)   'the learner must guess the smallest possible language compatible with the input at each stage of the learning procedure' (Clark and Roberts 1993:304–5)

This principle has the important conceptual advantage of being founded upon what appears to be a clear fact about language acquisition: that acquirers do not have access to negative evidence. Because of this, it is impossible for an acquirer to retreat from a superset hypothesis, since the only evidence that would force this to happen would be evidence regarding the impossibility of certain strings, but this is negative evidence and hence unavailable (the child apparently cannot learn from experience that English is *not* a null-subject language; merely hearing overt pronominal subjects is not enough). Consequently, acquisition would seem to have to proceed on a highly conservative basis as described in (7).

Conceptually well-motivated though it may be, the Subset Principle has arguably foundered as a useful principle for guiding the setting of parameters in language acquisition, since most parameters seem to define intersecting languages rather than languages in a subset-superset relation (taking a language to be the set of strings generated by a grammar). This is particularly clear in the case of word-order parameters, such as 'OV' vs. 'VO', since the parameter defining these options defines an intersecting set of grammatical strings. The same is true of many other important axes of variation (again, whether we call these 'parameters' or not is immaterial): ergativity, wh-movement, polysynthesis, and in fact null subjects (the classical null-subject parameter forbids overt expletives in null-subject languages, thus allowing a class of grammatical sentences in non-null-subject languages which is forbidden in null-subject languages). Hence the Subset Principle, for all its conceptual elegance, appears unsuited to accounting for 'parameter-setting'. Moreover, extremely well-known facts about language acquisition militate against it: children are known to overgeneralize in all areas, and hence they must have a mechanism for 'retreat' from superset traps. It may be that Bayesian learning algorithms can play a role here, although they seem inherently ill-suited to accounting for language acquisition (without a very rich 'prior', i.e. UG) since they predict convergence on subsets of predetermined available hypothesis sets.

For these reasons, we leave the Subset Principle aside, whilst recognizing its potential conceptual validity as a third-factor learning strategy (Biberauer and Roberts (2009) show that it may be useful in accounting for the diachronic loss of certain kinds of formal optionality, as well as for what they call 'restriction of function'). We are thus left with Input Generalization and Feature Economy, both powerful, defeasible, domain-general strategies.

To recapitulate: our thesis is that a residual notion of parameter can be constructed from the interaction of the mildly underspecified UG, the nature of the PLD (in particular P-expression) and the third-factor, computationally conservative strategies of Input Generalization and Feature Economy (with the Subset Principle left in abeyance). We consider this position conceptually preferable to Newmeyer's return to some entirely unclear and apparently retrograde notion of language-specific rule, and to Boeckx's unsupported assertion that narrow syntax must be invariant. We now turn to the empirical support for this general position.

4.5 On narrow-syntactic parameters

A corollary of the idea that Narrow Syntax is invariant across languages is that all linguistic variation is a matter of 'externalization', of giving the language of thought a form such that it can be communicated to others. In Berwick and Chomsky's words (2011:37–8):

> Parameterization and diversity, then, would be mostly—possibly entirely—restricted to externalization. That is pretty much what we seem to find: a computational system efficiently generating expressions interpretable at the semantic–pragmatic interface, with diversity resulting from complex and highly varied modes of externalization, which, furthermore, are readily susceptible to historical change.

Certain developments in syntactic theory, which predate the distinction between the narrow and broad language faculty introduced by Hauser et al. (2002), accord particularly well with this approach. One such development is the theory of movement as construction of a chain of copies by merging the same constituent more than once. If UG does not dictate which copy is to be pronounced, this allows variation, and this variation is located in the postsyntactic derivation of PF, where pronunciation is determined. Huang's (1982) wh-movement parameter would, in this light, be a matter of which copy in a wh-chain is pronounced, the higher or the lower copy (Brody 1995; Groat and O'Neil 1996). This idea could be applied to movement in general: Wherever we find a case of movement in language A but seemingly not in language B, this would mean that the movement does apply in language B as well, a chain of copies is derived, but it's the lowest copy which is pronounced. The movement is universal, a property of Narrow Syntax; how it is externalized, i.e. pronounced, is subject to variation.

Morphological expressions of syntactic relations, such as case or agreement, would also be a matter of post-syntactic derivation: Narrow Syntax would dictate, say, that finite T enters a probe-goal relation with an argument (the subject), but how this is externalized, as morphological case or agreement or both or neither, would be subject to variation.

The idea that all variation is a matter of externalization has been enthusiastically embraced by various scholars subscribing to the Minimalist Program, though mostly in a programmatic fashion (as indeed in Chomsky's own work). An exception is Halldór Sigurðsson, who in a series of recent works, including Sigurðsson (2009, 2011a), and especially (2011b), has tried to formalize this general idea and apply it to certain syntactic, or morphosyntactic, phenomena. The following is a very rough characterization of the theory articulated in Sigurðsson (2011b).

First, Sigurðsson makes a distinction between I-language and E-language: I-language is innate, a biological property of the human mind, basically invariant across languages and individuals ('apart from peripheral concept variation'); It is the language of thought. E-language, on the other hand, is what we use to communicate our thoughts to other people. It is learnt on the basis of experience ('by imitation'), subject to cross-linguistic (cultural) variation—though within the limits set by UG and other mental capacities that enter into linguistic activity. Much as we discussed earlier, Sigurðsson assumes that variation is allowed wherever UG does not specify a particular syntactic relation or structure or feature arrangement: the underspecification approach to variation. Sigurðsson describes in some detail a radically minimalist theory of UG where the building blocks are a single 'initial root' and a single 'initial feature' making up the Universal Lexicon (UL), which are filled with content from a repository of concepts, largely or wholly universal, including substantive concepts and grammatical concepts (tense, number, etc.), which are 'transformed into I-language elements by repeatedly copying or filling or loading' the initial root and the initial feature, and which are combined into complex expressions by a single operation Merge, deriving I-language representations that are the same across speakers and languages.

What is E-language, then? How does it relate to I-language? Sigurðsson does not spell out explicitly how the system as a whole is meant to operate, but we take it that the idea is that the derivation of a sentence means first constructing an I-language representation, employing UG, UL, and the concept mine, and then assigning E-language form to it (deriving an E-language representation from it) using other resources. There is a question as to how big a chunk of I-language structure the grammar needs in order to be able to assign E-language form to it (the issue of the role of phases in the system)—we put this question aside.

If I-language representations are constructed by Narrow Syntax (I-syntax, in Sigurðsson's terms), then E-language representations are, by implication, derived by Broad Syntax (E-syntax). But what is Broad Syntax? Sigurðsson discusses some E-language derivations, specifically derivation of sentences with chains of co-referential arguments where the person feature is crucially involved (sentences like *John says that he wants coffee*), and sentences exhibiting tense agreement across sentences (like *John said that he was ill*), showing how the underlying I-language relations are realized differently across languages, and he formulates some generalizations about the relation between I-language and E-language on that basis. The examples that Sigurðsson focuses on concern specifically how certain I-language relations are expressed as overt (or sometimes covert) morphological categories (case, agreement, tense marking), the point being that this is not a matter of I-syntax, but takes place in 'a component that "sees" syntax but is out of semantic/syntactic "reach" (deep PF, comprising abstract morphology)'.

We do not wish to take issue with this. We do want to question the assumption that even a broader notion of PF or morphology, incorporating some aspects of what used to be seen as syntax, is sufficient to account for all cross-linguistic syntactic variation.

We take it that the following is a theoretically coherent position: Broad Syntax is Narrow Syntax plus a set of formally different rule systems. Narrow Syntax builds hierarchic structures (by external and internal Merge) and establishes certain relations between the constituents (by Agree). Furthermore, Narrow Syntax is universal, deriving I-language representations, 'thoughts', which have the same syntax across languages and individuals. The other rule systems operate on the structures built by Narrow Syntax, but they allow variation (of systematic nature) which means that E-language representations show systematic variation across languages.

It's a theoretically coherent position, but we would claim it's empirically untenable: There is E-language variation which can't be due to just variation in vocabulary insertion, selective spell-out, linearization, morphology, and phonology. That is to say, there is E-language variation which involves syntactic structure building: external and internal Merge.

We might consider the possibility that Broad Syntax includes syntactic, structure-building rules which are post-Narrow Syntax and which do allow variation. We take this to be a theoretically untenable (or at least highly questionable) position: If the operations employed (Merge and Agree) are the same, then how could they be subject to variation in one part of the grammar but not the other?

The traditional P&P position, though slightly updated here, is that there is syntax, deriving LF representations interpreted at the C-I interface, and there are post-syntactic systems (selective spell-out, morphology, etc.) deriving PF representations interpreted at the A-P interface. Clearly a lot of the cross-linguistic variation is due to the post-syntactic systems. However, the traditional P&P position, which we agree with, is that syntax is flexible enough to allow for some limited variation (parametric variation). As stated earlier, this position is not jeopardized by the 'minimal UG' idea, following Hauser et al. (2002) and much subsequent work. In fact, the opposite is the case: Being minimally specified, UG allows variation in syntax, the structure-building module. The consequence is that the same 'thought' can have I-language representations which are different in some respects, although we would still expect them to have the same basic syntactic structure.

In the following we will discuss one specific case which we hope is sufficient to make the point we wish to make: That 'the same thought' can be expressed in two syntactically distinct ways, which can only be accounted for if variation is allowed in the syntax (now often called Narrow Syntax).

4.6 Case study: Answers to yes/no questions

In English and many other languages the minimal answer to a yes/no question consists of a particle, either an affirmative or a negative particle, yes or no.

(8)   Q(uestion):   Does Anna drink coffee?
      A(nswer):   Yes.

In many other languages the affirmative answer is expressed by echoing the finite verb of the question.

(9)   Q: Juo-ko Anna kahvia?   [Finnish]
          drinks-Q Anna coffee
          'Does Anna drink coffee?'

      A: Juo.
          drinks
          'Yes.'

The answers express the same thought, the externalization of that thought is quite different.

A crucial question, obviously, is what counts as 'the same thought'. As a working operational definition, two expressions convey the same thought if they are truth-conditionally equivalent and interchangeable in the same discourse context. Under this definition, (8) and (9) do express the same thought. In any context where a question can be answered 'Yes' in English, conveying affirmation, the corresponding question can be answered with a verb echoing the finite verb of the question in Finnish, conveying affirmation.[2]

What is the structure of the thought in (8) and (9)? A yes/no question is a sentence where polarity is left open. In a declarative sentence, polarity is fixed as either affirmative or negative, in a yes/no question it is a variable with two possible values, affirmative or negative. The question solicits an answer which assigns a value to the variable such that the sentence expresses a true proposition (see Holmberg 2001).[3]

Take [+POL] to mean 'affirmative', [−POL] to mean 'negative', and [uPOL] to mean 'unvalued polarity', where the possible values are + and −. The structure of the affirmative answer to the question 'Does Anna drink coffee?', in Finnish or English, is then:

---

[2] There are some exceptions. For example, if the question has narrow focus on some constituent (other than polarity) the affirmative answer in English can be *yes*, but it cannot be the echoed verb of the question in Finnish. Another case is when the question is a conjunction such as 'Did John come, and did he bring some food?' In this case Finnish cannot answer by an echoed verb, but will, instead, resort to an affirmative particle corresponding to *yes*. Space does not allow discussion of these cases, but they do not jeopardize the conclusions we draw from the comparison of Finnish and English in the text. In fact, they are explained by the fact that the (narrow-)syntactic derivation of the affirmative answer in Finnish is very different from the derivation of 'the same answer' in English.

[3] This is semantically equivalent to the question soliciting a choice between the two alternative propositions p and ¬p denoted by the question such that the selected proposition is true (Hamblin 1958). The claim made in Holmberg (2001, in press) and the text here is that the syntax of the question-answer pair involves an operator-variable relation.

(10)

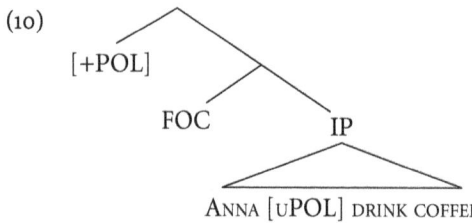

ANNA [uPOL] DRINK COFFEE

The answer is derived by ellipsis, since typically all that is pronounced is the morphological expression of [+POL] (i.e. *yes* in English). The IP can be deleted as long as it is identical to the IP of the question.[4]

Following Holmberg (2001) we assume that the answer is an identificational focus construction. In É. Kiss's (2006) terms, the IP names a list of alternatives (namely, Anna does or does not drink coffee), and [+POL] specifies the content of the list (in the relevant time and place). The syntactic relation between the focused [+POL] and the variable [uPOL] is an operator-variable relation: The operator assigns a value to the variable.

(11)

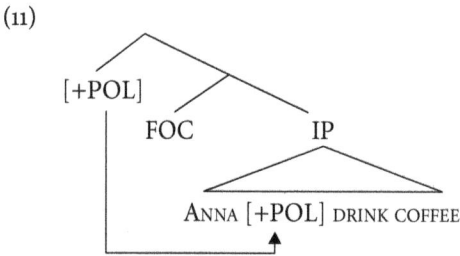

ANNA [+POL] DRINK COFFEE

In English, the externalization of (11) is straightforward: [+POL] is pronounced *yes*, FOC is null, and the IP is also (typically) null because of ellipsis.

(12)

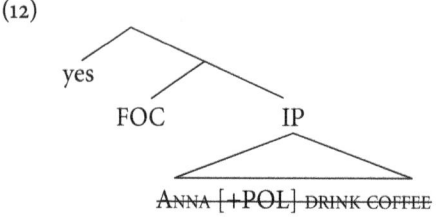

ANNA [+POL] DRINK COFFEE

---

[4] The way this is modelled in Holmberg (2001) is that there is no deletion in (10), but instead the LF of the IP of the question is copied into the IP position of the answer. In most respects this is formally equivalent to 'deletion under identity'.

The externalization of (11) in Finnish is more complicated. At first blush, it looks like it could be derived by V-movement to spec,FocP, with ellipsis of the IP. Indeed, if the whole sentence is pronounced in the answer, as it can be, the word order is VSO, as in (13), while the word order of an unmarked declarative in Finnish is SVO:

(13) Juo Anna kahvia.
      drinks Anna coffee
      'Yes, she does drink coffee.'

However, the answer may consist of more than just the finite verb: It can be a string of verbs: auxiliary and restructuring verbs optionally followed by the main verb.

(14) Q: Saa-ko Anna juoda kahvia?
         can-Q Anna drink coffee

      A: Saa juoda (Anna kahvia).
         can drink
         'Yes (Anna can drink coffee).'

According to Holmberg (2001), the derivation of the affirmative answer involves remnant movement of IP to spec, FOC, more precisely, remnant movement of a [+POL]-marked IP to the focus position, while a negative answer is correspondingly derived by remnant movement of a [−Pol]-marked IP to the focus position.[5] This remnant movement must be preceded by (a) V-movement of the main verb out of vP, and (b) topicalization of the rest of the vP (the predicate). The topicalization does not target a designated topic position in the CP-domain (unlike many instances of topicalization in other languages; cf. Rizzi 1997), but targets the highest A-position in IP, spec,FinP; see Holmberg and Nikanne (2002) for evidence that the position is indeed the specifier of the head encoding finiteness, and Holmberg (2001) for arguments that Finnish has vP-topicalization and that it is a step in the derivation of verb answers. The derived representation of the answer in (14) is (15):[6]

---

[5] The negative answer would be (i), employing the standard sentential negation, which can be spelled out alone or together with the verb.

(i) Ei (juo).
     not drinks
     'No.'

[6] The relation between the focused PolP and its copy is the same as in other, more familiar cases of fragment answers, as in (i) with roughly the structure of (ii) (Merchant 2004):

  (i) Who did Bill see?
       John.
  (ii) [$_{FocP}$ John Foc [$_{IP}$ Bill saw <John>]]

(15)

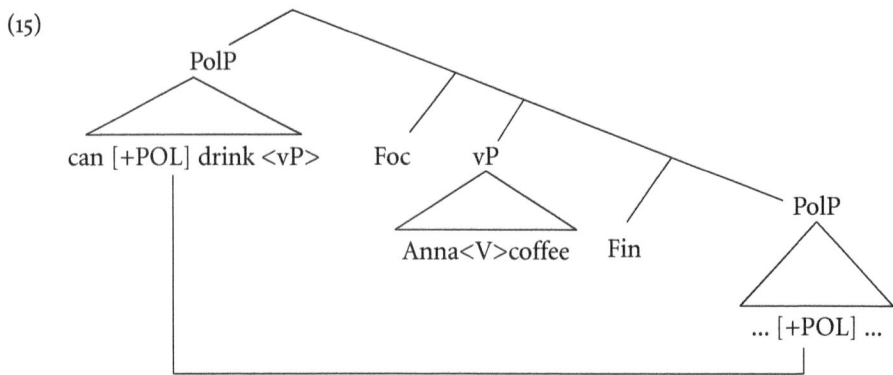

Clearly, 'externalization' in this case involves complex syntactic derivation. The derived structure contains the essential components in (10), also seen in the English version (12), but where in (12) the focused affirmative operator is just the feature [+POL] spelled out as a particle, the affirmative operator in the Finnish version is a reduced sentence, an IP, or more precisely, a Pol(arity)P with affirmative value (Holmberg 2001).

According to the architecture of the grammar suggested by the quotation from Berwick and Chomsky in the previous section, adopted and elaborated by Sigurðsson (2011b), (10) would be the universal I-language representation of an affirmative answer derived by Narrow Syntax (or I-syntax), which entails that (12) and (15) would be Broad-Syntactic articulations of this representation. We believe facts from answers to yes/no questions in Finnish and English are incompatible with this hypothesis.

Why does English not avail itself of the 'verb-echo' option?[7] We will consider Swedish instead, to avoid the complication arising from the fact that English employs the auxiliary *do* in questions.[8] So, why can't Swedish use the verb-echo option?

(16) Q: Dricker Anna kaffe?   [Swedish]
         drinks Anna coffee
         'Does Anna drink coffee?'

      A: Ja.
         yes

      A: *Dricker.
         drinks

---

[7] Finnish can use an affirmative particle as an alternative to echoing the verb, perhaps not surprisingly, given the simpler syntactic derivation. That said, there are languages which rely entirely on verb-answers, for instance Scots Gaelic (David Adger, p.c.).

[8] Another complication is that English also has *She does* as an alternative affirmative answer form (to the question *Does she drink coffee?*). This alternative has a very different structure from the Finnish verb answer, being derived by VP ellipsis. See Holmberg (2001) who shows that Finnish, too, has this alternative answer form, with very similar discourse properties.

The difference does not involve the null subject parameter: Finnish does not allow a null referential subject in the 3rd person but has verb-answers in all persons. This is one of the arguments in Holmberg (2001) in favour of the derivation of verb-answers by V or VP-movement to the C-domain with ellipsis of IP, instead of subject pro-drop and VP-ellipsis (see also arguments in Jones (1999) against analysing verb-answers in Welsh as derived by VP-ellipsis; see Goldberg (2005) on verb-stranding VP-ellipsis).

There are two or three operations in the derivation of the Finnish answer (15) that do not occur in Swedish: (a) The finite verb does not raise out of vP in Swedish except as part of the V2 rule (i.e. only in main clauses); (b) The non-finite main verb does not move out of vP in Swedish, as required for the main verb to end up in the focused remnant-fronted IP/PolP, and (c) Swedish does not have topic-fronting of the kind required to derive the remnant IP/PolP. We put finite verb raising aside, because of the complication posed by V2. Finnish shows direct evidence ('E-language evidence') of non-finite main verb movement in sentences like (17a), compared with the Swedish (b):

(17) a. Anna ei saa (enää) juoda (enää) kahvia.   [Finnish]
        Anna not can (any.longer) drink (any.longer) coffee

   b. *Anna får inte (längre) dricka (*längre) kaffe
        Anna can not (any.longer) drink (any.longer) coffee

According to Holmberg (2001, 2007), the topicalization of vP seen in (15) is a special case of the topicalization seen in (18), argued in Holmberg and Nikanne (2002) to be EPP-driven movement to the highest A-position in the sentence; Finnish is a 'topic-prominent language' in this sense. Swedish is not.

(18) Tämän kirjan   on kirjoittanut Graham Greene.   [Finnish]
      this   book.ACC has written   Graham Greene.NOM
      'This book is written by Graham Greene.'

(19) *Den här boken har skrivit Graham Greene.   [Swedish]
       this here book has written Graham Greene

What kind of movement is the fronting rule in (18)? It is topicalization, in that the object is interpreted as an aboutness topic while the subject is information focus (the best translation into English is often a passive). Holmberg and Nikanne (2002) show, with a battery of arguments, that the position of the object in (18) is the same as that of the subject in unmarked sentences (rather than being a designated topic position in the C-domain). This is shown, for example, by the fact that it can be preceded by the fronted verb in questions, as in (20a), to be compared with the unmarked, subject-first sentence (20b).

(20) a. On-ko tämän kirjan kirjoittanut Graham Greene?   [Finnish]
        has-Q this   book written   Graham Greene
        'Is this book by Graham Greene?'

 b. On-ko Graham Greene kirjoittanut tämän kirjan?
    has-Q Graham Greene written   this   book
    'Has Graham Greene written this book?'

The structure of (18) is roughly (21).

(21)

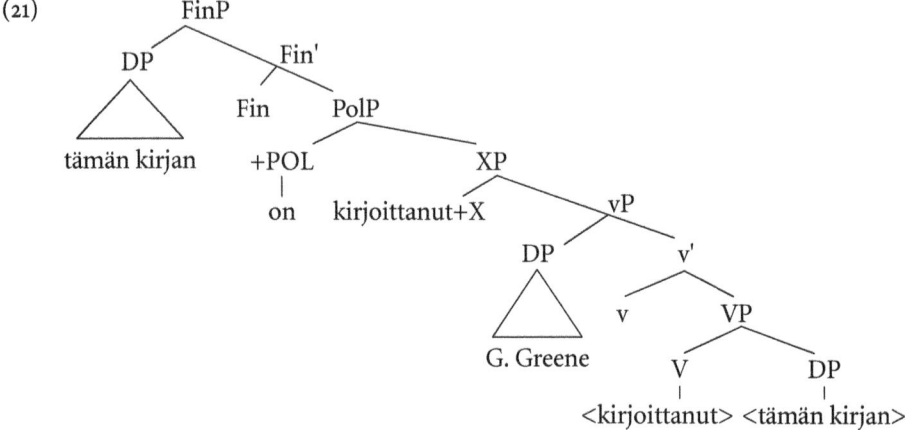

The claim in Holmberg (2001) is that in the verb answer, the entire vP moves to spec,FinP.

(22)

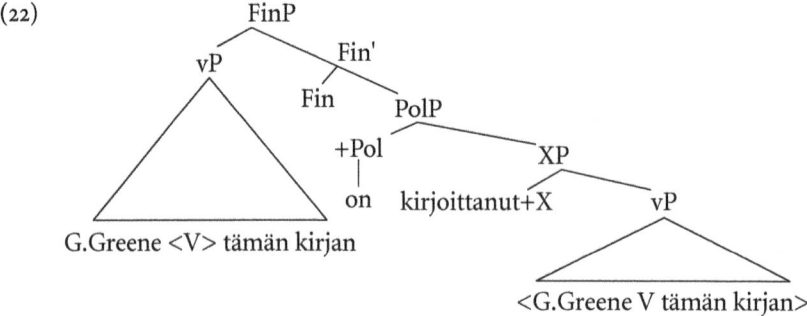

The answer is then derived by merging Foc, and moving/remerging the affirmative-marked PolP with FocP. When spelled out, typically leaving the topicalized vP null, the order is (23), a well-formed affirmative reply in Finnish to the question 'Has Graham Greene written this book?'

(23)   On kirjoittanut (Graham Greene tämän kirjan)   [Finnish]
       has written   Graham Greene this   book
       'Yes (he has).'

If the main verb does not move, but remains inside vP, it will be topicalized along with the rest of the vP. After movement of PolP, the spelled-out form will be (24), also a well-formed reply in Finnish.

(24) On (Graham Greene kirjoittanut tämän kirjan).   [Finnish]
      has Graham Greene written   this   book
      'Yes (he has).'

We mentioned the possibility that Huang's (1982) wh-parameter, i.e. the distinction
between languages that have wh-movement and languages that have wh-in-situ, could
be a case of selective spell-out: Wh-movement (formation of a wh-chain) would be
universal, but languages differ with respect to which copy is pronounced. This would
put the wh-parameter firmly in the post-syntactic module of the grammar. Can topicalization, as seen in (21), be another such case? Could it be that English (25), when
spoken in a context where *this book* is the topic and *Graham Greene* is information
focus, has the object moved to a topic position, just like Finnish, but with the difference that the lower copy is pronounced, instead of the higher, as in Finnish?[9]

(25) Graham Greene has written this book.

Since topicalization as in (18) is crucial in the derivation of verb answers (being the
case where vP is topicalized, with or without the main verb), if English (25) can be
derived by object topicalization, but with the lower copy spelled out, we might at least
seriously consider the possibility that English (and Swedish) affirmative answers are
derived exactly as in Finnish, except with variation as regards spell-out of the chains
derived.

This is where the argument becomes relevant that the topic position in Finnish is the
same position where we find the subject in unmarked sentences, regardless of whether
the subject is a topic or not, i.e. the highest A-position. The subject and the object are
competing for the same position.[10] Transferring this to English (assuming, for the sake
of argument, that Narrow Syntax is universal), it can't be the case that (25) instantiates
a chain where a copy of the object is in the highest A-position, because a copy of the
subject is (by all known syntactic criteria).

Instead, where the syntax of English and Swedish allows only movement of the subject to the high A-position, the syntax of Finnish allows movement of other referential,
topicalizable expressions as well, under certain conditions. The exact formal account
of this variation is controversial (see Holmberg and Nikanne 2002; Miyagawa 2010).
Plausibly it involves variation in the unvalued features of Fin: In English and Swedish,

---

[9] We switch to English here, because the argument is a little more complicated in Swedish, due to the
V2 property.
[10] The object and the subject can both precede the finite verb, as in (i).

(i) Kahvia Anna juo.
     coffee Anna drinks
     'It is coffee that Anna drinks.'

The interpretation in that case is contrastive focus on the object (the initial constituent) and topic on the
subject. In this case, the object is clearly in the C-domain. See Vilkuna (1995); Holmberg and Nikanne
(2002).

Fin can only ever attract the argument probed by the unvalued φ-features of Fin (the subject); not so in Finnish. As a consequence, the thought expressed by (18) cannot be expressed in this syntactic form in English or Swedish. The closest you can come is the passive *This book was written by Graham Greene*. It is a matter of definitions whether we want to classify them as expressing the same thought.[11]

If Holmberg (2001) is right, the topicalization possibility is crucial in the derivation of verb answers in Finnish, being a case where topicalization moves the entire vP (with or without the main verb), followed by remnant movement of the PolP to spec,FocP. If so, this would be another case where a syntactic (in Chomskyan terms, Narrow-Syntactic) difference, ultimately variation in the unvalued, movement-triggering features of Fin, has overt E-language effects in a variety of constructions.

To summarize, we have discussed a case, namely two types of answers to yes/no questions in two or three languages, where the E-language expressions are radically different, yet both are instantiations of the same universal structure. The differences are not a matter of vocabulary choice or morphological rules, including spell-out rules. Instead, the syntactic construction of the universal structure proceeds quite differently in the two cases, employing Agree and internal merge in different ways. There are good reasons to believe that this is not just construction-specific variation, but is a consequence of certain systematic differences in the employment of Agree and Move/internal merge, ultimately due at least in part to variation in the feature content of Fin in the two types of languages. That is to say, there is parametric variation in (narrow) syntax.

The answers in English and Finnish nevertheless instantiate the same universal structure (10). However, we would claim that this is not an I-language representation which is the input to the E-language system (in Sigurðsson's (2011b) model). It is not a representation that is actually employed in the derivation of the answers in English or Finnish, even though it happens to be very close to the syntactic representation of the English answer, but is an abstraction over the I-language representations (LFs) of answers to yes/no questions in English, Finnish, and arguably all human languages. It is the linguists' representation of the shared syntactic structure of a particular type of expression, not a representation in the mind of the language user. At that level of abstraction, we may have complete syntactic uniformity across languages.

---

[11] The fact that Finnish does not have a passive with an agent phrase, meaning that topicalization as in (18) really is the closest counterpart to the English passive *This book is written by Graham Greene*, is an argument that they do express the same thought (see Manninen and Nelson 2004 on the Finnish so-called passive). The fact that Finnish topicalization is more restricted than the English passive, in particular by excluding fronting of indefinite objects, argues that they don't express the same thought.

4.7 Conclusion

In this chapter we have argued that the notion of 'parameter' still has merit for the theory of syntax, and in particular for comparative syntax and the general attempt to construct a theory of the innate linguistic endowment, Universal Grammar. More specifically, we have argued for two things: first, a general 'emergentist' approach to parameters, arguing that, like many other linguistically significant notions, they emerge from the interaction of the three factors of language design discussed in Chomsky (2005) and elsewhere. Second, we argued, *pace* Berwick and Chomsky (2011) and Sigurðsson (2011b), that there must be parametric variation in the narrow syntax.

5

Cross-linguistic variation in the syntax of subjects

ANNA CARDINALETTI

5.1 Introduction: On language variation

Chomsky's (2001:2) Uniformity Principle in (1) states that grammar contains an invariant computational system, a universal set of formal features that drive syntactic operations, and a universal set of features which are interpretable at the interface:

(1) In the absence of compelling evidence to the contrary, assume languages to be uniform, with variety restricted to easily detectable properties of utterances.

If (1) is correct, a parameter like the one in (2), very often suggested in the literature on pro-drop (Romance) languages (Contreras 1991; Dobrovie-Sorin 1994; Barbosa 1997; Cornilescu 1997; Alexiadou and Anagnostopoulou 1998; Picallo 1998; Pollock 1998; Poletto 2000; Manzini and Savoia 2002; Carstens 2005, among many others; see also Jelinek (1984, 2006) on so-called non-configurational languages), cannot exist:

(2) ##Parameter: in null-subject languages, preverbal DP subjects are topics and/or sit in A' positions;
       in non-null-subject languages, preverbal DP subjects are 'real' subjects and sit in A positions.

This kind of parameter is theoretically and empirically wrong. It implies a semantic difference between the two sentences in (3) which is theoretically unexpected under (1) since it is not easily detectable:

(3) a. Gianni parla inglese.
     b. John speaks English.

No such semantic difference indeed exists. Like any other phrase, subject DPs can be topics, but need not be. Preverbal DP subjects in Italian behave differently from topics, as in e.g. English (Cardinaletti 1997a, 2004; Rizzi 2005, 2006b). The same has been shown for other pro-drop languages, e.g. Spanish (Suñer 2003) and Portuguese (Costa and Duarte 2002). Preverbal DP subjects are characterized by the property which in previous work I have called 'Subject of Predication', and which can be formalized as a Subject feature that is distinct from Phi-features/Case (Cardinaletti 2004). The existence of this feature is confirmed by the fact that XPs which do not check Phi-features/Case can be attracted to the preverbal subject position (Cardinaletti 1997a, 2004; Belletti and Rizzi 1988), as shown in (4) (also see section 5.2.6):

(4) a. A Gianni è piaciuto il regalo.
      to Gianni is pleased the gift
      'Gianni liked the gift.'

     b. Su Gianni è caduta una grande disgrazia.
      on Gianni is fallen a big misfortune

     c. La causa della rivolta sono Gianni e Maria.
      the cause of the riot are Gianni and Maria

The Subject feature is interpretable at the interface and available in all languages, in Italian as in English, and no language variation indeed appears to exist with regard to the 'subject' properties of preverbal DP subjects. This proposal has been further developed in works by Rizzi (2006b) and Rizzi and Shlonsky (2006, 2007) in terms of a Subject criterion.

The (relevant portion of) clause structure assumed here is depicted in (5). The Subject feature is merged with TP, and projects a SubjP. A subject field can be identified which contains a lower subject position hosting weak pronouns (which check grammatical features), and a higher subject position which hosts DPs or XPs (which check the Subject feature) (see below for a refinement of (5)):

(5) [$_{FinP}$ [$_{SubjP}$ {DP/XP} [$_{TP}$ {weak pronoun} [$_{VP}$]]]]

Excluding the existence of parameters like the one in (2), a successful working hypothesis is that parameters are limited to properties of the functional lexicon, an idea which goes back to Borer (1984). This hypothesis can be exemplified rather easily by the data in (6) concerning subject-verb agreement in expletive constructions: agreement is with the associate unless the expletive pronoun has a fully specified set of phi and case features. This is an easily detectable property—in Chomsky's sense. If the morphological make-up of the lexical elements that are used as expletives is analysed, it is clear that French *il* is fully specified as far as case information is concerned, whereas Italian *pro* and German *es* are not (Chomsky 1995; Cardinaletti 1997b):

(6)   a. Il arrive / *arrivent trois filles.

     b. *pro* *arriva / arrivano tre ragazze.

     c. Es *kommt / kommen drei Leute.

This working hypothesis leads to the idea that language acquisition reduces to lexical acquisition. Empirical work on language acquisition shows that parameters (e.g. pro-drop, word-order, V/2, overt/covert *wh*-movement, etc.) are set as early as the first multi-word utterances are produced (see Guasti (2002) for an overview). This is what Rizzi (2006a), calls 'group A' parameters. However, much work in language acquisition has also shown that functional elements (e.g. determiners, clitic pronouns, auxiliaries, copulas, etc.) are often omitted in early acquisition (the 'group B' parameters, which give rise to parametric discontinuity). These elements turn out to be 'pronounced' late.

This state of affairs seems somehow contradictory. Functional elements are those elements that encode the properties responsible for cross-linguistic variation, these properties must be learnt in order to fix parameters; still, the lexical items that spell out functional elements are not present in the first utterances. Another dimension of parametric variation is at stake here. Sigurðsson (2003:330) formulates the 'silence principle': 'Languages have meaningful silent features; any meaningful feature may be silent'. In other words, 'language variation consists of numerous choices, whether or not to assign physical expressions to logically present categories' (p.332). Similarly, Kayne (2005a) takes [±pronunciation of functional elements] to be another possible source of cross-linguistic variation.

Children have to learn whether functional elements are pronounced in their language, or not. This might take some time, as happens with lexical acquisition in general; it indeed takes time for children to arrive at the target lexical items.[1]

This reasoning suggests that functional projections are present in the child grammar even if they are not pronounced by children in the first stages of language acquisition. In spite of not being pronounced, their properties are detected and used by children to build target-like sentences from the very first stages (see e.g. Giusti 2012 for an analysis of determiner omission in child language compatible with the structural presence of DP in their grammar, *pace* Chierchia et al. 2000).

In this chapter, by focusing on two dimensions of cross-linguistic variation, I discuss the hypothesis that parameters are limited to properties of the functional lexicon, which have an impact on the core computational operations. In one case, variation concerns the probe head and the operation Move: the features which drive verb movement can be associated to different functional heads in the clausal skeleton. In the other case, variation concerns Spell-Out, i.e. the availability of lexical items which spell out syntactic features, an instance of variation which can concern both probes and goals (of the functional type, such as clitic and weak pronouns). The chapter discusses

---

[1] L. Rizzi has suggested another possibility, namely that pronunciation is avoided because it is costly.

examples from Romance and Germanic languages, but the discussed generalizations have a wider cross-linguistic significance.

5.2 Variation in subject placement in interrogative sentences

In closely related Romance and Germanic languages, the relative position of the subject and the finite verb in interrogative sentences is notoriously subject to variation. In English and German, both pronouns and DPs can be inverted with the verb; in French, subject-verb inversion is restricted to clitic pronouns, but a special construction with two subjects, called Complex inversion, is also found; in Northern Italian dialects (NIDs), subject-verb inversion is restricted to clitic pronouns; finally, no instance of subject-verb inversion occurs in Italian.

To understand this variation, I assume a rich array of functional projections in the clausal space identified as the subject field in (5). I also suggest that the semantic Q-feature encoded in the left-periphery of the clause, which is interpreted at the interface and arguably belongs to the universal set of features, cannot be the source of variation (*pace* Rizzi 1996, who analyses subject-verb inversion, i.e. verb movement to the C-layer, as a way to endow the left-peripheral interrogative head with the wh-feature). The universal Q-feature should be distinguished from a variable 'edge' [V] feature that attracts the finite verb or auxiliary, which can be associated to different functional heads of the clausal skeleton.

5.2.1 English, German, etc.: Subject DP–verb inversion

In English and German interrogative sentences, subjects follow the auxiliary or the verb:

(7) a. Did he/John do that?
    b. Has he/John ever done that?

(8) a. Machte er/Hans das?
    b. Hat er/Hans das gemacht?

The traditional analysis since den Besten (1983) assumes verb/auxiliary movement to the C layer. In the more elaborated clause structure proposed by Rizzi (1997), the attracting head is identified with Fin (Rizzi 1997:303). Fin precedes both subject positions identified in (5):

(9) a. [$_{FinP}$ did [$_{SubjP}$ John/he ~~did~~ [$_{TP}$ ~~John/he did~~ [$_{VP}$ ~~John/he~~ do that]]]]
    b. [$_{FinP}$ did [$_{SubjP}$ ~~did~~ [$_{TP}$ he   ~~did~~ [$_{VP}$ ~~he~~ do that]]]]

In English, the [V] feature which attracts the inflected verb in interrogative sentences is associated with the Fin head, and produces subject–verb inversion with any type of subject, both strong subjects, as in (9a), and weak subjects, as in (9b). The same happens in German and other Germanic languages.

5.2.2 *Northern Italian dialects (NIDs) and French: Subject clitic–verb inversion*

In Romance languages, subject – verb inversion is more limited. In French and Northern Italian dialects, subject DPs do not invert with the verb or the auxiliary, (10) and (11), respectively, and subject–verb inversion is only found with subject clitic pronouns (12b)–(13b,d):[2]

(10) a. *Fait Jean cela?
          does Jean that?

      b. *A Jean fait cela?
          has Jean done that?

(11) a. *'be:və Giuan?
          drink-3sg Giuan?

      b. *A Giuan bu'vid?
          has Giuan drunk?

(12) a. Il dort   all persons
          he sleep-3sg

      b. Dort-il?
          sleep-3sg-he?

(13) a. əl 'be:və   2sg, 3sg, 3pl
          he drink-3sg

---

[2] Unless otherwise indicated, all dialectal data come from the Emilian dialect of Donceto (Piacenza). The pattern in (13) is however very common across Northern Italian dialects. The surface forms of subject clitics in Donceto are indicated in the paradigms in (i) (notice that the preverbal optional [ə] in (ia) is not a subject clitic—Cardinaletti and Repetti 2008, 2010a,b, *contra* previous analyses):

(i) a. declarative sentences   b. interrogative sentences
         (ə) 'be:v   'be:v   -jə?
         ət 'be:v   'be:v   -ət?
         əl 'be:v?   'be:və   -l?
         (ə) bu'vum   bu'vum   -jə?
         (ə) bu'vi   bu'vi: -v?
         i' be:vən   'be:vən -jə?
         I, you, he, etc. drink(s)   do(es) I, you, he, etc. drink?

The underlying forms of subject clitics are provided in

(ii) a. proclitic subject pronouns   b. enclitic subject pronouns
         1st -   -   i   i
         2nd t   -   t   v
         3rd l   i   l   i

b. 'beːvə-l?
   drink-3sg-he?

c. 'beːv   1sg, 1pl, 2pl
   [I] drink-1sg

d. 'beːv-jə?
   drink-1sg-I?

Compared to French, subject-inversion in NIDs displays a complication. The pattern in (13a,b), illustrated with the 3rd person singular, is found with a subset of persons, namely 2sg, 3sg, 3pl. In the other three persons of the paradigm (1sg, 1pl, 2pl), illustrated in (13c,d) with the 1st person singular, declarative sentences are pro-drop (13c); in the corresponding interrogative sentence in (13d), an enclitic pronoun shows up which is not there in declarative sentences. This important difference with Italian, where no enclitic pronoun is ever present, will be discussed later.

I start from the assumption that when a subject clitic is present (as in (13a, b, d)), it is the real subject of the sentence, and no *pro* is present (Cardinaletti and Repetti 2008, 2010a, *contra* previous analyses). In a sense to be made more precise, Northern Italian dialects are partial *pro*-drop languages.

In (14)–(16), the derivations of interrogative sentences in French and the two sets of persons of NIDs are provided: the verb is attracted to the Y position, which is structurally higher than TP, but lower than SubjP, and subject clitic-verb inversion is produced (see Cardinaletti and Repetti 2008, 2010a for the detailed analysis):[3]

(14)   French: all persons
       a. declaratives: [$_{TP}$ il dort [$_{VP}$ il dort]]
       b. interrogatives: [$_{YP}$ dort [$_{XP}$ il dort [$_{TP}$ il dort [$_{VP}$ il dort]]]]

(15)   NIDs: 2sg, 3sg, 3pl
       a. declaratives: [$_{XP}$ əl beːvə [$_{TP}$ əl beːvə [$_{VP}$ əl beːvə]]]
       b. interrogatives: [$_{YP}$ beːvə [$_{XP}$ l beːvə [$_{TP}$ l beːvə [$_{VP}$ l beːvə]]]]

(16)   NIDs: 1sg, 1pl, 2pl
       a. declaratives: [$_{TP}$ *pro* beːv [$_{VP}$ *pro* beːv]]
       b. interrogatives: [$_{YP}$ beːv [$_{XP}$ jə beːv [$_{TP}$ jə beːv [$_{VP}$ jə beːv]]]]

In French and Northern Italian dialects, the [V] feature which attracts the inflected verb in interrogative sentences is associated to the Y head. This only produces inversion with subject clitic pronouns.

---

[3] For the XP projection, see section 5.3. To establish the precise nature of the YP projection, further cross-linguistic investigation is needed.

5.2.3 *French Complex Inversion*

Consider French Complex Inversion, where an enclitic subject pronoun co-occurs with a preverbal subject DP (see Kayne 1983b; Kayne 1994:139, fn.15; Rizzi and Roberts 1989; Vecchiato 2000; Boeckx 2001, among many others):

(17)   Quand **Pierre** / **lui** a-t-il téléphoné?
        when Pierre / he has-he called?

I suggest that in (17), the verb moves to the Subject head, a step further up with respect to simple clitic-verb inversion. The derivation is shown in (18):[4]

(18)   Quand [$_{SubjP}$ **Pierre** / **lui** a-t [$_{YP}$ ~~a-t~~ [$_{XP}$ il ~~a~~ [$_{TP}$ ~~il a~~ [$_{VP}$ ~~il~~ téléphoné]]]]]?

The proposal in (18) is supported by the data in (19). With (aggressively) non D-linked wh-phrases (19a) and non dislocable subjects, e.g. negative quantifiers (19b), the subject and the raised verb are adjacent, a fact which can be interpreted by saying that they occur in one and the same projection (SubjP in (18)):[5]

(19)   a. Qui diable Jean (*selon toi) a-t-il invité?
            whom the hell Jean (according to you) has-he invited
            'According to you, whom the hell did Jean invite?'

        b. Qui (diable) personne (*selon toi) n'a-t-il invité?
            whom (the hell) nobody (according to you) not has-he invited?

That a head different from the Y head is involved here is confirmed by the fact that Complex inversion is not allowed in Northern Italian dialects (Brandi and Cordin 1989:134). This is a minimal difference between French and Northern Italian dialects.

In conclusion, French Subj has a [V] feature which attracts the inflected verb in interrogative sentences. The subject DP raises to specSubjP, and Complex Inversion is obtained.

---

[4] SpecSubjP is an illicit position for weak subject pronouns, as is shown by the well-known fact that they are not allowed in Complex Inversion (Kayne 1983; Rizzi and Roberts 1989). Compare (17) with (i):

(i) * Quand **il** a-t-il téléphoné?
      when he has-he called?

[5] With other wh-phrases and other subjects, parentheticals and topics can occur both between the subject and the verb, as in the a. sentences, and between the wh-phrase and the subject, as in the b. sentences (Laenzlinger and Musolino 1995:83, 85):

(i) a. Où Jean, finalement, est-il allé?
        where Jean finally has-he gone?
    b. Où, finalement, Jean est-il allé?
        where finally Jean has-he gone?

(ii) a. Où Jean, ce livre, l'a-t-il acheté?
         where Jean this book it-has-he bought?
     b. Où ce livre Jean l'a-t-il acheté?
         where this book Jean it-has-he bought

5.2.4 *Italian: TP-internal verb movement*

Italian is another language in which no subject-verb inversion with DPs is found in interrogative sentences. This fact means that no verb movement to Fin takes place:

(20) a. *Fa Gianni/lui questo?
 does Gianni/he that?

   b. *Ha Gianni/lui fatto questo?
 has Gianni/he done that?

The comparison of Italian with Northern Italian dialects shows that in Italian, the verb does not raise to Y either. As we have seen, in Northern Italian dialects, subject enclitics appear in interrogatives in persons of the paradigm that display null subjects in declaratives. The pro-drop status of Italian would, in principle, not be incompatible with enclitic subjects in interrogative sentences. However, Italian does not display subject enclitics. The absence of subject enclitics in Italian is therefore to be interpreted as the absence of verb movement to Y.

In Italian interrogative clauses, only TP-internal verb movement occurs. The verb moves from the aspectual field (in Cinque's 1999 hierarchy) to the modal field and does not cross over either of the subject positions, which explains why no subject–verb inversion is ever found in Italian. Although it is clearly impossible to establish the position of a null subject with respect to the verb, the landing site of verb movement can be detected by checking its position with respect to adverbs. In declarative sentences (21a), the finite verb occurs lower than habitual (*di solito* 'usually') and repetitive (*di nuovo* 'again') adverbs (Cinque 1999:180, n.80; 214, n.7); in interrogative sentences (21b), the finite verb must instead occur in the modal field higher than repetitive adverbs (Cardinaletti 2007:60–62):[6]

(21) a. [$_{CP}$ [$_{TP}$ *pro* [$_{ModP}$ [$_{HabP}$ di solito {dorme} [$_{AspP}$ di nuovo {dorme}
   [$_{VP}$...

   b. [$_{CP}$ dove [$_{TP}$ *pro* [$_{ModP}$ {dorme} [$_{HabP}$ di solito {dorme} [$_{AspP}$
    where   [he]   sleeps   usually
   di nuovo ~~dorme~~ [$_{VP}$...
   again

In Italian, the [V] feature which attracts the inflected verb in interrogative sentences is not associated with heads higher than Mod, which explains why no subject–verb inversion ever takes place in this language. The comparison of Italian with the minimally different Northern Italian dialects confirms that this is a correct conclusion.

---

[6] Notice that while Cinque (1999:11, 106) considers habitual adverbs as the highest adverbs in the aspectual field ('lower adverbs'), Coniglio (2006:77–9) discusses several arguments to treat habitual adverbs as the lowest adverbs in the modal field ('higher adverbs').

5.2.5 *Intermediate conclusion*

The data discussed so far have shown an instance of minimal variation in verb placement in interrogative sentences. As summarized in (22b), interrogatives may cross-linguistically differ in the location of the verb with respect to the subject. Assuming the cartography of functional projections in (22a), this variation can be attributed to the height in clause structure of the head reached by the verb (or auxiliary):

(22)	a.	Fin	Subj	Y	T/Mod
	b. Italian: no inversion	*	*	*	V
	NIDs: inverted clitic pronouns	*	*	V	
	French: inverted clitic pronouns, Complex Inversion	*	V		
	Engl/Germ: inverted pronouns, inverted DPs	V			

The [V] feature that drives verb movement is associated with different syntactic heads of the clausal skeleton: the Fin head in English and German, the Subj head in French, the Y head in Northern Italian dialects, a IP-internal modal head in Italian. The cross-linguistic variation discussed so far can be regarded as an instance of variation in the way feature are bundled in the probe heads. As Chomsky (2008:135) suggests, 'one element of parameter-setting is assembly of features into lexical items (LIs), which we can take to be atoms for further computation and the locus of parameters'.

Notice that this instance of variation in verb placement cannot be triggered by the semantic Q-feature that characterizes interrogative sentences, an interface feature which does not give rise to variation.

As pointed out by Biberauer and Roberts (2010:276), however, verb movement can be taken to contribute to the interrogative meaning of the sentence because of its 'optional' character and the hypothesis by Chomsky (2001:34) that 'optional operations can apply only if they have an effect on outcome'.

That the observed variation cannot be regarded as a mere phonological matter is confirmed by other data which show that verb placement interacts in an interesting and complicated way with subject placement. We turn to these data in the next sections.

5.2.6 *Some related properties: Subject PPs*

Other syntactic properties are presumably related to the property discussed so far. They may be taken to represent the positive evidence required in language acquisition to establish which clausal head contains the [V] feature, the easily detectable property in Chomsky's (2001) words reported in (1).

In order to explain why English doesn't display any subject PPs, Rizzi and Shlonsky (2006:345) suggest that T-to-Subj movement takes place in English declarative sentences. As a consequence, preverbal DPs always check nominative Case, which excludes the occurrence of 'subject' PPs which do not check this feature.[7] This analysis can be easily extended to French, which displays the same restriction.

T-to-Subj movement in declaratives must be related to the verb movement possibilities in interrogatives. As we have seen, in English and French interrogative sentences, the verb moves higher than in Italian. Adopting Rizzi and Shlonsky's (2006) proposal, the same difference can be claimed to exist in declaratives. If in Italian, T-to-Subj does not take place in declaratives either, nominative case is always checked in TP, and PPs, which need not check nominative Case, can occur in specSubjP. The existence of 'Subject' PPs in Italian is accounted for. In (4a,b), repeated here as (23a,b), a dative and a locative subject, respectively, are exemplified:[8]

(23) a. A Gianni è piaciuto il regalo.
         to Gianni is pleased the gift
         'Gianni liked the gift.'

      b. Su Gianni è caduta una grande disgrazia.
         on Gianni is fallen a big misfortune

Notice that the same possibility holds in Northern Italian dialects. The data in (24) come from the dialect of Venice (Paolo Chinellato, personal communication):

(24) a. A Nane ghe ze piazùo el regalo.
         to Gianni to-him is pleased the gift
         'Gianni liked the gift.'

      b. Su de iù ze vegnùa zo na gran desgrassia.
         on him is come down a big misfortune

The piece of data in (24) is compatible with the previously discussed interrogative data. In Northern Italian dialects, there is no T-to-Subject movement in interrogative sentences, which explains why they do not display Complex inversion (nor DP-verb inversion since the verb does not further move to Fin). The verb stops in the lower head Y, which only produces subject clitic–verb inversion.

As for the difference between Italian and Northern Italian dialects, subject clitic–verb inversion represents the crucial empirical evidence for the assumption that the verb feature is associated to Y in the latter languages, but not in the former.

---

[7] In English Locative inversion, the PP targets a projection higher than the subject position, as shown by the fact that the PP cannot invert with the auxiliary (i) (Rizzi and Shlonsky 2006:344; also see Chomsky 2008:162, n.67):

(i) *Is in the room sitting my old brother?

Other differences between English and Italian, discussed in Cardinaletti (2004:156, n.8), are the possibility of Italian PPs co-occurring with A'-movements and their compatibility with non-bridge verbs. See however Collins (1997) for a different analysis.

[8] Similarly, in Italian inverse copular sentences (4c), agreement is with the postverbal subject and not with the preverbal predicate (while in English, agreement is with the raised predicate).

5.2.7 *Optional vs. obligatory verb movement*

Another dimension of variation is the obligatoriness vs. optionality of syntactic move-ment. Subj-to-Fin movement (as in English and German) is obligatory and all subjects follow the raised verb (cf. *where he has lived?*, *wo er hat gelebt?*). T-to-Y movement (as in French and NIDs) is instead optional. When the verb does not raise to Y, a clitic or weak subject pronoun intervenes between the wh-phrase and the verb.[9] The data in (25)–(27) exemplify this word order in French (Poletto and Pollock 2004:293), three Northern Italian dialects (the Emilian dialect of Gazzoli, Piacenza (Cardinaletti and Repetti 2010b:50), Triestino (Poletto 1993:228), Venetian (Poletto 2000:29) respec-tively), and a non-pro-drop variety of Spanish which displays weak pronouns, namely Caribbean Spanish (Ordóñez and Olarrea 2006):

(25)   a. Où il va?
          where he goes?

       b. Qui t'as vu?
          whom you have seen?

(26)   a. ?õːd õ va?
          where he goes

       b. Cossa la dise?
          what she says?

       c. Coss' ti ga?
          what you have?
          'What's the matter with you?'

(27)   Qué tú quieres?
       what you want?

Interestingly, (28) shows agrammatic productions by aphasic patients who speak Northern Italian dialects: the dialect of Schio in (28a) and the dialect of Venice in (28b) (Chinellato 2003:38–9). Aphasic patients do not have access to subject clitic pronouns (and to clitic pronouns in general). Since subject–verb inversion necessarily involves a clitic pronoun, they use the alternative strategy of forming interrogatives without moving the verb. This strategy is compatible with the use of a preverbal weak subject

---

[9] This difference between (obligatory) Subj-to-Fin and (optional) T-to-Y movement might be related to the fact that the former concerns heads of different layers of clause structure (the IP and CP layer, respec-tively), while the latter takes place inside the same layer (the IP layer). I will not discuss this point further here.

pronoun, which aphasic patients build by adding an initial vowel [e] to the clitic pronoun in order to obtain a bi-syllabic element (Cardinaletti and Starke 1999):[10]

(28)   a. Cossa elo beve?
       b. Cossa eo beve?
         what he drinks?

This piece of evidence confirms that the configuration 'wh – subject – verb' is possible in languages in which the verb does not raise as high as in English or German.

On the basis of the evidence in (25)–(28), the same configuration can be assumed in a pro-drop language like Italian in which the verb does not raise to Y: a (weak) null pronominal subject is located between the wh-phrase and the verb:

(29)   [$_{CP}$ dove [$_{TP}$ *pro* dorme [$_{VP}$ ~~pro dorme~~]]]? (see (21b))
       where [he] sleeps

5.2.8 Clitic/weak vs. strong subjects

While clitic/weak pronouns can appear in the order 'wh – subject – verb' (25)–(28), full DPs and strong pronouns cannot. (30) is an Italian example,[11] (31) presents data from

---

[10] Aphasic patients also use this strategy in yes-no questions instead of clitic–verb inversion. The pronouns *elo* and *eo* do exist in the dialects of Schio and Venice, but have a different distribution. They are ungrammatical in sentences like (28) (Chinellato 2003:39–42).

[11] The restriction is not found with the wh-item *perché* 'why' in main clauses:

(i) Perché Gianni è arrivato in ritardo?
    why Gianni is arrived late?

As suggested by Rizzi (2001), *perché* does not necessarily move to the left periphery, but can be merged in the much higher specIntP and does not therefore interact with subject movement. Subjects are, however, expectedly ungrammatical if *perché* is moved out of embedded clauses (Cardinaletti 2007:62):

(ii) *Perché Gianni ha detto [che berrà la birra ~~perché~~]?
     why Gianni has said that [he] will-drink the beer?

D-linked wh-phrases allow preverbal subjects. (30) contrasts with (iii):

(iii) In quale stanza Gianni dorme?
      in which room Gianni sleeps?

D-linked wh-phrases are attracted by a Topic feature (Starke 2001 among others) and do not interfere with subject placement, like Topics in general:

(iv) In quella stanza Gianni ci dorme da due anni.
      in that room Gianni there sleeps from two years
      'Gianni has been sleeping in that room for two years.'

Differently from Spanish (Torrego 1984), no amelioration is found in Italian with wh-PPs. Sentence (v) is as bad as with a non-prepositional wh-phrase, unless stress on *chi* turns it into a D-linked wh-item (a possibility which is available with any wh-item except weak *che* 'what'):

(v) *Con chi Gianni parla?
    with whom John speaks?

For embedded sentences, see n.17

the dialects of Gazzoli and Trieste, respectively,[12] (32) is French (Poletto and Pollock 2004:293),[13] and (33) is Caribbean Spanish (Ordoñez and Olarrea 2006):

(30)   *Dove Gianni dorme?
        where Gianni sleeps?

(31)   a. *õ:d Giani va?
           where Giani goes?

        b. *Cossa la mama dise?
           what the mother says?

(32)   a. ?*Où Yves va?
           where Yves goes?

        b. ?*Qui Paul a vu?
           whom Paul has seen?

(33)   *Qué José quiere?
        what José wants?

In no case can a DP occur between the wh-phrase and the verb. The same restriction is manifested in the agrammatic productions by the aphasic patients who speak Northern Italian varieties. Although they produce a weak pronoun in between the wh-phrase and the verb (28), they never produce sentences like (34) in which a strong pronoun or a full DP occur between the wh-phrase and the verb (Chinellato 2003:38–9):

(34)   a. *Cossa lu / Paolo beve?
        b. *Cossa iù / Paolo beve?
           what he / Paolo drinks?

5.2.9 *Some generalizations*

As we have just seen, whether the configuration 'wh – subject – verb' is possible or not depends on the type of subject. Only pronominal subjects can show up in that position, while DP subjects and strong pronouns cannot. Nor can any other elements which occur in specSubjP, such as locative and dative PPs and predicative DPs in inverse copular sentences (4):

(35)   a. *Cosa a Gianni è piaciuto di più?
           what to Gianni is pleased most
           'What did Gianni like most?'

---

[12] Poletto (1993:230) provides the Triestino example (31b) as grammatical. The speakers I have consulted however judge this sentence as ungrammatical, as in other NIDs.

[13] Boeckx (2001:52) takes (32b) to be possible as a concealed Complex Inversion. This is not in contradiction with what is being suggested here.

b. *Cosa su Gianni è caduto ieri?
   what on Gianni has fallen yesterday?

c. *Chi la causa della rivolta è stato?
   who the cause of the riot has been?

The structure in (5) assumed here allows us to express the observed difference in structural terms. Whereas weak subjects in specTP are permitted in interrogatives, strong subjects in specSubjP are excluded from occurring between the *wh*-phrase and the verb. This seems to be quite a general property of Romance languages, not only the ones analysed so far (Italian, French, and NIDs), but many others (Spanish, Catalan, European Portuguese, Romanian). The same generalization is found in languages of other language families: Arabic (Fassi Fehri 1993), Bulgarian (Bošković 2004), Macedonian (Kochovska 2006), Basque (Uriagereka 1999), and Bantu (Carstens 2005).

French, Northern Italian dialects, and Caribbean Spanish show that the restriction against preverbal full subjects in wh-questions is not related to pro-drop and cannot be attributed to the Topic status of the preverbal subject (*pace* many previous proposals which have tried to deal with this fact, e.g. Poletto 2000, Barbosa 2001, Zubizarreta 2001, among others), nor is it to be understood as an intervention effect of the subject (*pace* Carstens 2005, who suggests that the wh-phrase must move through the subject position, which must therefore be regarded as an A-bar position). Notice that a Relativized minimality (Rizzi 1990) approach is not easily helpful either, since no features are shared by the subject and the wh-phrase: as we have seen, the restriction operates whether they are of the same category or different (DPs or PPs), and whether the wh-phrase is an argument or an adjunct.

The restriction is however not universal. In interrogative sentences, strong subjects in specSubjP are possible in those languages like English and German in which the verb (or the auxiliary) raises to the C layer (i.e. to Fin in Rizzi's (1997) fine-grained structural approach, see (9)).[14]

It can be shown that this is again not a 'global' parameter but involves specific lexical choices. Internally to Italian, subject–verb inversion is found in those very few cases in which the verb moves to Fin: in Aux-to-Comp (36a) (Rizzi 1982), with some particular verbal forms such as the conditional (36b) (Poletto 2000:156), and in cases like (36c),

---

[14] Other languages such as Brazilian Portuguese do not seem to display the restriction. They however allow for an overt complementizer to occur in questions, which could be regarded as a strategy parallel to T-to-C movement (Cardinaletti 2007:70, fn.12). This strategy is presumably at work in other languages like Hebrew and creole languages that allow a DP to follow the wh-phrase, an issue raised by Luigi Rizzi. This instance of language variation might be related to the fact that in embedded sentences, Italian allows both wh- and subject movement, compare (30) with (i):

(i) Non so dove Gianni dorma.
   [I] not know where Gianni sleeps

where verb movement is somehow licensed, in a way to be made more precise, by the modal particle *poi* (Marco Coniglio, personal communication):[15]

(36) a. Avendo Gianni parlato al direttore, ...
         having Gianni spoken to-the director

      b. Cosa mai avrebbe Gianni potuto fare in quel frangente?
         what ever would-have Gianni been-able do on that occasion?

      c. ?Cosa ha Gianni poi fatto con quell'articolo?
         what has Gianni then done with that paper?

Notice also that the unavailability of preverbal full subjects only arises in the presence of overt *wh*-movement. It is not found in yes-no questions, as in (37), and in in-situ (echo) *wh*-questions, as in (38), which confirms that the restriction is syntactic and should not be related to the semantic properties of interrogatives:

(37) a. Gianni ha invitato Maria?
      b. Jean a invité Marie?
         Gianni/Jean has invited Maria/Marie?

(38) a. Gianni ha invitato chi?
      b. Jean a invité qui?
         Gianni/Jean has invited who?

The data discussed so far show that there is a clear interaction between the scope of verb movement and the availability of the subject position that hosts strong subjects. Again, this looks like a syntactic fact, not just a phonological fact. Phonology could be sensitive to the presence or absence of lexical elements, requiring for instance adjacency between two lexical items, but cannot distinguish between strong and weak subjects, which are syntactically different, nor between the different functional projections SubjP and TP which host them.[16]

A tentative account of the generalizations discussed has been proposed in Cardinaletti (2009), where it is shown that other constructions of Italian, such as Resumptive Preposing and, for some speakers, Focalization display similar facts. In all these cases, in which syntactic movement activates the specFin position, the Fin and the Subj heads interact in such a way that Fin itself satisfies the Subject criterion (see Rizzi and Shlonsky 2006). A subject DP (or PP) is therefore not attracted to specSubjP, but occurs postverbally. This mechanism is however not available when T-to-Subj-to-Fin

---

[15] This might be related to the fact that although modal particles occur inside the IP layer, they are licensed by heads of the left periphery (Zimmermann 2004a,b; Coniglio 2009, 2011; Cardinaletti 2011).

[16] That the restriction cannot be accounted for in terms of an adjacency requirement is confirmed by the fact that in addition to weak pronouns, stylistically fronted phrases and adverbs can intervene between the wh-phrase and the verb (Cardinaletti 2007). These elements do not occur in specSubjP, but in positions lower than TP.

movement takes place, as in English and Germanic wh-questions. In this case, a subject DP is attracted to the preverbal subject position, as in simple declarative sentences.

Notice that no language variation is found with regard to the occurrence of weak pronominal subjects in the lower subject position (SpecTP in (5)). Pronominal subjects are possible in both situations, whether the verb moves higher, as in English or German (9b), or stays lower than the subject pronoun, as in Italian (29) and the non-null subject languages analysed in (25)–(28). In other words, pronominal subject placement is independent of the Subject criterion (or the EPP feature, as formulated by Chomsky (2008)). With weak pronouns, Feature matching (between the pronominal subject and the relevant functional head) must occur in a very local configuration, what is traditionally known as a spec-head configuration. Internal Merge is obligatory here, and the pronominal goal is always spelled out at the probe.

5.2.10 *An account based on phases and feature inheritance*

The restriction discussed in the previous section can be understood if Chomsky's (2001, 2008) phase theory is adopted and in particular his proposal that T inherits properties of C. Chomsky (2008:157) suggests that 'EPP can be reformulated in terms of feature inheritance': the Edge Feature, the feature that attracts elements, 'can be inherited from the phase head along with the Agree feature'.

Given this proposal, the interaction of verb movement and subject placement can be understood as follows. In the absence of T-to-C movement (i.e. Subj-to-Fin movement under the the clause structure assumptions adopted here, (5)), a wh-phrase and the subject (DP or PP) cannot raise both because their movement should be triggered by one and the same Edge Feature (EF): the EF of C should attract the wh-phrase, the EF of T inherited from the phase head C should attract the subject. This looks problematic, either movement can take place. However, when T-to-C movement takes place, both wh- and subject movement become possible because T-to-C makes the two heads *share* the Edge Feature of C.[17]

5.3 Micro-variation in pro-drop

Another instance of cross-linguistic variation in the syntax of subjects is the well studied pro-drop parameter. I will look here at a minimal difference between Italian and Northern Italian dialects: while Italian displays 3rd person null subjects, these dialects do not. This difference is illustrated by the contrast in (39). The two sets of languages

---

[17] In embedded sentences, both wh- and subject movement are possible, compare (30) with (i). Here, the wh-phrase is attracted by the Edge feature of C, while the Agree feature of C-T seeks the subject DP (Chomsky 2008:148–52):

(i) Non so dove Gianni dorma.
   [I] not know where Gianni sleeps

however behave alike as far as 1st and 2nd persons are concerned (40) (I will come back to the 2sg case in sections 5.3.4 and 5.3.5):

(39) a. beve   bevono
      b. əl 'be:və   i 'be:vən
         he drink-3sg they drink-3pl

(40) a. bevo   beviamo   bevi   bevete
      b. 'be:v   bu'vum   ət 'be:v   bu'vi
         [I] drink-1sg [we] drink-1pl you drink-2sg [you] drink-2pl

As said in section 5.2.2, I assume that the overt pronouns in (39b) are the real subjects of the sentence, and no *pro* is present. The clitic pronoun values the features of the head X merged with TP. Following Roberts (2010a,b), Cardinaletti and Repetti (2010a) have assumed that the head X, the incorporation host, has no EPP feature, which means that the weak pronoun *pro* is not a possible goal for X. The derivation for the persons which display a subject clitic pronoun is given in (41c), compared to Italian in (41a) and the pro-drop persons in (41b):[18]

(41) a.   [$_{TP}$*pro* bevo [$_{VP}$ ~~pro~~ ~~bevo~~]]   Italian
      b.   [$_{TP}$*pro* 'be:v [$_{VP}$ ~~pro~~ ~~'be:v~~]]   NIDs: 1sg,1pl,2pl
      c. [$_{XP}$ əl 'be:və [$_{TP}$~~əl~~ ~~'be:və~~ [$_{VP}$ ~~əl~~ ~~'be:və~~]]] NIDs: 3sg,3pl

How can the minimal difference between Italian and these closely related languages be expressed? To answer this question, we address the issue of the correlation between richness of verbal inflection and *pro*-drop which attracted the attention of a great number of researchers and is notoriously a very delicate question (e.g. Taraldsen 1978; Rizzi 1982; Huang 1984; Jaeggli and Safir 1989; Kenstowicz 1989; Roberts 1993; Speas 2006; Holmberg 2010b; Roberts 2010a, just to name a few). The discussion here will add new questions to both the empirical and the theoretical debate.

---

[18] The clitic-doubling sentence in (i) shows that the X Projection occurs lower than SubjP, which hosts strong subject pronouns and full subject DPs (see (5)):

(i) [$_{SubjP}$ ly / l ɔm [$_{XP}$əl 'be:və[$_{TP}$~~əl~~ ~~be:və~~ [$_{VP}$ ~~əl~~ ~~be:və~~]]]]
    he / the man he drinks

Due to their derivation, clitic pronouns, such as *əl* in (41c), occur higher than weak pronouns, such as *pro* in (41b) (Cardinaletti and Starke 1999). This generalization can be easily exemplified with dative pronouns: *gli* 'to him' is a clitic pronoun, *loro* 'to them' a weak pronoun:

(ii) a. Maria **gli**   ha   dato ~~gli~~ un libro ~~gli~~
        Mary to-him   has given   a book
     b. Maria ha dato **loro**   un libro ~~loro~~
        Mary has given to-them a book
        'Mary has given him/them a book.'

5.3.1 *Italian vs. NIDs*

If English and French are compared to Italian, poverty of inflection seems to be easy to state. This seems confirmed by a subset of Northern Italian dialects, which includes dialects like Paduan and Bellunese in (42): clitic pronouns appear in the three persons of the paradigm in which no morphological distinctions on the verb are found:

(42) a. *Paduan*   b. *Bellunese*

vegno	magne
te *vien*	te *magna*
el *vien*	al *magna*
vegnemo	magnon
vegni	magné
i *vien*	i *magna*
'I come, etc.'	'I eat, etc.'

Taking into account other verbs and other dialects, however, 'poverty of inflection' does not explain the distribution of subject clitic pronouns in the paradigm. In Paduan, other verbs display more verbal distinctions than the verb in (42a), see (43c). In the Emilian dialect of Donceto, verbal inflection is rich in that the distinction between 3rd person singular and plural is morphologically marked as in Italian (43a,b). Still clitic pronouns appear in exactly the same persons as in (42) (Cardinaletti and Repetti 2010a:129):[19]

(43) a. *Donceto*   b. *Donceto*   c. *Paduan*   d. *Paduan*   e. *Bellunese*

a. *Donceto*	b. *Donceto*	c. *Paduan*	d. *Paduan*	e. *Bellunese*
be:v	læ:v	magno	vegno	magne
ət be:v	ət læ:v	te magni	te *vien*	te *magna*
əl be:və	əl læ:və	el *magna*	el *vien*	al *magna*
bu'vum	la'vum	magnemo	vegnemo	magnon
bu'vi	la'væ	magné	vegni	magné
i 'be:vən	i 'læ:vən	i *magna*	i *vien*	i *magna*
'I drink, etc.'	'I wash, etc.'	'I eat, etc.'	'I come, etc.'	'I eat, etc.'

These data from minimally different languages, which exemplify what Kayne (2000a) calls micro-parametric variation, confirm that there is no easy relationship between richness of inflection and *pro* drop.

5.3.2 *Is pro-drop UG-restricted?*

In a study of clitic doubling in French, Kayne (2000a:176) suggests that *pro*-drop is UG restricted: A covert subject *pro* can only be 3rd person, and there is no such item as a 1st or 2nd person *pro*. This means that in the 1st and 2nd person, the subject is indeed overt and corresponds to the verbal agreement suffix, which must be analysed

---

[19] See Renzi and Vanelli (1983:§1.2.1) for the same observation for other dialects.

as an incorporated subject pronoun. The corollary of this proposal is that an agreement suffix having the properties of a pronoun can only be 1st or 2nd person. Evidence is provided by Italian 1st and 2nd person plural inflection morphology, which is similar to person morphemes used in other points of the pronominal system, for instance in the 1st and 2nd person singular object pronouns:[20]

(44)   a. 1pl: bevia-m-o (we drink)   see *me, mi* (me)
       b. 2pl: beve-t-e (you:pl drink) see *te, ti* (you:sg)

In this proposal, 3rd person pro-drop is not directly related to rich inflection. The difference between Italian and Italian dialects can be expressed as follows: Italian possesses a 3rd person *pro*, while NIDs do not have any 3rd person *pro*. This approach implies that there may be two 'lexical' sources for variation:

(45)   a. ± availability of the lexical item *pro* (which is only 3rd person, by hypothesis)
       b. ± 'pronominal' T (i.e., ± incorporated $1^{st}/2^{nd}$ pronouns on T)

The four types of languages which are produced by the combination of these two parameters are summarized in (46):

(46)

	+'pronominal' T	−'pronominal' T
+pro	Italian: 'pro-drop' in all persons, i.e.: - (apparent) pro-drop in 1st and 2nd person; - pro-drop in 3rd person	???: overt, non-incorporated pronouns in 1st and 2nd person; pro-drop in 3rd person
−pro	NIDs: - (apparent) pro-drop in 1st and 2nd person; - no pro-drop in 3rd person	English: no pro-drop

Some questions for this proposal are raised by partial *pro* drop languages such as Finnish, which are similar to Italian as far as 1st and 2nd persons are concerned, but different in the 3rd person singular, which gets a different interpretation in the two languages: definite in Italian (47a) versus generic in Finnish (47b) (Holmberg 2005):

(47)   a. Qui non può fumare.
       b. Täällä ei saa polttaa.
          here not may smoke

---

[20] Kayne's proposal is similar to other proposals which take verbal inflection to be the subject of the clause (e.g. Alexiadou and Anagnostopoulou 1998), but it is more restricted in that verbal inflection can have this property only in the 1st and 2nd person. These proposals, however, share the idea that the nature of verbal inflection is categorially different in null-subject languages and non-null-subject languages like French and German, a hypothesis with non-trivial consequences, as far as I can see.

Since both languages possess 3rd person *pro*, the difference in interpretation cannot be easily expressed. Similarly, this system cannot express in a straightforward way the difference between Italian and Hebrew, where the distribution of *pro* is much more constrained. Example (48) shows that while 1st and 2nd pronouns can be analysed as incorporated, as in Italian (Shlonsky 2009), the differences in the 3rd person (referential pro-drop in Italian vs. non-referential pro-drop in Hebrew) need further assumptions.

(48)   Lamad-ti albanit.
        studied-1sg Albanian

Other questions are raised by the Northern Italian dialects themselves. If in NIDs, 1st and 2nd person verbal inflections are incorporated pronouns, what are the elements that follow the verbal inflection in interrogative sentences as in (49b) (see fn. 2)?

(49)   a. bu'vu-**m**.   b. bu'vu-**m**-jə?
           drink-1pl   drink-1pl-1pl
           'We drink / We are drinking.'   'Do we drink? / Are we drinking?'

Elements like *jə* in (49b) look like subject pronouns; they are so etymologically (they derive from Latin pronouns, Rohlfs (1968:150); Vanelli (1984, 1987), among others). Are there two incorporated subject pronouns in (49b)? This seems unlikely. Notice also that (49b) displays the same morpheme order as in the 3rd persons (50), where the verbal inflection is followed by the enclitic subject pronoun (see (13b) and fn. 2):[21]

(50)   a. 'be:v-ə-l?   b. 'be:v-ən-jə?
           drink-3sg-3sg   drink-3pl-3pl
           'Does he drink? / Is he drinking?'   'Do they drink? / Are they drinking?'

A further question is raised by the overt subject clitic pronoun in (40b): why do 2sg subject clitics differ from 1pl and 2pl subject clitics in that they never incorporate in declarative sentences and always appear in proclitic position? Notice that proclitic 2sg subjects are found in all Northern Italian dialects that have subject clitics (Renzi and Vanelli 1983). One possible structural answer could be that the 2sg features are the highest person features in the hierarchical structure, which cannot be moved across by the verb in declarative sentences (in interrogatives, they can, see fn. 2). Person features however seem to be hierarchically ordered in a different way, with first person higher than second person (De Crousaz and Shlonsky 2003; Bianchi 2006; Cardinaletti 2008, among others).

Because of all these reasons, a UG-restricted account of pro-drop cannot be adopted. Another account of the difference between Italian and NIDs should be looked for.

---

[21] On the phonological derivation of the syncretic 1st and 3rd person plural forms *jə* in (49b) and (50b), see Cardinaletti and Repetti (2008).

5.3.3 *A different account*

I would like to take a slightly different path and follow Holmberg's (2005) proposal, which allows us to assume the existence of *pro* in all persons of the paradigm, as in the traditional account of pro-drop since Rizzi (1982).

Holmberg's (2005) minimalist account of pro-drop reverses the licensing relationship with respect to previous approaches. *Pro* must be seen as a pronoun with interpretable syntactic features, but no phonological features, i.e. a non-pronounced personal pronoun. Like an overt pronoun, *pro* values the uninterpretable phi-features of T. The property which singles out pro-drop languages like Italian is a D feature in T (see also Holmberg 2010b). The presence of the D-feature in T 'means that a null φP that enters into an Agree relation with I can be interpreted as definite, referring to an individual or a group' (Holmberg 2005:555). The easily detectable property to distinguish pro-drop from non-pro-drop languages is the existence of overt weak pronouns (including overt expletives, which are universally weak, Cardinaletti and Starke 1999).

In this account, the difference between Italian and Northern Italian dialects can be seen as a lexical difference: the availability of different pronouns for 1st and 2nd person on the one side and 3rd person on the other. In Italian, 1st and 2nd person *pros* bear interpretable [person] features and value the uninterpretable [person] features of T, while 3rd person *pros* bear interpretable [number] features and value the uninterpretable [number] features of T. In the Northern Italian dialects, only *person* silent pronouns are found which value the uninterpretable [person] features of T, but not *number* 3rd person silent pronouns. Therefore, in the 3rd persons, subject pronouns are overt. Since the overt pronouns are clitic in these languages, the derivation activates the [*u*number] head X which is merged with TP, as shown in (41c).

In conclusion, in Holmberg's approach, pro-drop is not directly related to the richness of inflection. To possess overt or null pronouns in the different persons of the paradigm is a lexical property. Differently from Italian, NIDs do not include [number] null subjects in their lexicon, independently of whether 3rd person verbal inflection is rich, as in Donceto (43a,b), or not, as in Paduan (43c,d) and Bellunese (43e).

5.3.4 *On 2nd person singular pronouns and Italian subjunctives*

The question concerning the 2nd person singular in NIDs is still open: why does the 2nd person singular behave differently from the other set of persons in (40b)? In other words, why do NIDs always display a 2sg overt pronoun? As we see from the comparison between (43a–c) and (43d–e), poverty of inflection cannot provide a straightforward answer in this case either. In e.g. the dialect of Donceto, the 2nd and 3rd persons singular are morphologically distinct (*be:v* vs. *be:və*, *læ:v* vs. *læ:və*), as in Italian, still a clitic subject pronoun is necessarily overt in the former language, but not in the latter.

Notice that the 2nd person singular also behaves in a peculiar way inside Italian. The present subjunctive in (51) and the past subjunctive in (52) are two cases in which Italian behaves like a non-pro-drop language as far as the 2nd person singular is concerned. The subject must be spelled out as the 2sg overt pronoun *tu* (51b)–(52b):

(51) a. Crede che [*pro* sia ricco], ma non lo sono / *non lo sei / non lo è.
        [he] thinks that [I/*you/he] amSUBJ / *areSUBJ / isSUBJ rich, but [I] am /
        *[you] are / [he] is not

      b. Crede che [**tu** sia ricco], ma non lo sei.
        [he] thinks that you areSUBJ rich, but [you] are not

(52) a. Credeva che [*pro* fossi ricco], ma non lo sono / *non lo sei.
        [he] thought that [I / *you] wasSUBJ / *wereSUBJ rich, but [I] am / *[you] are
        not

      b. Credeva che [**tu** fossi ricco].
        [he] thought that you wereSUBJ rich

The sentences in (53) show that like the overt pronouns of non null-subject languages, *tu* is weak: among other properties, it cannot occur in postverbal position (53a) and cannot be topicalized (53b) (Cardinaletti 1997a:51f, 2004:126f):

(53) a. *Crede che venga tu.
        [he] thinks that comesSUBJ you

      b. *Tu crede che venga.
        you [he] thinks that comesSUBJ

Notice that the Italian present subjunctive paradigm displays three identical verbal forms, *sia* in (51) (past subjunctives only display two identical forms, see the 1st and the 2nd person singular *fossi* in (52)). This seems to lead us back to the hypothesis that some connection indeed exists between poor verbal inflection and lack of pro-drop. However, while the 2nd person singular needs to be overtly realized, the syncretism of the 1st and 3rd person verbal forms is compatible with the presence of null subjects (51a).[22] These data confirm the conclusion of section 5.3.1 that poverty of inflection need be qualified in order to understand whether there is a systematic relationship between verbal syncretism and pro-drop.

---

[22] The 3rd person interpretation of the null subject in (51a) is possible in a context in which the 3rd person referent has already been introduced into the discourse. In an out-of-the-blue context, however, only the 1st person interpretation of *pro* is possible, made available by the Speaker head (Sigurðsson 2004; Giorgi 2010).

5.3.5 *On syncretisms*

In Italian, another instance of verbal syncretism which is compatible with pro-drop is shown in (54). The sentence is ambiguous between the meaning 'I am here' and the meaning 'they are here', still no overt subject is necessary here:[23]

(54)   Sono qui.
       [I] be-1sg / [they] be-3pl here
       'I am here / They are here.'

Consider other cases in which null subjects are licensed in spite of poor verbal inflection. As shown in (55), in Southern Italian dialects like Abruzzese, three persons of the paradigm are identical (D'Alessandro and Roberts 2010), still no overt subject is necessary. The difference between the data in (55) and those in (43) is puzzling:[24]

(55)   *Abruzzese*
       magne
       migne
       magne
       magneme
       magnete
       magne
       'I eat, etc.'

The data show that the $1^{st}/3^{rd}$ person syncretism is compatible with null subjects (as in Italian present subjunctive (51a) and present indicative of *essere* 'be' (54), and in Abruzzese (55)), whereas other instances of syncretism are not compatible with null subjects: 1st and 2nd person (as in Italian present and past subjunctives (51)–(52), and NIDs like Donceto (43a,b)), and 2nd and 3rd person (as in Italian present subjunctives, and NIDs like Paduan and Bellunese (43d,e)). The data are summarized in (56):

(56)	a. *Abruzzese*	b.	*Italian*		c. *Donceto*	d. *Paduan*		e. *Bellunese*
	magne	sia	**fossi**		**be:v**	vegno		**magne**
	migne	tu sia	tu **fossi**		ət **be:v**	te vien	te **magna**
	magne	sia	fosse		əl **be:və**	el vien	al **magna**
	magneme	siamo	fossimo		bu'vum	vegnemo	magnon
	magnete	siate	foste		bu'vi	vegni	magné
	magne	siano	fossero	i	'be:vən	i vien	i **magna**
	eat	beSUBJ	beSUBJ-PAST		drink	come	eat

---

[23] As pointed out in fn. 22, ambiguity only arises in contexts in which the 3rd person referents have already been introduced into discourse. Otherwise, the 1st person interpretation is more salient.
[24] Spanish systematically displays the same situation as Abruzzese.

The generalization can be understood if person features are decomposed into smaller features, as often suggested in the recent literature (e.g. Harley and Ritter 2002). If person features are decomposed into [±Participant] and [±Author] (Halle 1997; Nevins 2007), we arrive at the feature system in (57) for the three persons singular. The features that the persons of the paradigm share are shown in (58):

(57) a. 1sg [+Participant, +Author]
      b. 2sg [+Participant, −Author]
      c. 3sg [−Participant, −Author]

(58) a. 1sg and 2sg: [+Participant]
      b. 2sg and 3sg: [−Author]

In this system, 1st and 3rd person are characterized by different values of the same features: [+Participant, +Author] vs. [−Participant, −Author]. Whether verbal inflection is identical in the two cases or not does not seem crucial since the two persons are featurally one the opposite of the other. The actual choice between the two interpretations is a discourse matter. While the 1st person interpretation is more salient in out-of-the blue contexts, the 3rd person interpretation becomes available if a referent is found in the discourse (see fn. 22 and 23).

In the other instances of syncretisms, however, the two persons share the same values for the same features. If verbal inflection does not resolve the ambiguity, the subject cannot remain non-overt. In particular, the recovery of the combination of features [+Participant, −Author] is more difficult to obtain than the other two persons if neither the pronoun nor the verbal morphology are overtly marked.[25] This is what happens in NIDs and in Italian subjunctives.

As pointed out by Luigi Rizzi, there is an interesting difference between present and past subjunctives when a 1st person plural subject occurs in the main clause (for sentences with a 1st person singular main subject, see Cardinaletti 1997a:60, n.25):

(59) a. Speriamo che *pro* sia in grado di aiutarci.
         [we] hope that [*I / *you / he] *amsubj / *aresubj / issubj able to help-us

      b. Speravamo che *pro* fossi in grado di aiutarci.
         [we] hoped that [*I / you] *wassubj / weresubj able to help-us

When the 1st person interpretation of *pro* is excluded for independent reasons (overlapping reference), the 2nd person interpretation becomes available in past subjunctives

---

[25] The proposal that the 2nd person is less salient in the discourse than the 1st or 3rd person (Manzini and Savoia 2005:119) seems confirmed by German Topic-drop constructions (Cardinaletti 1990), where the empty subject is also more often interpreted as 1st and 3rd person than 2nd person. This asymmetry cannot be related to verbal inflection since German 2nd person singular happens to always be morphologically distinct from the other persons of the verbal paradigm.

(59b), while in present subjunctives (59a), the 3rd person interpretation still prevails. In order to get the 2nd person interpretation, an overt subject pronoun is required: *Speriamo che **tu** sia in grado di aiutarci* (see (51b)).

The difficulty of recovering a 2nd person is confirmed by the observation that the polite form of address of Italian, in spite of being morphologically 3rd person singular, requires an overt subject pronoun in the present subjunctive:[26]

(60)   a. *Crede che [*pro* sia ricco], ma (lei) non lo è.
          [he] thinks that [you] aresubj rich, but (you) are not

       b. Crede che [**lei** sia ricco], ma (lei) non lo è.
          [he] thinks that you aresubj rich, but (you) are not

As pointed out by Richie Kayne, it can be relevant to the discussion that for some speakers of Italian, there is an appreciable improvement in sentences like (51a) if the verb is reflexive:

(61)   ?Crede che [*pro* ti sia comportato male].
       [he] thinks that [you] REFL aresubj behaved badly

Although this improvement is not shared by all speakers, it seems to go in the expected direction. The more liberal speakers rely on the 2nd person reflexive pronoun to recover the features of the null subject. Why this is not a general strategy used by all Italian speakers remains an open question.

The data discussed in this section show that the interpretation of *pro* is not simply a matter of grammatical licensing. As Holmberg (2005:560) puts it: 'Narrow syntax is oblivious to whether pronouns or inflectional affixes do or do not end up being pronounced. Sentence processing, by contrast, is obviously highly dependent on phonological features: if the subject is null, and the agreement on the finite verb is also null or not sufficiently distinct, then recovery of the subject's features will fail, or will rely on information from the discourse.'

In conclusion, the complex interaction between pronounced/unpronounced verbal inflections, i.e. the morphemes that realize the probe heads, and pronounced/unpronounced pronominal subjects, i.e. the morphemes that realize the goals, does not seem to be entirely syntactic in nature, but raises questions related to sentence processing and efficiency of computation. We are presumably dealing here with a third factor condition ('language-independent principles of data processing, structural architecture, and computational efficiency', Chomsky 2005:9) on sentence processing.

---

[26] The gender mismatch between the subject pronoun *lei* 'you' (homophonous to the 3rd person singular feminine pronoun *lei* 'she') and the masculine adjective *ricco* 'rich' guarantees that we are dealing with the form of polite address.

5.4 Conclusion

In this chapter, two instances of language variation in the syntax of subjects have been discussed. First, we have seen that in closely related languages, the feature that drives verb movement is associated with different heads of the clausal skeleton, i.e. it is bundled with the different features that are encoded in these heads. This lexical difference has consequences in other aspects of syntax, namely, in the placement of subjects. Verb placement and subject placement interact in a complicated way, which cannot be captured, it seems to us, in purely phonological nor in purely semantic terms.

Second, we have seen that languages may differ in the null subjects their lexicon contains, whether only 1st and 2nd person or also 3rd person. We have also seen that the use of a null or an overt pronoun, when both are possible in the language, does not seem to be entirely syntactic in nature, but it interacts in a complex way with discourse. This observation might also help in understanding the unavailability of a 2sg *pro* in languages in which verbal syncretisms do not resolve the ambiguity between 1st and 2nd or 2nd and 3rd interpretations.

6

Contact and change in a Minimalist theory of variation

RICARDO ETXEPARE

6.1 Introduction

This chapter addresses a case of diachronic change resulting from Basque-French contact. The Navarro-Labourdin variety of North-Eastern Basque (the major Basque variety spoken in France) undergoes a set of related changes during the nineteenth century.[1] Those changes affect the distribution of the dative case and its agreement properties (Pikabea 1998). The outcome of these changes is the emergence of a dative alternation, of the sort observed in various forms in many languages. Most of those changes, I will claim, can be accounted for by a single grammatical factor (a parameter), that arises as a consequence of contact with French. This grammatical factor is the presence of a phonologically null Path denoting adposition that arises through contact with French and distinguishes the underlying grammars of north-eastern Basque from those corresponding to central and western varieties. Part of the analysis in this chapter will therefore consist of a classical reduction of several clustering differences in terms of a single parameter.

Not all variation observed in the Navarro-Labourdin variety, however, can be directly attributed to the presence of this single grammatical factor: some systematic variation arises as a consequence of the interaction of that parameter with principles of interface economy. This phenomenon illustrates the workings of what Chomsky calls

[1] I wish to thank the participants and the audience at the workshop 'Linguistic Variation in the Minimalist Framework' held in Barcelona in January 2010 for very valuable input in the writing of this chapter, as well as the organizers for their invitation to participate in such an exciting event. I would also like to thank the audience of the Edisyn meeting held in Donostia-San Sebastian in June 2010. On a more personal basis, I would like to thank Bernard Oyharçabal, Javier Ormazabal, Beatriz Fernandez, and Pablo Albizu for valuable comments and discussion. I gladly acknowledge financial support from the projects ANR-07-CORP-033 and FFI2011-29218, and IT769-13.

'third factor' effects in the determination of the attained I-languages (Chomsky 2005). The changes affecting north-eastern varieties of Basque can thus be viewed as a direct instantiation of the combined effects of the three basic factors shaping natural language: external factors related to the nature of the input, as determined by the contact situation, internal structural properties related to UG, as illustrated by the functional lexicon and its combinatory properties, and general conditions of efficiency of computation and representation, not specific to language.

6.2 Datives in Central and Western Basque

Before we address those changes, we need to know how dative marking was before those changes occurred. The system, as attested by actual dialectal variation and a rich literary corpus, was identical to what we see today in central and western dialects, and in the standard variety. The following is a summary of those properties (see Oyharçabal 2010, for a recent description and analysis).

6.2.1 Dative case

Dative is one of the so called grammatical cases in Basque. Those are cases which mark a determiner phrase as argumental. It shares this property with ergative and absolutive cases. Dative DPs agree with the auxiliary in number and person. The dative usually marks the recipient or beneficiary of the action:

(1) a. Jonek   Mikeli   eskutitz bat   bidali dio
        Jon-ERG Mikel-DAT letter   one-ABS sent   AUX[ditransitive]
        'Jon sent a letter to Mikel'

     b. Jonek   Mikeli   autoa   konpondu dio
        Jon-ERG Mikel-DAT car-DET-ABS fixed   AUX[ditransitive]
        'Jon fixed the car for Mikel'

     c. Jonek   Mikeli   euskara   irakatsi dio
        Jon-ERG Mikel-DAT basque-ABS taught   AUX[ditransitive]
        'Jon taught Basque to Mikel'

Basque also employs dative marking for some non-participant roles in ditransitive constructions, such as ethical datives, datives of interest (2b), and possessor raising constructions (2a). Dative case also marks subjects of psychological predicates of the *piacere* class (2c) (Belletti and Rizzi 1988):

(2) a. Jonek   Mikeli   besoa   hautsi dio
        Jon-ERG Mikel-DAT arm-DET-ABS broken   AUX[3sA-3sD-3sE]
        'Jon broke Mikel's arm'
        [Context: A trainer about her trainee]

b. Egunero 10 kilometro korritzen dit
   daily   10 kilometre run-HAB   AUX[3sA-1sD-3sE]
   'She runs 10 kilometres every day (and that affects me)'

c. Joni   liburuak   gustatzen zaizkio
   Jon-DAT books-ABS like-HAB   AUX[3plA-3sD]
   'Jon likes books'

6.2.2 *Case, agreement, and the pre-dative suffix*

Dative case and agreement are not the only ways in which Basque marks the presence of a dative argument. Finite sentences containing a dative argument require a particular affix (*-i-/-ki-* see Trask 1995) in the inflected auxiliary, which has been variously called *dative-flag* (Rezac 2006) or *pre-dative affix* (Hualde and Ortiz de Urbina 2003).[2] The dative-flag precedes the agreement affix cross-referencing the dative argument. Take an unaccusative verb like *nator* 'I come':

(3) N-ator
     1sA-ROOT
     'I come'

The form in (3) can be extended to include reference to a dative argument, the end-point or beneficiary of the coming event. In that case, the agreement affix corresponding to the dative argument is preceded by the pre-dative affix (Hualde and Ortiz de Urbina 2003:207):

(4) N-ator-ki-zu
     1sA-ROOT-PREDAT-2sD
     'I come to you'

In other words, the presence of a dative argument in a Basque finite sentence requires three things: (i) a dative case suffix; (ii) agreement in person and number; and (iii) an independent inflectional head which signals that the sentence has a dative.

6.2.3 *The DP-status of the dative*

It is generally admitted, for central and western dialects, that dative arguments are Case-marked DPs. Only DPs trigger agreement on the verb, and datives, as we saw, do. Only DPs enter into binding relations as antecedents, and this is the case with dative DPs too. Compare in this regard (5a), with a dative argument, and (5b), with a postpositional phrase:

(5) a. Jonek   Mireni$_i$ bere$_i$ buruaz hitzegin dio
        Jon-ERG Miren-DAT POSS head   talked AUX[3sA-3sD-3sE]
        'Jon talked to Miren about herself'

---

[2] Historically, the dative-flag can be traced back to the root of the verb *egin* 'do'. There is considerable dialectal variation in the kind of morphological object which instantiates the dative flag (see Laka 1993).

   b. *Jonek   Mirenekin$_i$ bere$_i$ buruaz   hitzegin zuen
       Jon-ERG Miren-with POSS head-INSTR talked   AUX[3sA-3sE]
       'Jon talked with Miren about herself'

The dative argument typically c-commands and precedes the theme in Basque (see Fernandez 1997 and Elordieta 2001 for a thorough discussion).

6.3 Changes in the North-Eastern varieties

The north-eastern Navarro-Labourdin variety presents a series of contrasting properties in both the distribution of the case marker and its agreement properties. First, the scope of the dative case suffix seems to expand to include the marking of spatial functions of different sorts (sections 6.3.1 and 6.3.2), as well as the aspectual status of the event as unbounded (sections 6.3.3 and 6.3.4). Then, the dative case-suffix seems to only optionally agree with the auxiliary (section 6.3.5).

6.3.1 *Spatial datives*

In the Navarro-Labourdin variety, the dative marks the spatial goal of the event or situation:

(6) a. Erretora   badoa elizako   atearen   gakoari   (Lz.I, 235)
        priest-DET goes church-GEN door-GEN lock-DAT
        'The priest goes to the door-lock of the church'

     b. Balkoin bat, bideari   emaiten   duena   (Etc. OM, 130)
        balcony one, road-DAT give-HAB AUX[tr]-REL-DET
        'A balcony that looks onto the road'

     c. Alemanen   tankak oldartzen   zirela   Maginot harresiari
        German-GEN tanks charge-GER AUX-COMP Maginot fence-DAT
        'As the German tanks charged against the Maginot line'   (Lz, VII, 53)

     d. Hurbiltzen   da poliki-poliki bonetari   (LZ, I, 113)
        approach-GER is slowly   beret-DAT
        'He slowly approaches the beret'

Central and western varieties, as well as the Navarro-Labourdin variety before the nineteenth century, only admit spatial postpositions or complex postpositional phrases (see next subsection) in that case:

(7) a. Erretora   badoa elizako   ate   gakora
        priest-DET goes church-GEN door lock-ALL
        'The priest goes to the door-lock'

b. Balkoin bat, bide**ra**   ematen   duena
balcony one, road-ALL give-HAB AUX[tr]-REL-DET
'A balcony that looks over the road'

c. Alemanen   tankeak oldartzen zirela   Maginot harresia**ren kontra**
German-GEN tanks   charge   AUX-COMP Maginot fence-GEN   against
'As the German tanks charged against the Maginot line'

d. Hurbiltzen da   poliki-poliki txapela**ren ingurura**
draw.near AUX slowly   beret-GEN vicinity-ALL
'He slowly approaches the beret'

6.3.2 *Datives in complex postpositions*

There is a set of postpositions in Basque which encode directional paths. Those postpositions, starting in the nineteenth century, select DP grounds which are marked with a dative case suffix in the Navarro-Labourdin variety:

(8) a. Mendia-**ri**   gora   b. Mendia-**ri**   behera
        mountain-DAT   up   mountain-DAT   down
        'Up the mountain'   'Down the mountain'

     c. Pareta-**ri**   kontra   d. Jujea-**ri**   bisean-bis
        wall-DAT   against   judge-DAT   vis-à-vis
        'Against the wall'   'Vis-à-vis the judge'

     e. Etxea-**ri**   parrez-par f. Har-**i**   buruz
        house-DAT   face-to-face   that-DAT   towards
        'Facing the house'   'Towards that'

DPs encoding the ground of a spatial relation are selected by inessive postpositions or genitive cases in the rest of the Basque varieties in those cases:

(9) a. Mendia-**n**   gora   b. Mendia-**n**   behera
        mountain.in   up   mountain.in   down
        'Up the mountain'   'Down the mountain'

     c. Pareta-**ren**   kontra   d. Jujea-**ren**   aurrez-aurre
        wall-GEN   against   judge-GEN   vis-à-vis
        'Against the wall'   'In front of the judge'

     e. Etxea-**ren**   parrez-par f. Ha-**ren-gana**
        house-GEN   face-INSTR-face   PRON-GEN-INE-ALL
        'In front of the house'   'Towards her/him'

6.3.3 *Datives in complements of aspectual verbs*

Aspectual verbs of the atelic sort select for dative nominalized clauses in Navarro-Labourdin (see section 6.3.1), as the progressive and inchoative aspectual verbs in (10):

(10) a. Eta horren   ahultzeari   ari   zirezte
       and that-GEN weaken-NOM-DET-DAT PROG are
       'And you are weakening that'

   b. Josteari   *lotu* da
      sew-NOM-DAT tied is
      'He started sewing'

Those same complements are headed by the inessive postposition in central and western varieties. The central counterpart of (10a) would thus be (11), modulo lexical and morphological differences:

(11) Eta horren   ahultzen   ari   zirezte
     and that-GEN weaken-NOM-INESS PROG are
     'And you are weakening that'

6.3.4 *Datives in atelic verbs*

The dative also shows up in the object of a handful of unergative and semelfactive predicates:

(12) a. Horr-i   pentsatu   b. Atea-ri   jo
        that-DAT   think   door-DAT   knock
        'To think about that'   'Knock on the door'

Central and western dialects mark those same arguments with the inessive postposition:

(13) a. Horreta-n   pentsatu   b. Atea-n   jo
        that-IN   think   door-IN   knock
        'To think about that'   'To knock on the door'

6.3.5 *Optional agreement and word order*

Apart from the extension in the range of uses of the dative, north-eastern Basque also shows what seems like optional agreement[3] with the dative argument in ditransitive constructions (Oyharçabal 1992; Ortiz de Urbina 1994; Fernandez and Ortiz de Urbina 2010; Etxepare and Oyharçabal 2009, forthcoming).

(14) a. Amak   semeari   opari bat igorri dio
        mother-ERG son-DET-DAT present one sent   AUX[3sE-3sD-3sA]
        'The mother sent a present to the son'

---

[3] The non-agreeing structures are a typical repair strategy for the *me-lui* or Person/Case constraints observable in the Basque agreeing ditransitive construction (see Rezac 2009) in other varieties. The extension of this phenomenon in the Basque dialectal domain is not clear at present.

b. Amak   opari   bat igorri du   semeari
   mother-ERG present one sent   AUX[3sE-3sA] son-DET-DAT
   'The mother sent a present to the son'

Note that the alternation involves three things: the agreement and the dative flag on the one hand, and the relative order of the O and the IO on the other. The unmarked order of the non-agreeing cases seems to favour the order O-IO with the indirect object in postverbal position (see Etxepare and Oyharçabal 2009).

6.4 Poverty of Stimulus situations under contact

6.4.1 *French à meets the Basque dative*

Pikabea (1998) observes that at least a subset of the changes involved can be directly attributed to French contact, under the hypothesis that the eastern dative largely correlates with the surface distribution of the French dative preposition. The Basque dative cases reviewed earlier seem to arise in those contexts where French shows the preposition *à*:

(15)   a. Il est allé à la porte   MOTION VERBS
           he went to the door

        b. Il a commencé à travailler   ASPECTUAL COMPLEMENTS
           he has started to work

        c. Il a pensé à ça   ATELIC UNERGATIVES
           he has thought about that

        d. Il a frappé à la porte   SEMELFACTIVES
           he has knocked at the door

        e. Il a envoyé un présent à son fils   CAUSED MOTION VERBS
           he has sent a present to his son

But the correlation is not strictly speaking right if one takes into account the full set of spatial datives. French *à* has a purely locative reading. It cannot express direction by itself (Troberg 2008), as seen in the contrast between French (16a) and Basque (16b):

(16)   a. *Votre chambre regarde sur/*à   la   colline
           Your   room   looks   over/PREP the hill
           'Your room looks onto the hill'

        b. Balkoin bat bideari   emaiten duena
           balcony one road-DAT give-GER AUX(tr)-REL-DET
           'A balcony that looks onto the road'

Ruwet (1982) notes that French *à* can only accompany DPs that can be independently conceptualized as places:

(17)   Pierre était couché sur/contre/devant/*à son tigre apprivoisé
       Pierre was in   bed PREP   his tiger favourite
       'Pierre lay down in bed on/against/in front of/ *a his favourite tiger'

As Torrego (2002) notes, only those Romance varieties that have a stative dative preposition *a* license possessive *habere*, French among them. This suggests that the basic meaning of the French preposition *à* must be locative, or related to a Place function. The locative occurrences of *à* (18a) can not be reproduced by the dative in Basque, as shown in (18b):

(18)   a. Il est à la maison
       b. *Etxeari   da
          home-DET-DAT is
          'She/he is home'

This suggests that if Pikabea is right in attributing the Navarro-Labourdin dative spreading to the influence of French, the French-looking Basque datives cannot be directly modelled on the surface distribution of the French datives. I will defend the idea that underlying the Navarro-Labourdin dative spreading is a reanalysis of the French preposition *à* as a directional one. Pikabea notes, based on textual evidence, that the syntactic context where the spatial, non-agreeing dative first appears are ditransitive predicates involving caused motion or caused possession (cf. 14b). I will come back to this in section 6.6.

6.4.2 *Complex postpositional phrases*

There is another grammatical context where the French influence cannot be direct. There is no French (nor Gascon or Bearnais, see Cardaillac 1976; Palay 1980; Hourcade 1986; Haase 1992) correlate of the presence of the dative in complex postpositional phrases:

(19)   a. Pareta-**ri**   kontra   b. Contre   le   mur
          wall-DAT   against   against the   wall

Assuming, as is commonly taken to be the case, that the source behind the changes in 6.3.1 to 6.3.5 is French, the complex postpositional phrases constitute a clear case of the Poverty of Stimulus situation. That is, whereas certain aspects of the distribution of the dative case suffix could eventually be accounted for in terms parallel to the French prepositional dative, some other aspects, notably their presence in complex postpositional structures, are not amenable to that scenario, for the simple reason that they lack a French structural correlate. There is therefore, no direct source in French for anything like 6.4.1 and 6.4.2.

6.4.3 *Summary*

The changes occurring in the Navarro-Labourdin variety in the nineteenth century are summarized in the following table. The table also shows whether the relevant properties are attested in Central Basque varieties and French: dative in complex postpositional phrases:

(20)   Changes in nineteenth-century Navarro-Labourdin Basque in comparison to Central Basque and French

NAVARRO-LABOURDIN BASQUE	FRENCH	CENTRAL BASQUE
Goal Datives	Goal Datives	*Non-attested*
Aspectual Datives	Aspectual Datives	*Non-attested*
Datives in unergative Predicates	Datives in unergative Predicates	*Non-attested*
Non-agreeing Datives	Non-agreeing Datives	*Non-attested*
Complex Postpositions	*Non-attested*	*Non-attested*

The table suggests that the place we have to look at to understand the change is the domain of complex postpositions. That is the spot where a trivial account in terms of E-language correspondences fails.

6.5 Hypotheses

The related changes undergone by the Navarro-Labourdin variety will be accounted for along the following lines: first, Navarro-Labourdin Basque borrows a silent directional adposition modelled on the basis of the French dative preposition. A reanalysis of the French dative preposition as a directional one precedes the borrowing. This silent adposition licenses a dative case in the ground DP. Furthermore, the directional adposition can be inserted in more than one position in the clause structure, and extends beyond those syntactic contexts where French *à* occurs. Unlike the extant lexical adpositions in Basque, which merge both Path and Place features, this silent adposition is not complex, and stands in an elsewhere relation with the lexical adpositions. Anticipating some of the discussion that follows, the basic micro-parameter that underlies the related changes described in sections 6.3.1–6.3.5 and that distinguishes central and Navarro-Labourdin varieties can be formulated as in (21):

(21)   The lexical inventory of Navarro-Labourdin adpositions contains a lexical entry for the feature [d-Path] (directional Path)

Getting to (21) is the object of 6.6 in this chapter.

The emerging adpositional forms exist together with a different strategy to express oblique arguments in Basque, shared by all dialects: an applicative strategy. Under this view, the agreement alternation is not optional agreement, but a phenomenon similar to the dative alternation in English (and related alternations in other languages), where the borrowed adpositional structure plays the role of the prepositional construction. The applicative construction, on the other hand, undergoes a process of specialization in the Navarro-Labourdin varieties that restricts the range of applied objects to those DPs that can introduce a discourse variable. I will call this phenomenon Specialization. The processes of borrowing, structural generalization, lexical integration, and specialization reflect the workings of different components of the grammar. In the case of what I call Specialization, it illustrates the working of the 'third factor' in language design proposed by Chomsky (2005) in the context of the Minimalist Program. Discussing the agreement alternation and its proper analysis will be the object of 6.7.

6.6 Datives and adpositions

As a first step in getting to (21), let us ask ourselves, what determines the distribution of spatial datives in motion predicates? How do they relate to lexical postpositions?

6.6.1 Spatial Datives and predicate classes

6.6.1.1 Motion verbs and unbounded paths Let us take as a starting point the verb *itzuli*. It has two related meanings in Basque: it means either 'return, come back', or 'turn towards something'. In its first reading, it takes an allative DP as the target of motion (22a). In its second meaning, it takes a dative DP as the target of an oriented path (22b):

(22) a. Maiterengana   itzuli   zen
          Maite-GEN-INE-ALL turned was
          'He/she returned to (where) Maite (was)'

      b. Itzuli   zen Maiteri   (Etchepare 1958:94)
          turned was Maite-DAT
          'He/she turned towards Maite'

Jackendoff (1990) provides the following conceptual schema for the 'turn towards' meaning:

(23) *Itzuli* 'Turn towards'
      [EVENT INCH ([STATE ORIENT ([Thing Subject], [Path Object])])]

Compared to the basic conceptual function GO underlying the 'return' reading of the verb, the conceptual representation of 'turn towards' contains the basic conceptual function ORIENT, which does not imply motion into a goal. ORIENT has two arguments, one being the Figure of the relation, and the other one being a directional or unbounded Path, which in turn selects a spatial Ground. The above contrast suggests the following hypothesis: spatial datives occur with those predicates that do not represent a transfer. The turning motion leaves the Theme in a certain position vis-à-vis the spatial goal (*Maite*, in 22b), but does not take it into the spatial Goal. The latter requires an overt adposition (22a).

Bihurtu in (24) is another verb that obeys a similar pattern. *Bihurtu* also has two different meanings: it means either 'return' or 'to turn against'. The first meaning requires an allative goal, and entails that the theme has moved to a physical or abstract place. The second one does not give rise to such an entailment, it only means that the subject stands in a resisting or rebelling attitude vis-à-vis a certain goal:

(24) a. Lege zaharretara bihurtu   dira
         old   law-PL-ALL turned.back is
         'They returned to the old laws'

      b. Ez   da... lege zaharreri   bihurtuko den   gizon bat   (LZ,II, 30)
         NEG is   old law-PL-DAT turn-FUT is-REL man   one
         'He is not a man who will turn against old laws'

Abiatu 'depart, to set in motion to a goal' can take an allative or a dative goal. The two cases do not have an identical meaning:

(25) a. Bidera   abiatu da
         road-ALL moved is
         'He moved to the road'

      b. Abiatzen   gaituk beraz   bideari   (LZ, V, 61)
         move-GER we.are therefore road-DAT
         'We therefore set out on our way'

With the allative postposition, the predicate expresses a motion taking the theme to a physical space, the road. With the dative, it means that the subject has set in her/his way, with no further implication that a goal is within reach.

The verb *erori* provides a further example of the alternation between the dative and the allative. With an allative postposition *erori* means 'fall' and the allative locates the physical space where the falling ends (26a). Our corpus also shows the variant in (26b), with a dative ground, where *erori* means 'fall under' or 'be inclined to/towards'. In the latter case, no motion is entailed:

(26) a. Lurrera   erori da
         floor-ALL fallen is
         'He/she fell on the floor'

      b. Jainkoaren nahi sainduari erortzen diren   arima jenerosak
         god-GEN   will holly-DAT fall-HAB AUX-COMP spirit generous-DET-PL
                                                                (Etc. BEB, 109)
         'Those generous spirits who are inclined towards god's holy will'

Verbs like *jarraiki/segitu* 'follow' or *hurbildu* 'approach' also require dative. They lexically entail that the theme has not reached the goal but follows a path that is goal-oriented:

(27) a. Etsenplu oneri... jarraiki da bere... urhatsetan (Etc., FE, 114)
       example good-DAT follow is his steps-INE
       'He follows the good examples in all his steps'

    b. Hurbiltzen da polliki bonetari (LZ., I, 113)
       approach-GER is slowly beret-DAT
       'He slowly approaches the beret'

If this is what underlies the use of dative ground DPs, we can make sense of the fact that verbs like *arrive* or *come*, which denote an attained spatial goal, are incompatible with the dative:

(28) a. *Etxeari liburua heldu da
       house-DAT book-DET arrived is
       the book arrived to the house

    b. *Etxeari eskale bat etorri da
       house-DAT beggar one come is
       a beggar came home

The data suggest the following partition in the set of Path exponents in Basque:

(29) a. Allative -> Bounded Path (Spatial Goal, TO)
    b. Dative -> Unbounded Path (Oriented Path, TOWARDS)

6.6.1.2 Stative verbs The directional element associated to the dative suffix is particularly prominent when the predicate itself is such that it cannot contribute one. Stative verbs like (30a,b) are a case in point:

(30) a. Balkoin bat,... bideari emaiten duena (Etc. OM, 130)
       balcony one road-DAT give-HAB AUX(tr)-REL-DET
       'A balcony that looks onto the road'

    b. Lehena salbu, oro Kaliforniako itsasoari dagoen lur zerrendan
       first except all California-GEN sea-DAT is-REL land stretch-INE
       (L.P., 52)
       'Except the first one, all of them in the stretch of land looking (lit. *which is*) onto California'

(30a) involves a complex predicate formed by the light verb *eman* 'give' and a dative goal. The complex verb is a stative predicate that does not involve an abstract motion. The directional component is directly contributed by the dative ground. An even more clear case is (30b), where the copula *egon* 'to be' physically locates the subject *oro* 'all', but contributes nothing that could be interpreted as an orientation function. It is the presence of the dative ground that adds the directional component.[4]

6.6.1.3 Directed change of state   Consider the following cases:

(31) a. Heien egitateeri   begiak   hetsi   ditut   (LZ., II, 74)
         their   deeds-DAT   eyes   close   AUX(tr)
         'I closed the eyes to their deeds'

      b. Aphal dezagun   burua   jainkoaren nahi   sainduari   (Etc. FE, 179)
         lower AUX(tr)   head-DET   god's   will   holly-DAT
         'Let us bow to god's holy will'

      c. Ederrak   idekitzen   du   gogoa   egiari   (Sal., 180)
         beauty-ERG open-HAB   AUX(tr)   mind-DET   truth-DAT
         'Beauty opens the mind to the truth'

      d. Haien erranari   behar dugu   nahitaez   plegatu   (LZ.,IV,138)
         their words-DAT   must   AUX(tr)   obligatorily   yield
         'We must submit to what they say'

In all cases, the absolutive argument (the Figure) undergoes a change of state, and this change leaves it in a particular orientation vis-à-vis the Reference Point (someone else's deeds, god's will, truth or someone else's words in (31)). But there is no movement that will take the figure into the Ground. I assume that a relevant part of the conceptual structure underlying those predicates involves the function ORIENT, as in the previous cases:

(32) [EVENT CAUSE ([Thing…], [STATE ORIENT ([Thing…], [Path …])

---

[4] Jackendoff (1983:173) proposes the following conceptual structure for cases like 'to look onto':

(i) [STATE ORIENT([Thing x], [Path y])]

Other stative verbs denote psychological states where the Ground constitutes the target of that state. Those grounds also display dative in the Navarro-Labourdin variety:

(ii) a. Erne   egon momentuaren kausitzeari
          attentive be   moment-GEN find-NOM-DET-DAT
          'Be attentive to the right moment'
      b. Ohartu zara horri?
          aware   AUX   that-DAT
          'Did you notice that?'

Jackendoff (1983) proposes a conceptual structure similar to (i) for those cases, with a diacritic in the orientation function that circumscribes it to the psychological domain:

(iii) [STATE ORIENT_{PSYCHOLOGICAL} ([Thing x], [Path y])]

For a full list of the types of verbs and their relation to the orientation function see Etxepare and Oyharçabal 2013.

6.6.1.4 The dative as the elsewhere case   Let us take up again the generalization in (29) that we drew on the basis of motion verbs:

(33)   a. Allative -> Bounded Path (Spatial Goal, TO)
       b. Dative -> Unbounded Path (Oriented Path, TOWARDS)

The corpus presents cases where the dative seems to occupy the place of the allative, if we were to blindly follow the schema in (33). Consider for instance the following examples with the verb *joan* 'go':

(34)   a. Erretora badoa elizako   atearen   **gakoari**   (LZ., I, 235)
           priest   goes   church-GEN   door-GEN lock-DAT
           'The priest goes to the door-lock of the church'

       b. *Erretora badoa elizako   atearen   **gakora**
            priest   goes   church-GEN   door-GEN lock-ALL

(35)   a. Solas   berri bati   zoazin gehienen   beharriak   (LZ.,V,119)
           conversation   new   one-DAT went   most-GEN-PL   ear-DET-PL
           'Most ears were directed to a new conversation'

       b. ??Beharri gehienak   solas   berri batera   zoazin
            ear   most-DET-PL conversation   new   one-ALL went

The occurrence of the dative is surprising here, since the conceptual function expressed by the simple verb *joan* in Basque is GO, and it requires a spatial goal. One way to address this problem would be to take the predicates in (37)–(38) to denote motion along an unbounded path. Under this interpretation, the priest goes towards the door-lock, and the ears are set towards a new conversation. The issue, however, is why the allative is impossible.[5] As shown by Aurnague (2001), the allative does not only express a spatial goal, it also requires that the Figure be included in or supported by the Ground or Spatial Goal. The following, for instance, is also impossible (Aurnague, 2001:197):

(36)   *Ganibetara joan da
         knife-ALL gone is
         'He went to the knife'

This is a topological property that we should not ascribe to the Path function itself, witness the dative cases. Rather, it seems to be a property of the inessive declension case in Basque (Aurnague, 2001:103–12). It is commonplace in the Basque grammatical tradition to consider that allative suffixes somehow contain inessive ones. One piece of

---

[5] The allative is impossible even if we add the suffix *-antz*, which contributes the 'towards' meaning in the complex allative postposition *-rantz* (<ra+antz):

(1)   ??Beharri guziak   solas   berri baterantz   zoazin
       ear   all-DET-PL   conversation   new   one-ALL-towards went

dialectal evidence is provided by those dialects where the allative suffix (the allomorph *-lat* in those cases) overtly follows an inessive suffix, as in some varieties of Souletin:[6]

(37) Etxe-a(*n)-lat
      house-DET-(-INE)-ALL
      'To the house'

A natural way of accounting for this dependency is to say that the allative suffix is a complex category, one that spells out both Path and Place features (Kracht 2000; Caha 2009). This allows us to account for another property of allatives: they are incompatible with animate DPs (38a), a restriction which can be already observed with the inessive (38b):

(38) a. *Jon-era
         Jon-ALL
         'To Jon'

      b. *Jon-en
         Jon-INE
         'In Jon'

In the latter case, Basque uses a special inessive suffix *–gan*, preceded by a genitive suffix (39a). The allative is added to that suffix in directional contexts (39b), supporting the idea that allative embeds inessive and spells out both Path and Place in cases like (36):

(39) a. Jon-en-gan   b. Jon-en-gan-a
         Jon-GEN-INE   Jon-GEN-INE-ALL
         'In Jon'   'To Jon'

This restriction in animacy is typologically a common one in the area of locative adpositions, see Aristar (1996), and Kuryłowicz (1964), for a classical reference. So the restrictions imposed by the allative are inherited from the inessive. When compared to the allative, the dative shows no such restriction: it does not mind whether the DP Ground is animate or not, or whether it includes or supports the Figure. The only thing it cares about is encoding a Path feature. This Path feature can occur in predicates expressing either the GO or the ORIENT function, to use Jackendoff's terms. This suggests the following distribution:

(40)

	Animate	Inanimate
Place+Path	ALL	ALL
Path	DAT	DAT

---

[6] With the inessive unexpressed, but indicated by the presence of a determiner, impossible in the complement of allative adpositions (see Hualde and Ortiz de Urbina 2003:187–8). I thank Bernard Oyharçabal for pointing this out to me.

According to (40), the dative is associated to the expression of simple Paths. The table in (40) invites the conclusion that the dative stands in an elsewhere relation vis-à-vis the declension suffix allative. The latter has a richer specification (it includes the inessive), and it is obligatory in those cases where the relevant topological relations between Figure and Ground meet the semantic description of the declension suffix. The dative surfaces in the rest of the cases. (41) summarizes the distribution of the spatial dative in Navarro-Labourdin varieties:

(41)   All dative grounds are associated to a directional Path.

6.6.2 *A syntactic representation for the Dative Grounds*

Consider the stative predicate in (42a). If Ramchand (2008) is right in claiming that purely stative copulas like *egon* 'to be'[7] do not map into any of the basic primitives out of which other predicate classes are built, the Dative Ground cannot constitute an argument. For this type of element, Ramchand proposes the category of Rhemes, terms that contribute to specify the relevant predication. For the specific case of the stative predication in (42a), I will propose that the Rheme merges as a complement to the locative copula (42b):

(42)   a. Itsasoari dago
            sea-DAT is
            'It is looking onto the sea/It is oriented towards the sea'

        b. ...BE [$_\text{AdpositionalPhrase}$ ... $\emptyset_\text{PATH}$ [[DP]K_DAT]

The Dative must be associated to a directional Path. The copula *egon* by itself does not express a Path function.

Rhemes can otherwise be merged to any of the basic building blocks of event structure, either to the Process head (which contributes dynamicity) or to the Result State. For the verbs of Directed Change of State, which are mostly deadjectival, I will propose the following structure, with the Path adposition merging directly to the adjective heading the Result State:

(43)   a. We close the eyes to their deeds
        b. [We Init° [Eyes Proc° [(eyes) Res° closed [$\emptyset_\text{PATH}$ [$_\text{KP}$ [Deeds] K°...]]

In (43), the Adpositional Phrase modifies the underlying Result State by merging a directional Path to the adjective.

In the case of motion verbs, the Path function would be merged as a Rheme to the Process head (44):

(44)   ...Proc [$\emptyset_\text{PATH}$ [$_\text{KP}$[DP] K_DAT...]] (Directional Path)

---

[7] More precisely, 'to be in a location'. The copula *egon* contrasts with the copula *izan* 'to be' in much the way Spanish *estar* contrasts with Spanish *ser* (see Etxepare 2003).

The dative Ground cannot merge to the Result State head, because the latter (following Ramchand) does not admit directional paths, and the Dative Ground implies the presence of a silent Path head:

(45) *Etxeari   heldu da
      house-DAT arrived is

6.6.3 *Aspectually determined datives*

6.6.3.1 Aspectual verbs Atelic aspectual verbs like *hasi* 'start', *lotu* 'set to', or *bermatu* 'keep on', among others, take Dative nominalized clauses:

(46) a. Ordu berean   abiatu zen fraide muthilak biltzeari   (Etc., OM, 106)
         time same-INE set   was friar   boys   gather-NOMLZ-DAT
         'He set immediately to gather the young friars'

      b. Horren   hedatzeari   bermatzen zen   (Etc., OM, 222)
         that-GEN extend-NOMLZ-DAT set-on   AUX
         'He kept on spreading that'

      c. Lotu zen lan   huni
         tied was work this-DAT
         'He went on to work on this'

      d. Laster jarri nintzen eskol   emaiteari   (Oztibarre, fieldwork)
         soon   sit   was-1SG school teach-NOMLZ-DAT
         'I soon started teaching'

The atelic verbs in (46) represent abstract Paths: they all involve a change of state from a situation where the subject is at rest to one in which he or she is engaged in an activity that has no definite end-point. It is fair to conclude that they are one more instance of the kind of Dative Ground discussed in the previous sections, now operating in the aspectual realm. A piece of evidence in favour of this conclusion is that telic aspectual verbs (those selecting a Result Phrase) do not admit the dative marker:

(47) a. *Bukatu du   egiteari
         finished AUX do-NOMLZ-DAT
         'He/she finished doing that'

      b. *Lortu   zuen egiteari
         managed AUX do-NOMLZ-DAT
         'He/she managed to do it'

The latter are good in all Basque dialects with an inessive suffix:

(48) Bukatu/lortu   du   egi-te-n
      finished/managed AUX(tr) do-NOMLZ-INE
      'He/she finished doing it/He/she managed to do it'

If inessive case suffixes encode a [Place] feature, the Navarro-Labourdin dative cases must encode something more than that. By hypothesis, they encode [Path].

It is a delicate matter to situate the relevant aspectual head in the clause structure. Is it directly generated in the lower portion of the VP (Ramchand's First Phase), or does it belong in a higher projection, external to the VP? There is a sense in which we want to separate these cases from the sort of Place and Path functions that operate in the first phase domain of verbs like *joan* 'go'. Take central dialects for a moment:

(49) Eskola ematen   jarri zen
      school give-NOM-INE sit   AUX
      'He/she started teaching'

The Central equivalent of the Navarro-Labourdin dative is an inessive. But the ines-sive suffix here does not obey at least some of the topological restrictions at work in the case of first-phase syntax. There is no obvious sense, for instance, in which the Figure must be supported by the Ground. The argument can be carried over to the arguably more complex cases in north-eastern dialects. Let me suggest that unlike with the verbs of motion, this dative case-suffix is generated separately above the vP (Kayne 2005b), and takes a nominalized clausal complement (50a). If the suffixal sta-tus of the dative case is to be attributed to the movement of the nominalized clause, the final structure must approach (50b):

(50) a. …$\emptyset_{PATH}$ [K° [D° [Init … Proc…]]] ->
      b. …$\emptyset_{PATH}$ [$_{KP}$ [$_{DP}$ D [Init … Proc…] K_{DAT} …]

Another piece of evidence can be adduced in support of the view that the [Path] feature in the case of aspectual verbs is located outside VP. The dative suffix in those cases triggers the aspectual coercion of simple nominals:

(51) a. Zer motari   ari   haiz   hor ?   (LZ., I, 265)
         what type-DAT PROG AUX(intr) there
         'What type (of wine) are you [trying] there?'

      b. Kondea   bere ezpatari   lotzen da   (LZ., II, 124)
         count-DET his sword-DAT tie-HAB is
         'The Count starts [using] his sword'

The dative attaches directly to the object of the hidden eventuality (in brackets in the translation), and triggers a reading where the object is involved in some unspecified event. No such effect is obtained by means of other adpositions, be they inessive ones or allatives (52a,b):

(52) a. Kondea   bere ezpatara   lotzen da
         count-DET his sword-ALL tie-GER is
         'The count gets tied to his own sword'

b. *Zer   mota-ra/-tan ari   haiz hor?
   what type-ALL/INE PROG AUX there

This suggests that the silent Path adposition responsible for the coercion effect is higher than the allative and the inessive of simple motion verbs, and embeds a tacit verbal structure:

(53)   Ø_PATH [K° [D° [_VP Init…DP]]]

6.6.3.2 *Atelic predicates*   Once the directional Path adposition is found in the complement of atelic aspectual operators, it is not surprising to find it in the complement of unergative verbs too, yielding atelic predicates like (54a–c):

(54)   a. Bainan herriak ez dezake   ihardok ikastegiari   (Sal., 183)
           but the people NEG can(tr) resist   school-DET-DAT
           'But the people cannot resist school'

        b. Athe guzieri jotzen du   (Etc., FE, 65)
           door all-DAT knock-HAB AUX(tr)
           'He/she knocks on all doors'

        c. Horri   pentsatzen dut
           that-DAT think-GER AUX(tr)
           'I'm thinking of that'

Those verbs denote an activity, and the activity has a target, but the event has no inherent endpoint. The aspectual contribution of the dative is manifest in the case of the verb *pentsatu* 'think', which alternates with an absolutive object:

(55)   a. Hori pentsatu dut   (bi minututan)
           that thought AUX(tr) in two minutes
           'I thought that in two minutes'

        b. Horri   pentsatu dut   (*bi minututan)
           that-DAT think   AUX(tr)   in two minutes
           'I thought about that in two minutes'

The direct object of *think* in (55a) is a measuring object directly merged to the Process head as a Rheme, and not a direct argument of the verb. The simplest option is to think of the dative structure in (55b) as involving a VP external aspectual structure, akin to the one proposed for aspectual complements. One piece of evidence for this is given by the comparison with central varieties, where the adposition that triggers the aspectual interpretation is inessive:

(56)   Horreta-n pentsatzen du
        that-INE   think-HAB AUX
        'He/she thinks about that'

If Ramchand is right in claiming that complements of Process heads cannot be Place denoting entities, but must denote Paths or other scalar entities, then the inessive here cannot be the direct complement of the Process head. Ramchand also suggests that semelfactive aspect could be represented in a VP-external position, as proposed by Rothstein (2004).

6.6.3.3 Summary　A look at the types of predicates that present Dative Grounds reveals a set of different configurations whose common factor is the presence of a silent directional Path adposition, that licenses the Dative Ground:

(57)　a. ...BE [Ø$_{PATH}$ [[DP]K$_{DAT}$...]]　　　　　　　　　　　　　　　Stative

　　b. .... Proc [Ø$_{PATH}$ [$_{KP}$[DP] K$_{DAT}$...]]　　　　　　　　　　　Motion

　　c. ...Res° closed [Ø$_{PATH}$ [$_{KP}$ [DP] K$_{DAT}$...]]　　Directed Change of State

　　d. ...Ø$_{PATH}$ [$_{KP}$ [D° [Init ...Proc...]] K$_{DAT}$...]　　　　　　Aspectual

The silent adposition spreads across the verbal structure occupying all those places where a directional Path function is compositionally allowed. There is no further restriction on the distribution of the silent directional head. To this, we can add those configurations where the dative Ground is not selected by a predicate. This is the case for the adjunct dative phrase in (58), which measures the extension of the event:

(58)　a. ...gainetik beherekoari larderiatu zituen hango　　botijesak
　　　　upper.from low-GEN-DAT threatened AUX(tr) there-GEN shopkeepers
　　　　'He threatened those shopkeepers from the most important to the lesser one'

　　b. ...[Ø$_{PATH}$ [[DP]K$_{DAT}$...]] PP-Adjunct

6.6.4 Adpositional structures in Basque

Under the hypothesis defended here, Spatial Datives surface as part of a syntactic structure including a directional Path. Our analysis has proposed a two part syntactic representation that splits the relevant construction into a silent Path head and a Place denoting dative:

(59)　[$_{PP}$ P$_{PATH}$ [$_{KP}$ [DP] K...]]

But there a is simpler analysis, one that expands the semantic range of the dative:

(60)　DAT = {unbounded Path}

This is in fact the analysis proposed for non-agreeing datives by Albizu (2001) and Fernandez and Ortiz de Urbina (2010), as well as Etxepare and Oyharçabal (2009). This analysis assimilates the dative case marked Grounds to adpositional phrases directly. The diachronic change effected during the nineteenth century would therefore be one that touches on the range of interpretations that the dative can have. I will in what follows argue against this view, but that will require a brief detour to the (spatial) adpositional system of Basque.

6.6.4.1 Adpositions and spatial nouns   The domain of spatial relations in Basque is expressed by means of three different sets of elements: (i) Locative suffixes; (ii) spatial nouns; and (iii) invariant postpositions encoding direction among possibly other things (de Rijk 1990; 2008; Eguzkitza 1998; Hualde 2002). The basic locative suffixes[8] are three, the inessive (a), the allative (b), and the ablative (c):

(61)   a. Etxea-**n**   b. Etxe-**ra**   c. Etxe-**tik**
         house-DET-INE   house-ALL   house-ABL
         'In the house'   'To the house'   'From the house'

Apart from those basic locative suffixes, Basque has a rich set of spatial nouns that combine with those suffixes to express various spatial relations:

(62)   a. Etxe-a-ren   **aurre**-a-n
         house-DET-GEN   front-D-INE
         'In front of the house'

       b. Zuhaitz-en   **arte**-tik
         tree-DET-GEN   among/between the trees
         'From between the trees'

       c. Ohe-a-ren   **azpi**-ra
         bed-DET-GEN   side.below-ALL
         '(To) below the bed'

       d. Erreka-a-ren   **ondo**-tik
         river-DET-GEN   proximity-ABL
         'From next to the river'

       e. Etxearen   **atze**-tik
         house-DET-GEN   behind-ABL
         'From behind the house'

       f. Teilatuaren   **gain**-e-a-n
         roof-DET-GEN   surface-DET-INE
         'On the roof'

       g. Erreka-a-ren   **inguru**-a-n
         river-DET-GEN   vicinity-DET-INE
         'Around the river'

Those spatial nouns define an area projected from the Ground DP. According to de Rijk (1990), spatial nouns are 'real' nouns: they select a genitive complement (62a–g), and can be selected by elements that typically select nominal phrases, like articles or demonstratives. In that case, they have referential uses (63a,b):

---

[8] Three other suffixes are built on the allative by the addition of further material: -*rantz* 'towards' (see fn. 2), -*raino* expressing a spatial endpoint, and -*rarte* expressing a temporal endpoint (English 'until/till').

(63) a. Etxearen   aurrea   konpondu beharra   dago
         house-GEN front-DET fix   need-DET is
         'The front-side of the house should be fixed'

  b. Inguru hura arras hondatua zen
     vicinity that very ravaged was
     'That area was completely ravaged'

The referential uses, however, introduce a different meaning when compared to bare spatial nouns in complex postpositional structures. *Aurre* 'front' means two very different things in (a,b):

(64) a. Etxearen   aurrea
         house-GEN front-DET
         'The façade of the house'

  b. Etxearen   aurrean
     house-GEN front-INE
     'In front of the house' / 'In the façade of the house'

Under the referential reading (64a), the noun only refers to a part of the house. In (64b) on the other hand, it can refer to the space in front of the house, an area projected from the ground element.

If we introduce a modifier that forces us to go beyond the simple nominal head, we lose the projective meaning:

(65) Etxearen   aurre zikinean
     house-DET-GEN front dirty-INE
     'In the dirty façade of the house'

The same happens if we insert number:

(66) Etxearen   aurreak
     house-DET-GEN front-DET-PL
     'The façades of the house'

Furthermore, not all spatial nouns can be independently used as nouns without a degree of allomorphy, cf. *arte* (spatial noun) vs. *tarte* (space in between, ordinary noun). Those properties suggest treating the spatial nouns as what Svenonius (2006) calls Axial Parts, part of the functional structure of the PP. The notion of Axial Part is drawn from Jackendoff (1996:14): 'The axial parts of an object—its top, bottom, front, back, sides, and ends..., unlike standard parts such as handle or leg,...have no distinctive shape. Rather, they are regions of the object (or its boundary) determined by their relation to the object's axes. The up-down axis determines top and bottom, the front/back axis determines front and back, and a complex set of criteria distinguishing horizontal axes deterlines sides and ends.' The elements that locate the Figure with respect to a projected space are assimilated to functional heads under Svenonius' hypothesis, and occupy a designated position in the clausal architecture (67a). The Basque complex postpositional phrases would look like (67b) under this view:

(67)   a. [$_{\text{PlaceP}}$ Place° [$_{\text{AxialP}}$ AxialP° [$_{\text{DP}_{\text{Ground}}}$ D° NP]]]

      b. [[[[etxe $_{\text{GroundP}}$]-a $_{\text{DP}}$] –ren $_{\text{CaseP}}$] aurre $_{\text{AxP}}$] -a $_{\text{DP}}$]i –n] $_{\text{PlaceP}}$

Independent evidence for this particular hierarchy is provided by the fact that the projective interpretation of spatial nouns only becomes possible when the spatial noun is selected by an adposition.

The nominal category of the Axial Part head has some consequences in the internal structure of the PP: the Ground is case-marked genitive, as corresponds to binominal structures (68a). At the same time, case-marking can be avoided by incorporation into the Axial noun (Baker 1988b), yielding a form of compounding (68b).

(68)   a. Etxearen   aurrean
       house-DET-GEN front-DET-INE
       'In front of the house'

      b. Etxe-aurrean
       house.front-INE
       'In front of the house'

6.6.4.2 Invariant postpositions   Basque also possesses a third type of postpositional head, which typically encodes directionality, besides possibly other things, and has an invariant form. In Central Basque, the most common invariant postpositions are the following:

(69)   a. Paretaren   kontra   b. Aldapan   gora
       wall-GEN   against   slope-INE   up
       'Against the wall'   'Up the slope'

      c. Aldapan   behera   d. Oihanean   barna
       slope-INE   down   wood-INE   through
       'Down the slope'   'Through the wood'

      e. Basoan   zehar   f. Basoaz   kanpo
       wood-INE   towards   wood-INST out
       'Towards the wood'   'Out of the wood'

      g. Etxearen   parrez-par
       house-GEN   face.to.face
       'Facing the house'

These postpositions differ from the spatial nouns on several accounts: they do not have referential uses, do not show any of the nominal properties we saw, and select not the Ground, but another postpositional phrase, usually an inessive one. Unlike the other postpositional structures, which are pretty much invariant across the entire Basque domain, the latter ones allow a degree of dialectal variation. In the Navarro-Labourdin variety, a subset of them[9] present dative case-marked Grounds:

(70) a. **Etxeari**   buruz   b. **Oihanari**   barna
         house-DET-DAT   towards   woods   through
         'Towards the house'   'Through the woods'

      c. **Paretari**   kontra   d. **Patarrari**   behera
         wall-DAT   against   slope-DET-DAT   down
         'Against the wall'   'Down the slope'

      e. **Patarrari**   gora   f. **Etxeari**   parrez-par
         slope-DET-DAT   up   house-DAT   face.to.face
         'Up the slope'   'Facing the house'

If we look at the postpositional structures in (70), it is evident that the invariant postposition represents, in an overt fashion, the directional head.[10] But if the directional head is lexicalized by the invariant postpositions, then the dative suffix cannot be the exponent of the directional feature.

6.6.5 *A note on the borrowing context*

If what I said is right, then the dative lexicalizes something else than directional Path. One possibility is that it lexicalizes Place (the complement of Path):

(71) [$\emptyset$PATH [PlaceP[DP] KDAT...]]

The corpus (as well as one of the speakers consulted) has constructions where the dative seems to directly encode Place:[11]

(72) a. Muturra lurrari   sartua   (LZ, V, 115)
         mouth   ground-DAT put.in-DET
         'With the mouth inside the ground'

---

[9] The invariant postposition *buruz* 'towards' in (70a) only exists in north-eastern varieties, not in central ones. Then, our corpus does not show any dative ground with *zehar* 'across', and *kanpo* 'out'. It could be that the latter are 'telic', in the sense that they make crucial reference to the boundaries of a domain. Rare cases of dative marked grounds with those postpositions can be gathered nevertheless in nineteenth-century texts.

[10] For the directional component of *kontra* 'against', see Vandeloise's discussion (1986) of French *contre*. As noted by Vandeloise, you cannot throw something against the floor, at least not in French, nor in Basque. In order to throw something against something else, the Theme must follow an oblique path to the target. I take this to be telling us that *kontra* 'against' has a directional component to it.

[11] (72c) denotes a temporal location. Central dialects have an inessive suffix instead of the dative here:

(i) Zahartzean   gertatzen   da
     old.get-NOM-DET-INE   happen-GER is
     'That happens when you get old'

   b. Nolanahika   erabiltzen zuen dirua. …bil arau   haizeari   barrea
      irresponsibly employed   aux   money get-as-soon wind-DAT   spread
      'He used the money in an irresponsible way. As he got it, he spread it in the
      air'

   c. Zahartzeari   gertatzen   da (Fieldwork, Oztibarre)
      old.get-NOM-DET-DAT   happen-GER   is
      'That happens when you get old'

This raises the question of how the dative compares to the inessive, which also
encodes Place. According to Aurnague (2001) the two main topological functions of
the inessive are to express (physical) inclusion and support. Neither of the spatial relations expressed by the dative above (transparently) encode support or inclusion. This
seems to pose the same problem as the dative/allative alternation. The dative is not
possible as a locative in a general way:

(73)   a. *Jon etxeari dago
       b. Jean est à la maison

I take this to mean that the inessive spells out something more than just Place. I will
tentatively claim that it also lexicalizes Axial Part, when the latter is not independently
lexicalized. Unlike the inessive, the dative would only lexicalize [Place].

We did not say anything about how the borrowing from French may have occurred.
Diachronic evidence suggests that the changes in Basque started with verbs of motion.
Pikabea suggests, based on literary records, that the changes in ditransitive verbs of
caused motion and caused possession had already started by the middle of the eigh-
teenth century. This is therefore the earliest syntactic context where the change is
attested. If this is the case, the borrowed forms must have been modelled on structures roughly like this one:

(74)   (envoyer une lettre) [Path Ø [PlaceP à Jean]]

But this already reminds us of the Navarro-Labourdin directional Path structures:

(75)   a. [Path Ø [PlaceP à Jean]]
       b. [Path Ø [PlaceP Jon-i]]

I therefore conclude that the specific source for the change were structures like (75a).

6.7 Datives and agreement

Ditransitive predicates of the caused motion/caused possession type show apparent
optional agreement, as shown in (76)–(78), from the corpus. How should we deal with
this?

(76) a. Kasik   zituen   guziak bertzeri   emaiten zituen   (Etc., HH, 74)
almost he.had-COMP all-PL other-DAT give-HAB AUX[3sE-3plA]
'He used to give almost everything he had to others'

     b. Ondoko urtetan eman ziozkaten   aita   Chabagnori
next   years   give   AUX[3plE-3sD-3plA] father Chabagno-DAT
kargu batzu arras ohoragarriak   (Etch. HH, 79)
duty   some very important-PL
'In subsequent years they gave father Chabagno some very important duties'

(77) a. …behako bat bota dezan   ondoko   lagunaren
glance   one throw AUX[3sE-3sA] next-GEN friend-GEN
kopiari   (Etch. BEB, 9)
copy-DAT
…so that he may throw a look to the copy of the friend close to him

     b. Doi-doiako begi-ukaldia botatu nion
just-GEN   glance.blow throw AUX[3sE-3sD-3sA]
liburuari   (Etc.BEB, 66)
book-dat
I threw just a glance to the book

(78) a. Jeneralak   depexa hau igorri zion
general-ERG message this sent   AUX[3sE-3sD-3sA]
bere andreari   (Etc. BEB, 69)
his   wife-DET-DAT
'The general sent the following message to his wife'

     b. Igorri zituzten   Ameriketako buruzagieri sekulako…
sent   AUX[3plE-3plD-3plA] American   leaders-DAT amazing
ageriak (ibidem)
documents
'They sent amazing documents to the American leaders'

Remember that the adpositional structures modelled on (a reanalysis of French) *à* enter a language which had a way of encoding dative arguments in ditransitive constructions. A natural way of interpreting the apparent optionality then is not as such, but as the alternative use of two different syntactic structures: the old Basque one, and the new 'French' one.

Arregi and Ormazabal (2003), Ormazabal and Romero (2010), and Oyharçabal (2010) defend the idea that Basque agreeing datives are applicative constructions. Remember (see section 6.1.2) that the agreeing dative DP requires the presence of a further inflectional affix in the auxiliary, the so called *pre-dative affix* or *dative flag*. Seeing the pre-dative affix as an applicative head seems a natural step to make. The applicative head precedes the obligatory agreement affix cross-referencing the oblique argument. The non-agreeing Navarro-Labourdin ditransitive structures do not display the applicative affix either.

6.7.1 *The scope of the agreement alternation*

One of the prima facie intriguing facts about the Navarro-Labourdin system, is that the agreement alternation does not extend everywhere: some datives always show agreement. Projected possessors, for instance, require dative agreement in the inflected verb (79):

(79) a. Aitari   eskua   hunki   diot/*dut
         father-DAT hand-DET touched AUX[1sE-3sD-3sA]/[1sE-3sA]
         'I touched father's hand'

      b. Mahaiari hanka   kendu   diot/*dut
         table-DAT leg-DET pull.from AUX[1sE-3sD-3sA]/[1sE-3sA]
         I pulled out a leg to the table

      c. Piarresi   muntra   ebatsi diot/*dut
         Piarres-DAT watch-DET stolen   AUX[1sE-3sD-3sA]/[1sE-3sA]
         'I stole Peter's watch'

Predicates that introduce what we would call a 'dative of interest' obligatorily index the dative argument too. Consider the following case:

(80)   Esneak   Mireni   gaindi egin dio/*du
       Milk-DET-ERG Miren-DAT over   done AUX[1sE-3sD-3sA]/[1sE-3sA]
       'The milk boiled over on Miren'

The dative in (80) does not participate in the event. During the boiling over *Miren* may not even be present. Someone else may be handling the milk but the result be of interest to her. Perhaps she is the head of a cooking team, and somehow responsible for what her cooks are doing in the kitchen. She is affected by the outcome of the event, but she does not participate in it.

Another context where dative agreement is obligatory is in psychological predicates of the *piacere* class. (81) shows two canonical psychological predicates. These predicates have dative subjects and those subjects obligatorily agree with the inflected verb.

(81) a. Joni   bizia huts   eta ilun iduri zaio/*da
         Jon-DAT life   hollow and sad look AUX[3sD-3sA]
         'For Jon, life looks hollow and sad'

      b. Mireni   ez   zaio/*da   gustatu
         Miren-DAT NEG AUX[3sD-3sA] like
         'Miren didn't like it'

Summarizing: projected possessors, datives of interest, and dative subjects of psychological predicates must obligatorily agree with the inflected verb. All these cases belong in what some authors have called, in the context of applicative constructions, 'high applicatives' (see Pylkkanen 2002; Cuervo 2003; Jeong 2007 among others). In other words: the only domain where adpositional and applicative structures may alternate is in the domain of low applicatives, where the silent Path adposition contributes to the event-schema underlying caused possession and caused motion predicates. In Ramchand's terms, in First Phase syntax.

6.7.2 Double dative constructions

The idea that the apparent agreement alternation actually corresponds to the alternative use of two different basic structures for the dative invites the conclusion that both structures could in principle co-occur (as in Japanese, Miyagawa and Tsujioka, 2004).[12] The prediction is borne out, as shown by the cases in (82):

(82)   a. Hurbildu nion   urrikalmenduzko seinalea
          approach AUX[1sE-3sD-3sA] repentance-GEN   signal-ABS
          ezpaineri   (Etc, O, 164)
          lips-DAT
          'I approached *him* the signal for repentance *to his lips*'

       b. Barneari   farrasta   bat egiten   dautzun   manu
          interior-DAT impression one do-HAB AUX[3sE-2sD-3sA]-COMP order
          auhenezkoa
          painful
          'The painful orders that make *you* a big impression *inside*'

(82a) involves a projected possessor (the two datives are related by a part/whole relation). (82b) involves a spatial dative (*inside*), and a dative (*you*), which expresses the psychologically affected subject. The co-occurrence of both types of datives would show that they are merged in a different position in the clause structure.

6.7.3 Word order and syntactic structure

The applied object (the IO) generally c-commands and precedes the object. In the case of non-agreeing datives, speakers show a preference for the order O-IO. In the latter case, one can show that both the object and the indirect object are below the external aspect heads:

(83)   [RelC Op$_i$ Jonek igorri t$_i$ duena/*diona]   da [VP... liburu bat bere
                   Jon-ERG sent   AUX[TR]/[DITR]-REL-D is   book   one his
          anaiari]$_i$
          brother-DAT
          'What John sent is a book to his brother'

---

[12] I marked by italics in the translation the terms corresponding to the dative DPs in Basque.

(83) is a pseudo-cleft structure, where the gap in the lefthand term corresponds to the VP. The verbal root *igor-* 'send' has raised and merged to the participial head −*i* (see Laka 1990; Haddican 2008). The auxiliary in the relative clause cannot include dative agreement in this case. This suggests that the applied object, unlike the non-agreeing one, occupies a position higher than the VP. The object and the non-agreeing indirect object can also be replaced by a wh-word in wh-complements, when the latter ranges over VP complements. This is impossible for the agreeing cases:

(84) [Liburu bat Mireni],   horra zer   igorri duen/*dion
      book   a   Miren-DAT that what sent   AUX[3sE-3sA]/3sE-3sD-3sA]
      Jonek
      Jon-ERG
      'A book to Miren, that's what Jon sent'

The structural position of the object and the indirect object must therefore be below (participial) Aspect:

(85) T Aspect [$_{XP}$...Obj...Indirect O]

I will take the fact that the agreeing auxiliary is impossible in (83) and (84) to show that the agreeing dative is actually in a structural position beyond the aspectual phrase that licenses the gap and the wh-word. This accords well with the fact that the applicative morpheme is fused with the auxiliary and the temporal and agreement affixes, therefore beyond the aspectual head that marks the upper boundary of the Object. On the other hand, the applicative construction that alternates with the adpositional one must be a low applicative (Pylkkanen 2002). It is basically in the domain of motion and caused possession events that the alternation arises. We are therefore split into two contradictory requirements: the applied object must correspond to a low applicative, but all the relevant morphology that marks the construction as an applicative one is outside the verbal domain, and the agreeing IO consistently takes scope over the verb phrase. How can we accommodate those two seemingly contradictory requirements? I have argued in other work (Etxepare 2012; see also Preminger, 2009) that dative agreement in Basque is actually an instance of cliticization.[13] If this is correct, then we may account for those two properties in the following way, with the dative agreement affix selecting the object and taking the IO as its subject:

(86) Appl (Cl)+X Asp [$_V$. ... IO (Cl) O]

---

[13] One piece of evidence in favour of this idea is that the dative 3r person singular agreement affix (−*o*−) is the only lexicalized 3rd person singular affix in the entire Basque inflectional paradigm. There is *per se* no overt 3rd person singular agreement in Basque. That value always has zero exponence. I thank Javier Ormazabal for pointing this out to me. Also, as shown by Etxepare (2006), dative arguments do not allow long-distance agreement, available to absolutive arguments. Apparent instances of dative long-distance agreement only occur in restructuring contexts, which typically allow clitic climbing.

The derivation in (86) recalls Cuervo's (2003) and Ormazabal and Romero's (2007) analysis of Spanish dative clitic doubling as the raising of an applicative head (the dative clitic itself). I use X as the (unspecified) landing site of the clitic (the Basque 'agreement' morpheme $-o-$ in (83) and (84)). So the scope of the applied object, whose formal features are copied in the clitic, is beyond the aspectual projection.

6.7.4 *The agreement paradox and third factor effects in language change*

One intriguing difference concerning agreeing datives between Navarro-Labourdin and Central dialects is the fact that in the Navarro-Labourdin variety, according to the corpora used, dative agreement seems to be restricted to things which have a certain referential import. So for instance, anaphors and negative polarity items tend (overwhelmingly) not to agree:

(87) a. Bakea eman dezagun elgarri   (LZ., III, 48)
         break give AUX(tr) each.other-DAT
         'Let's give a break to each other'

      b. Nehori   aipatu   duzuia gure artekoa?   (LZ., II, 236)
         anyone-DAT mentioned AUX(tr) our   in.between
         'Have you mentioned our thing to anyone?'

      c. Maizegi dugu   gure buruari   galde   egiten
         too.often AUX(tr) our   head-DAT question do-HAB
         'We ask ourselves too often'

This is not the case in Central dialects, where agreement is the rule for any dative DP. Diachronically, the agreement restrictions in the Navarro-Labourdin variety emerged together with the agreement alternation itself. Referentiality constraints of a similar sort have also been observed in double object constructions in English (see Bresnan et al. 2007) and seem to arise in applicative constructions generally (see Peterson 2007). But a paradox arises when we try to state the conditions for that. A straightforward formulation of the referentiality restrictions in the north eastern agreeing cases would read as follows:

(88)   Applicative head selects $F'_{Agr} \leq F_{Agr}$

(88) is intended to express that the agreement related to the applicative head selects a subset (F') of the features generally involved in agreement in Basque, with F a feature matrix including the whole set of phi-features available in agreement. F', a subset of F, would be delimited in such a way that it would semantically map into denotata possessing a 'referential import'. One way of thinking concretely of this would be to restrict dative agreement to those DPs which introduce discourse referents, in the sense of Karttunen (1976). Thinking of F' as whatever encodes 'referential import', (88) would capture the restriction on (applicative) dative agreement if the dative DP does

not possess a feature matched in F'. This logic is only available if we put the set of syntactic categories involved in agreement in correspondence to whatever 'referential import' translates into—a very problematic move. The thing is that the restrictions cannot be formulated in such a rigid and general way, no matter how we refine them. This is so because the only contexts in which those restrictions are operative are the contexts where a structural alternation with the adpositional construction is available. In the high applicatives, where the agreement indexes are the same, there is no restriction in what kind of dative can agree:

(89) a. Ez   zaio   nehori   gustatzen
         NEG AUX[3sD-3sA] anyone-DAT like-HAB
         'No one likes it'

      b. Bere buruari   zuen   duintasun apurra   kendu
         his   head-DAT AUX[3sE-3sD-3sA]-REL dignity   little-DET took.away
         dio
         AUX(ditr)
         'He took away from himself the little dignity he had'

      c. Lagunek   elkarri   ihes   egin diote
         friends-ERG each.other-DAT run.away do   AUX[3plE-3sD-3sA]
         'They ran away from each other (and that affects them)'

The restrictions therefore, cannot be stated as restrictions on the kind of feature that the Applicative head checks. It must be relativized to the contexts where the applicative construction and the adpositional one concur. In other words, it arises in those cases where the dative clitic raises from a low applicative position:

(90)   Appl agreement involves DPs with a certain 'referential import' only when the applicative construction alternates with the adpositional construction

If what distinguishes applicative from adpositional structures in the context of dative constructions is raising of the applicative morpheme (see recently Ormazabal and Romero 2010), the semantic effects described in (90) can be related to Chomsky's (2001) idea that external merge and internal merge express two different types of semantic properties: predication and argument selection by external merge, discourse related properties by internal merge. The difference between low applicatives and high applicatives in Basque is that low applicatives undergo internal merge to some higher position. This is not so for high applicatives, witness the double dative configurations in section 6.7.2. So the restrictions only apply when the clitic raises to a higher position.

A different matter is which species of third factor effect appropriately accounts for (90). In Chomsky's view, (90) would eventually follow from the special status of

Phase borders, assuming applicative constructions to introduce a Phase.[14] When displacement to an edge position occurs, creating a non-trivial chain, the head of the chain can receive a 'surface' interpretation, with 'surface' interpretation meaning the kind of interpretive restriction associated to, say, object shift in Scandinavian languages, or inner topicalization of the sort observed in romance languages (Belletti 2005; Uriagereka 2008). Languages would be distinguished by whether they possess the relevant peripheral feature or not. This would be an interface optimalization strategy, whereby a position at the phonological edge of a phase is singled out to signal discourse prominence. This 'peripheral feature condition' would fall in the family of third factor concepts related to 'principles of structural architecture and developmental constraints that enter into canalization, organic form, and action over a wide range, including principles or efficient computation' (Chomsky 2005:6).

Uriagereka (2008) on the other hand, proposes to treat effects of this type as following from a learning strategy. Learners that find themselves in situations of interpretive conflict, where contextualized and non-contextualized readings of a same argument are possible, will tend to associate the most specific syntactic form with the most specific reading. He calls this the Learnability Wager (Uriagereka 2008:134):

(91)   Learnability Wager
       In situations of learning conflict, let whatever involves a more specific form correlate with whatever involves a more specific interpretation

The learnability wager falls in the family of third factor effects associated to 'principles of data analysis that might be used in language acquisition and other domains' Chomsky (2005:6). I leave open for the moment the precise status of the referential constraints observed in ditransitive constructions in the context of third factor effects.

---

[14] We will not go into this, but refer to Uriagereka (1999) for a discussion of the 'phasal' or opaque status of structures whose specifier is occupied by an agreeing argument in Basque. McGinnis (2002) argues that high applicatives, but not low ones, constitute phases. The distinction accounts for several syntactic differences covered by the terms *symmetric* and non-symmetric *applicatives*. The Basque referential restrictions cannot be directly accommodated into this view, to the extent that those restrictions crucially involve clitic climbing from a low applicative. One possibility, if we look at the Basque cases from this angle, is that clitic climbing targets a high applicative position, marked by the pre-dative flag in the auxiliary, itself a Phase.

7

Towards elegant parameters: Language variation reduces to the size of lexically-stored trees

MICHAL STARKE

7.1 Introduction

Three decades after the 'Principles and Parameters' revolution in language variation, we still have no theory of variation. Thirty years ago, if some element moved in one language but not in another, a movement rule would be added to one language but not to the other. Today, a feature 'I want to move' ('EPP', 'strength', etc.) is added to the elements of one language but not of the other. In both cases (and in all attempts between them), variation is expressed by stipulating it. Instead of a theory, we have brute-force markers.

This chapter presents a theory of parameters.* An approach which has no stipulated markers (no 'EPP features', 'edge features', 'strength of features', etc.), deriving variation from the very shape of lexical items—and as a side-effect provides a principled space of possible parameters. The solution is simple: once lexical items are seen to spell out entire syntactic phrases, some lexemes will be bigger phrases, some will be smaller phrases. I explore the conjecture that this is all we need for variation, showing that this difference is sufficient to account for all major types of syntactic variation.

The failure to come up with a theory of parameters is partly a casualty of the very success of the Principles and Parameters research programme. The heart of Principles and Parameters (P&P, Chomsky (1981)) is the idea that most of grammar—perhaps all of it—is invariant across languages, i.e. the 'principles' part. Parameters are secondary in that they presuppose the principles: they only make sense against a backdrop of pre-established principles. Parameters are simply the 'residue' left once the invariant

* Many thanks to Carme Picallo for her patience and support during the writing up of this paper.

principles are factored out, whatever that residue turns out to be.[1] The search for invariant abstract principles has been a spectacular success (by the modest standards of nascent sciences such as linguistics): there is a broad consensus on the existence of phrase structure made out a functional sequence of head-complement relationships, of locality principles, of binding principles, etc. applicable across languages, and even on the general outline of these principles—a striking contrast to the state of affairs barely 30 years ago. That success has however left the study of variation in a dark and inhospitable place.

In the early days of P&P, there was plenty of space in the theoretical apparatus to implement variation: Grammars could vary either lexically (perhaps complementizers vary as to whether they induce subjacency effects or not) or inside their principles (principles could contain parameters inside themselves, the classical historical illustration being 'clauses require [±overt] subjects', and as a result, adult grammars would vary in their principles). As research advanced, the theoretical space open for implementing variation gradually closed down, to the extent that the most promising contemporary approaches lead to a landscape in which there is apparently no space left for variation at all.

The first move in that direction, a standard move by now, was to eliminate parametric variation from grammar itself, and restrict it to the lexicon. According to that line of thinking, principles are invariant across languages, but they are exquisitely sensitive to the grammatical properties of lexical items. The second move, was the rise of fine-grained representations, i.e. cartography, the functional sequence, etc. As years went by, results piled up showing that the ingredients of syntax are smaller and more numerous than classically thought, and hence syntactic representations are bigger and more fine-grained than classically thought. To almost everybody's surprise, the order in which those new ingredients ('phrases', 'projection', 'functional categories') occurred in syntactic representations turned out to be also largely or entirely invariant across languages. This path of research is quickly leading in the direction of one feature per terminal, and invariant content and order of phrases across languages. This is a spectacular success for the invariant part of grammar ('principles'), but it just as spectacularly shrinks the theoretical space available to express variation: under that view, both the content and the order of features is invariant cross-linguistically. Not only are grammatical principles invariant, but the features and underlying representations they operate on are also invariant.

This is a barren landscape for a variation-theorist—everything has become invariant. Even the idea that variation is lexical is beyond limits: since lexical items are made

---

[1] Diagnosing the health of P&P by looking at the state of the theory of parameters thus rests on a fundamental misunderstanding of P&P. (Similarly for claims about Minimalism and related approach being post P&P rather than another instantiation of P&P). The current lack of a satisfying approach to parameters is certainly something we need to solve—and that's the aim of this chapter—but it is not a good barometer of the overall health of P&P.

out of grammatical 'features', saying that variation is lexical amounts to saying that variation will be variation in features. And this clashes with the road leading us to features being invariant in their content and order in the functional sequence. At this point, it looks like we broke our last tool for expressing variation—the only escape being to invent parochial features amounting to 'I want to move' or 'I am different from the other language'—such as 'EPP' features or 'edge' features. Not everybody is at the end of that road (yet), but the further down the road one is, the more desperate the variation problem looks. And yet, there is a simple way out. No matter how much invariance we are led to accept in the principles, representations, and features, there is an elegant solution to the parameter problem.

7.2 The solution

That solution builds on the idea of phrasal spellout. Assume an underlying syntactic structure of the type:

(1)

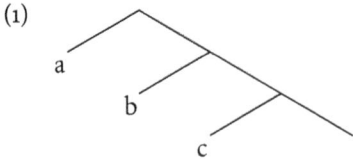

The idea of phrasal spellout is that an entire (sub)constituent such as for instance [b [c]] in the structure in (1) can be spelled out by one lexical item, e.g. 'how' in English:

(2)

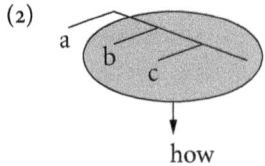

how

Given this technology, developed in the nanosyntax framework independently of variation (Starke 2002), lexical items come in various 'sizes': they spell out either bigger or smaller constituents. This opens the possibility that in the next language we look at, the counterpart of 'how' spells out a slightly different amount of structure; for instance, the Slovak 'jak' might be:

(3)

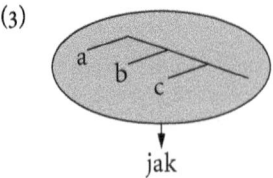

jak

At this point, we have language variation without diacritic markers such as strength of features: all grammatical processes involving the 'a' layer, aP, will affect the Slovak 'jak' but not the English 'how'—or more generally Slovak wh-phrases but not English wh-phrases.

The conjecture is that such 'size differences' are enough to express all cross-linguistic syntactic variation. What we thought of as 'parameters' are just differing sizes of lexical items. In this chapter, I restrict myself to the theoretical side of this claim: can this indeed derive the known categories of syntactic variation, or is there a principled limit to this solution?

At first sight, it looks like there is a catch. To see it, let's start by looking more closely at the notion of phrasal spellout. The motivation for it runs something like this (see the nanosyntax work for a more detailed walkthrough, e.g. Starke (2009) for an overview of the architecture, Caha (2009) for a detailed case-study and an introduction): as syntactic representations become bigger, their terminals become more fine-grained, until they reach the point of being 'submorphemic', i.e. smaller than individual morphemes. Syntactic trees with even moderate amounts of functional projections have long passed the 'submorphemic terminals' point. If terminals are smaller than individual morphemes, it follows that morphemes cannot feed syntax: they are too big, too coarse, they do not provide the right granularity of ingredients to build syntactic trees. Rather, it is only after some steps of derivation that a constituent large enough to correspond to a morpheme is created. It thus follows that the lexicon comes strictly after syntax and lexemes correspond to entire phrasal constituents.[2]

(4)

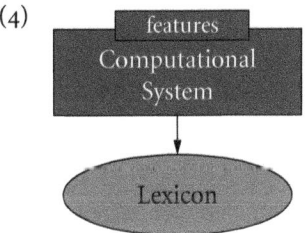

And this is where the catch comes: if the lexicon is strictly after syntax, the lexicon comes too late to ever influence the course of syntax.[3] And therefore, the size of the constituent spelled out by e.g. 'how' or 'jak' will never be able to influence the working

---

[2] The architecture remains neutral on whether the features feed syntax from the 'outside' or whether they are part of the computational system itself. The point is that only atomic features are available at the beginning of a computation. Grouping of features is done exclusively by syntax, and hence only available after syntax. (There is thus no concept of 'bundles', these are simply syntactic phrases.)

[3] This 'too late' problem is not shared by other so-called late insertion approaches, such as Cardinaletti and Starke (1993), Halle and Marantz (1993), and originally den Besten (1976), Otero (1976). In all those approaches, there is pre-syntactic lexicon of bundles as well as a post-syntactic one (ultimately because these approaches do not have phrasal spellout). Such architectures thus have a pre-syntactic 'early' locus for variation.

of the syntactic computational system. If this were so, parameters could not be reduced to the size of lexical items.

Luckily, there is a simple solution to this 'too late' problem, and in fact, that solution is already included in the Nanosyntax framework. It comes from idioms and semi-regular morphology, so let's look at that, as it will not only solve our new problem, but it will also give us tools for the discussion of variation.

Idioms are *prima facie* an important source of support for phrasal spellout. Within the traditional approach, there is no easy way to handle multi-word idiomatic expressions, as witnessed by the clunkiness of the existing attempts at handling idioms while at the same time confining spellout to terminals. Under phrasal spellout, idioms are natural: they are cases in which a relatively high-level constituent has been stored (see also Jackendoff 1997). The traditional example of 'kick the bucket' can now be rendered as an entire VP stored in the lexicon, or rather as the modern-day equivalent of such a VP (e.g. a syntactic layer including AspP).

There are many interesting technical and empirical issues to address about storing idioms as phrasal constituents, but only one of them is directly relevant to our concerns here: put simply, multi-word idiomatic expressions are made out of regular words, with their regular allomorphies and quirks of lexical insertion. Those words are therefore themselves the result of spellout operations at lower hierarchical levels of the syntactic structure (e.g. the lexical insertion of 'bucket' in 'kick the bucket' or of 'took' in 'took to the cleaners'). We thus have a series of lower-level spellout operations ('kick', 'the', 'bucket') and one higher-level spellout operation identifying the whole VP/AspP as corresponding to the lexical entry of the idiom.

Given this setup, the VP/AspP-level spellout operation must know about the outcome of the previous lower-level spellout operations: It is only if the lower-level operations chose 'bucket' over 'jar', 'horse' or 'plate' that the idiom will be applicable. The spellout of the higher constituent must somehow 'remember' the outcome of the spellout of the lower-level constituents. This means (inter alia) that the architectural schema in (4) must be modified to add the equivalent of a feedback loop after spellout:

(5)

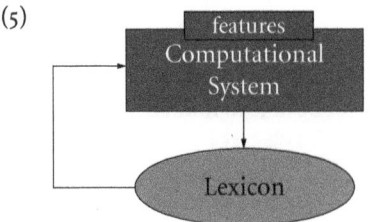

This way the choice of 'bucket' over 'jar' will be visible to the next computational cycle, and the idiom 'kick the bucket' can be correctly restricted to cases where 'bucket' was spelled out earlier.

As a by-product, we have now solved our 'too late' problem: given the feedback loop from spellout back into the syntactic computational system, syntax does have access to prior lexical choices. Lexical choices can in principle affect further computation, and hence there is a logical sense in which spelling out a syntactic structure with 'how' in (2) may lead to different consequences than spelling out a syntactic structure with 'jak' in (3). We are in business again.

There are at least three different ways in which the 'size' of (the syntactic structure of) a lexical item can affect further computation. Let's start with the simplest.

7.3 Size makes syntactic layers unavailable

Suppose that a structure such as (1) is lexicalized differently in two languages, for instance as in (2) versus (3), repeated here:

(6)

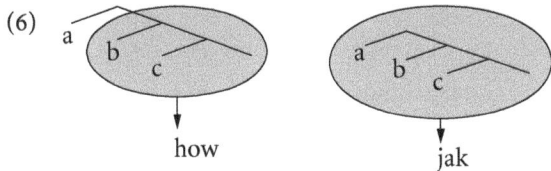

how   jak

The a layer, aP, will be 'eaten up' in one language and hence unavailable for use by independent lexical items, whereas it will be available for such use in the other language. As a result, one language will have some visible constructions targeting aP whereas the other language will lack such constructions.

To make things concrete, here are a couple of illustrations of this logic. Consider for instance the following indefinites in English and French:

(7) someone   quelqu'un
     something   quelque chose
     somewhere   quelque part

Although the English and French series share many properties, they curiously differ as to whether they enter into the 'or other' construction:

(8) someone or other (fell down)
     something or other (fell down)
     ?He must have put this somewhere or other

French also has this construction, as in:

(9) Il a bien dû le mettre à un endroit ou un autre
     He has well must it put in a place or an other
     'He must have put it in some place or other'

But French indefinites systematically refuse to enter that construction:

(10)   *quelqu'un ou un autre (est tombé)
        *quelque chose ou un(e) autre (est tombé(e))
        *Il a bien dû le mettre quelque part ou un(e) autre

This English/French asymmetry can be expressed by a size difference between English and French indefinites: if the 'or other' construction attaches to aP, and French indefinites spell out *abc* while English indefinites spell out only *bc*, then aP is available in English and 'or other' can attach to it (presumably followed by movement of the indefinite), but it is unavailable with French indefinites, as illustrated in (11):[4]

(11)

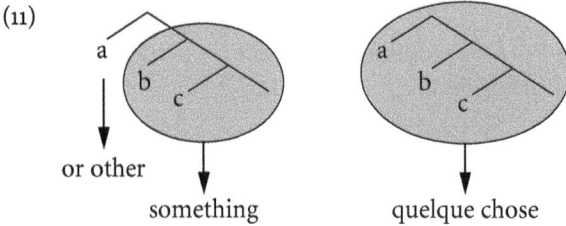

The point here is not to argue for a particular analysis of this construction, but rather to show that parameters seen as size differences are able to handle the type of variation in which a construction is available in one language but not the other. In other words, at least some 'parameters' are expressible in terms of structural size.

Here is another example of the same logic, again offered for illustrative purposes. The Germanic verbs in English can be found with a few constructions which are not available to the Latinate verbs of English: verb-particle constructions, resultative constructions. Again, such a situation fits into the same pattern: if Latinate verbs spell out a larger syntactic structure than Germanic verbs, the Germanic verbs will leave some layer of structure available for further use while Latinate verbs will 'eat out' those layers:

---

[4] Readers familiar with Nanosyntax may object here that the technical definition of spellout in Nanosyntax derives the 'superset principle' as a theorem and hence the French indefinites should be able to shrink to accommodate the 'or other' construction. If we were to pursue this analysis of indefinites, we would thus need to treat French indefinites as 'unshrinkable', in a way reminiscent of the R-state adjectival passives in Starke (2006).

This would in fact be natural: these indefinites are clearly composite expressions, i.e. idioms composed of 'quelque' and 'chose', 'un', etc. Technically they would thus be lexical items referring to other lexical items ('pointers'), and such cases are known to be unshrinkable.

(12)   a. 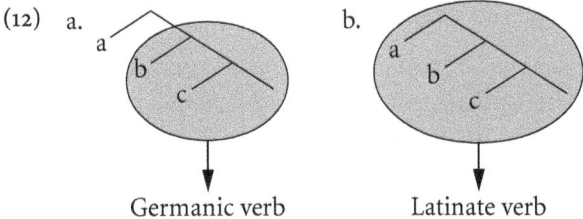 b.

Germanic verb   Latinate verb

As before, if particles, resultatives, etc. target aP, it follows that Germanic verbs will be compatible with particles, resultatives, etc. while Latinate verbs will not. Extending this reasoning cross-linguistically, if the verbs of say Italian or French are not found in particle constructions and do not have resultatives, we would conclude that the Italian or French verb spell out the larger structure as in (12b).

Again, we would have a case of a 'parameter' (the presence vs. absence of classical resultative constructions in English vs. Italian) reducing to a simple size effect: Italian verbs spell out a slightly larger syntactic structure than the Germanic verbs in English.

This reasoning extends to another familiar type of cross-linguistic variation: some languages are described as 'lacking some functional projection' present in another language—a situation which has led to controversies about whether all functional layers are always present but somehow silent, or whether they can be genuinely absent. Consider the situation we just saw, however: if all verbs of Italian (or French) spell out the bigger structure (12b), and some other language has verbs spelling out the smaller structure (12a), in such a situation, aP will never be 'visible' in Italian (or French) but will be visible in other languages. In this case, it will thus appear as if Italian or French 'lack a functional projection' which is present in other languages. Again, a familiar case of language variation reduces to the differing sizes of lexical items in different languages.

To push this example one step further, take the following statement about Mandarin Chinese:

Tai (1984) claims that there are no simple monosyllabic accomplishment verbs in Mandarin, and to derive an accomplishment verb with the attainment of a goal, a resultative V-V compound must be formed.

(Su 2009:7)

This suggests that the feature distinguishing accomplishment verbs is lexicalized by the verb stem in English but not in Mandarin. As a result, we expect the syntactic layer projecting this feature to be syntactically available in Mandarin but not in English. This would derive syntactic variation from independently needed lexical variation: Mandarin verbs lexicalize 'smaller' structures than English verbs (which in turn has obvious connections to the widespread presence of 'complex predicate' construction in Asian languages as compared to their lesser use in European languages: if Asian verbs spell out smaller constituents, other material needs to step in to spell out the remaining projections).

7.4 Size triggers spellout-triggered movement

Size differences can trigger another type of syntactic variation: movement differences. Let us start with what we could call 'spellout driven movement', before addressing more traditional movements such as wh-movement.

Finding selective triggers for movement, such that there is movement in one language but not the other, is a notoriously difficult task. Consider a situation such as the following:

(13)

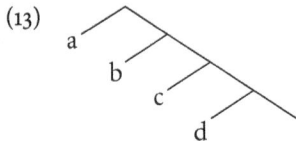

With two lexical items to spell it out:

(14)   a. kick   ← →   [[c] d]
       b. ed   ← →   [[a] b]

Assume we came to the stage of the derivation in which we have built cP:

(15)

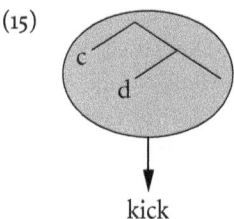

This constituent can be spelled out with the lexical entry (14a) as 'kick'. Compare this to the situation in which we have built the tree up to aP:

(16)

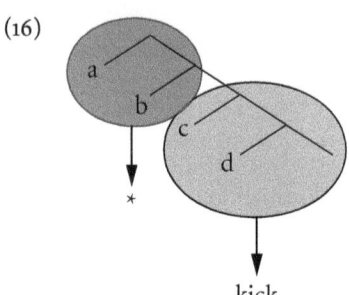

Here we have a problem: this tree cannot spell out. There is no single lexical item that covers abcd, so we need to resort to the two lexical items covering ab and cd respectively. As before, the lexical item (14a) matches the constituent [c [d]] and presents no problem. The lexical item (14b), on the other hand, cannot be used: it matches a constituent [a [b]], but there is no such constituent in the structure, i.e. there is no constituent made up of ab to the exclusion of anything else.

If this structure is to be spelled out, something must be done to save it: last resort movement driven by the need to spell out. The constituent [c [d]] moves out as a last resort, so as to create the configuration:

(17)

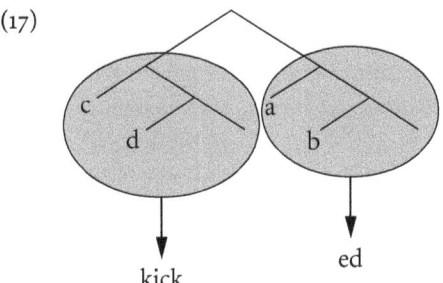

The structure can now be spelled out: as before, [c [d]] corresponds to 'kick' and [a [b]] matches the lexical item (14b) and hence spells out as 'ed', yielding 'kick-ed'.

In a language containing a lexical item [a [b [c [d]]]], no movement is necessary, the structure can be spelled out as is. We have thus derived both movement and its variation without postulating any feature or other property dedicated to (selectively) triggering it.

These movements happen in order to succeed at spellout.

This style of movement trigger is not limited to morphological entities. The same logic applied high up in the syntactic tree will trigger movement of large syntactic constituents. For instance a syntactically complex complementizer, perhaps spelling out ForceP and FinitenessP in Rizzi's (1997) system, will yield movement of the entire clause around the complementizer, so as to create a configuration in which [force [fin]] is a constituent matching the lexical entry of the complementizer.

This technology, in fact, predicts an interesting split between two types of movements: spellout driven movements that swap the order of two constituents, no matter how big, and which have no detectable semantic or classically syntactic triggers, versus classical feature-driven movements which do have detectable semantics, which reconstruct, etc. Spellout-driven movements are remarkably similar to the movements often postulated in the remnant movement literature, and it is an interesting conjecture that those remnant-like movements have resisted an analysis in terms of classical triggers precisely because they are 'spellout driven' in the sense mentioned.

As before, there is a lot more to say on this topic, among others how to derive the difference between triggering a 'cyclic'-like movement (specifier to specifier) versus remnant-like (complement to specifier within an fseq), but here I limit myself to our core point: it is possible to reduce syntactic variation to lexical size effects, including variation with respect to one class of movements (thereby doing without EPP features and their ilk).

7.5 Size creates the illusion of *wh-* in situ

Finally, let us turn to classical feature-driven movements, such as wh-movement. Again, I leave a detailed discussion for a separate occasion, concentrating on the logic of deriving variation here.

How can we express the fact that some grammars, such as English, require wh-movement (of the first wh element), while other grammars, such as French, don't? Here we need to distinguish two issues: (i) why do wh-expressions move at all? (ii) why do wh-expressions sometimes move (visibly) and sometimes not move (visibly)?

As is well known, locality facts suggest that movement takes place in both types of languages. One part of the puzzle is thus straightforward: all wh-expressions are always moved to the left periphery, in all relevant constructions, in all languages. Translated into theoretical terms: the *wh* feature is always moved/attracted/displaced to some projection in the vicinity of the complementizer, in all languages and all relevant constructions. What of the variation then?

As it turns out, this type of variation is also expressible in terms of lexical size. Assume the representations (2)–(3) for wh-elements, now transposed to English versus French question words:

(18)

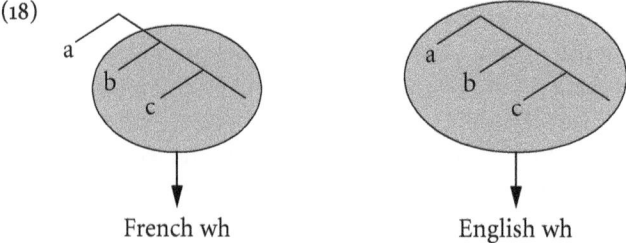

French wh   English wh

Assume further that French has a null morpheme spelling out aP. The first consequence is that bP will move over aP, by the logic of spellout-driven movement discussed already:

(19)

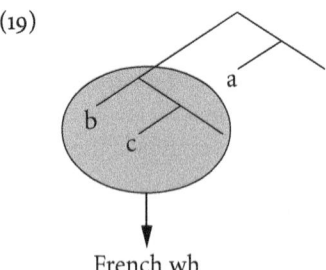

French wh

If aP is the layer targeted by wh-movement, i.e. a is the question feature, English will have audible wh-movement but French will not—though they will both show locality effects. This is because aP is contained in English wh-words and hence remains a constituent with bP and cP. In such a configuration, displacing aP necessarily pied-pipes bP and cP, resulting in audible displacement. By contrast, since aP is not contained in the wh-words of French, the French aP is stranded by bP+cP (as depicted in (19)) and moving aP moves the null morpheme, leaving bP+cP untouched, thereby providing the twin consequence of locality effects and wh-in-situ.[5]

It thus turns out that all major types of cross-linguistic variations can be expressed in terms of lexical elements spelling out bigger or smaller syntactic structures: the presence or absence of a construction or functional projection in one language but not the other, and the presence or absence of overt movement in one language but not the other. We have thus opened the way for a clean theory of parameters, one without technical notions invented only to notate variation.

7.6 Conclusion

This chapter presents a novel approach to parameters, which does away with notational markers such as EPP features, strong features, or other diacritics dedicated to expressing variation. Parameters, i.e. cross-linguistic variation, can be expressed in terms of lexical elements spelling out bigger or smaller subconstituents of the syntactic structure being built by the computational system:

(20)

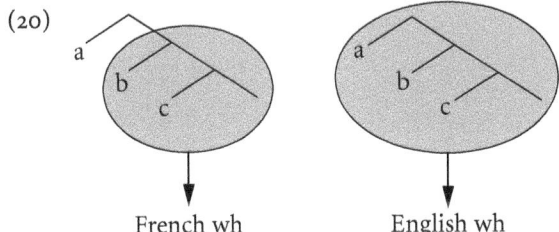

French wh   English wh

The oval represents the lexically stored element, the black tree represents the structure being built by the computational system and waiting to be spelled out. In such a situation, grammatical processes moving aP will affect bigger lexical items (the second type), and grammatical processes populating aP will be available with the smaller lexical items (the first type).

This simple technology is sufficient to cover all major types of parameters, and also defines the space of possible parameters: the syntax of two languages can differ only insofar as their lexical elements spell out bigger or smaller syntactic phrases.

---

[5] Notice this reasoning does not require anything like the lexical integrity principle, at this stage.

After three decades of Principles and Parameters tradition, this is to my knowledge the first explanatory theory of (the format and working of) parameters—as opposed to descriptive diacritics marking loci of variation. In this theory, 'parameters' reduce to the amount of structure that lexical items spell out. Of course, being the only principled game in town is a comfortable position, but detailed case studies will have to tell us whether it is also the correct position.

Part II

Variation without Parameters

8

What Principles and Parameters got wrong

CEDRIC BOECKX

8.1 In critical condition

This chapter is based on a presentation I made at the *Linguistic Variation in the Minimalist Framework* workshop.* Quite appropriately, the workshop, which focused on the character of linguistic variation and the role of parameters in the context of linguistic minimalism, took place in the Sant Pau hospital complex in Barcelona—a distinguished, UNESCO-protected setting for a distinguished patient: the Principles-and-Parameters model. Judging from textbooks, the Principles-and-Parameters model counts as the standard model or consensus view within generative grammar. It is customarily said to be the model that solved 'Plato's problem' (the logical problem of language acquisition), and made minimalist explorations possible. Yet, I contend that some of the most deeply-embedded tenets of the Principles-and-Parameters approach,

* Thanks to Carme Picallo for organizing, and inviting me to, one of the most stimulating workshops that I ever attended. Apart from minor elaboration and reorganization of the material, I have not deviated from what I presented at the workshop referred to in the text as the 'Barcelona meeting'. I have tried as much as possible to incorporate the questions and reactions I got during the event, as well as comments from two anonymous reviewers. Where appropriate, I have also addressed issues raised by other presenters, or re-emphasize some of the points I raised which I felt had not been adequately addressed by others. The present work is very much work in progress, and I refer readers to Boeckx (To appear b) and Boeckx (To appear a) for related discussion. Some of the issues raised here were originally voiced in presentations dating back to 2004 and now documented in Boeckx (2008b, 2011a) and Boeckx et al. (2009). I remain grateful to the organizers of these venues for the opportunity they offered me to begin to reflect on parameters and the nature of linguistic variation. I am also extremely grateful to Fritz Newmeyer and Guillermo Lorenzo for writing very thoughtful reviews of Boeckx (2006) (see Newmeyer 2008, Lorenzo 2007), where some of my needlessly conservative statements were correctly criticized. Last, but not least, I want to thank the participants at the Barcelona meeting, especially Ian Roberts and Anders Holmberg for engaging with the issues I raised. The present work is supported by a Marie Curie International Reintegration Grant from the European Union (PIRG-GA-2009-256413), research funds from the Fundació Bosch i Gimpera, and a grant from the Spanish Ministry of Economy and Competitiveness (FFI-2010-20634; PI: Boeckx).

and in particular the idea of Parameter, have outlived their usefulness. I claim (for reasons to be developed in this chapter) that if one takes minimalism and biolinguistics seriously, one should abandon the notion of Parameter, the more so given its diminishing empirical validity (on the latter, see especially Newmeyer 2005).

Please note that I am referring here to the substantive notion of Parameter (hence the upper-case *P*), a notion introduced into linguistic theory by Noam Chomsky (see Chomsky 1980, 1981).[1] I should note right away that I am aware of the existence of a much watered-down notion of parameter (lower-case *p*), which I think is currently used massively in the relevant literature to provide artificial life support to the Principles-and-Parameters model. This notion of parameter is not what I am focusing on here, as it is clearly devoid of any theoretical teeth, hence for me does not even begin to exist in a theoretical context. But, of course, if one wishes to use the term 'parameter' as a synonym for 'difference', then who am I to deny that there are 'parameters' between John's English and Koji's Japanese? But when one does use 'parameter' thus, one should explicitly recognize that 'parameter' is 'nothing but jargon for language-particular rule' (Newmeyer 2005). I take it that advocates of Principles-and-Parameters model are trying (or at any rate, should try) to advocate something stronger (and more interesting), though (but see section 8.2).

I am also aware that many colleagues that share my 'Chomskyan' persuasion think that by claiming that there are no parameters, I am throwing the baby out with the bathwater, that without parameters we are going back to the days of Skinner, or Tomasello, or Joos, that I forget that Principles-and-Parameters is an open and flexible programme, that it is so much more superior to the rule-based approaches that preceded it, that no one is *that* kind of parameter-advocate any more (referring to the classical notion of Parameter articulated in Chomsky 1981), and so on, and so on.

My overall reaction to these objections is that no, I am not trying to belittle the achievements of research on 'comparative syntax'. I agree that the Principles-and-Parameters model was a very significant move in the field. Contrary to what preceded it, the Parameter-based model has the (scientific) merit of being wrong. And yes, I am aware that the Principles-and-Parameters model is a broad framework that can be stretched in many different directions, but—much like Fodor and Piattelli-Palmarini

---

[1] Rizzi (1978), often given as the source of the notion 'parameter', in fact credits Chomsky for the suggestion. For what is perhaps the earliest mention of the term 'parameter' in the generative literature, see Chomsky (1977):

Even if conditions are language- or rule-particular, there are limits to the possible diversity of grammar. Thus, such conditions can be regarded as parameters that have to be fixed (for the language, or for particular rules, in the worst case), in language learning. ... It has often been supposed that conditions on application of rules must be quite general, even universal, to be significant, but that need not be the case if establishing a 'parametric' condition permits us to reduce substantially the class of possible rules.

It is interesting to observe, in the context of what follows in the text, that Chomsky talks about rules.

(2010) pointed out recently in a different, though not altogether dissimilar context[2] — there is a point at which even stretchable material breaks.

As for the idea that no one entertains any more the idea of Parameter I am criticizing, I beg to differ. For one thing, I do not know of many other notions of Parameters — at least, if one insists (as I think one should) on a substantive, non-vacuous notion of Parameter. As for the fear of Skinner's ghost, I think it can be safely put to rest. Yes, I will put more emphasis on environmental factors when I sketch my alternative (section 8.4), suggesting that we ignore insights from Piaget to Tomasello at our own peril, but from there to say that I am giving up on Chomsky and buying into Skinner is too much of a stretch. I will argue in favour of a very lean (and invariant) Universal Grammar. But I will not reject UG completely. Finally, to those who think that by discarding the notion of Parameter, I am reviving the spectre of infinite variation (the notorious Joos statement that 'languages can differ without limit as to either extent or direction' so often cited by Chomsky), let me point out a few things:

(i)   It is not at all clear that the idea of actual infinite variation was ever entertained even by scholars of Joos's persuasion (see Biberauer 2008 for relevant discussion, accompanied by citations);

(ii) Even a minimal amount of syntactic invariance suffices to avoid infinite variation;

(iii) It is not at all clear that the exponential growth of parameters that syntacticians are willing to entertain is so much better a situation for the learner than a model without parameters at all;

(iv) I am reminded of an observation once made by Tony Kroch to the effect that after first denying the existence of error in language acquisition (an obvious rhetorical move), we have come to acknowledge the existence of errors, and treat them as a rich source of information. We should do the same in the context of rule-learning.

It is interesting to note that after receiving much opposition during talks I gave where I deny the existence of Parameters, many an advocate of Parameters came to me and confessed that they also felt the number of parameters had got out of hand, that when it exceeded 30, they became suspicious, that they felt the term is used as a taxonomic device only, etc. I am reminded of an opening passage in Gould (1977):

I have had the same most curious experience more than twenty times: A colleague takes me aside, make sure that no one is looking, check for bugging devices, and admits in markedly

---

[2] The focus of Fodor and Piattelli-Palmarini's (2010) critical examination of natural selection and Darwinism is not altogether dissimilar from the current one because like them, I am questioning a consensus view that appears to be quite successful and, in fact, looks like 'the only game in town'. Like them, I also want to show that the notion at the heart of this consensus view does not have the causal/explanatory power it is claimed, or assumed, to have. Finally, like them, I also think that the proponents of the view I am criticizing are prone to mischaracterize critiques.

lowered voice: 'You know, just between you, me and this wall, I think there really is something to it after all.' The clothing of disrepute is diaphanous before any good naturalist's experience. I feel like the honest little boy before the naked emperor.

There is no denying that there is something wrong (deeply wrong) with Parameters. Not logically, of course. The beautiful simplicity of the logic of Parameters (well captured in Baker 2001) was in fact what I suspect persuaded many linguists to adopt it. As I will indicate, the problem is not logical, but *bio*-logical.[3] This may come as a surprise to some readers, as the idea of parameter clearly originated from Chomsky's familiarity with work in biology (an inspiration acknowledged by Chomsky on various occasions; see e.g. Chomsky 1980; Berwick and Chomsky 2011). But it is important to bear in mind that the regulatory networks that are now part and parcel of biology (molecular Evo-Devo) are used to account for differences across species, not within species. The linguistic variation we are talking about is intra-specific, and the appeal to Evo-Devo remains an analogy. So, when I say later in this chapter that biology tells us it is high time we rethink the role of Parameters, I appeal here to biolinguistics— biology relativized to the language organ. Moreover, theoretically (in the context of the Minimalist Program), the notion of Parameter so obviously does not fit. Even at the empirical level (the weakest in my opinion, in terms of persuasion), cracks have started to show. The empirical challenge mounted by Newmeyer (2005)—the now obvious break-downs of all alleged macro-parameters—has not been met. Roberts and Holmberg (2005) should be given credit for trying, but the response did little to alleviate Newmeyer's doubts (see Newmeyer 2006), and recent statements like the following should make us pause:

As for parameters, things are perhaps even worse. I cannot get into this topic here, but I believe that the notion 'parameter' has hardly been developed beyond the traditional observation that there are 'differences' among languages, like with respect to pro-drop or the order of head and complement. In short, the interesting principles were mostly discovered before Minimalism and the notion 'parameter' has always remained underdeveloped from a theoretical point of view.

(Koster 2010)

It is interesting to note in this context that after observing that very few linguists have taken the time to lay down a few guidelines for what counts as a Parameter, and after trying to offer such guidelines ('definitions'), Smith and Law (2009) conclude on a grim note (confirming the suspicion of Newmeyer 2005, but also of others such as Culicover 1999): 'The preceding discussion implies that many of the parameters postulated in the literature are, by our criteria, accidents rather than reflecting genuine, but not exceptionless, generalizations.' Smith and Law are far from explicit about which of the parameters postulated in the literature remain as genuine parameters by their

---

[3] In this I strongly disagree with Narita (2010), where Fukui's work on macroparameters is said to not only meet 'biological adequacy' but is even said to be preferable on biological grounds.

standard. They only mention *pro*-drop and head-directionality, but those are precisely the 'parameters' that began their theoretical lives as *bona fide* (macro-)parameters, only to see their scope diminish to the level of micro-parameters and possibly item-specific rules. If these are the standing parameters Smith and Law have in mind, it is conceivable that there are even fewer parameters than they think—perhaps as few as zero.

The clearest indication of the problematic trajectory of the parameter model is to be found in the gap between theoretical work and language acquisition studies. Recall that the raison d'être of the model is 'Plato's problem', the logical problem of language acquisition. However, even a quick survey of the current literature on parameters reveals that it is increasingly used as a tool to investigate what, following Fasanella-Seligrat (2011), we may call 'Greenberg's problem' (consider Baker 2010; Baker and McCloskey 2007).[4] Principles and Parameters have been pressed into typological service.[5] But as Newmeyer (2005) correctly stresses, the model is one that was designed to answer what is the set of possible languages, not what is the set of probable languages (on this point, see also Hale and Reiss 2008). In and of itself, the typological extension would not be so problematic if it weren't for the fact that as work on formal typology increased, productive work linking theoretical constructs with acquisition data is in a state of free fall. Part of the reason for this rests, I believe, with theoretical linguists, whose works fail to make new testable acquisitional predictions, hence the disengagement on the part of acquisition specialists.

At the workshop on which this chapter is based, Luigi Rizzi expressed his disagreement with me on this point, adding that it is the field of language acquisition as a whole that is once again dominated by empiricist biases. Perhaps Rizzi is right, but I think it's too easy to move all the blame away from the theoretical linguists. By blackboxing development, as the standard Principles-and-Parameters model undeniably does (see Longa and Lorenzo 2008), it is certainly hard for acquisitionists to find something to

---

[4] At the Barcelona meeting, Ian Roberts clearly illustrated this typological tendency, when he said 'So, for example looking at the head parameter again, we know that if we phrase it in maximally category-neutral terms, then it just doesn't work. There are too many disharmonic languages around. And if you phrase it in maximally microparametric terms, maybe restating it for each category in each language, or even for each lexical item in each language, we just don't make any crosslinguistic predictions'. This is correct, but it again points to focus on Greenberg's problem. The focus should be on I-languages.

[5] Luigi Rizzi points out the existence of significant results arrived at by focusing on typology, such as (in his view) Cinque (2005), and much of the work on cartography. Without getting into the adequacy of Cinque's account (see Abels and Neeleman 2006), or the cartography project as a whole (see Boeckx 2008a, To appear b; Fortuny 2008 for relevant discussion), I note that Cinque's conclusion does not bear on patterns of variation (Parameters), but on patterns of *non*-variation (Universals). As such, they do not diminish my feeling that talk of Parameters is inappropriate in a typological context.

In the context of typology, let me remind the reader of Odden's correct remark that 'It is misguided to attribute every accidentally true statement about human language to UG, for doing so trivializes the theory of UG itself.' (Odden, 1988)

work with.[6] For example, Wexler's (1998) proposal, which takes many parameters to be set before experimental work could detect the parameter setting process has the net effect of alienating the acquisition community. True, Rizzi (2006a) discusses examples of late parameter setting, and non-unformity between child language and adult language. Tellingly, he ends up appealing to performance and maturational factors to account for the late setting of the relevant parameters, which illustrates perfectly the point that I want to make: on its own, the structure of parametric theory is silent on the developmental process we call language acquisition.

It is interesting to note that this very state of affairs was anticipated back in the early 1980s, when the notion of Parameter setting and its attendant switchboard metaphor (Chomsky 1986a) emerged. Lasnik (2002) points out the following:

in the very very early 1980s, maybe 1980 or '81, when Noam in his class was laying out the theory in relation to the question of language acquisition and there was a lot of discussion in the class about how the big problem was why language acquisition is so rapid, given that language is such a complicated thing—but as the theory was laid out it occurred to me: Jeez, we've almost reached the point where the question should be turned around. So I raised my hand and said: 'Don't we have a new question, now—Why is language acquisition so slow?' ... 'Why doesn't it take six minutes?' Interestingly, at that same era when the theory of parameters began to be very popular, there was a lot of work in theory and acquisition and learnability. Parameters was just the breakthrough we had been waiting for. It's been observed all around the world that kids go through discrete stages independent of the language, etc. That's an interesting fact we have to explain and the theory of parameters is designed to explain that. But I never completely believed that at the time and I still don't completely believe it. If the theory of parameters explains stages, those stages shouldn't last more than a couple of minutes each. There's gotta be something else that explains stages.

[6] After the Barcelona meeting, I came across the following passage, from Yang (2010), whose opinion converges with mine:

There was a time when parameters featured in child language as prominently as in comparative studies. Nina Hyams's (1986) ground-breaking work was the first major effort to directly apply the parameter theory of variation to the problem of acquisition. In recent years, however, parameters have been relegated to the background. The retreat is predictable when broad claims are made that children and adults share the identical grammatical system (Pinker 1984) or that linguistic parameters are set very early (Wexler 1998). Even if we accepted these broad assertions, a responsible account of acquisition would still require the articulation of a learning process: a child born in Beijing will acquire a different grammatical system or parameter setting from a child born in New York City, and it would be nice to know how that happens. Unfortunately, influential models of parameter setting (e.g. Gibson and Wexler 1994, but see Sakas and Fodor 2001) have failed to deliver formal results (Niyogi and Berwick 1996), and it has been difficult to bridge the empirical gap between child language and specific parameter settings in the UG space (Bloom 1993; Valian 1991; Wang et al. 1992; Yang 2002). The explanation of child language, which does differ from adult language, falls upon either performance limitations or discontinuities in the grammatical system, both of which presumably mature with age and general cognitive development—not thanks to parameters.

The failure (typical of the breakdown of macroparameters reviewed in Newmeyer 2005) of what is perhaps the major attempt in recent years to find converging evidence from cross-linguistic and acquisition data, Snyder's (1995, 2001, 2002) predictions regarding the 'Compounding Parameter' (see e.g. Son 2006; Boeckx (To appear b)), is another blow to the Principles-and-Parameters model.

What Lasnik is stressing is that the burden of the acquisition problem falls on something other than Parameters. At the very least, it shows that Parameters are not sufficient to 'solve' Plato's problem. You need to appeal to (non-grammar-based) 'strategies' (see e.g. Yang 2004, Pearl 2007). The discussion in this chapter will suggest that Parameters may not even be necessary. But before making that point I want to stress how inappropriate the Principles and Parameters approach is when applied to Greenberg's problem. Because of the very nature of the problem (distribution of grammatical systems that are, of necessity, full of historical residues and arbitrary properties), one is led to entertain incoherent notions such as the existence of a 'High Analyticity' parameter (Huang 2005) (a continuous notion disguised as a discrete state[7]), or, when not all expected consequences of a parameter hold in a particular grammatical system, one is led to untenable conclusions such as 'th[is] language is in flux' (Bošković 2008a). Grammatical systems may be highly analytic or in flux, but only in the E-language sense, not in the I-language sense with which Parameters must necessarily be associated.

As I pointed out in passing, it is no surprise that such incoherent notions are entertained, due to the fact that what typologists describe are not proper objects of biolinguistic inquiry. In the words of Chomsky (1995):

Thus, what we call 'English' or 'French' or 'Spanish' and so on, even under idealizations to idiolects in homogeneous speech communities, reflect the Norman conquest, proximity to Germanic areas, a Basque substratum, and other factors that cannot be regarded as properties of the language faculty. Pursuing the obvious reasoning, it is hard to imagine that the properties of the language faculty—a real object of the natural world—are instantiated in any observed system. Similar assumptions are taken for granted in the study of organisms generally.

As a result, Parameter-based typological inquiry (especially those of the macro-parameter type) fall into the same problems that plagued most claims about holistic types from the nineteenth century and the pre-Greenbergian twentieth century: 'they have not been substantiated and have fallen into oblivion' (Haspelmath 2008). As Otero (1976) pointed out almost 40 years ago, '[i]t hardly needs to be added that these archetypes are nowhere to be found.' So, why look for them through Parameter-lenses?[8]

In addition to this undesirable move towards typology, work on Parameters suffers from the disappearance of principles caused by the advent of linguistic minimalism.

---

[7] If Japanese is less analytic than Chinese, but more so than French, is it + or − analytic?

[8] At the Barcelona meeting, Ian Roberts pointed out that a line in Chinese really looks different from a line in Mohawk. True, but nothing ought to follow from this at the level of abstraction that one is used to in generative linguistics. Perhaps the problem is Mark Baker's (1999) confidently stated assumption that 'languages [do not] differ only in relatively superficial ways', that they are more like 'Swiss watches than piles of sand.' See Boeckx (To appear b, 2012a) for detailed discussion of this choice of metaphor, and why it leads us astray.

The dramatic reduction of principles has been pushed to the limit in recent years, with the recognition that movement is just another instance of Merge. This leaves virtually no room for Parameters, in the classical sense of the term. Recall that Parameters in Chomsky (1981) were not independent from Principles. Contrary to what the name 'Principles-and-Parameters' may suggest, it is not the case that some condition can be a Principle or a Parameter in that model: Parameters are principles (more precisely, principles with a choice point to be fixed embedded in them). If Principles disappear, Parameters can't be maintained. Although theoretical linguists have been slow at recognizing this (or at least, slow at making this explicit),[9] researchers in language acquisition have had it very clear, hence their 'maximalist' (as opposed to 'minimalist'), top-down (as opposed to 'bottom-up') theoretical assumptions (well illustrated in Longa and Lorenzo 2008; Lorenzo and Longa 2009).[10] Incidentally, the same maximalist assumptions appear necessary in the works of Mark Baker, who seeks to maintain the idea that '[t]here are some parameters within the statements of the general principles that shape natural language syntax' (Baker 2008b).

The clash between Parameters and the minimalist drive is well captured in the following quote from van Riemsdijk (2008):

One of the main problems that we now face is the question of how the actual repercussions of such highly general principles of physical/biological organization in the grammar of specific languages can be insightfully represented.... It would be absurd to propose that the constraint[s] [them]sel[ves] [are] parametrized.[11]

Koster (2010) is right in saying that 'the notion "parameter" has always remained underdeveloped from a theoretical point of view.' With the advent of the Minimalist Program, I claim that it is impossible to entertain a theoretically sound, substantive, contentful notion of Parameter. (I examine in this chapter the claims to the contrary that were expressed at the Barcelona meeting by Luigi Rizzi, Anders Holmberg, Ian Roberts, and Ángel Gallego).

Of course, it may well be the case that the minimalist trend towards approaching UG from below is on the wrong track. There may well be many principles with room in them for parameters, but recent trends in biology gives us reason to doubt this

[9] When I began to reflect on this issue, I could only find the following statement by Eduardo Raposo: 'There are no real objects called "parameters" in UG. This in no way implies that the search for the systematic ways in which languages vary [notice again the typological as opposed to acquisitional concern—CB] has no place in linguistics. It just means that the search is lexical in nature.' (Raposo 2002). More recently, Hornstein (2009) has also expressed scepticism towards the notion of parameter in a minimalist context. For relevant discussion, see also Richards (2008, 2009); Samuels (2011).

[10] None of the parameters illustrating the logic of Principles-and-Parameters (the switchboard metaphor with cascading effects) are embedded in principles that have retained currency (cf. bounding nodes, theta-criterion). Other illustrations of this Parametric logic still await a technical formulation (many examples in Baker's hierarchy, notions like analyticity, Compounding, etc.).

[11] Do we really want to say, as Baker and Collins (2006) do, that general economy principles like Attract Closest are choice points for language learners?

possibility. As I discuss in Boeckx (To appear b, 2012c), the revival of embryology ('generative biology') under the rubric of 'Evo-Devo', with its emphasis on developmental and phenotypic plasticity, epigenetics, and the emergence of theories such as niche construction, stresses organismic processes as opposed to genetic blueprints, interactions (the interactome as opposed to the genome; the triple helix as opposed to the double helix),[12] as opposed to programs. As such it seems tailor-made for minimalist explorations, especially once these discard lexical blueprints or programs (i.e. numerations, parameter-hierarchies, pre-formed functional sequences, etc.), and truly explore interface-based explanations. Much like the emerging expanded synthesis in biology, linguistics will have to embrace pluralism, get rid of isolationist (i.e. modular, self-sufficient) tendencies, and revisit the works of old foes to treat them as friends. Like the modern synthesis did, the classical Principles-and-Parameters model blackboxed development, and dreamt of a single-level, reductionist theory to capture the generation of variation. Much like what happened in linguistics, biologists were in part attempting to exorcize the ghosts of Lamarck. Linguists were attempting to minimize if not Skinnerian, at least Piagetian tendencies. But biology (and, I contend, linguistics) is now mature enough to accommodate some of the insights of alternative visions without any existentialist dilemma. Much like modern biology, modern linguistics will have to soften its stance of various issues,[13] especially those touching on specificity and innateness (Massimo Piattelli-Palmarini would talk about this in terms of leaving behind the (necessary) age of specificity; see Piattelli-Palmarini 2010). The range of processes explored are likely to be more abstract (less-task-dependent) and generic, nothing like the Parameters of old.

As Yang (2010) points out, 'one needs to be mindful of the limited structural modification that would have been plausible under the extremely brief history of Homo sapiens evolution.' In Hornstein's words, '[t]he short time scale suggests that the linguistic specificity of FL as envisaged by GB must be a mirage.' (Hornstein 2009).

These passages express well the point of view at the heart of Hauser, Chomsky, and Fitch (2002), who, more than anything, want to draw attention to the richness of the Faculty of Language in the Broad Sense, and the many difficulties of

---

[12] Here linguists have to be particularly careful and appreciate the interactionism implied by terms like 'triple helix.' The three strands identified by Lewontin correspond fairly closely to the three factors in Chomsky (2005), but linguists seem to have the unfortunate tendency to view these three factors as separate (or at least separable from one another)—for example, when they ask if a given process is a third factor principle, or when they ask—see Gallego (2011)—which factor is the source of variation. Biologists like Lewontin are right to stress that the explanation lies in how *all* the factors interact with one another.

[13] If they don't, they are doomed to face what we may call 'Piattelli-Palmarini's dilemma'. As I pointed out in Boeckx (2006, 2010b), when Piattelli-Palmarini (1989) (rightly) cast doubt on adaptationist scenarios in the context of language evolution, there was no alternative, given the rich-UG model he assumed. The non-adaptationist alternative invoking laws of form didn't look too promising either. How could very general laws of form yield the degree of specificity that the UG model he assumed was made of? It took minimalism (and the extended synthesis in biology) to help us bridge this gap, and make the laws of form conjecture plausible.

assuming a high degree of linguistic specificity (a rich Faculty of Language in the Narrow Sense). This is the point where (as Jackendoff and Pinker correctly pointed out) the Hauser-Chomsky-and-Fitch vision meets minimalism, which takes a deflationist stance on Universal Grammar ('approaching it from below'). To repeat, minimalism may well be wrong, but (unlike the Principles-and-Parameters model) is at least on firmer biological ground. Given what we already know about the biological foundations of language, and what we can reasonably anticipate from future developments in biology, there won't be any explanatory room, or causal role for Parameters. True, both minimalism and the new biology ('Evo-Devo') are works in progress (programs, not theories), and, as Yogi Berra reminded us, it's hard to make predictions, especially about the future, but right now, Parameters go against the grain in both cases, and the model in which the notion of Parameter is based is out of step with both movements. As a result, a linguist sensitive to biolinguistics should be suspicious of Parameters.

To sum up this section, I have argued that one finds four instances of worrisome disconnects in the context the Parametric model:[14]

(i) A serious discrepancy between the rhetoric of success ('having solved Plato's problem, . . . ') and the empirical results to show for it;

(ii) A growing distance between theoretical work on Parameters and the use of the latter in acquisition studies;

(iii) A clash between the minimalist elimination of principles and the maintenance of parametrized principles;

(iv) An unquestionable feeling of lagging behind in light of new directions in biology regarding the origin of diversity and the underlying specificity of traits.

8.2   A last-gasp attempt: *'Le paramètre est mort; vive le paramètre!'*

In light of the range of problems for Parameters raised by F. Newmeyer, myself, and others, a few generative syntacticians have decided to rise to the challenge and defend the notion. Anders Holmberg and Ian Roberts have done just that, but, as I will show in this section, I remain unconvinced, in part because they end up endorsing a definition of parameter which I used in Boeckx et al. (2009) to demonstrate the absence of Parameters. As far as I can see, they agree with me in many respects, but fail to draw the obvious conclusion: that Parameters don't exist.

---

[14] Especially worrisome are the theoretical/conceptual disconnects. The empirical problems, though interesting, are always very weak on their own. As Darwin once remarked (in a letter to Henry Fawcett), 'How odd is it that anyone should not see that all observation must be for or against some view if it is to be of any service.'

Many syntacticians now realize that a minimalist, bottom-up approach to Universal Grammar doesn't fit well with the classical notion of Parameter (with upper-case *P*—the only notion worth its theoretical salt, in my opinion), but either implicitly or explictly, they have adopted a slogan suggested to me by Henk van Riemsdijk (personal communication): '*Le paramètre est mort; vive le paramètre!*' This is a version of the formula used in France to mark the unbroken chain of command, the continuity of the monarchy following the death of the king ('*Le roi est mort; vive le roi!*'). Paraphrasing Henk, we may say that 'the GB parameter is dead, long live the minimalist parameter!'

The problem with this view (which I am not ascribing to Henk) is that it is not clear what a minimalist notion of a parameter could be. As I discussed in Boeckx (2009 et al.), minimalist inquiry points to the idea that Parameters don't exist; they are not real theoretical objects, they are epiphenoma. Points of variation (lower-case *parameter*, if you want) arise where properties of the biologically-determined initial state of the language faculty remain silent, and where systems with which the language faculty (in the narrow sense) interacts, forces a choice to be made.[15] For example, taking linear order to be determined outside narrow syntax (following Chomsky 1995), I suggested we may think of the effect of a micro-parametric, head-specific head-parameter as arising from the fact that Merge produces an unordered pair which must be linearized one way or another to satisfy demands ultimately due to the linear requirement imposed by the physics of speech (or externalization more generally). Holmberg and Roberts seem to adopt this point of view when they say, as they did at the Barcelona meeting (see also Roberts and Holmberg 2010, Introduction), that 'P&P theory [i.e. the notion of Parameter] is compatible with current minimalist theorizing, once parameters are seen as effects of the absence of UG specification, but where the range of variation allowed is nevertheless constrained (often by extralinguistic factors).' Whereas they continue to defend the notion of parameter after endorsing this view, I reject it. The reason I do so is that as Holmberg and Roberts themselves

---

[15] Smith and Law (2009) points out that such epiphenoma may have been genetically assimilated, making them real parameters. Although I take genetic assimilation (or accommodation) to be real, I seriously doubt that genes accommodate epigenetic effects of this specificity. For the non-specificity of genetic coding, especially in the context of complex cognitive traits like language, see Benítez-Burraco (2009), Lorenzo and Longa (2003). To the extent that one can speak of assimilation in the case of linguistic variation, it takes place at the phenotypic level, where assimilation is simply another term for learning (see West-Eberhard 2003).

Smith and Law also question the reasoning that led me to claim that parameters are epiphenoma on grounds that 'the physical necessity for linearization may be the ultimate cause of the parameter but the skew distribution of the world's languages and the consistency of head direction within a language suggest that the parameter does exist: The physical constraint has led to grammaticalization [genetic assimilation] of the parameter.' I disagree. Notice, first of all, the typological concern again. But setting this aside, Smith and Law's argument is factually incorrect. They still seem to assume that parameters like head-directionality have a macro-parameter, language-consistent profile. That this is not the case was one of the motivations behind Kayne (1994). I thought this much could be taken for granted by now.

acknowledged at the Barcelona meeting, once this underspecification view is adopted, 'the notion of parameter is almost empty; it really doesn't have much content.' Well, if it doesn't have much content, if it's almost empty, why do we maintain its existence?

Let me repeat that if by parameter we simply mean difference (within a limited range), then everyone (even linguists of a non-Chomskyan persuasion) would be willing to recognize the existence of parameters. But P&P theory, and the notion of Parameter in particular, would be far away from the alleged breakthrough it was. (Try to impose the reading where 'parameter' is almost empty onto Chomsky (1981) and you will see what I mean.) I tend to agree with Baker (2005) and Luigi Rizzi (in Boeckx et al. 2009; Rizzi 2009b) that the only notion of parameter worth fighting for is one that treats variation in terms of overspecification within UG, not underspecification—precisely the notion that clashes with the 'Approaching UG from Below' movement and with the new biology.

Elsewhere, Holmberg (2010a) has again defended the notion of 'parameter' in terms of underspecification, saying that '[a] parameter is not a principle plus something, it's a principle minus something.' The problem is that 'a principle minus something' is just a *façon de parler*, not a Parameter (*qua* parametrized principle), at least in a minimalist context, where principles are (in the best-case scenario) generic processes or laws. Minimalist principles are completely divorced from differences, they do not contain 'minuses'. The 'minuses' arise at the meta level, when linguists look at how these principles interact with the rest of the mind. Not being language-specific, their formulation cannot contain language-specific vocabulary by means of which the 'minuses' could be defined. The correct conclusion to draw from the statement that parameters are not principles plus something is that parameters aren't, period. Their fate is that of the passive and other constructions in Chomsky (1981): taxonomic devices that are not genuine properties of the language organ.

In addition to endorsing an underspecification view, Holmberg (2010a) defends the notion of Parameter by pointing out that, contrary to claims in Newmeyer (2005) (see also Boeckx (To appear b, chap. 4)) one can find empirical effects of parameters of the sort that motivated the whole parametric approach: 'octopus' or cascade effects that were intended to show how parameters facilitates the acquisition task ('macroparameter'). Remember the following passages from Chomsky (1981):

If these parameters are embedded in a theory of UG that is sufficiently rich in structure, then the languages that are determined by fixing their values one way or another will appear to be quite diverse (. . .); yet at the same time, limited evidence, just sufficient to fix the parameters of UG, will determine a grammar that may be very intricate and will in general lack grounding in experience in the sense of an inductive basis.   (p. 4)

[. . .] there are certain complexes of properties typical of particular types of language; such collections of properties should be explained in terms of the choice of parameters in one or another subsystem. In a tightly integrated theory with fairly rich internal structure, change in a single parameter may have complex effects, ... Ideally, we hope to find that complexes of proper-

ties ... are reducible to a single parameter, fixed in one or another way. For analogous considerations concerning language change, see Lightfoot 1979.   (p. 6)

Holmberg (2010a) discusses contrasting data from Mainland Scandinavian and
Insular Scandinavian (as well as parallel data from Finnish) to show how differences
in properties like Stylistic Fronting, Quirky subjects, and the like can be made to follow from agreement properties (along the lines originally argued for in Holmberg
and Platzack 1995; see also Ott (2009)). However, upon closer scrutiny, this kind of
empirical evidence does not militate in favour of maintaining 'parameters' as interesting theoretical constructs. The reason for this is that for a given grammatical property
to have collateral effects does not speak directly to Plato's problem.[16] The reason cascade effects were seen as evidence in favour of the Principles-and-Parameters in the
early days of the model (when such effects seemed much more numerous than they
turned out to be; cf. Newmeyer 2005; Boeckx (To appear b)) is that they were effects
for which it was hard to imagine what kind of evidence the child could use to learn
them from the available data. If these effects could be made to follow automatically
from other properties of the grammar for which the child could use the available data
as evidence, the acquisition task was dramatically simplified. The lack of *that-t*-effects
in *pro*-drop languages discussed in Rizzi (1982) was just such an effect. (Unfortunately,
this particular prediction, as so many others with the same profile, turned out to be
empirically incorrect; see Newmeyer 2005; Nicolis 2008; Rizzi and Shlonsky 2007.)

As I stressed already, Parameters were intended to be used in the context of Plato's
problem, not in the context of Greenberg's problem. The mere fact of finding cascade 'effects' is not an argument for the existence of a parameter if these effects could
be learned by the child acquiring the language using primary linguistic data.[17] I do
not have space to go through Holmberg's evidence here, but I suspect most of the
effects he discussed are reasonably salient in the data available to the child, and as
such could be learned even in the absence of a parametric structure. Once again, I
cannot stress enough that typological concerns should take a backseat in a generative context. As a final illustration of this methodological imperative, let me mention the existence of 'fundamental *syntactic* (and semantic) difference between English

---

[16] I remember discussing this point with Juan Uriagereka many years ago. I am glad he voiced concerns
similar to mine in Lohndal and Uriagereka (2010).

[17] I note here in passing that I am not at all convinced that the specific effects discussed by Holmberg,
which were repeated at the Barcelona meeting, really are that different from one another (a very real possibility, as Holmberg himself acknowledged during the meeting). It is always possible to make numerous cascade
effects emerge if one cuts the theoretical vocabulary of constructions very thinly: e.g. instead of Quirky (i.e.
non-nominative) subjects, one could speak of Genitive Subjects, Dative Subjects, and Accusative Subjects,
thereby making three effects emerge where there is only one. Kayne (2005b) seems to make the same point
when he writes 'It has occasionally been thought that the term "parameter" itself should only be used when
there is such a notable or "dramatic" range of effects. I will not, however, pursue that way of thinking here.
In part that is because what seems "dramatic" depends on expectations that may themselves be somewhat
arbitrary.'

and Serbo-Croatian' that led Bošković (2008b) to postulate a parameter according to which language may or may not make syntactic use of a D-layer in nominal structures (if they don't, nominal structures are NPs). Bošković shows that assuming this difference leads to significant generalizations of the following sort (Bošković 2010 lists many more):

- Only languages without articles may allow left-branch extraction of the sort illustrated here by means of Serbo-Croatian *lijepe je on vidio djevojke* 'beautiful he saw [*t* girls]'
- Only languages without articles may allow adjunct extraction from NPs
- Only languages without articles may allow scrambling
- Only languages with articles may allow clitic doubling

Notice the important modal auxiliary 'may' in all of these statements. As Bošković discusses, some languages lacking an overt definite article (hence, *prima facie* qualifying for an NP-, as opposed to a DP-status) do not necessarily allow for the options opened to them. What this means is that these options are sub-'parameters' to be set by the child. But now notice that the DP-/NP-parameter does no work for this particular instance of Plato's problem: if the child does not know whether her language will allow left branch extraction even once it has set the DP/NP-parameter appropriately, she will have to look for evidence in the primary linguistic data to find out. Given the paucity of examples of adjunct extraction from NPs, for example, one can see that the NP/DP macro-parameter is of little help. Once again, Plato's problem got confused with Greenberg's problem. Bošković (2008b) explicitly commits what I like to call the typological fallacy when he writes in the context of the generalizations he has identified: 'My main argument for a fundamental difference in the structure of [NPs] in languages with and those without articles concerns a number of generalizations where articles play a crucial role . . . The generalizations could turn out to be strong tendencies, which would still call for an explanation.' It is true that an explanation is called for, but why should it be an explanation *in terms of parameters*?[18]

8.3 How did we get there? The root of the problem

In this section I would like to turn to the reason why the notion of Parameter has retained currency despite all the problems it has faced (for a long time), and show that once this reason is identified, 'parameter' becomes an even more dubious notion, biolinguistically speaking. The reason I have in mind is the belief that the well-documented shift from Parameter as specification on principle to Parameter as lex-

---

[18] I agree with Smith and Law (2009) that assuming that all differences must be treated in parametric terms—as Kayne (2005b) does when he writes 'I will consequently freely use the term "parameter" to characterize all cross-linguistic syntactic differences'—renders the notion of parameter completely vacuous.

ical specification nonetheless allowed us to retain a restrictive notion of Parameter. This belief was well expressed by Luigi Rizzi at the Barcelona meeting (see also Rizzi 2009b), who took the shift (known as the 'Borer-Chomsky' conjecture) to have been 'significant'. Although it changed the locus of variation, according to Rizzi, it maintained 'a version of the switchboard model'.

The Borer-Chomsky conjecture is standardly formulated as follows:

All parameters of variation are attributable to differences in features of particular items (e.g. the functional heads) in the lexicon.   (Baker 2008b)

In the words of the authors of the conjecture themselves:

Parametric variation is restricted to the lexicon, and insofar as syntactic computation is concerned, to a narrow category of morphological properties, primarily inflectional.

(Chomsky 2001)

The availability of variation [is restricted] to the possibilities which are offered by one single component: the inflectional component.   (Borer 1984)

Not only did this shift to lexical parameters solve problems that became obvious shortly after Chomsky (1981) (reviewed by Rizzi at the Barcelona meeting), it was seen as a step forward in the direction of solving Plato's problem, as '[a]ssociating parameter values with lexical entries reduces them to the one part of a language which clearly must be learned anyway: the lexicon.' (Borer 1984)

In my opinion, the problem was indeed right there: what we wanted to understand (the nature of variation) was relegated to the part of the language organ that we understand the least: the lexicon. Consider Rizzi's proposal (made at the Barcelona meeting; see also Rizzi 2009b):

(1) A parameter is an instruction for a certain syntactic action expressed as a feature on a lexical item and made operative when the lexical item enters syntax as a head.

Rizzi takes this statement to be a model of simplicity and restrictiveness, but I beg to differ. It would be a model of simplicity and restrictiveness, if we had an idea of what counts as a possible feature on a lexical item, and what is a head. Notions like lexical feature and head are very common in syntactic discourse, but from a minimalist/biolinguistic perspective, they remain poorly understood. Kayne (2005b) recognizes this, when he writes 'What this brings out is something that I think has always been implicit in the proposal that parameters are restricted to features of functional elements, namely that the features in question must be simple and limited in type, in some sense to be made precise. ...Reaching an adequate characterization of what it means to be an appropriate feature in this sense is one of the primary challenges faced by (comparative) syntax.' In other words, in the absence of a restrictive theory of what a lexical entry is, the Borer-Chomsky conjecture brings us no closer to understanding the nature of linguistic diversity.

Very few attempts have been made at coming up with such a theory of lexical entries. Adger (2010) (alongside Adger and Svenonius 2011) is the most explicit discussion of the nature of lexical entries (pre-syntactic feature bundles) within minimalism that I know of, and, as I argue in Boeckx (To appear b), Adger's discussion and specific proposal shows how far we are from a restrictive, biolinguistically plausible theory of lexical entries. Adger opens his paper with a (biolinguistic) challenge. Its goal is to 'explore the consequences of the idea that structure embedding in human language is only ever syntactic (that is, that there is a single engine for the generation of structure and the engine is the syntax' (an idea familiar in recent works by Marantz, and Borer, and directly related to the proposal in Hauser, Chomsky, and Fitch 2002). As Adger correctly observes 'if structure embedding is only syntactic, then the feature structures that are the basic atoms of syntax (i.e. lexical items) cannot involve embedding of one feature inside another.' In so doing, Adger notes, this minimalist approach 'contrasts rather starkly with work in other approaches which take lexical items to have rich featural structure' (all feature-unification frameworks, such as HPSG, and LFG). I think Adger is exactly right in his desire to restrict embedding to the domain of syntax (i.e. pre-syntactic lexical entries should be completely flat), but as readers familiar with his paper know, Adger is forced to propose a fair amount of embedding inside his minimalist lexical entries. As far as I can see, *all* proposals concerning the format of parameters within the Chomsky-Borer conjecture have to do so as well: they have to encode parametric properties as features of features, which implies embedding.

As I have discussed in a series of publications (Boeckx 2009b, 2011b,c, 2012a,b, To appear b), the reason why pre-syntactic embedding is unavoidable in current syntactic models is because *all* syntactic frameworks (not only minimalist models) suffer from what I have called 'lexicocentrism'—the view that 'derivations are driven by morphological [i.e. featural] properties to which syntactic variation of languages is restricted.' (Chomsky 1993b: 44). This is in fact the view enshrined in most minimalist textbooks (see e.g. Adger 2003; Hornstein et al. 2006), the view that lies behind such notions as 'Last Resort' and 'triggered Merge', and that makes it possible to claim that 'labels can be eliminated' (Collins 2002), that 'syntax is crash-proof' (Frampton and Gutmann 2002), etc. This is the view that Rizzi's format for lexical parameters relies on. A similar view was endorsed by Holmberg and Roberts at the Barcelona meeting, who take 'parameters to correspond to the things that are let open by UG, such as the distribution of formal features.' This is also the view advocated by Ángel Gallego at the same meeting, for it is necessary for him to be able to entertain the idea that there is variation pre-syntactically. Gallego claims that this sort of variation is 'restricted to (i) Selection of the set of features for a given language L from the set of features made available by UG; and (ii) the way these features are assembled to create lexical items of L.' But what is 'assembling', exactly? Unfortunately, we are not told. The only reasonable answer within minimalism is Merge, meaning that the assembling takes place in narrow syntax, not pre-syntactically; meaning that the ('parametric') consequences of this assembling will only be detected post-syntactically.[19]

This effectively means that if as Rizzi, Holmberg, Roberts, and Gallego claim, variation arises solely as a result of how features are assembled (which features are found on a given lexical item), this result will, of necessity, be felt post-syntactically. We are thus led to the assertion in Boeckx (2011a) that narrow syntax is invariant (symmetric under variation). Not only don't we find good examples of syntactic parameters (Newmeyer 2005; Boeckx (To appear b), among others), there cannot be any syntactic parameters if we adopt the minimalist idea that principles are not parametrizable (due to their natural law-like character) and the biolinguistically motivated ban on pre-syntactic embedding.

It should now be clear to the reader that the problem with the attempts to make the Borer-Chomsky conjecture precise is just one aspect of a bigger problem: the heavy dependence on the lexicon, and what counts as a possible feature/lexical entry. This is a problem that plagues the cartographic approach, and indeed minimalism as a whole. It is too easy to invent features and 'bundle them' pre-syntactically because once in the pre-syntactic lexicon, they are taken for granted. What is needed is, as I argue in Boeckx (To appear b), a full-blown adoption of Borer's exoskeletal model (a more radical model than even Borer is willing to explore), one that leads to the idea that all lexical entries are alike: all lexical items are flat, consisting—as far as syntax goes—of a single property (the property that makes them mergeable, sometimes called the 'edge feature'; cf. Chomsky 2008). With such a lexicon, Merge becomes free (what I like to call a 'Merge α' model) and becomes crucial in every grammatical explanation. Defeating lexicocentrism means endorsing a super version of syntactocentrism, where Parameters are but one of the casualties.

Ian Roberts pointed out at the Barcelona meeting that 'to exclude parameters from narrow syntax would be to impose a condition on this part of the grammar which has neither conceptual motivation, nor, as far as we are aware, any empirical motivation.' The discussion already in this chapter makes it clear that my claim that narrow syntax is immune to variation is not an extra condition imposed; it follows from a truly minimalist view on what narrow syntax is. Although good evidence for syntactic parameters is hard to find (in fact, I think, it is completely lacking), it has always

---

[19] This confinement of variation to post-syntactic components is one of the ways in which the model advocated here differs from the nano-syntactic model (Starke 2009, this volume). Although nano-syntacticians also dramatically reduce the size of pre-syntactic lexical entries, they allow for syntactic compounds to re-enter (feed back into) the syntactic derivation and therefore influence subsequent stages. Another difference, which became clear following a question raised to Michal Starke by Luigi Rizzi at the Barcelona meeting, is that at least some instances of movement (of the 'long-distance' kind) are assumed to be feature-driven in this model. This is because the nano-features used in the model have projecting semantic properties (crucial for the establishment of the functional sequence, the version of cartography assumed in nano-syntax), unlike in the model I defend. This makes nano-syntax a model much closer to Generative Semantics than what is claimed by its proponents.

been hard, for me at least, to see what would make this true. That is, why shouldn't narrow syntax be subject to variation? As long as narrow syntax is lexically determined (feature-driven), it is indeed impossible to exclude variation from narrow syntax other than by fiat (as Roberts notes). But as soon as we adopt a truly exoskeletal approach to the lexicon, as soon as we allow ourselves to construct (i.e. explain) properties of the lexicon, we make it theoretically impossible to state 'parameters' at the level of narrow syntax. The only option left would be to parametrize the basic processes like Merge and Transfer, which I take to be ruled out a priori. What we end up with is a situation reminiscent of what Kayne (1994) achieved: by formulating a more restrictive theory of syntax, one excludes patterns of variation. To borrow a line from Kayne's presentation at the Barcelona meeting, 'some properties of the language faculty are too deeply built in to be possible loci of variation.' The Minimalist Program, allied to biolinguistic desiderata, suggests that the whole of narrow syntax is just too deeply built in (third factors) to be a locus of variation.

Let me add two more comments regarding the absence of variation within narrow syntax.

Elsewhere (Roberts 2010c), Ian Roberts suggests that reducing everything to PF-variation is a wrong move, as 'we expect PF parameters to be symmetrical, in the sense that the entire logical space of variation ought to be filled, and attested in the world's languages.' I see no reason to adopt this point of view, and every to adopt the opposite. There is massive evidence that PF conditions are far more asymmetric in their effects than narrow syntax processes. If Merge is free and symmetric, the evidence of gaps are likely to be the result of non-syntactic factors (witness Blevins 2004).

On numerous occasions, Richard Kayne has told me that my claim that syntactic variation does not exist, but morphological, or morphophonological variation does, seems to depend on a seemingly arbitrary definition of the term 'syntax.' Kayne takes recent trends such as Hale and Keyser (1993, 2002) and Halle and Marantz (1993) to be attempts to reduce morphology to syntax. But I disagree. I do not think it is a trivial matter of terminology, it's an issue of level of representation and explanation. This is a point that Hale and Keyser were well aware of, and which they addressed explicitly in the context of their 'l-syntax' vs. 's-syntax' distinction. Here is what they wrote:

> We have proposed that argument structure is a syntax, but we have also separated it from s-syntax, ... probably an onerous distinction, perhaps nothing more than a temporary terminological convenience. [BUT]
>
> We must nevertheless assume that there is *something* lexical about any verbal/lexical entry. ... What is it that is lexical about the entry corresponding to *shelve*? Clearly, it is a lexical fact that *shelve* exists as a simple transitive verb in English. ... in reality all verbs are to some extent phrasal idioms, that is, syntactic structures that must be learned as the conventional 'names' for various dynamic events.

In effect, Hale and Keyser are pointing out that their 'l-syntax' is a syntax in the representational sense (a post-syntax, a morphology, in my terminology), whereas 's-syntax' is a syntax in the dynamic, derivational sense (narrow syntax, for me). Confusing the two would be like confusing genetics and epigenetics. One is static, the other one dynamic. One relies on the other, but they are not to be collapsed. Hence, it is important to be clear about which level is subject to variation. That is to say, it is important to distinguish between the (I am claiming, invariant) mechanism that produces the variation (narrow/s-syntax) and the selection step that corresponds to l-syntax/morphology.

8.4 An alternative, in light of and in line with the new biology

At this point it is worth reflecting on what an alternative approach to Plato's problem might look like. In this section I will only be able to make a few general remarks, and hint at a few research directions (see Boeckx (To appear b) for development).

It seems to me that the first thing to be clear about is that one should resist the temptation to take the Principles-and-Parameters model to be the only game in town. (Neo-Darwinians made the same mistake with natural selection; cf. Fodor and Piattelli-Palmarini 2010; Pigliucci and Müller 2010). The major mistake made by the Principles-and-Parameters model, much like the one made by the neo-Darwinians, was to rely on metaphors (cf. the switchboard metaphor, the artificial selection imagery, etc.) more than on actual causal-mechanistic processes. It was also deeply wrong to think that a single-level theory (a single mechanism) would be sufficient. As the new biology is telling us, a more pluralistic, multi-factorial, interactionist approach is needed. Blevins (2004) has begun to do it in the context of phonology. I think this sort of approach should be pursued. Instead of putting genes in the driver's seat, biologists like West-Eberhard (2003) (see also the various contributions in Pigliucci and Müller 2010) are now urging everyone to take genes to be followers, not leaders, stabilizing structural options, rather than generating these. We should adopt the same perspective in linguistics. As I suggest in Boeckx (To appear b), the neo-constructionist, realizational, post-syntactic PF-models that are becoming more and more influential should be used to view lexical features not as leaders, but as followers, as stabilizing, rather than dictating the construction of structural options.

The emerging picture is one where at least as far as the post-syntactic grammatical component is concerned, we are dealing with a variety of 'constructions' in something like the notion of construction in Construction Grammar, although crucially for me, these constructions are constructed by a narrow syntactic component that looks nothing like a Construction Grammar.[20] The post-syntactic constructions will be stabilized, selected (l-syntactic/morphological) forms, and will invariably be language-specific,[21] and often morpheme-specific. Sometimes, they will even be lexical-item-specific (word-islands in Tomasello's sense). We'll thus find idioms of varying lexical specificity, as Jackendoff (2005, 2010) correctly points out. (The mistake is to confuse this with the syntactic engine that constructs all of these.) The varying degree of specificity could, and in my view should, be related to the debate about micro- vs. macro-parameters.

In Boeckx (2011a) I suggested that points of underspecification (in the sense also used by Holmberg and Roberts cited earlier) would indeed be very local effects (I called them 'nano-parameters' to make this clear), but, once fixed (as local rules) could 'grow' into macro-parametric effects if coupled with what I called a Superset Bias, a learning strategy (an economy guideline for memory) that would seek to retain the same direction of stabilization in subsequent learning acts, unless there is too much evidence against it in the primary linguistic data (this sort of epigenetic bias is frequent in nature; cf. West-Eberhard 2003; it also makes a lot of computational sense, see Mobbs 2008). Independently, Roberts and Holmberg (2010) formulate a similar idea (going back to Roberts 2007), which they call a Markedness convention. According to them, 'there is a preference for a given feature of a functional head to generalize to other functional heads.' Details of implementation aside, the Markedness Convention and the Superset Bias have the potential effect of capturing typological tendencies (the focus of Greenberg's problem). Because it's only a bias, it predicts exceptions, and is thus better equipped than macro-parametric approaches of the classical type.[22]

Through this learning bias (and, no doubt, other non-langage-specific, 'third-factor' principles) it may be possible to *construct*[23] something like a 'parametric' structure like Baker's (2001) Parameter Hierarchy, as opposed to assuming that it is part of our biological endowment (an instance of the classic debate between epigenetics vs. preformationism). But I want to stress that the resulting 'parametric' structure, built inductively,[24] is likely to be more web-like than tree-like. It will be more like a subway map than a vertical hierarchy of the sort Baker (2001) anticipated. It will be reminiscent

---

[20] Construction Grammar takes Constructions as idiomatic, non-decomposable templates, which is clearly non-explanatory.

[21] They may even be sociolect-specific, which would allow us to incorporate some of the insights made in their respective presentations by David Adger and Sjef Barbiers at the Barcelona meeting.

[22] Contra Newmeyer (2005) I do not think that processing biases will be sufficient to account for typological generalizations, although they too may play a role.

[23] Another case of neo-constructionism/exoskeletallity in linguistic analysis. As I stress in Boeckx (To appear b), if UG is to be approached from below, all hierarchies from the cartographic representations/function sequences to Baker's Parameter Hierarchy, must be constructed. As Epstein and Seely (2006) correctly point out, 'if you have not grown [/constructed] it, you have not explained it.'

[24] In work in progress I am exploring the possibility of arriving at such a structure using a hierarchical Bayesian model of the sort proposed by Kemp et al. (2007), which I think makes sense given the success of linguistically well-informed Bayesian learning in the context of language acquisition (Yang 2002, 2004, 2010; Pearl 2007).

of networks explored in complex systems. Due to the numerous intersections it will contain, it is likely to be a factor in explaining why language acquisition takes time (cf. Lasnik's dilemma discussed earlier in this chapter), and why acquisitionists have found evidence of parallel learning paths (cf. the works of Stephen Crain and Rozz Thornston discussed in Boeckx 2009a, chap. 6).

Although Roberts and Holmberg adopt a similar idea with their Markedness convention (correctly pointing out that with it there is no need to formulate a theoretical difference between micro- and macro-parametric variation), they are wrong in using expressions like 'parameters become more micro' over time (the micro-/macro-options are entertained in parallel at the point of selection/learning). They are also wrong in taking their Markedness Convention to help construct top-down decision trees (networks, which they liken to epigenetic landscapes) that mirror the child's learning path. I would advocate a more bottom-up strategy for constructing the decision tree, in line with the new biology's recognition that epigenetic landscapes, useful as they are, are static representations that must also be constructed from the ground up, lest they miss the actual dynamical process that has true causal power (see again West-Eberhard 2003). Until we do so, we cannot claim that we are describing the actual learning path taken by the child.

I would like to conclude this section by pointing out that the emerging research programme to address Plato's problem is actually much closer to Hagit Borer's original vision, a vision obscured by the blanket statement of the 'Chomsky-Borer Conjecture'. It is true that Borer (1984) wrote that 'the availability of variation [is restricted] to the possibilities which are offered by one single component: the inflectional component.' But I don't think she meant this in the way that was explored subsequently in Ouhalla (1991), Webelhuth (1992), Fukui (2006), which Chomsky made standard ('Parametric variation is restricted to the lexicon, and insofar as syntactic computation is concerned, to a narrow category of morphological properties, primarily inflectional'). As the following passage (much richer than the portion of it that is usually quoted 'Associating parameter values with lexical entries reduces them to the one part of a language which clearly must be learned anyway: the lexicon') reveals, Borer was talking about learning (constructing) rules. (Like Yogi Berra, Borer could say that she never said half of the things she said.):

> The inventory of inflectional rules and of grammatical formatives is idiosyncratic and learned on the basis of input data. If all interlanguage variation is attributable to that system, the burden of learning is placed exactly on that component of grammar for which there is strong evidence of learning: the vocabulary and its idiosyncratic properties. We no longer have to assume that the data to which the child is exposed bear directly on universal principles, nor do we have to assume that the child actively selects between competing grammatical systems.   (Borer 1984)

By saying that 'We no longer have to assume that the data to which the child is exposed bear directly on universal principles, nor do we have to assume that the child actively selects between competing grammatical systems', I think Borer was essentially saying that by divorcing variation from syntactic principles, we no longer need a parametric theory to support language acquisition. This is the view I have expressed in this chapter.

Note again that this return to rules is not a return to the dark ages of unconstrained variation. After all, the parameter format proposed by Roberts and Holmberg (2009), like the parameter schemata of Longobardi (2005), are much like rule formats in Chomsky and Halle (1968).[25]

8.5 Conclusion: Why this is all good news and real progress

It is to be expected in a new field like (bio-)linguistics that conceptual change happens fairly rapidly. Linguists who have grown with the Principles-and-Parameters model have gradually updated their thinking (say, from parametrized principles to lexical parameters), but without necessarily paying attention to the fact that in so doing, they have stepped well outside of the original boundaries of the model. In and of itself, this is not a bad thing, so long as explanatory demands continue to be met. Unfortunately, in the case of parameters, this is not the case. Greenberg's problem has too frequently replaced Plato's problem, and the notion of Parameter (upper-case *P*) has lost its explanatory, causal role, to the point of being replaced by a misleading homonym, parameter (lower-case *p*), a fancy term for difference. As we saw, when one attempts to formulate a notion of parameter that is consistent with minimalist/biolinguistic demands, one is forced to conclude that 'the notion of parameter is almost empty; it really doesn't have much content' (Holmberg/Roberts). What a Pyrrhic victory for defenders of the Principles-and-Parameters model!

However, I have been at pains to show that the demise of the concept of Parameter is very good news for minimalists. It's a move in the right direction (in the direction of better integration with the rest of biolinguistics). It is sometimes said that Minimalism 'led to relatively few new insights in our understanding of phenomena in the first half of the nineties. This is probably because it did not generate new analytical tools, and thus failed to generate novel ways of looking at well-known paradigms or expand and solve old problems, an essential ingredient for progress to be made at this point' (Koopman 2000). I completely disagree with this statement, and believe that the gradual move away from Parameters indicates substantive empirical progress.

---

[25] It is interesting to note that the format for parameters put forth by Holmberg and Roberts during the Barcelona meeting—Q(ff ∈ C) [P(f)] (for some quantification Q over a set of features FF included in the set of categories C, some predicate P defined by the theory of grammar like 'is a label of', 'agrees', 'attracts' holds of this set)—does not contain any explicit choice point, unlike the parameters of old. It's really a rule/construction format; an idiomatic template à la Hale and Keyser (1993). It is in fact the very same schema argued for by Reiss (2003) and Samuels (2009) for the formulation of phonological rules.

Minimalism—with its emphasis on movement as (internal) merge, post-syntactic morphology, and so on—has made it possible to convert once-syntactic parameters into post-syntactic construction schemata. That is to say, minimalism has contributed to showing that the classical Principles-and-Parameters vision was wrong; the character of linguistic variation is not infinite, but it is not Parametric either. Let me repeat that this is not a return to Skinner and Joos, much like the new biology is not a return to Lamarck. As the debate between Newmeyer and Holmberg/Roberts made clear (Newmeyer 2005; Roberts and Holmberg 2005; Newmeyer 2006), statements like 'Place the Verb before its Object' could be seen as either a rule (Newmeyer) or a parameter value. Minimalism (of the Merge α kind) gives us what Kayne (1994) rightly characterized as the 'all too infrequent pleasure of seeing the theory choose the analysis.'

The recognition that Parameters do not survive the move to beyond explanatory adequacy is really good news. As Frisch (1999) notes:

For the traditional formalist, it is actually desirable for some linguistic patterns, especially those that are gradient, to be explained by [other] principles. The remainder ... might be a simpler, cleaner, and more accurate picture of the nature of the innate language faculty and its role in delimiting the set of possible human languages.

Newmeyer (2005) writes that statement once made by Pierre Pica to the effect that there are no (macro)parameters 'is a cause for disappointment, not rejoicing.' I disagree. It is a cause for rejoicing in light of the attempt to approach UG from below. Once UG is seen to be much more underspecified than we thought, the very existence of variation receives a straightforward rationale: there is variation precisely because the genome does not fix all the details of Universal Grammar. There is in fact so much underspecification that the explosion of parameters we have witnessed in the past 20 years is exactly what we expect. A Minimalist view of language makes variation inevitable.

Yang and Roeper (2011) write that 'Minimalism has not supplemented the basic architecture of P&P of the task of language acquisition'. But this statement (and similar ones, like my claim that parametric variation is a matter of virtual conceptual necessity in Boeckx 2006) can only be maintained at the descriptive level,[26] that is, if we understand parameter as devoid of causal effect. At what Marr (1982) would call the algorithmic level, Parameters are nowhere to be found. It now remains to work out the pluralistic alternative I have hinted at in the preceding page, or some other, and

---

[26] A similar conclusion holds for the very remark Massimo Piattelli-Palmarini and I made in Boeckx and Piattelli-Palmarini (2005), where we said that 'a parametric model of language acquisition is "logically" necessary.'

to rewrite our history of the field,[27] bearing in mind the words of the late Tony Judt, who once[28] said that '[t]he historian's task is not to disrupt for the sake of it, but it is to tell what is almost always an uncomfortable story and explain why the discomfort is part of the truth we need to live well and live properly. . . . A well-organized society is one in which we know the truth about ourselves collectively, not one in which we tell pleasant lies about ourselves.'

---

[27] Amundson (2005) has done exactly this in the context of the alleged explanatory success of the Modern Synthesis in biology.

[28] Interview conducted by Donald A. Yerxa, *Historically Speaking: The Bulletin of the Historical Society*, January/February 2006.

9

Variability and grammatical architecture

DAVID ADGER

9.1 Introduction

This chapter is an attempt to connect formal minimalist syntactic theorizing with empirical problems raised by sociolinguistic investigation.[1] This work is an extension of previous collaborations with sociolinguists over the past eight years (Adger and Smith 2005; Adger 2006; Adger 2007; Adger and Smith 2010; Cheshire et al. 2013). In current sociolinguistic work there is only a small interest in generative syntactic models for sociolinguistic phenomena. The syntactic models generative linguists provide are considered by many sociolinguists to be orthogonal (perhaps even inimical) to their interests. Similarly, there has been scant interest in generative syntax in modelling structured variability in morphosyntactic data (with a number of notable exceptions, some of which are mentioned). In some of the work I've done over the past eight years or so, I've been interested in exploring how generative models of syntax, devised with quite different goals in mind, might be useful for the analytical purposes of sociolinguistics. This chapter reviews the basic ideas of this research programme, raises some problems for it, and sketches some ways forward. What will be crucial here is not the sociolinguistic side of relevant data, but rather the question of how to theoretically model community-internal variability, and more specifically person-internal variability.

There are a number of models in the literature which have attempted to tackle this issue: Tony Kroch has proposed that there are competing, multiple grammars (Kroch 1994) each categorically generating a variant, so that individuals who control

[1] Many thanks to the audience at the Barcelona Workshop on Linguistic Variation in the Minimalist Framework, January 2010, and to Terje Lohndal and Peter Svenonius for comments on an earlier draft. Thanks, too, to Jenny Cheshire, Naomi Nagy, Sali Tagliamonte, and Jennifer Smith for much needed sociolinguistic advice.

multiple grammars have access to multiple variants, giving rise to intra-personal variability. More recently, Nevins and Parrott (2010) have developed a system involving a
probabilistic version of the Distributed Morphology operation of Impoverishment,
resurrecting the basic proposals of Labov (1969), in a modern theoretical setting.
A more standard route, within generative syntax, pursues a view originally developed
by Henry (1995), which ties the mechanisms of variation to optional movement.

The line of attack that I'm going to pursue here is different from these. It connects with issues addressed elsewhere in this volume. Cedric Boeckx, in his contribution, raised questions of 'memorization' or 'idiomaticity', and how those concepts
relate to non-compositionality. Sjef Barbiers, in his contribution, raises the same issue
but discusses it in terms of 'conventionalization', connecting this to questions of frequency. This will also be a concern for me. Of course, these are live issues in the debate
between generative grammar and construction grammar (see Goldberg 2003; Lidz and
Williams 2009; Goldberg 2013; Adger 2012, 2013a). Proponents of the latter believe that
grammar effectively emerges from the conventionalization of frequent collocations
of items. The approach I'll pursue is effectively 'Construction Grammar in Reverse':
grammar is a constraining factor in acquisition, providing the representational skeleton upon which the form meaning relationship takes flesh (cf. Borer 2003). The actual
morphosyntactic properties of a particular language (especially the form and properties of morphemes) are a conventionalization of distributional occurrences, for which
frequency may be an important factor, but the nature of these is severely constrained
by the operation of universal grammar in a way that I will specify. The eventual aim
of the general research programme is to connect specifically minimalist theories of
syntactic representations to empirical issues of interest to sociolinguists.

9.2 Internal factors

The particular empirical domain I'll focus on is what sociolinguists call internal factors
(Labov 1994). These are individual-internal factors connected to grammatical features
and structures (or possibly to the processing of grammatical features and structures)
that impact upon the choice of a particular variant in a particular context. I'll focus
on two examples. The first is from Buckie, a small fishing village in the North East of
Scotland. The example comes from joint work with Jennifer Smith, a native of Buckie
and a sociolinguist who has spent some time working there (Smith 2000). As an example of the phenomenon I am interested in, consider (1):

(1) a. Buckie boats were a' bonny graint.
         'Buckie boats were all nicely grained.'

     b. The mothers was roaring at ye comin' in.
         'The mothers were shouting at you to come in.'

All speakers in this particular speech community allow this kind of variation (Adger and Smith 2010). In both examples there are plural subjects but the form of the verb is variable; in (1a) there is an apparently agreeing auxiliary *were* and in (1b) we find the apparently non-agreeing form *was*. We find this pattern also with certain pronouns. I've given, in (2) below, a table with the frequencies found in the Buckie corpus of 39 speakers (19 male, 20 female, spanning three generations), all born and raised in the community (see Smith 2000 for details of this corpus):

(2)   Distribution of *was* with different Subject Types. N = 4904

Subject	percentage of *was*	N
1st singular	100	691
2nd singular	69	161
3rd singular	100	2290
1st plural	67	368
2nd plural	10	10
3rd plural	0	435
Singular NPs	100	762
Plural NPs	56	187

For 2nd person singular and 1st person plural, we see that two thirds of the time the form is *was*, whereas in Standard English we expect *were*. All speakers allow this variation throughout the paradigm reported here, although we don't have sufficient numbers in this data to show that all speakers have this pattern of frequency distribution. Following standard practice in sociolinguistic variationist research, the data is presented for the whole community, embodying the idea that the individual's grammar is reflected in the aggregate at community level (e.g. Labov 1972). Similarly, for plural noun phrases (examples like 1a and 1b), we find 56 per cent *was*. Again all speakers allow this variability. Any analysis of the general pattern that proposes that, in Buckie, the patterns can be accounted for by simply substituting *was* in place of Standard English *were* is untenable, since, as can be seen in the table, the 3rd plural pronoun *they* has only the *were* form, apparently displaying obligatory agreement.

Variable agreement with plural NP subjects appears also with main verbs in the present tense, as well as with present tense *be*:

(3)   a. The money that that lads *is* making is nae canny compared to what I made.
'The money that those boys are making isn't good compared to what I made.'

      b. Aye, and some of them *are* drawing dole on three, four different names.
'Yes, and some of them are receiving unemployment benefit using three or four different names.'

(4)   a. What bairns walk any distance?
'What children walk any distance?'

b. When they go back, the teachers asks them to write something and they send them till's

'When they go back, the teachers ask them to write something and they send them back to us.'

In (3) and (4), we find a plural subject in both (a) and (b) examples, but variation in whether the verb is marked with the −*s*.

Furthermore, with the pronominal *they*, the present tense main verb, just like the past and present auxiliary, appears with plural agreement (i.e. no −*s* is possible). There is just 0.6% appearance of −*s* with *they* in present tense (N = 1271). Adger and Smith (2010) show that these are all narrative presents with the verbs *say/tell*, and they argue that −*s* here is performing a distinct function (that is, that there is a special morpheme −*s* that variably marks narrative present irrespective of the form of the subject). The conclusion that the grammar of Buckie rules out −*s* when the subject is *they* is backed up by judgement data we carried out on the individuals who were recorded for the initial corpus gathering phase of the research. We took cases where −*s* appeared with a plural subject and swapped in *they* in the same context. This led to uniform rejection by our speakers:

(5)   *When they comes up to see us there   Buckie judgement

(6)   *When they gets home   Buckie judgement

(7)   *They does na do it yet   Buckie judgement

(8)   *They does na get what that cats get   Buckie judgement

(9)   *They is up in Elgin   Buckie judgement

This phenomenon of variable agreement which becomes obligatory in the presence of a pronoun has been tackled in the literature by various people: Henry (1995) developed a proposal about the manifestation of this phenomenon in Belfast English which related it to differential possibilities in where pronominal vs. non-pronominal subjects could be syntactically placed and how this syntactic placement impacts on agreement morphology. Tortora and den Dikken (2010) extend this idea to Appalachian English, although more recently Bernstein and Zanuttini (2010) have proposed a featural perspective on this close to what Jennifer Smith and I argued for. As mentioned previously, Nevins and Parrott (2010) developed a proposal that ties the pattern to variable application of impoverishment rules, ultimately tied to markedness effects.

Adger and Smith (2005) proposed a basic architecture for such variable phenomena that was further developed in Adger (2006, 2007) and Adger and Smith (2010). What we argued is that the explanation of the variability is to be tied only to the featural composition of the agreeing finite element, and it has nothing to do with the syntactic position of the relata. Further, the general approach developed a learning procedure which generates underspecified lexical items whose random combination leads to predictions of differential proportions of variants, rather than by embedding probabilities into morphological spellout rules, like the Nevins and Parrott proposal. Finally, the system allows individuals to have a single grammar, distinguishing variability from bilingualism. In fact, Adger (2006) points out that if UG is minimal, containing just the Merge operation plus constraints on the mapping of syntactic representations to semantic and morphophonological interpretations, there can't be multiple grammars in any meaningful sense: rather we have multiple individual lexical items which share interpretations and which constitute the basis of the variability, and it is these items that are chosen in different speech contexts, rather than whole grammars. Of course, since these items are typically functional items, choosing one version over another will potentially have grammatical effects. Adger and Smith (2010) provide a number of arguments that this is the right way to approach the Buckie data outlined.

An important consequence of the model developed in this work is that no radical change is required in the architecture of current minimalist syntactic theory. We already have all the technology at our disposal to tackle this issue: the featural representation of functional categories and the matching of morphological feature matrices to syntactic ones (as in, for example, vocabulary items in Distributed Morphology).

To see how this theory works schematically, take some functional category X, specified with features F, G, and H, and take three vocabulary items, each of which matches one of these features:

(10)   a. X[F, G, H]
      b. (i) [F] $<->$ i
         (ii) [G] $<->$ j
         (iii) [H] $<->$ j

The syntax builds X, and then X needs to be 'vocabularized'. Any of (bi–iii) will match, and so any can vocabularize X. On the assumption that the choice of vocabulary item is random, then we expect each of (bi–iii) to be inserted 33% of the time. However, if there is homonymy in the vocabulary list, as in (10b), then the surface forms will be unevenly distributed in terms of their frequency. In the schematic example given here, we will see 66% j to 33% i, approximately.

The idea, then, is that the variability arises because of an underspecification of the relation between the syntactic feature bundles and their morphological exponents; variability in the frequency of the forms emerges because of homonymy in the set of relevant exponents, and I proposed an algorithm (Adger 2006) that generates the set of exponents from the input, and termed this approach to variation *Combinatory Variability*.[2]

---

[2] Adger (2006) implements the proposal in a lexicalist fashion, allowing the lexical items underlying the morphological exponents to be underspecified. However, as noted in that paper, the proposal can also be expressed in terms of underspecification between the syntactic features on a lexical item and their morphological exponents, which is the implementation offered in Adger and Smith (2010).

The system is different in one important respect to standard models of the morphology syntax interface that involve underspecification, though: it does not incorporate a Subset Principle for resolving competition between lexical entries, at least not as a grammatical principle. The algorithm in Adger (2006) does reduce a certain amount of homophony, and therefore incorporates the intuition that a morphological learner generalizes beyond its input data (see also Pertsova 2007), but the algorithm produces what Adger (2007) calls a Pool of Variants, any of which can in principle be inserted. I showed that this was the right result in a number of cases.

The categoricity of agreement with pronominal *they* arises because of parametric variation in the usual sense: Buckie, like Welsh, but unlike Standard English, bundles a pronominal feature, [+/−pronominal], in with person and number features in its finite agreement head (see Adger and Smith 2010 for details). The checking of this pronominal feature is what leads to the impossibility of *they* with −s.

However, this basic story is not quite satisfying. It lacks a place for the internal factors mentioned in (at least) two important ways. The first is frequency effects: it is well known in the variationist literature that the frequency of a particular lexical item can impact on how robust the variability is: more frequent verbs, such as auxiliaries, appear more frequently with −s (see the discussion in section 9.4 on frequent verbs and grammatical change). In fact, it is generally true that variation is more robust for items that are more frequent (this is strikingly attested in historical change, see for example Ellegard (1953) on *do*; see also Erker and Guy (2012) for a nuancing of this idea in a synchronic corpus). For example, in Buckie frequent verbs like *be* or *do* (even just focusing on their main verb uses), when compared with less frequent verbs like *kick* or *interrupt*, have a higher proportion of −s with plural subjects (again, see section 9.4 for the data). There is no obvious way in the combinatorial variability system as developed so far to capture that.

The second issue is how grammatical properties can influence the choice of a variant. As first noted in the Labovian tradition (e.g. Labov 1969), it turns out that there are grammatical effects on how frequent variants are. Grammatical features don't merely determine whether a structure is grammatical or ungrammatical; for variable cases, they rather impact on the probability that one variant rather than another will appear. That is, beyond the social effects on variability, which are well known (Labov 2001), there are also grammatical effects on variability. In general these effects are more 'global' than simply the features of a lexical item. This is the problem of internal factors mentioned.

For example, take verbal −s (as the appearance of −s on verbs with plural subjects is often known): it turns out that in Buckie it is more likely that verbal −s will appear in subject relative clause constructions than it is that it will appear in non relatives (chi squared = 197.568 with one degree of freedom, two-tailed p-value less than 0.0001):

(11)

Subject relatives vs. other			
Subject relatives		other	
%	N	%	N
42	53	34	327

It appears that the syntactic context matters in this case. The interesting thing about this kind of effect is that the syntactic context impacts not on the grammaticality or ungrammaticality of a particular form, but rather on the probability of that form. All the context does is push the observed frequencies in one direction or the other.

Again the combinatorial variability model as it stands apparently has no obvious way of doing this. What the model states is just this: the agreeing verb form is just V plus some set of agreement and tense features. But we seem to need more information: specifically whether the clause that the verb appears in is a relative clause. The question is how we get that information into the system.

This internal factors question then raises a further issue about the empirical data: are there constraints or limits on the nature of the internal factors and if so, what characterizes these? Are they derivative of functional or surface relevant properties of the data, or are they constrained by the nature of the syntactic representation?

These are the issues in the theory of variation that I want to tackle: variability, frequency, and internal-factor effects.

9.3 Connecting syntactic structure to variable form

What I want to do now looks extremely disconnected from this. I'm going to briefly explore the standard theory of how Merge works, and develop a particular perspective on how information flows in a syntactic representation which is reliant on the common distinction between extended projections and specifiers (Grimshaw 1991). In the system I sketch here (see further Adger 2013b), I'll show that the information high up in an extended projection can have an effect on what is vocabularized low in that projection. The way that spellout, or morphological vocabularization to be more exact, is executed in this theory will give us a handle on frequency effects as well as on the limits of the impact of internal factors.

Merge is standardly taken to be binary, I have given in (12) a (slightly simplified) definition from Collins and Stabler (2011), who formalize certain aspects of minimalism, that clarifies the stipulations inherent in Merge:

(12) Let W be a workspace and let A, B be syntactic objects where A, B belong to W and A and B are distinct. Then, external merge of A, B is equal to the set {A,B}.

Note that this definition (and all others I'm aware of that are set theoretic) has a crucial stipulation in it: that A and B are distinct. One might ask why that stipulation is there. If we remove it then we have the Merge of A and A being simply the set {A}.

In fact, the idea of removing this stipulation and allowing *Self Merge* has been proposed already in the literature. Guimarães (2000) suggested it and developed a system that constrained it by ruling certain applications of Self Merge out. Kayne (2010) uses it as a way of distinguishing nominal from verbal extended projections. Both Guimarães and Kayne strictly limit the application of Self Merge. For example, Kayne says in a footnote in his paper, 'alongside {x} there seems to be no need for {{x}}, which would be unavailable in principle if every merge operation must directly involve a head.'

In Adger (2013b), I propose jettisoning that assumption (that every Merge operation must involve a head), simplifying the theory of phrase structure by removing both the distinctness condition on Merge and the requirement that Merge always involves a head. That proposal then creates a system that generates unary branching structures of the kind that the classical bare phrase structure system standardly rules out (Chomsky 1995). In (13), the root Self-Merges to give a set of cardinality 1, whose member is root. We can then Self-Merge that set, giving a new set, of cardinality 1, whose member is {root}. Continuing, we generate a potentially infinite sequence of elements (the set containing that root, the set containing the set containing that root, and so on). We can represent this data structure in a more familiar form as a unary branching tree, where each x stands in for the position of a new pair of set brackets:

(13)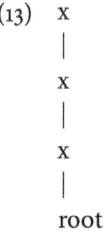

The immediate issue to address then is that of the label of these various constituents. The absence of labels might be one way to rule out iterated Self Merge: there is nothing to give the output of Self Merge a label (cf. the related idea in the footnote from Kayne (2010) discussed). In a system like that of Chomsky (1995), where labels of higher structure are always predicted from the set of labels in the contained structure, however, that proposal would still allow a structure where the label of the root is repeated at every level, requiring a further principle (perhaps an economy principle, as suggested by an anonymous referee) to rule that out. Alternatively, in a label free system like that of Collins (2002), one might allow labelless representations like (13) but take them to be ruled out by the principles that map syntactic structures to the interfaces. However, Collins (2002) is actually an argument not for the elimination of labels, but rather for the redundancy of triggered Merge and labels. Accepting the logical force of the argument, but taking the opposite line to Collins, then, I suggested in Adger (2013b) that we jettison triggered Merge (following Chomsky 2004) and instead have an exocentric labelling system.

In such a system, labels are given exogenously, by something outside the core computational system: for example, one might take a language-external cognitive schema to apply to the fractionated structure that is given by the syntax, thereby labelling that structure with what are known commonly as functional categories (cf. Chomsky 2007:14). More concretely, assume an antecedently given conceptual distinction between kind, sortal and substance concepts (see, for example, Li et al. 2009; Xu 2010). These cognitive distinctions are represented as linguistic distinctions via labels of pieces of structure (e.g. the label Ki(nd) or Cl(assifier) from Svenonius (2008b), following Zamparelli (2000) and Borer (2005)). The conceptual relationships between the cognitive distinctions are represented as syntactic relations between labelled structures (e.g. dominance, identity). Syntax provides a bare structure, which is labelled by cognitive schemata to give structures rooted by a lexical item dominated by a series of functional category labels: since these schemata are finite in size, the structures labelled by them are also finite, so syntax using just Self Merge provides a finite set of labelled structures (effectively, fragments of unary branching extended projections).

However, I take it to be false that the functional structure is identically represented in all languages for every root, or we would expect no variation at all. Rather language acquirers make use of what is universal (the finite set of structures generated by Self Merge and labelling) during the process of language development and associate the structures UG allows them to generate with distributional regularities in the data. The relevant regularities include morphophonological regularities (that is, what morphemes the label, or series of labels, are associated with) and morphosyntactic regularities (properties of these structures relevant to their co-occurrence with other structures). The outcome of this process is, then, a set of structures that are effectively annotated by morphophonological and morphosyntactic properties (syntactic features). I take the morphosyntactic annotations to be what bear the core 'parametric' properties discussed by Rizzi in his contribution to this volume: syntactic content and instructions for syntactic actions (see also Adger and Svenonius's (2011) distinction between first order and second order features).

The process of acquisition is then, in this model, a process that matches the possible unary extended projections with systematic regularities in the primary linguistic data (morphemes, for example), and associates these with both morphophonological and syntactic properties. Once acquisition reaches a more or less steady state, the acquirer has, in effect, compiled a lexicon the elements of which contain fairly rich morphophonological and syntactic information. The outcome of the process of lexicon compilation is one that associates fragments of unary extended projections with both morphological and syntactic properties. These pre-compiled lexical items are available for language use and correspond to fairly classical morphemes.

A simple example of language variability to help clarify the working of these concepts is the difference between the English morpheme *child* and the Scottish Gaelic morpheme *clann*. The English morpheme is a singular count noun, while the

Gaelic morpheme is what Acquaviva (2008) calls a 'lexical plural': *clann* is used to refer to a group of children, but is grammatically singular, occurring with, for example, a singular article (*a' clann*, the.fem.sing children; **na clann*, the.fem.pl children). In order to refer to a single child, a paraphrase *daoine cloinne*, person children.gen.sing, literally 'person of children' is used. In the system developed here, English *child* is the spellout of the structure that results from a series of Self Merge operations that add count semantics to a root (following Borer 2005). Its plural, *children*, is the spellout of a structure that additionally has had a plural label added to it (call this Pl). This label is, when present, interpreted as adding a plural semantics, but, in addition, it carries a plural grammatical feature (e.g. [–singular], following Noyer 1992, or Harbour 2004), a result of distributional regularities in the data available to an English child that effectively activates the syntactic relevance of the functional category label. *Clann*, on the other hand, is a root that has no spellout in the absence of a plural label. *Clann* is the spellout of the whole unary extended projection (the root, the functional structure that adds count semantics, and the functional structure that adds plural semantics. More concretely, there is a spellout for Pl-Cl-N-child, but no spellout for Cl-N-Child). The idea that a morpheme can 'span' a sequence of functional categories has its antecedents in Williams's (2003) analysis of auxiliaries. However, for *clann*, there is no grammatical (syntactic) feature [–singular] on this label because the distributional regularities in the data do not associate *clann* with this property. Gaelic does possess a grammatically plural label, which is associated with a variety of spellouts depending on noun class, gender, etc.; for example, the plural of *sùil*, 'eye' is the affixed form *sùilean*. In such cases the plural functional category Pl bears a plural syntactic feature [–singular]. Of course, the fact that *clann* already encompasses the plural functional category means that it's impossible to pluralize *clann*, in this way. Gaelic *clann* differs from English *children*, in that the latter includes while the former lacks, a precompiled association of morphophonological information (effectively the suffix *–ren* and its impact on the root) and morphosyntactic information (the annotation of [–singular] on the Pl functional category label).

Another aspect of variation that this system allows is a version of Brody's (2000) proposal that the syntactic action associated with a functional label might be an instruction to the spellout systems to pronounce the whole sequence in a particular position (Brody annotates this position with a diacritic which is interpreted by the spellout systems as an instruction to pronounce the whole word at that position in the structure, see Adger and Svenonius (2011), Adger (2013b), and especially Svenonius (2012) for recent discussion). For example, in a V2 language, where the finite verb is spelled out in C, we can take the label for declarative C to bear an instruction that the phonology of the entire finite extended projection is to be linearized at C (see further for more detail and an example). That is, the C[+finite]-T fragment of the projection line is associated with an annotation that requires the morphophonology of the whole projection line to be at C (that is, the spellout of the verb, its aspectual markers, and tense and agreement markers are all spelled out in the structural position C). This is importantly different from the proposal made by Starke (this volume) who takes variation between systems to involve the spellout of whole tree structures as a single morpheme. In that system, the generalization that all finite verbs appear in C is not trivially implementable.[3]

In addition to this kind of variation between and within languages, dependent on the presence or absence of a syntactically active feature, on the 'span' of functional categories lexicalized by a morpheme, and on the position at which the morpheme is pronounced, languages also have labels associated with particular syntactic requirements, for example, the requirement that a particular label have a specifier: for T this would give rise to EPP effects, while, for a V2 language, it would apply to the C which is the spellout point for finite extended projections just discussed. Again, this involves associating fragments of extended projections with distributional regularities. It is notable that the available distributional regularities seem to be extremely restricted, confined to the shape of the morpheme, its position, and its relationship to its specifier.

Self Merge, then, generates an infinite set of sequences which are rooted. Some (finite) subset of this contains sequences whose parts are labelled; a further subset of this is extracted during acquisition and associated with morphophonological and morphosyntactic information. Some (perhaps most) morphemes will lexicalize more than one label in a unary extended projection, giving the effect of insertion of morphophonological material at non-terminal points of a structure.[4] Let us call the acquired set of such pairings between labelled unary extended projections and morphosyntactic and morphophonological representations the Compiled Vocabulary, adapting the Distributed Morphology term for this (Halle and Marantz 1994).

In addition to Self Merge, the system also has standard (binary) set-Merge in both its internal and external manifestations. Because of this, the system generates an infinite set (because of recursion) of tree structures whose nodes may branch (in which case we have a specifier structure) or not. This system, although derivational, is very similar in its yield to Brody's (2000) Mirror Theory system of phrase structure. It is a consequence of both systems that the syntactic complement relation is reserved for extended projections (see Adger (2013b) for argument that this consequence is beneficial).

To see the system in action, applied to the data that concerns us here, take, for example, a fragment of the Buckie sentence in (4b):

---

[3] This observation about the architecture and the argument that V2 is problematic for a Nanosyntactic approach to spellouts of non-terminals is due to Peter Svenonius.

[4] This architecture shares, with Nanosyntax (Starke 2009; Caha 2009) the idea that morphemes are associated with non-terminal structures, but with Mirror Theory, the idea that morphological structures are associated with unary branching head-head sequences. See Ramchand (2008) for a slightly different implementation of a similar intuition involving an autosegmental style association line architecture, and Adger et al. (2009), Bye and Svenonius (2012), and Adger (2013b) for further developments and applications of the idea.

(14)   The teachers asks them

The verb root *ask* here Self-Merges giving a syntactic object that contains just the root. This object is then labelled as a V (presumably there is a small set of choices as to how roots are labelled, Baker 2003). If Borer (2005) is correct, then the choice of label here is available to a speaker throughout his/her life, so that roots can be ambiguously nominal or verbal.

The label V bears some feature that provides a well formed interpretation when a specifier is Merged as an object (or further Self Merge leads to an aspectual category, as in Ramchand (2008), that bears such a feature), allowing Merge of *them* followed by further Self Merge which is labelled v, which allows Merge of the subject, as is standard. Further Self Merge builds T, Internal Merge raises the subject, and further Self Merge builds matrix C. So much is fairly standard, with Self Merge and Labelling taking the place of external merge of heads. The final structure is a 'telescoped' structure, similar to Brody's:

(15)

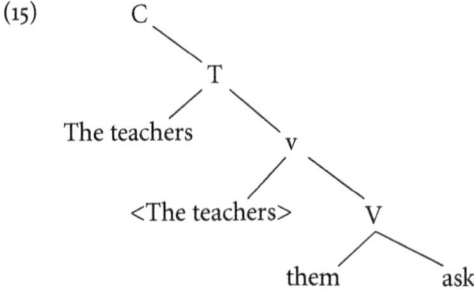

With this in place, let us turn in more detail to how these structures are spelled out. In Brody's system, a core principle is Mirror, which states that:

(16)   'The syntactic relation "X complement of Y" is identical to an inverse-order morphological relation "X specifier of Y" '(Brody 2000:42)

Brody's system gives us an agglutinative interpretation of the morphology, so that the morphological structure associated with (15) is:

(17)

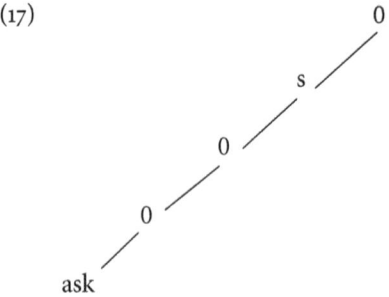

The second part of Brody's system is the diacritic mark, mentioned already, that specifies at which point of the extended projection (what Brody calls the extended word) the morphological form is pronounced. If v bears this mark, then the word *asks* will be spelled out 'in' v: that is, it will be spelled out after the subject and before the object.

I adopt this proposal here, combining it with the idea, already discussed, that overt, apparently atomic, morphemes may 'span' more than one category label. For example, the relevant compiled vocabulary item is [be V v T[past] C] <-> *was*, capturing the suppletion. Note however, that in addition to this, in the absence of any further stipulation, we also have to have [be V v T[past] C] vocabularized as be-0-ed-0, since each of these labels, at least in principle, and probably in this case in actuality, has a vocabularization independently of the others. The root [be-V] needs to be associated with *be*, [v] presumably can have a zero realization, as can [C], and T[past] has an *ed* realization with regular verbs.

Standardly, one would appeal to a blocking principle (Kiparsky 1973) to rule out *beed* as the past tense of *be*. However, given the framework outlined for dealing with variation, blocking cannot be a principle of grammar, it must rather be a fact about the routinization of structures that is emergent from the learning process, so both *was* and *beed* have to coexist as possible vocabularizations of this syntactic structure (where by vocabularization, I just mean the morphophonological properties associated with the built syntactic object). As well as the item *was* in the Compiled Vocabulary, the grammar allows the construction of a set of alternative forms, including the regular, but non-occurring, *beed*. In terms of the Combinatorial Variability model, they are both in the Pool of Variants, however *beed* is so low in that Pool of Variants (that is, its probability is minuscule compared to *was* because its frequency in the input during acquisition is so low) that although it matches the category label sequence, it is never (or very rarely) going to be put to use.

During development the child is using all of the syntactic resources given to her by UG to build up syntactic structures and to linearize them into morphological chunks. However, as the child's development progresses, variation emerges as a result of the tension between the child's generated structures and the evidence from the input. This variation then reduces as the child begins to attempt to match the frequency of her caregivers' variants (Smith et al. 2007). The evidence for the non-routinized version *beed* is very low, so the variation vanishes from the child's production (although not from the child's I-language). Blocking is then simply a side effect of this process: the routinized version is associated with such a high probability that the regular version is judged as unacceptable.

Given this, a non-suppletive structure like *asks* will also exist in (at least) two forms, a routinized version (or perhaps more than one of these, see later discussion) and the version that is the algorithmic output of the linearization of the syntax (the equivalent of *beed*).

In situations where the child's input is variable, more than one vocabularization of a single extended projection segment is possible: one of these will be the output of the morphological linearization of the structure on a label by label basis, but the child's input may consist of only routinized suppletive forms (for example, *was* and *were*), and so the child will have these forms matched to sequences of syntactic categories and keep them both in the pool of variants.

With this framework in mind, consider again the variable agreement in Buckie. Maintaining the approach sketched already, we have two vocabularizations for the root *ask* in the context where it has a plural NP subject: *ask* and *asks*. Adger and Smith (2010) show that an application of Adger's (2006) algorithm to the Buckie data results in a system that allows T with a NP[−singular] subject to bear, via agreement, a feature [−singular] associated with a zero phonology and a feature [−pronominal] associated with the phonology *−s*. This results in a choice of which is spelled out (see Adger and Smith 2010 for details), giving rise to the variable effect.

The latter of these forms itself has both a routinized and a generated source. The more frequent the verb *ask* is in the input, the more routinized its forms are. It is always possible to generate the *−s* form, (as indeed it is for the −0 form) by associating the relevant feature with the relevant morphophonological signal in essentially an agglutinative fashion, but there may be no routinized form. In the absence of such a routinized form, or if such a form is barely routinized, then there will only be one way to get to the *−s* form: linearize the syntax into an appropriate morphology. But a compiled Vocabulary Item is, of course, more immediately accessible, creating a downward pressure on the use of the syntactically computed version. In this way, the system captures the generalization that the variability between the forms is more robust for frequent verbs than for infrequent ones.

The approach also gives us a handle on the problem of internal factors. Indeed it begins to give shape to a possible theory of internal factors. Note that in the structures generated by the theory, C is actually part of the possible vocabularization of the verb. Although the verb is pronounced 'in' v, C is part of the projection line, and hence a vocabularization that results in a verbal *−s* form may span C, and hence the relative/non-relative specification of C will be relevant to that vocabularization.

Thinking about the higher proportion of *−s* in relatives in Buckie, we can see this as combinatorial variability applied not to a feature bundle at the head (i.e. X^0) level of structure, as in the theory presented in Adger (2006), but rather to a sequence of labels, where certain vocabulary items span the C that appears in a relative clause (C[rel]), while others don't. Putting aside the featural details covered in Adger (2006) and Adger and Smith (2010), we would have something like the following:[5]

---

[5] Actually the data we have shows this effect for subject relatives (we don't have the relevant data for object relatives), so the relevant features will have to include the phi-features on T shared with the subject, if, indeed the effect is restricted to just subjects.

(18) a. [V v T C[rel]] $< - > $ –s
      b. [V v T] $< - >$ –s
      c. [V v T] $< - >$ –0

Now in a non-relative, only (b) and (c) match the syntactic context, predicting a rough equality in the frequency of each variant. However, in a relative clause, all of (18a–c) are available for insertion, which predicts a higher frequency of the surface form –*s*. Of course, this is a toy example, as numerous other factors will be relevant (the featural content of the subject and hence T, possible aspectual information contributed by v (see e.g. Poplack and Tagliamonte 1989) or an Asp projection, the frequency of the verb root itself, etc.). However, even in this toy case we can see that the system constrains the set of potentially relevant internal factors to be those that are encoded in the projection line of the verb. We predict, then, that this kind of agreement variation cannot be affected by, for example, the number of the subject of a clause embedded by the agreeing verb, or the subject of a sentential subject of the verb. To my knowledge this has never been tested because it was thought to be so unlikely. The theory here makes a robust prediction that it is unlikely.

9.4 Language change and variability

Let me now turn to some broader issues connected to questions of acquisition and change. In terms of acquisition, of course, the approach outlined here allows us to connect fairly well with some of the work that has been done by proponents of Construction Grammar and their predecessors (e.g. Bybee 2006, and for work on variable agreement systems see, especially, Pietsch 2005), who have pointed out that there are frequency effects in the process of development that potentially have an impact on frequencies in corpora and on ease of processing. However, the Combinatorial Variability system allows us to do this while keeping the notion of frequency or probability firmly outside the grammar: it is relevant only for questions of lexical access during production. The grammar generates a restricted range of variants depending on the syntax (the Pool of Variants) and then some function will apply to the Pool of Variants to select a single one in any occasion of use. The structure of the Pool of Variants, how homonyms are distributed within it and whether there are both generated and routinized forms, has a direct impact on the frequency distribution of the surface forms. In addition, the Pool of Variants may be externally structured by the processing systems that effect lexical access: some items are generally highly routinized and easily accessible, so that when they appear within the Pool of Variants this property itself has an effect on whether that item is chosen.

On the question of language change there are two interesting phenomena I want to briefly mention here. The first is related to the loss of variability and the emergence of a possible parametric setting, while the second is related to the emergence of grammatical structuring in previously unstructured variation.

In Buckie there is a change happening in variable agreement. Older speakers use more −s forms with plural NP subjects than younger speakers as is seen in the following table, which includes all kinds of apparently singular agreement with plural subjects (*was, is,* other auxiliaries and main verbs) (chi squared value is 64.674, with two degrees of freedom and a two-tailed p value of less that 0.0001):[6]

(19)

Distribution −s in plural NP contexts by age. N = 380					
old		middle		young	
%	N	%	N	%	N
73	59	24	136	32	185

There's an interesting dip in the middle-aged speakers which appears in many of the variables which have been investigated for this corpus (see Smith 2000). Smith argues convincingly that this is due to a particular sociolinguistic factor connected to language standardization for middle-aged females which depresses the numbers.

What is interesting in the context of the approach developed here is that this change is affecting auxiliaries more than it is affecting main verbs:

(20)

Distribution −s with plural NP by age and verb type. N = 375						
	old (chi squared = 0.632, p = 0.4267)		middle (chi squared = 18.657, p less than 0.0001)		young (chi squared = 31.391, p less than 0.0001)	
	%	N	%	N	%	N
auxiliaries and copulae	56	32	69	92	71	130
main verbs	44	25	31	42	29	54

In the older generation, there is no significant effect of whether the −s appears on an auxiliary or on a main verb. In the middle and younger generations a marked shift appears and there is a highly significant effect of auxiliary versus main verbs. Given the theory of intra-personal variability sketched earlier, we can attribute this change to the frequency difference alluded to already (and in fact to the further effect of the suppletive forms of the auxiliaries, which implies that they must span the sequence of labels). Given that children track the frequencies of their caregivers with some exactitude (Smith et al. 2007), the existence of change in the frequencies of variables seems odd. However, at some point in development, children alter their frequency of use of particular variables. This is possibly connected to changes in how the developing

---

[6] This discussion reports joint empirical work with Jennifer Smith.

child fixes its linguistic affiliation, changing from its family to its peer group, or at least adding to its linguistic repertoire. Assume that children alter this frequency uniformly, depressing their use of a particular variant by a stable amount. In such a case, the more frequent verbs will maintain a higher proportion of use of the disfavoured variant, an effect heightened by the upward pressure exerted by the accessibility of these compiled forms. However, the grammatical system is still the same: the grammar still produces plural NP subjects with –s and we would predict that novel verbs, for example, would be grammatical in both forms. Low frequency verbs that are variable would arise just via application of the grammatical principles involving the linearization and vocabu-larization of category labels. However, given the frequency of auxiliaries, we then see a bifurcation between auxiliaries and main verbs that depends precisely on the fact that auxiliaries are in almost every sentence, whereas the different main verbs are much rarer. Now, when these speakers bring up the next generation, after iteration of the process, the variable agreement, depending on its sociolinguistic status, may become yet more disfavoured until at some point the bifurcation between auxiliary and non-auxiliary verbs becomes so sharp that acquirers attribute what was a variable distinc-tion to a categorical property of grammar (for example the auxiliary/main split). This would then correspond to the emergence of a parametric distinction between varieties that develops from the loss of variation interacting with frequency effects.

The other side of language change is explored in Cheshire et al. (2013). In that paper we examine the appearance of a new condition on variation in the speech of a group of London teenagers. The study shows that, for both the teenagers and the older gener-ation, both *who* and *that* can be used as subject relativizers with animate antecedents of the relative clause, just as in Standard English:

(21) apparently a chav is like someone that wears like big gold chains

(22) I'm the only one who's gone to college

As in Standard English, *who* does not appear with inanimates. However, although the frequency of *who* as a subject relativizer with animates is the same in each gener-ation, there are very different conditions on the use of *who*. The younger generation is statistically more likely to use *who* than *that* when the antecedent of the relative is an ongoing topic of the discourse. No such effect is found for the older generation, so what we see is the emergence of a structuring of the variation.[7]

We capture this behaviour within the kind of system developed here by specifying the relativizers as follows:

(23) a. [C, relativizer:+] <-> *that*
      b. [C, relativizer:+, animate:+] <-> *who*
      c. [C, relativizer:+, animate:+, topic:+] <-> *who*

---

[7] In fact, this effect only holds for the teenage group from multilingual inner-city London. Another group that was investigated, from a non-multilingual part of London, does not show this effect.

Any of these feature bundles can occur with an animate topical antecedent. However, when the antecedent is non-topical the vocabularizations in (23) are not all possible: non-topical antecedents can only appear with (a) (pronounced as *that*) and (b) (pronounced as *who*). Schematically, we have the following situation:

(24)   a. NP[animate:+, topic:+] (a) *that*, (b) *who*, (c) *who*
       b. NP[animate:+, topic:−] (a) *that*, (b) *who*

This captures the higher proportion of relativizers pronounced as *who* that occur when the antecedent is topical: since both (b) and (c) can be used with a topic, but only (b) with a non-topic, topics are expected to occur with *who* more often than with *that*, while there is no such expectation for non-topics.

Cheshire et al. argue that the availability of the topic feature in the specification of the relative complementizer (we take *who* just to be a realization of C) arises because of the multilingual environment the speakers develop their linguistic competence within, an environment which includes many languages which have grammatical marking for topicality and other information packaging features (see the paper for discussion). However, what is crucial for the discussion here is that the co-opting of this feature creates a differentiation in the Pool of Variants available to speakers in topical vs. non-topical syntactic environments, and hence a difference in the frequencies with which the variants are produced in the different environments. That imbalance may then lead to a change in the grammatical system, in this case actuated by the multilingual environment rather than the attenuation of grammatical contexts due to sociolinguistic pressure to differentiate generational usage patterns.

9.5 Conclusion

At a general architectural level, the system developed here and in the cited papers allows us to maintain a strictly modular grammatical architecture, which keeps the theory of syntax fairly pristine, both in terms of the mechanisms and operations involved, and in terms of the theoretical vocabulary over which they operate. Moreover, it provides the wherewithal for theoretical linguists to begin to address questions of individual variability, frequency, and the way that internal factors structure variability, topics that have not been addressed in generative grammar for many years. At the same time, this system connects well with current sociolinguistic work on language variability and change, and provides a viable grammatical architecture for sociolinguists interested in linking their work with linguistic theory.

10

Syntactic doubling and deletion as a source of variation

SJEF BARBIERS

10.1 Introduction

In syntactic doubling constructions (a subset of) the features of a morpheme are expressed phonologically twice. Examples of subject pronoun doubling in Flemish are given in (1) and (2). (1) is a case of full (i.e. identical) doubling, (2) a case of partial doubling.[1,2] This phenomenon is called doubling because the same semantic content can be expressed with a single instance of the subject pronoun, both in the relevant dialects and in the related standard language:

(1) **Zij**   heeft **zij**   daar niks   mee te maken.
    she.STRONG has   she.STRONG there nothing with to do
    'She has got nothing to do with it.'

(2) **Ze**   heeft **zij**   daar niks   mee te maken.
    she.WEAK has   she.STRONG there nothing with to do
    'She has got nothing to do with it.'

It has become clear recently that syntactic doubling is a pervasive phenomenon cross-linguistically.[3] The first hypothesis on which this chapter builds is that syntactic doubling is a core property of the syntax of natural language and that it is necessary for full interpretation at the level of Logical Form. More specifically, a local syntactic configuration of the type [a b a] is necessary to express monadic predication.[4]

---

[1] For a cross-linguistic overview of syntactic doubling constructions and possible analyses see Barbiers (2008).

[2] I do not discuss reduplication, cases in which (part of) a morpheme is doubled to form a new, complex morpheme, as this seems to involve a phenomenon with different characteristics. Cf. Inkelas and Zoll (2005).

[3] See Barbiers, Koeneman, Lekakou, and van der Ham (2008).

[4] See Barbiers (1995).

The second hypothesis of this chapter is that syntactic doubling is an important source of cross-linguistic and intralinguistic variation. Syntactic doubling involves local redundancy of features. As is well known, redundancy of such features often allows these features to be left unexpressed at the level of Phonological Form (PF) under the condition of local recoverability. Given this condition, a local syntactic doubling configuration [a b a] can give rise to three different realizations at PF: [a b a], [a b], [b a].[5] The PF-realizations [a b] and [b a] thus involve cases of hidden syntactic doubling.

If the hypothesis is correct that syntactic doubling is a core property of natural language and if the three PF-realization options are real, this defines a research programme in which we have to look for cases of [a b] and [b a] that in fact involve syntactic doubling underlyingly. The case study discussed in this chapter in support of the two hypotheses involves focus particle doubling in Dutch. In the unmarked case, a single focus particle is enough in Dutch (3) and (4), but the particle can be optionally doubled, as (5) shows:

(3) **Maar** één student ken   ik.
     only one student know I
     'I know only one student.'

(4) Eén student ken   ik **maar**.
     one student know I only
     'I know only one student.'

(5) **Maar** één student ken   ik **maar**.
     only one student know I only
     'I know only one student.'

I argue that the cases in which there is only one visible particle involve hidden focus particle doubling, where one of the particles is left unpronounced. The second particle is necessary to make full semantic interpretation of the first particle possible, and triggers movement of the first particle. Since that particle is attached to a constituent and can pied pipe this constituent, this gives rise to additional word order options.

10.2 Background: Some remarks on the theory of syntactic variation

The theoretical background of this chapter is the Minimalist Program, in particular the hypothesis that there is no variation in the syntactic module of the grammar.[6] According to this hypothesis, all apparent syntactic variation can be reduced to variation

---

[5] The option [b] is ruled out as [a] is not recoverable from that PF-realization. Similarly for the option [a].

[6] Chomsky (1995). The model of the mental grammar includes the following modules: Lexicon (a list of morphemes with their meanings and sound forms), Syntax (the module that contains the combinatorial rules), Logical Form (LF; the module that provides the semantic representation on the basis of the output structure from Syntax), and Phonological Form (PF; the module that spells out the syntactic structure phonologically).

in specification of morphemes in the Lexicon, in particular morphosyntactic feature specification, and to spell out options at PF. Optionality arises in the mapping from the syntactic module to PF, not in the syntactic module itself. A syntactic structure built in the syntactic component feeds into PF and LF. At PF, various spell out options are available for this syntactic structure. Consequently, the various spell out options are syntactically and semantically equivalent.

While variation in lexical specification and spell out options at PF constitute grammar internal sources of language variation, it is also plausible that there are grammar external, i.e. sociolinguistic factors determining part of the language variation patterns. In the domain of the Lexicon, and in particular phonotaxis, we are used to the distinction between possible and impossible words, and within the class of possible words between actual and non-realized words. Impossible words are words that the grammar rules out (e.g. English *rtap*), possible words are words that the grammar allows. Within the latter class, the actual words are in the Lexicon of the relevant language (e.g. English *part*), while the non-realized words (e.g. English *tarp*) are not in the Lexicon because they haven't been conventionalized.

If it is true that the grammar generates semantically and syntactically equivalent options, and if it is also the case that languages can pick one or more of these options but do not necessarily exploit all of them, then we have to assume that the structures resulting from PF spell out can be conventionalized and stored in the Lexicon as well. This implies that at the level of phrases we also have to distinguish between possible and impossible structures, and within the class of possible structures between actual and unrealized structures. This may perhaps seem controversial but the assumption is necessary anyway in view of proposals that verbs and pronouns are stored in the Lexicon as syntactic phrases.[7]

The distinction between actual and unrealized structures at the level of phrases has a very important methodological consequence. When a particular structure is reported to be absent in a language, we do not know in advance whether the pattern is impossible because it violates certain syntactic principles, or whether it is absent just because it has not been conventionalized. The distinction also raises an intriguing sociolinguistic question. Empirical domains for which spell out options at PF have been made plausible seem to differ with respect to whether the different options covary with sociolinguistic factors. For example, the different word order options in verb clusters correspond to particular geographic areas and are subject to normative pressure.[8] On the other hand, the various options found in multiple PP Extraposition and in the focus particle patterns discussed in this chapter do not seem to correlate with any sociolinguistic factor.[9] This deserves further research. It may be that frequency

---

[7] E.g. Hale and Keyser (1993); Déchaine and Wiltschko (2002).

[8] See Barbiers (2005).

[9] This issue has not been investigated systematically for the whole Dutch language area for PP Extraposition and focus particles, unlike verb cluster ordering. However, whereas we find ample claims in the literature about verb cluster orders that are typical for a particular geographical area before it was inves-

is playing a role here, and that the frequency of a particular option has to pass a certain threshold in order for it to be exploitable by sociolinguistic factors.

It is not unusual in the generative framework to abstract away from certain types of variation, in particular microvariation, as the main goal of the enterprise is to find those building principles that all language varieties have in common. However, if variation is a property that makes language special among cognitive systems,[10] if there are no macroparameters but only microparameters in the sense of Kayne (2000b), and if, as stated already, it is not a priori clear which part of grammatical variation can be explained by intragrammatical factors and which part by extragrammatical factors, it is essential to study grammatical variation in all its tiny details, both from an internal and external perspective.

10.3 Syntactic doubling as a problem for good language design

Syntactic doubling was defined above as in (6):

(6)   Syntactic doubling
      (A subset of) the features of a morpheme are expressed phonologically twice or more.

At first sight, syntactic doubling seems to violate major principles of good language design, or, in Minimalist terms, it seems to be an imperfection, as the duplicate does not seem to contribute to the semantic interpretation of the clause. The main claim of this section is that syntactic doubling is a core property of natural language syntax, necessary for full interpretation. For the sake of concreteness, we start with a number of examples of syntactic doubling.

10.3.1 Syntactic doubling in varieties of Dutch

Most examples of syntactic doubling in this section are from the Syntactic Atlas of the Dutch Dialects, a recent survey of 267 dialects of Dutch spoken in The Netherlands, Belgium, and north-western France.[11] The sentence in (7) is a case of doubling because

---

tigated systematically (see references cited in Barbiers, van der Auwera, Bennis, De Vogelaer, and Devos 2008), I am not aware of any such claims concerning PP Extraposition and focus particle patterns.

[10] The claim that variability is a characteristic property of language that sets it apart from other cognitive modules is forcefully made in Evans and Levinson (2009). The question is, however, whether other cognitive modules have been studied in a sufficiently fine-grained way to conclude that they lack inherent variability. Evans and Levinson's claim that the importance of variability is not recognized in the generative framework is false in view of the immense body of comparative phonological and syntactic work that has been carried out by generative grammarians and the goal of generative grammar to provide a theory of language variation.

[11] Barbiers et al. (2005); Barbiers, van der Auwera, Bennis, De Vogelaer, and Devos (2008). For a description of the project, see Barbiers and Bennis (2007) and Barbiers et al. (2007).

the nominal group contains both an indefinite determiner and the numeral ONE. Both have the features [indefinite], [singular]:[12]

(7) Indefinite determiner doubled by ONE
     Ge zet **unn**-en arig-en   vent (**in-ne**) N.Brabantish
     you are a.MASC strange.MASC guy   one.MASC
     'You are one strange guy.'

The colloquial Dutch phrases in (8) involve possessive doubling. In (8a–d) the possessors agree with the possessive pronoun in person, gender, and number. The phrase in (8d) is a case of partial doubling, as the possessor *hem* 'him' does not have the possessive feature of the possessive head *z'n* 'his'. These cases of agreement, in fact all cases of agreement, fall under the header of syntactic doubling given the definition in (6):[13,14]

(8) Possessive doubling
     a. **Jan** **z'n** boek
        John his book
        'John's book'

     b. **Maria** **d'r** boek
        Mary her book
        'Mary's book'

     c. **de jongens hun** boek
        the boys   their book
        'the boys' book'

     d. **hem** **z'n** boek
        him his book
        'his book'

The sentence in (9) is a case of optional partial complementizer doubling. The complementizer *dat* 'that' has the features [finite, subordinate], while the complementizer *of* 'if' has the features [Q, finite, subordinate]:

(9) Complementizer doubling
     Ik weet niet wie (**of**) (**dat**) er   komt. Coll. Dutch
     I   know not   who if   that   there comes
     'I don't know who will come.'

---

[12] See Barbiers (2007) for a more precise analysis of the features of the indefinite determiner and ONE. See SAND I, map 80a, for the geographic distribution of this and related constructions.

[13] The case feature of *hem* 'him', if it is one, is not doubled here. The hidden assumption w.r.t. the phrases in (8) is that the possessive pronoun doubles the immediately preceding constituent. Given cases like (8a–c) it is clear that it cannot be the other way around.

[14] See Weiß (2008) for similar constructions in varieties of German.

The complementizers IF and THAT are between brackets which means that they can but do not have to be there.[15] The fact that one or both complementizers can be silent in this construction is remarkable as complementizer deletion is normally impossible in varieties of Dutch. The deletability of complementizers here plausibly has to do with the presence of another complementizer and *wie* 'who'.

Aspectual auxiliaries can double in certain West Flemish dialects. In (10), we find doubling of *gaan*:[16]

(10)   Aspectual auxiliary doubling

    da-n-ze   in den lak **(goan) goan** vissen   West-Flemish

    that.PL-they in the lake go   go   fish

    'that they go fishing in the lake'

Cases like (11) of so called periphrastic DO can also be considered to involve doubling:[17]

(11)   Periphrastic DO

    Ik **doe** de kopjes **afwassen** Zeeuws, N-Brabantish. D. Limburg

    I do the cups   wash

    'I'll wash the cups.'

Particularly interesting is (partial) wh-pronoun doubling, of which Dutch has five different variants, given in (12): with one wh-element (12a), with two identical wh-elements (12b), with two distinct wh-pronouns (12c), with a wh-element and a relative pronoun (12d,e). Optionality arises here too, as there are many speakers who allow more than one option. The variants in (12a–c) do not have a clear geographic distribution, while the variants in (12d,e) occur in a very restricted area:

(12)   WH-pronoun doubling (Barbiers et al. 2009)

    a. **Wie** denk je   dat ik gezien heb?   Dutch

       who think you that I seen   have

       All: 'Who do you think I saw?'

    b. **Wie** denk je   **wie** ik gezien heb?   Coll. Dutch

       who think you who I seen   have

    c. **Wat** denk je   **wie** ik gezien heb?   Coll. Dutch

       what think you who I seen   have

    d. **Wie** denk je   **die** ik gezien heb?   Restr. areas

       who think you REL I   seen   have

---

[15] See SAND I, map 16a for the geographic distribution of these variants.

[16] See Haegeman (1990), van Riemsdijk (2002).

[17] See SAND II, maps 41b–43b for the geographic distribution of the periphrastic DO construction in declarative, imperative, and interrogative clauses.

e. **Wat** denk je **die** ik gezien heb?   Restr. areas
   what think you REL I seen   have

Similar doubling patterns occur in long relativization. Here we find a clearer geographic distribution:[18]

(13) Relative pronoun doubling
      Dit is de man **die** ik denk **die** ik gezien heb.
      this is the man REL I think REL I seen   have
      'This is the man that I think that I saw.'

There is no correlation between wh-doubling patterns and relative pronoun doubling patterns, e.g. full (identical) doubling of wh-pronouns (*wie-wie*) does not occur in the same dialects in which full (identical) doubling of relative pronouns (*die-die*) occurs.[19]

Doubling is not restricted to two elements. Many of the doubling types illustrated already, allow for tripling or even quadrupling. An extreme example is the combination of subject pronoun doubling, complementizer agreement, and verbal agreement in (14), in which the plural feature is expressed four times:

(14) Subject pronoun doubling and agreement
      da-**n**-**ze**-**ziender**   rijker zij-**n**   West Flemish
      that.PL-they.WEAK-they.STRONG richer are.PL
      'that they are richer'

All of these doubling constructions seem to violate principles of good language design and all of them raise similar analytical and theoretical questions. Yet, it is unlikely that the various doubling cases represent a unified phenomenon. Some seem to be the result of purely formal syntactic requirements, e.g. wh-doubling and subject pronoun doubling, which have been analysed as multiple spell out of copies in a movement chain.[20] In other types of doubling constructions, semantic interpretation is playing a role too, as in the focus particle doubling construction illustrated in (15), to be discussed later:

(15) Focus particle doubling
      (**Maar**) twee boeken ken   ik (**maar**)   Coll. Dutch
      only   two books   know I only
      'I know only two of the books.'

---

[18] See SAND I, maps 85a,b. For a full description and formal analysis of this variation, see Boef (2013).
[19] See SAND I.
[20] Cf. Barbiers et al. (2009) for an analysis of Wh-doubling, and van Craenenbroeck and van Koppen (2008) for an analysis of subject pronoun doubling along these lines.

10.3.2 *How doubling seems to violate good language design*

If we were to design a syntax for natural language from scratch, the five principles in Table 10.1 would be good criteria for the quality of this design. Syntactic doubling seems to violate all of them. The first principle, Universality or the Universal Base Hypothesis, says that all languages have the same syntactic structure.[21] The fact that syntactic doubling can be optional within a language variety, or completely ungrammatical in a closely related language variety contradicts this principle if it is to be analysed as a phenomenon in the syntactic component of the grammar.

The second principle, Compositionality seems to be violated too.[22] If the task of the syntactic module is to combine simple meanings of individual morphemes into complex meanings of phrases and sentences, then the presence of semantically superfluous morphemes is unexpected, and languages without (particular) syntactic doubling constructions show that such doubling morphemes are superfluous indeed. Put differently, if a language has a particular construction with and without doubling, the variant with doubling is expected to add something to the semantic interpretation.

The third principle says more or less the same but now from a syntactic perspective. If we adopt the Minimalist hypothesis that syntax is economical, not containing any superfluous elements or steps in the derivation, syntactic doubling is a problem. A construction with a doubled pronoun seems to be less economical than the same construction with a single occurrence of this pronoun.

The fourth principle, the principle of Explicitness, says that a syntactic construction should not contain any hidden elements. If the non-doubling counterpart of a doubling construction contains elements that are not spelled out at PF, then variation in doubling is a problem for this principle too. We know, of course, that there can be a lot of hidden material in a sentence, so this principle is violated massively by constructions other than doubling. So the questions to be asked here are: (i) When/how can syntax deviate from maximal explicitness? (ii) Does doubling satisfy the principle

---

TABLE 10.1. **Principles of good language design**

I	Universality	Strongest version: All languages have the same syntactic structure
II	Compositionality	Every step and every element in a syntactic structure directly contributes to semantic interpretation
III	Economy	No superfluous derivational steps or elements
IV	Explicitness	No hidden elements
V	Uniqueness	For each type of semantic relation (e.g. predication), there is exactly one syntactic configuration; => no optionality

---

[21] Cf. Cinque (1999).   [22] Cf. Frege (1892).

of Explicitness? We will see later that the answer to the latter question is yes and that the non-doubling counterparts of these doubling constructions can be considered as maximally explicit too because they satisfy a condition of local recoverability of hidden material.

The fifth and final principle of good language design is what we may call Uniqueness. According to this principle, every type of semantic relation corresponds to exactly one type of syntactic configuration. The Uniformity of Theta Assignment Hypothesis is an instance of this principle.[23] If that principle holds for the syntax of natural language, and if doubling is a syntactic phenomenon, then the intralinguistic optionality and cross-linguistic variability of doubling is a problem, as it shows that one semantic relation may correspond to more than one syntactic configuration.

10.4 Syntactic doubling as a core property of good language design

10.4.1 Origins of syntactic doubling

The task is now to develop an analysis of syntactic doubling such that it does not violate these five principles of good language design. This analysis should also explain why syntactic doubling is such a pervasive phenomenon, possible with every functional element in language.[24] Rather than taking it as an imperfection, I take it to be a core property of natural language syntax. Analyses of doubling based on this assumption will take the form of (16):

(16)   The computational system requires doubling under conditions to be specified. In such conditions, non-doubling arises when one or more duplicates are left unexpressed at PF under the condition of local recoverability.

We will see that an analysis based on (16) can satisfy all the principles of good language design described in section 10.3.2. An example of this type of analysis is the analysis of doubling in movement chains in Nunes (2004). In his approach, syntactic doubling is the normal case because the computational system requires elements to be copied to positions higher up in the structure. The fact that multiple spell out of copies in movement chains is nevertheless rare is due to Antisymmetry requirements.[25]

Nunes' analysis roughly works as follows. In a long wh-question such as *Who do you think I have met?* the wh-element that belongs to the embedded clause is copied up to the initial position of the embedded clause and subsequently, it is copied up to the

---

[23] Cf. Baker (1988a).

[24] See the papers in Barbiers, Koeneman, Lekakou, and van der Ham (2008). In the language varieties discussed there, syntactic doubling usually involves at least one functional element. Doubling involving two lexical elements seems to be much more rare, the only case reported for these language varieties being lexical verb doubling in verb fronting constructions as we find it, e.g. in Spanish and Hungarian (cf. Vicente 2007).

[25] Cf. Kayne (1994).

first position of the main clause. The computational reasons for this have been amply discussed in the literature and need not concern us here. The result of the two copying operations is schematically given in (17):

(17)   [MAIN CLAUSE wh   ...   [EMBEDDED CLAUSE wh   ....   wh   ...]]

If no other conditions were active, the spell out of (17) would be **Who do you think** **who I have met who**, with tripling of *who*. However, according to the antisymmetry linearization algorithm, a structure such as (17) cannot be spelled out. The reason is that the three wh-copies count as one and the same element, and this element is both hierarchically higher and lower than the intervening material. This provides a contradictory linearization instruction to the spell out component and the structure is ruled out. The structure is saved when the lower copies of wh are deleted, i.e. remain silent at PF.

Thus, in Nunes' analysis doubling is the normal case but it is often obscured because the linearization component requires most copies to be deleted, which is possible because they are part of the same chain and hence recoverable. In those cases where we see actual doubling at the surface, an offending copy has survived due to a morphological reanalysis process (e.g. morphological reanalysis of the wh-copy with an embedded complementizer) which makes it distinct from the higher copy.

An approach of the type in (16) for configurations that are more local than wh-chains is proposed in Barbiers (1995). The central hypothesis of this proposal is that the syntactic configuration in (18) is the basic unit of semantic interpretation:

(18)   Basic unit for semantic interpretation

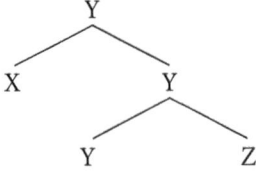

Semantic interpretation: Y(X,Z), where X ≠ Z => dyadic predication
e.g. [X *the book* [Y *on* [Z *the table*]]]

If it is true that (18) is the basic unit for interpretation, this implies that every predicative head has exactly two arguments. This is OK for dyadic predication, but a problem for monadic predication relations such as between *blue* and *the flowers* in *The flowers are blue*, where *blue* seems to have only one argument: blue(the flowers).

By hypothesis, the dyadic predication relation in (18) is reduced to a monadic one if the two arguments of the predicative head are formally identical. This is the case if argument X is a copy of argument Z, as in (19), or if Z is an agreement morpheme that has a subset of the morphosyntactic features of X, as in (20):[26]

---

[26] Movement from complement to specifier position violates the anti-locality condition of Grohman (2003). Explanations for empirical phenomena based on the anti-locality condition should be reconsidered if the hypothesis proposed here is correct.

(19)

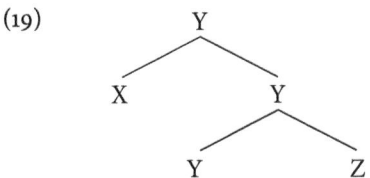

the flowers blue   ~~the flowers~~
Interpretation: Y(X,Z), where X = Z => monadic predication

(20)

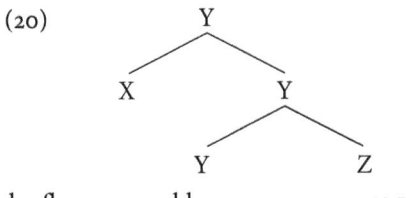

les fleurs.FEM.PL bleu   –es.FEM.PL
Interpretation: Y(X,Z), where features of X = features of Z => monadic predication

Thus, the configurations in (19) and (20) are more local cases of syntactic doubling. This doubling arises as a consequence of the principle in (21):

(21)   Principle of Semantic Interpretation (hypothesis)
   (i) Dyadic predication Y(X,Z) if X immediately c-commands Y, and Y immediately c-commands Z.
   (ii) Monadic predication Y(X) if X immediately c-commands Y, and Y immediately c-commands Z, and the features of Z are a subset of the features of X, or the converse.[27]

10.4.2 Syntactic doubling as a source of syntactic variation

According to the hypothesis discussed in the previous section, monadic predication always comes with doubling, either because a predicative head takes an argument as its specifier and an agreement morpheme agreeing with this specifier as its complement, or because the complement of the predicative head is copied to its specifier. Both configurations in (19) and (20) involve local redundancy. Local redundancy may give rise to unexpressed elements at the level of spell out. Thus the phenomenon of pro-drop can be interpreted as a case in which a subject pronoun in SpecIP is not pronounced under (partial) formal identity with an agreement morpheme on the finite verb in I. Similarly, we expect this to be possible in configurations such as (19) and (20). The

---

[27] In this chapter 'subset' should not be understood as proper subset. So the features of a morpheme are a subset of the features of another morpheme if the feature bundles of the two morphemes are identical, or if the features of one morpheme are a proper subset of the features of the other morpheme.

interaction between semantic (LF-)requirements and spell out (PF-)requirements is summarized in (22):

(22)   Doubling and Deletion Hypothesis (DaD)
    (i) Local syntactic doubling is necessary for monadic predication.
    (ii) Redundant (i.e. doubled) features can be silent at PF if locally recoverable.

The local redundancy in the configurations in (19) and (20) makes invisibility of the element in complement or specifier position possible or, if linearization requirements play a role here as well, even necessary. As a result, there will be many cases of hidden doubling in natural languages.

The DaD Hypothesis in (22) makes clear predictions with respect to what kinds of cross-linguistic syntactic variation we expect to find. It also makes it possible to reduce head marking, dependent marking, and juxtaposition to one general configuration. Bouchard (2003) argues that head marking, dependent marking, juxtaposition, and superimposition are the only four logically possible ways to express a semantic relation between two elements in a linear structure. According to him, the restriction to these four options has nothing to do with principles of Universal Grammar, i.e. innate building principles specific for language. In a linear structure, there simply are no other ways to express a relation between two elements.

I put superimposition aside as it involves the complex interaction between two subsystems, e.g. syntax and tone. From the perspective of (22), then, the remaining three, head marking, dependent marking, and juxtaposition, can all be reduced to the same basic configuration in which the two arguments of a predicative head are formally identical. These three possibilities follow from the Principle of Semantic Interpretation (21), a good candidate for UG.

The typology predicted for head marking is now as given in (23). Where the typology says 'languages' one could also read 'constructions', as a language may choose option (i) for construction type C1 and option (ii) for construction type C2:

(23)   Predicted typology for head marking
    (i) Languages without agreement on Y: The features of Z (= agreement) are a subset of the features of X (= specifier), so Z can be PF-silent (e.g. Chinese).
    (ii) Pro-drop languages: The features of X (= specifier) are a subset of the features of Z (= agreement), so X can be PF-silent (e.g. Italian).
    (iii) Languages with agreement and without pro-drop (both X and Z spelled out) (e.g. German).
    (iv) No languages that lack both pronouns and agreement: violation of recoverability.

For dependent marking, something similar holds if the configuration of dependent marking is also a doubling configuration, as in (24). In this configuration, the feature Dative is locally present twice, once in a preposition, once as a Case feature:

(24) Morphological case as doubling

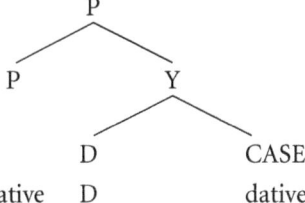

This predicts the typology in (25). Again, 'languages' can also be read as 'constructions':

(25) Predicted typology for dependent marking
    (i) Languages without Case and with prepositions (e.g. English)
    (ii) Languages without P but with Case (e.g. Finnish)
    (iii) Languages with Case and prepositions (e.g. German)
    (iv) No languages that lack both Case and prepositions: violation of recoverability

Finally, juxtaposition is predicted to come in three types. Given the configuration in (19), repeated here as (26), either the complement or the specifier can be spelled out, or both:

(26)

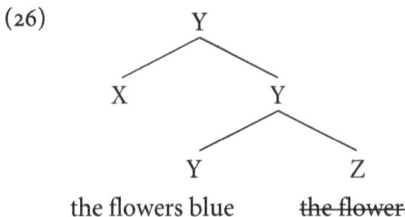

This predicts the typology in (27). Again, 'languages' can be read as 'constructions'.

(27) Predicted typology for juxtaposition
    (i) Languages that spell out the complement (e.g. VO languages; English)
    (ii) Languages that spell out the specifier (e.g. OV languages; Japanese)
    (iii) Languages that spell out both
    (iv) No languages where both specifier and complement are silent: violation of recoverability

As far as I know, languages of type (27-iii) that overtly spell out both the complement and the specifier in the configuration in (26) do not exist. If so, this directly follows from Antisymmetry. As was discussed already, for copies in a movement chain, Antisymmetry in principle rules out spell out of more than one copy as this would lead to contradictory input for the linearization component. Only if one of the copies undergoes morphological reanalysis with some head or if the two copies are not completely identical (e.g. one a pronoun, the other a full DP) is overt doubling expected to be possible. Some examples to which this analysis of juxtaposition has been applied include optional PP Extraposition as VP Intraposition and word order variation in verb clusters in Dutch.[28]

10.4.3 Diachronic cycles

The typologies in (23), (25), (27) are likely to form the base of diachronic cycles such as the Jespersen cycle.[29] From this perspective, such cycles are the result of two counteracting forces. The Principle of Semantic Interpretation requires the argument in a monadic predication relation to be structurally present twice, while such local redundancy can or must be avoided at PF. It can be avoided because PF-deletion of features is possible if the features are locally recoverable. It must be avoided in the case of full identity because this causes problems for linearization, as was discussed already. As soon as an element in such a configuration loses a feature due to independent processes, e.g. paradigmatic impoverishment or phonological weakening, this loss must be compensated for by the other element.

Thus, consider the following hypothetical scenario. Suppose a language has full and distinct person and number specification on the finite verb for each member of the paradigm such that subject pronouns can be silent.[30] Next, person inflection is lost in the plural by an independent morphological or phonological process, possibly under the influence of language contact. The consequence of this loss is that [person] has to be overtly expressed elsewhere, on the subject pronoun. If this subject pronoun also has a [plural] feature, the inflection on the verb now becomes fully redundant and is expected to disappear, i.e. to be no longer expressed phonologically. Similarly, if an overt morphosyntactic distinction is lost in the pronominal paradigm this is expected to be compensated for by an inflectional ending that represents the lost feature.

This scenario for diachronic cycles allows for various stages to become stable: if nothing happens to the inflectional paradigm, a language will retain the pro-drop property. If nothing happens to the pronominal paradigm, the verbal inflection will not change.

10.4.4 How syntactic doubling satisfies principles of good language design

If we handle syntactic doubling in the way described, then all principles of good language design are satisfied. One syntactic configuration underlies all monadic and

---

[28] Cf. Barbiers (1995) for PP Extraposition and Barbiers (2005) for word order variation in verb clusters.

[29] Cf. Jespersen (1917).

[30] This scenario presupposes that the relation between a subject pronoun and a finite verb involves monadic predication. This has to be worked out technically, which cannot be done in the present chapter due to limits of space.

dyadic predication relations in all languages, so Universality and Uniqueness are guaranteed and there is no optionality in the syntactic module of the grammar.

Monadic predication requires a local doubling configuration, so both elements in the doubling configuration contribute to semantic interpretation; neither of them is superfluous. Syntactic doubling therefore does not violate Compositionality.

There are no superfluous steps or elements in the derivation of monadic predication relations, so syntactic doubling conforms to the principle of Economy.

Finally, the derivation complies with the principle of Explicitness. Hidden elements only occur under local recoverability, i.e. a specifier of a head can be silent if the formally identical complement of that head is spelled out and vice versa.

10.5 Focus particle doubling in Dutch: A case of criterial doubling

So far we have identified two types of doubling. The first type arises when a constituent is copied to higher positions in a movement chain, such as in long wh-questions. Doubling is standard in such chains, but only becomes visible at PF if it does not violate conditions on linearization. The second type of doubling arises in monadic predication configurations, in which two arguments of a predicative head must be formally identical. In this section, we analyse a third type of doubling, criterial doubling which combines properties of both types of doubling.

Here is the analysis in a nutshell.[31] Focus particles such as *ook* 'also', *alleen* 'only', *zelfs* 'even', *maar* 'only', *al* 'already' are relations between two arguments.[32] When a focus particle is attached to a constituent (e.g. DP, PP, CP), a problem for full interpretation arises, as in such a configuration the particle has only one argument. A second particle is attached to a constituent that can serve as the second argument of the lower particle, e.g. to TP. The first particle is then copied into the Spec of the second particle, optionally pied piping the argument to which it was attached first. In the resulting configuration, the two particles share the two arguments, a case of absorption.[33] Because there is a particle in the head and in the specifier of the higher focus particle projection, spell out options arise. The idea that focus particle configurations should involve doubling was first proposed on theoretical grounds in Bayer (1996) for German and later in Kayne (2000b) for English. In both cases this involves abstract doubling, because German and English do not seem to have visible focus particle doubling. Overt focus

---

[31] This analysis was first presented at CGSW 18, 2003 at Durham. A squib version of this analysis appeared as Barbiers (2010).

[32] The semantics of focus particles is more complex than can be discussed in this chapter that concentrates on syntactic variation. For semantic analyses of focus particles see Rooth (1985, 1992); von Stechow (1991); Krifka (1992). Cf. Sudhoff (2010) for a comparison of these analyses. In the main text, I take the argument of a focus particles to be the constituent to which it is attached. This constituent may but need not coincide with the focus of the focus particle. The only requirement is that the focus has to be inside the argument of the focus particle.

[33] Cf. May (1985); Haegeman (1995), among others.

particle doubling in Dutch suggests that these ideas are on the right track. The analysis provided in this section also solves the distributional paradox that has been discussed many times in the literature.[34]

10.5.1 Introduction to focus particle doubling

The Dutch focus particle *maar* 'only' can be attached to constituents such as DP (28a), PP (28b) and to extended projections of the verb (28c). In traditional terms, the latter are cases of adverbial use, in which *maar* 'only' expresses durativity or repitition:

(28) a. [**Maar** [DP één boek]] ken   ik.
          only   one book   know I
          'I know only one book.'

     b. [PP **Maar** in één boek] staat   een handtekening.
              only in one book stands a   signature

     c. Jan   bleef **maar** praten.
          John kept   only   talking.
          'John kept on talking.'

Since [*maar één boek*] precedes the finite verb in verb second position and only one constituent can precede the finite verb in Dutch, [*maar één boek*] must be a constituent, and *maar* must be attached to the nominal group (DP) [*één boek*].[35]

When *maar* 'only' is attached to a DP or PP, it is optionally doubled elsewhere in the clause, as in (29a,b). This is a genuine case of doubling, not a case in which an adnominal or ad-adpositional focus particle is combined with an adverbial focus particle. As is shown in (29c,d), *maar* 'only' in its adverbial use cannot be combined with stative verbs such as *kennen* 'know' and *hebben* 'have', for reasons that need not concern us here. Since (29a) also involves the verb *kennen* 'know', we can conclude that the second instance of *maar* 'only' is possible because of the first instance of *maar* 'only'. The brackets indicate that one of the instances of *maar* 'only' can be left out without changing the meaning of the clause:

(29) a. (**Maar**) één boek ken   ik (**maar**).
          only   one book know I   only
          'I know only one book.'

     b. (**Maar**) aan één boek heb ik (**maar**) iets.
          only   on one book have I   only   something
          'Only one book is useful for me.'

---

[34] Cf. Büring and Hartmann (2001); Bayer (1996); Kayne (2000); Bouma et al. (2007), among many others.

[35] Contra Büring and Hartmann (2001). Read further in this section for a short discussion of the distributional paradox.

c. *Ik ken   het boek **maar**.
   I   know the book only

d. *Ik heb **maar** iets   aan het boek.
   I   have only   something on the book

There are other focus particles in Dutch that can be doubled, among others *wel* 'as many as' (30a) and *al* 'already' (30b):

(30) a. **(Wel)**   vijftig boeken heeft hij **(wel)**.
            as many as fifty   books   has he as many as / AFFIRM
            I. 'He has as many as fifty books.'
            II. 'He does have as many as fifty books.'

      b. **Al**   tien boeken heeft hij **al**.
           already ten books has he already
           'He already has ten books.'

There are two classes of focus particles in Dutch. Class 1 focus particles (31-i) allow identical doubling, class 2 focus particles (31-ii) do not allow identical doubling. That class 2 focus particles do not allow identical doubling is illustrated in (32). Interestingly, members of these two classes can be combined, and then the order is always fixed. The linear order is always class 2 particle – class 1 particle. This is illustrated in (33):

(31) Two classes of focus particles in Dutch:
      (i) Class 1 allows doubling: a.o. *maar* 'only', *wel* 'as much as', *al* 'already' (cf. 30)
      (ii) Class 2 does not allow doubling: a.o. *zelfs* 'even', *ook* 'also', *alleen* 'only' (cf. 32)
      (iii) Class 1 and Class 2 particles can be combined but only in the linear order
            Class 2 – Class 1 (cf. 33).

(32) a. **Alleen** Jan ken   ik (*****alleen**)
          only   John kn018 I   only

      b. **Ook** Jan ken   ik (*****ook**).[36]
          also John know I   also

      c. **Zelfs** Jan ken ik (*****zelfs**).
          even John know I   even

---

[36] Doubling of *ook* 'also' seems to be sometimes possible, as in (i).

(i) Nu   wil   ik het ook weten ook.
    now want I it also know also
    'I won't give up until I know it.'

Since examples of this type involve two instances of adverbial *ook* 'also', not combinations of adnominal or ad-adpositional and adverbial *ook* 'also', they are probably irrelevant for this chapter, and I put them aside.

(33) a. alleen maar 'only only'   - *maar alleen
        zelfs   al   'even already' - *al   zelfs

      b. Hij is nu ook al   / *al   ook boos op haar.
         he is now also already / already also angry at her
         'He is even angry at her now.'

The analysis that I will give of this phenomenon is that focus particles of class 1 are
functional heads in the extended verbal domain that trigger movement of focus particles of class 1 or 2 to their specifier positions. Since specifiers always precede heads,
the predicted linear order is Class 2 – Class 1.

10.5.2 *Focus particle doubling and the distributional paradox*

It is well known from the literature that focus particles show a distributional paradox
in German, Dutch, and English.[37] The paradox is that focus particles seem to be able
to attach to a constituent when it is in sentence initial position but not when it is
elsewhere in the clause. This is illustrated in (34). In (34a), the particle *ook* 'also' and
the PP [op Marie] precede the finite verb. If the generalization is correct that in verb
second languages like Dutch, maximally one constituent can precede the finite verb,
ook 'also' and the PP must form one constituent, so *ook* 'also' must be attached to this
PP. However, (34b) seems to indicate that the particle cannot be attached to PP. A
similar paradox occurs with *maar* 'only' (34c,d) and all other Dutch focus particles:

(34) a. **Ook** [pp op Marie] is hij boos   geweest.
         also at Mary   is he angry been
         'He has also been angry at Mary.'

      b. Hij is boos (*ook) [pp op Marie] geweest.
         he is angry also   at Mary   been

      c. **Maar** [pp op één jongen] is hij boos   geweest.
         only   at one boy   is he angry been

      d. Hij is boos (*maar) [pp op één jongen] geweest.
         he is angry only   at one boy   been

One of the solutions in the literature is that focus particles cannot attach to constituents at all and that in cases like (34a,c) the particle is attached to the entire clause
(CP), not to the clause initial constituent.[38] Such an analysis has various disadvantages,
which I mention briefly here: (i) It forces us to give up the generalization that only one
constituent can precede the finite verb in main clauses in verb second languages like
Dutch and German, an otherwise quite robust generalization; (ii) It wrongly predicts

---

[37] See Bouma et al. (2007) for a recent overview and references.
[38] Cf. Büring and Hartmann (2001).

that a clause initial focus particle can take the entire clause as its semantic argument in sentences like (35b); (iii) It wrongly predicts that a clause initial focus particle always takes wide scope with respect to the verb or quantified subjects (36):

(35) a. Jan heeft gewandeld en ook heeft hij gezwommen.
      John has walked and also has he swum
      'John has walked and also has he swum.'

    b. *Jan heeft gewandeld en ook hij heeft gezwommen.
      John has walked and also he has swum.

(36) Alleen vlees at niemand.
    only meat ate nobody
    I. only > no one: 'Meat was the only thing that nobody ate.'
    II. no one > only: 'There was nobody who only ate meat.'

My solution to the distributional paradox is the opposite, and in the spirit of Bayer (1996). I would like to propose that focus particles can attach to every constituent of the right semantic type, but that focus particles when attached to a constituent have to move to find the second argument. The derivation goes like this. In (37a), *Hij is boos ook op Marie geweest* lit. he is angry also at Mary been, [ook op Marie] 'also at Mary' is a constituent. The sentence is ungrammatical not because *ook* 'also' attaches to the PP, but because *ook* 'also' cannot stay in that position. It has to move to some high position in the middle field, as indicated in (37b). When it does that, it can pied-pipe the prepositional phrase, as in (37c), and the order will be *Hij is ook op Marie boos geweest*. From that position, the particle or the particle and the PP can move up to clause initial position (37d,e):

(37) a. *Hij is   boos [ook [~PP~op Marie]] geweest.
      he is   angry also   at Mary been

    b. Hij is ook   boos [o̶o̶k̶ [~PP~op Marie]] geweest.
      he is also   angry also   at Mary been

    c. Hij is [ook [~PP~op M.]] boos [o̶o̶k̶ [~PP~o̶p̶ M̶.̶]]   geweest.
      he is also at Mary angry also   at Mary been

    d. Ook is hij o̶o̶k̶   boos [o̶o̶k̶ [~PP~op Marie]] geweest.
      also is he also   angry also   at Mary been

    e. [Ook [~PP~ op Marie]] is hij {o̶o̶k̶ {̶~PP~o̶p̶ M̶a̶r̶i̶e̶}̶}̶ boos
      also   at Mary is he also   at Mary   angry
      {o̶o̶k̶ {̶~PP~ o̶p̶ M̶a̶r̶i̶e̶}̶}̶ geweest.
      also at Mary   been

The position in the middle field to which the focus particle must move can be made visible by introducing one of the category 1 particles, the ones that can double. This is given in (38a). In (38a), the particle *ook* 'also' has moved to the specifier of the projection of *al* 'already'. In (38b), *ook op Marie* 'also at Mary' as a whole has moved to this specifier position:

(38) a. Hij is ook **al**   boos ~~ook~~ op Marie geweest.
         he is also already angry also at Mary been
         'He has even been angry at Mary.'

      b. Hij is [ook op Marie] **al**   boos ~~[ook op Marie]~~ geweest.
         he is also at Mary already angry also at Mary   been.

Evidence that the triggering focus particle (*al* 'already' in (38a)) is a functional head while the moved focus particle (*ook* 'also' in (38b)) is a constituent in the specifier of that head comes from fronting. A functional head cannot be fronted in Dutch, while an element in specifier position can. Exactly this contrast we find between class 1 and class 2 focus particles, as illustrated in (39):

(39) a. *Al   is hij ook   op Marie ~~al~~   boos geweest.
          already is he already at Mary already angry been

      b. Ook is hij   op Marie al   boos geweest.
         even at he   at Mary already angry been

The derivations for (38) are given in (40):

(40) (38a): [....[ₐₗP   ook   [ₐₗ al [ₐₚ boos [ₚₚ ~~ook~~ [ₚₚ op Marie [....[39]
      (38b): [....[ₐₗP [ₚₚ ook op Marie] [ₐₗ al [ₐₚ boos [ₚₚ ~~ook~~[ₚₚ ~~op Marie~~ [....

Focus particle doubling arises when the moving particle is identical to the triggering particle. This is illustrated for *maar* 'only' in (41). In (41a), *maar* 'only' has carried along the PP *op één jongen* 'at one boy' in its way up. Again, overt doubling is not obligatory, as the variants of (41a) in (41b,c) show:

(41) a. Hij is **maar** op één jongen **maar** boos geweest.
         he is only   at one boy   only angry been

      b. Hij is **maar** op één jongen boos geweest.
         he is only   at one boy   angry been

      c. Hij is op één jongen **maar** boos geweest.
         he is at one boy   only angry been

The derivations of (41a–c) are given in (42). In all three cases, [ₚₚ *maar op één jongen*] 'only at one boy' is in the specifier of *maar* 'only'. In (42a), both the head and the

---

[39] One could assume that even in this derivation the PP is pied-piped by the focus particle, but spelled out in its base position and not in its landing site (cf. Bobaljik 2002 for such spell out options). However, if that were possible, we would expect it to be possible for the moved focus particle to be spelled out in its base position as well, contrary to fact.

specifier contain an instance of *maar* 'only'. Thus, one instance of *maar* 'only' is locally redundant and can be silent at PF. In (41b) the head *maar* is deleted. In (41c), *maar* in the specifier is deleted:

(42)   Derivations of (41a–c):

    a. [.... [$_{maarP}$ [$_{PP}$ maar op één jongen] [$_{maar}$ maar [$_{AP}$ boos [$_{PP}$ ~~maar op één jongen~~ [....

    b. (42a) + PF deletion of second *maar*

    c. (42a) + PF deletion of first *maar*

As we have seen in (38a) and (40), a class 2 focus particle can move to the specifier of the higher focus particle leaving behind the constituent to which is was attached in the base structure. If the derivations in (42) are correct, a class 1 particle should also be able to do this. The result with identical doubling is ungrammatical, however, as illustrated in (43a), while the result without doubling is grammatical (43b):

(43)   a. *Hij is **maar maar** boos ~~maar~~ op één jongen geweest.
        he is only   only   angry only   at   one boy   been

    b. Hij is **maar** ~~maar~~ boos ~~maar~~ op één jongen geweest.
        he is only   only   angry only   at   one boy   been

The explanation of this contrast is straightforward if we take (41)/(42) into account. There we have seen that a focus particle can be deleted at PF in a specifier-head configuration where both the specifier and the head contains a particle. The crucial difference between (41) and (43) is that in (43) the specifier contains only a focus particle, such that the two identical focus particles are linearly adjacent. If we make the additional assumption that under such circumstances a haplology rule applies obligatorily, the ungrammaticality of (43a) follows.[40]

The assumption that haplology effects occur in specifier head configurations with two identical elements is independently necessary. For example, in relative clauses in southern Dutch doubly filled comp dialects, SpecCP and C can both be filled if the relative pronoun in SpecCP and the complementizer in C are not homophonous, as in (44a). However, when the two elements are homophonous, one of the two has to disappear (44b):

(44)   a. de   man die   dat ik gezien heb
       the man who that I   seen   have

    b. het kind (*dat) dat ik gezien heb
       the child that   that I   seen   have

---

[40] See Neeleman and van de Koot (2006) for haplology rules. The obligatoriness of deletion of one of the particles also follows from Antisymmetry.

Summarizing, I have argued that a focus particle can attach to any constituent in its base position. If the particle stays there, the sentence is ungrammatical. The particle has to move up to the specifier of another focus particle, optionally pied piping the constituent to which it was attached. This explains the distributional paradox. A combination [focus particle – constituent] can occur in derived positions, such as the left-hand part of the middle field and the clause initial position, but not in base position. A focus particle attached to a constituent obligatorily occurs with a second focus particle. This gives rise to doubling when the two particles are identical. This doubling can then be obscured by optional or obligatory deletion of one of the focus particles which is allowed because the content of the deleted focus particle is locally redundant. Focus particles in Dutch thus provide evidence in support of the Doubling and Deletion Hypothesis presented in section 10.3. They both show overt doubling and the possibility of deletion of redundant material under local recoverability. This doubling conspiracy is a source of variation, in this case intralinguistic variation. At the surface, the variation is syntactic but it was shown that the number of syntactic positions can be kept constant and thus the apparent syntactic variation can be reduced to variation in PF spell out.

10.6 The trigger of focus particle movement and doubling

The analysis presented so far does not yet answer the question of why a second particle and movement to that particle is necessary. I would like to propose that movement to the second focus particle is required for full semantic interpretation. Focus particles are quantifiers. They are relations between two sets. For example, on one of the interpretations of the sentence in (45), *ook* 'also' is an inclusion or additive relation between [the books] and the set of other things that John has read:

(45)   Jan   heeft   ook   de   boeken   gelezen.
       John has   also the books   read

Let us assume that the other focus particles can be analysed as relations between two sets as well. If the two arguments that denote the two sets must be present in syntax, then a focus particle attached to a constituent such as DP or PP faces an interpretive problem. The constituent to which the particle is attached serves as its first argument, but since the particle is inside the DP or PP, it cannot find the second argument there. According to the Principle of Semantic Interpretation, dyadic relations require the following syntactic configuration:

(46)   Dyadic predication Y(X,Z) if X immediately c-commands Y, and Y immediately c-commands Z.

In many cases, this involves a Spec-Head-Complement configuration. If the focus particle is a head and its complement is its first argument, then there should be a second argument in the specifier of the particle of the right semantic type, e.g. in (45) it should be a constituent that denotes the set of other things that John read.

Thus, if nothing happens, the focus particle will be left with only one argument and the structure will be uninterpretable. The structure will be saved if the focus particle can be provided with a second argument. This is achieved in two steps. First, a second focus particle is attached to TP. TP denotes the second set, in the case of (45) the set of things John read.[41] In this stage, the lower focus particle has one argument, a DP or PP, and the higher focus particle also has one argument, TP. The lower focus particle now moves to the specifier of the higher particle. Here absorption takes place: the two focus particles interpretively become one and together express a relation between two arguments, the PP or DP, and TP.

10.7 The parallel between focus particles and negation

Interestingly, focus particles behave parallel to constituent negation in this respect.[42] We have seen that sentences such as (37a), repeated here as (47a), are ungrammatical because the particle has to move up. If we replace the constituent with the focus particle by a negative constituent we also get an ungrammatical sentence (47b). Such sentences are good if the negative PP moves in front of the adjective, as in (47c).[43] In West Flemish dialects, the negation *nie* 'not' optionally occurs in such cases, giving rise to doubling:

(47) a. *Hij is   boos [ook [pp op Marie]] geweest.
          he is   angry also   at   Mary   been

      b. *Hij is   boos [pp op niemand]   geweest.
          he is   angry   at nobody   been

      c. Hij is [pp op niemand] (nie) boos   geweest.
          he is   at nobody   not   angry   been
         'He has not been angry at anybody.'

The Doubling and Deletion Hypothesis predicts that in addition to overt doubling and optional deletion of the negative head (West Flemish as in (47c)), there should also be a language type in which the negative part of the specifier can be deleted, again entirely parallel to focus particle doubling configurations. Such languages do indeed exist. Various Brabantish dialects spoken in the Belgian province of Antwerp have *iemand nie* lit. someone not, meaning 'nobody' and *ergens nie* lit. somewhere not, meaning nowhere (cf. SAND 2, map 59a). The sentences in (48) illustrate the parallel

---

[41] In order for this to be possible, the constituent containing the focus should be turned into a variable, either in semantics or by moving the constituent that contains the focus out of TP.

[42] For the relation between negation, affirmation, and focus see Laka (1990).

[43] Cf. Haegeman (1995).

between deletion of a focus particle in the specifier of another focus particle and deletion of a negative morpheme in the specifier of another negative morpheme:

(48)   a. [Hij is [$_{maarP}$ [~~maar~~ op één jongen] [maar [boos geweest]]]].
      he is   only at one boy   only angry been
      'He has been angry at only one boy.'

    b. Hij heeft [$_{nieP}$[~~n~~-iemand] [nie [gezien]]]]
      he has no-one   not seen
      'He has not seen anybody.'

The fact that both focus particles and the negative morpheme in a negative word can be deleted in this configuration suggests that they have the same structural status. Put differently, the orthographic convention to write words such as *niemand* 'no one' as one word may be misleading. In view of the accessibility for deletion of the n- part of *niemand* and the lexical integrity condition which says that parts of words are not accessible to grammatical operations, *niemand* should be written as *n iemand*.[44] The fact that the variant *niemand ie*, with deletion of the initial *n-* of *nie*, is not attested, suggests that *nie* should not be analysed as *n ie*.

Another interesting issue raised by the parallel in (48) is that the various PF deletion options in the case of negation correspond to particular geographic areas. In West Flemish we find optional deletion of *nie* 'not', in Standard Dutch we find obligatory deletion of *nie*, and in some Brabantish dialects we find optional deletion of *n-* in the n-word. For the different variants in focus particle doubling configurations (41), no correlations between variants and geographic distribution have been observed. The question is why negation would differ from focus particles in this respect. The tentative explanation I would like to propose for this difference is that negative sentences are much more frequent than sentences with focus particles and that the frequency of a syntactic phenomenon has to be above a certain threshold in order for it to be sensitive to sociolinguistic factors.[45]

The fact that constituent negation and focus particles behave similarly in these configurations raises the question of what they have in common semantically and syntactically. Semantically, if we take n-words to be negative quantifiers, they face the same problem in their base position, namely that they lack the second argument needed for full semantic interpretation.

Focus particles and negation further have in common that they have a polarity feature [negative] or [positive]. An overview is given in (49):

---

[44] See Lapointe (1980) for the Lexical Integrity Hypothesis.

[45] This explanation has to remain tentative in this chapter because there are no frequency studies available, and also because there does not exist a systematic study of the geographic distribution of the different deletion patterns possible with focus particles.

(49) a. Focus particles with a [negative] feature
      Class I elements: *maar* 'only' and *pas* 'just'.
      Class II elements *alleen* 'only' and *slechts* 'only'.

      b. Focus particles with a [positive] feature
      Class I elements: *al* 'already', *wel* 'as many as'.
      Class II elements: *ook* 'also', *zelfs* 'even'.

Focus particles with a negative feature license negative polarity items such as the verb *hoeven* 'need'. This is illustrated in (50):

(50) Negative focus particles: *maar* 'only', *alleen* 'alone', *slechts* 'only'.
      a. Je   hoeft *(niet) te bellen.
         you   need   not   to call
         'You don't have to call.'

      b. Je   hoeft maar/alleen/slechts te bellen.
         you   need   only/alone/only   to call
         'You only have to call.'

The positive focus particles cannot occur in the scope of negation:

(51) Positive focus particles: *ook* 'also', *wel* 'as many as', *al* 'already'
      a. Al   tien boeken heeft Jan/*niemand al.
         already ten   books   has   John/nobody   already

      b. Wel   tien boeken heeft Jan/*niemand wel.
         as many as ten   books   has   John/nobody   as many as

      c. Hij/*niemand heeft ook   Jan   gezien.
         he/nobody   has   also   John seen

      d. Hij/*niemand heeft zelfs Jan   gezien.
         he/nobody   has   even   John seen

As was stated already, *al* 'already' and *maar* 'only' are the focus particles that trigger movement of a focus particle that is attached to a constituent. If this movement is feature driven and if movement presupposes morphosyntactic agreement, we expect that only negative focus particles can move to the specifier of *maar* 'only' while only positive focus particles can move to the specifier of *al* 'already'. This expectation is, however, not correct. In (52), the positive particle *ook* 'also' has moved to the specifier of the negative particle *maar* 'only':

(52) Marie is nu   ook maar boos ~~ook~~ op Jan.
      Mary is now also only angry also   at John.
      'Mary is now also angry at John.'

The features [positive] and [negative] are thus semantic features that do not take part in agreement relations that are necessary for movement.

It is also unlikely that an uninterpretable [focus] feature on the moving focus particle is responsible for focus particle movement. As we have seen in (43b), the higher focus particle and the focus particle moving to its specifier can be identical (in the case of (43b), both are *maar* 'only'). It is hard to see how the lower particle can check the higher one if they both have an uninterpretable [focus] feature.

The remaining possibility is that there is an agreement relation between the uninterpretable focus feature of the higher particle and the interpretable focus feature of a focused element inside the complement of the lower focus particle, but that raises the question of why the lower focus particle is present in the derivation at all. I conclude that focus particle movement in the focus particle doubling construction is not mediated by feature checking. Rather, the lower focus particle moves to the higher one for semantic reasons.

The feature content of the focus particles does play a role when it comes to deletion of a focus particle under local identity. As we have seen in (43), when the two particles are completely identical one of them can or must be deleted. When the two particles are not identical, only the lower focus particle can delete. This is illustrated in (53):

(53) a. Marie is alleen (maar) boos op Jan geweest.
          Mary   is only   (only)   angry at John been

      b. Marie is *(alleen) maar boos op Jan geweest.
          Mary   is only   only   angry at John been

This suggests that the features of *maar* 'only' are a proper subset of the features of *alleen* 'only', such that PF deletion of *maar* does not cause a recoverability problem while deletion of *alleen* 'only' does.

10.8 Conclusion

The central hypothesis of this chapter is that syntactic doubling is necessary for full interpretation at LF, while deletion of locally redundant material is possible and sometimes necessary at PF. This was dubbed the Doubling and Deletion Hypothesis (DaD). According to this hypothesis, syntactic doubling is a core property of the syntax of natural language and in interaction with deletion an important source of cross-linguistic and intralinguistic variation.

In addition to doubling in dependency chains, two main types of syntactic doubling configurations were discussed. The first type involves monadic predication configurations, in which the two local arguments of a predicative head are formally identical. For such configurations, the DaD Hypothesis was shown to make precise predictions with respect to the typology of head marking, dependent marking, and juxtaposition, and with respect to the properties of diachronic cycles such as the Jespersen cycle.

The second type of doubling configuration involves focus particles, which are analysed as quantifiers, i.e. relations between two sets, and therefore require two arguments in syntax. When they are attached to constituents such as DPs and PPs, they have only one argument, and doubling of the focus particle and movement of the lower particle to the higher one is necessary for full semantic interpretation. This was shown to resolve the distributional paradox known from the focus particle literature, and to explain the variation patterns found in Dutch focus particle constructions.

It was further shown that focus particles behave parallel to negation in this respect, which raises the question of why variation in the spell out of negation is sensitive to sociolinguistic factors such as geographic location, while variation in spell out of focus particles does not seem to be sensitive to such factors. It was tentatively suggested that this is due to the higher relative frequency of negative sentences as compared to sentences with focus particles, under the assumption that a type of construction has to reach a certain frequency threshold for it to be prone to sociolinguistic differentiation.

The DaD Hypothesis defines a research programme in that it predicts the existence of many other cases of hidden syntactic doubling. The programme invites reconsideration of analyses of criterial movement proposed in the literature (e.g. focus, negation, Whj).[46] The DaD Hypothesis should be tested against diachronic cycles such as the Jespersen cycle, pro-drop and agreement cycles, and Preposition-Case cycles.

---

[46] Cf. Rizzi (1991).

11

Some concluding remarks

M. CARME PICALLO

The preceding chapters responded to the workshop call (see Foreword) from several angles, while providing an excellent illustration of the themes currently under active research in the domain of syntactic variation within a minimalist agenda. As Minimalism constitutes a program admitting several ways of implementation, there are a number of research paths to follow, some of them undertaken in the individual contributions of this volume. The contributions show differences regarding how the program may be approached and illustrate the fact that several lines of inquiry are currently being followed, while highlighting a number of problems that need to be solved—or avenues that need to be explored—in order to have workable and explanatory models of syntactic diversity.

The contributions grouped in Part I of this volume (*The parametric approach*) defend the idea that the study of variation is an integral part of the study of syntax, while those grouped in Part II (*Variation without parameters*) support the idea that the observed diversity should largely be set aside in order to concentrate on the precise characterization of simple and invariant syntactic mechanisms. Specific differences mainly concern the issue of whether or not variation should be accounted for by feature properties; the theoretical import, content, and role of the notion *parameter*, and the degree of specification (or lack thereof) that should be assumed for the computational system. An exchange of ideas regarding some of these discrepancies took place after the presentations at the workshop. The aim of the discussion sessions was to facilitate a fruitful exchange of ideas among speakers and attendees on the various research lines that are being pursued. Some issues addressed at the end of each presentation have been incorporated by the authors in the individual chapters in this volume, either in the main text or in footnotes. This last chapter briefly summarizes some general comments or concerns that were raised by contributors and participants at the workshop.

A number of questions were centred on the assumption that specific feature properties should restrict the class of possible grammars. As the notion of syntactic feature occupies centre stage, any condition or principle applying to such building blocks of computation should have very restrictive consequences one way or another. However, a characterization of what a possible syntactic feature might be is still lacking, as well as an understanding of how some properties attributed to individual features—such as interpretability—may relate to our conceptual apparatus, or to other non-linguistic systems. A different but related issue is which types of mechanisms may trigger feature bundling, as their assembling to form lexical or functional items appears to be far from random (see Adger and Svenonius 2011 for discussion on these issues). Exactly what constitutes a lexical item, or what is a possible such item, and how lexicalization/categorization comes about are other concerns that were addressed. Note that the pool of building blocks that may form hierarchies of individual features by merging into one another in a cartographic space amounts to already assuming the existence of a 'lexicon', in this case of sub-morphemic units.

The rigid format for structural architecture proposed by cartographic approaches is highly restrictive. A much less restricted format to account for variation would be a non-uniform approach. Suppose that all possible features in the UG pool (assuming that the set of possible syntactic features had already been characterized) may not be present in all languages, but each language selects a subset of the available universal set, as suggested in Chomsky (2001). This hypothesis would amount to assuming that variation is already pre-syntactic, and resides primarily on the different feature sets being selected. Within this line of thought, the obvious question arises as to what the minimal (sub)set of selected features should be for syntactic computations to be able to proceed (i.e. are some features more principled/universal than others?). Also to be determined, if such a hypothetical non-uniform approach were to be taken, is whether or not variable feature selection would affect some types of features but not others (i.e. only uninterpretable/unvalued features, or interpretable features as well).

Other concerns were expressed on the issue of whether or not, under Minimalist tenets, progress is consistent with maintaining the notion of parameter. The sceptical stance on this matter derives from the assumption that UG is maximally underspecified. As the term 'parameter' is now divorced from language-specific principles, this notion may not amount to more than simply using a technical term to express the fact that languages differ. Hierarchical downward expansions, or parametric geometries, leave open the question of why, or how, a given option can acquire the status of being a default option—or a less marked option—to lie at the root, or in the higher echelons, of a hierarchy. Constructing such models by noting properties observed in a number of languages may only scratch at the surface of phenomena, and may divert attention from the search for primitives satisfying minimal design specifications. Critics of this system argued that parametric hierarchical proposals constitute reorganizations of observed facts and are an account for variation as complex as the phenomena to be accounted for. In the realm of acquisition, scepticism was also expressed regarding the proposal that such hierarchies should model learning paths, and that children perform computational decisions on the basis of abstract parametric hierarchies.

Massive variation is the expected outcome within a frame where UG is underspecified and its operations invariant or of a very generic nature. In other words, distributions based on observations of how lexical/functional elements behave in their exponents—on the properties of which parametric hypotheses generally rest—may not be good candidates to instruct core syntactic operations because they should be the result, not the origin, of much more abstract syntactic computations. Core operations of the faculty of language (such as recursion or minimal search) do not offer options for their application, but many different options should be possible in externalization processes, in particular if lexical insertion takes place post-syntactically.

The chapters in Part II of this volume adopt the tenet that variability is inevitable when the relation between combinations of abstract linguistic units and the possible realizations of their exponents is underspecified. Optionality in Spell Out may create apparent parameterization effects, and factors like frequency or conventionalization in the use of forms have an impact in lexical access during production. However, concerns were formulated to such maximally underspecified approaches to variation. The characterization of optionality must be sharpened when considering grammatical phenomena because an assessment of the impact of a myriad of non-linguistic factors on linguistic variation should be part of the process of finding out how to satisfy or how to restrict them. So far, a workable model for framing such non-linguistic factors in the linguistic system has not been offered and, with some exceptions, proposals on these lines remain largely programmatic and have offered no proof that all syntactic computations are absolutely invariant. Languages indeed allow a certain range of Spell Out options but, at the same time, show strong rigidity in other syntactic aspects, and the balance between rigidity and optionality should be modelled. Word order, for example, is not altered on an individual basis and does not vary on occasion. A radical underspecification view meets the challenge of explaining why the language acquirer rigidifies the language being learned in some dimensions but not in others. A related question is how to distinguish between externalization options that happen to be simply unrealized—but had the 'opportunity' to exist—and those whose impossibility may be a result of the cumulative effects of different pressures. Hypothetical options that cannot obtain should be ruled out on principled grounds.

With respect to frequency, its influence in the disappearance of some types of forms is not arguable. Also uncontroversial is its role in triggering some morphological changes, the typical one being the regularization of irregular verbs over time as, for example, has been documented in large quantitative analyses of English texts (Lieberman et al. 2007; Michel et al. 2011:180). A more interesting concern than quantification of variants would be to provide an empirical assessment of the importance of frequency, combined with other external conditions (such as language contact, among other things) to trigger 'parameterization' while assessing which syntactic conditions, if any, are able to feed or bleed a possible change in a given grammar.

The contributions to this volume and the questions they raise are thought-provoking in many ways. They show that syntactic diversity may be approached through different strategies while using a variety of analytical tools. They constitute an attempt to direct grammatical theory to better explanatory depths. Lying ahead is the task of finding good devices to sort out the many ingredients that comprise the faculty of language and the exciting prospect for researchers to theoretically evaluate them, and then put them to empirical test.

References

Abbot-Smith, K., E. Lieven, & M. Tomasello (2001). 'What children do and do not do with ungrammatical word orders', *Cognitive Development* 16: 1–14.

Abels, K. & A. Neeleman (2006). 'Universal 20 without the LCA', MS, University of Tromsø and University College London.

Aboh, E. (2004). *The Morphosyntax of Complement-Head Sequences*. New York: Oxford University Press.

Acquaviva, Paolo (2008). *Lexical Plurals: A Morphosemantic Approach*. Oxford: Oxford University Press.

Adger, David (2003). *Core Syntax: A Minimalist Approach*. Oxford: Oxford University Press.

Adger, David (2006). 'Combinatorial variability', *Journal of Linguistics* 42: 503–30.

Adger, David (2007). 'Variability and modularity: A response to Hudson', *Journal of Linguistics* 43: 695–700.

Adger, David (2010). 'A minimalist theory of feature structure', in A. Kibort & G. Corbett (eds), *Features: Perspectives on a Key Notion in Linguistics*, Oxford: Oxford University Press, 185–218.

Adger, David (2012). 'Constructions are not explanations' available at <http://ling.auf.net/lingbuzz/001675>.

Adger, David (2013a). 'Constructions and grammatical explanation', *Mind and Language*, 28.4: 466–78.

Adger, David (2013b). *A Syntax of Substance*. Cambridge, MA: MIT Press.

Adger, David, Daniel Harbour, & Laurel Watkins (2009). *Mirrors and Microparameters: Phrase Structure beyond Free Word Order*. Cambridge: Cambridge University Press.

Adger, David & Jennifer Smith (2005). 'Variation and the Minimalist Program', in L. Cornips & K. Corrigan (eds), *Syntax and Variation: Reconciling the Biological and the Social*. Amsterdam: John Benjamins, 149–78.

Adger, David & Jennifer Smith (2010). 'Variation in agreement: A lexical feature-based approach', *Lingua* 120: 1109–34.

Adger, David & Peter Svenonius (2011). 'Features in Minimalist Syntax', in C. Boeckx (ed.), *The Oxford Handbook of Linguistic Minimalism*. Oxford: Oxford University Press, 27–51.

Akhtar, Nameera (1999). 'Acquiring basic word order: evidence for data-driven learning of syntactic structure', *Journal of Child Language* 26: 339–56.

Akhtar, N. & M. Tomasello (1997). 'Young children's productivity with word order and verb morphology', *Developmental Psychology* 33: 952–65.

Albizu, Pablo (2001). 'Datibosintagmenizaerasintaktikoareninguruan: eztabaidarakooinarrizkozenbaitdatu', in B. Fernández & P. Albizu (eds), *Kasu eta KomunztaduraenGainean. On Case and Agreement*. Bilbao: University of the Basque Country, 49–70.

Alexiadou, Artemis & Elena Anagnostopoulou (1998). 'Parametrizing Agr: Word order, V-movement and EPP-checking', *Natural Language and Linguistic Theory* 16: 491–539.

Amberber, Mengistu (2005). 'Differential subject marking in Amharic', in Mengistu Amberber & Helen de Hoop (eds), *Competition and Variation in Natural Languages: The Case for Case*. Amsterdam: Elsevier, 295–319.

Amundson, Ron (2005). *The Changing Role of the Embryo in Evolutionary Thought: Roots of Evo-Devo*. Cambridge: Cambridge University Press.

Anagnastopoulou, Elena (2003). *The Syntax of Ditransitives: Evidence from Clitics*. Berlin: Mouton.

Anderson, Stephen (2005). *Aspects of the Theory of Clitics*. New York: Oxford University Press.

Aristar, Anthony (1996). 'The relationship between dative and locative. Kuryłowicz argument from a typological perspective'. *Diachronica* XIII.2: 207–24.

Arregi, Euridice & Javier Ormazabal (2003). 'Aditz ditrantsitiboen barne-egitura', in J. M. Makatzaga & B. Oyharçabal (eds), *P. Lafitteren sortzearen mendemugako biltzarra. Gramatika gaiak. Iker-14 (I)*. Bilbao: Euskaltzaindia, 119–36.

Aurnague, Michel (1996). 'Les noms de localisation interne: tentative de caractérisation sémantique à partir des données du basque et du français', *Cahiers de lexicologie* 69: 159–92.

Aurnague, Michel (2001). 'Entités et relations dans les descriptions spatiales: l'espace et son expression en basque et en français', Mémoire d'habilitation, Université de Toulouse-Le Mirail.

Bach, E. (1965). 'On some recurrent types of transformations', in C. W. Kreidler (ed.), *Report on the Sixteenth Annual Round Table Meeting on Linguistics and Language Studies*. Washington, D.C: Georgetown University Press, 3–18.

Baker, Mark (1988a). *Incorporation: A Theory of Grammatical Function Changing*. Chicago: Chicago University Press.

Baker, Mark (1988b). *The Syntax of Agreement and Concord*. Cambridge: Cambridge University Press.

Baker, Mark (1996). *The Polysynthesis Parameter*. Oxford: Oxford University Press.

Baker, Mark (1999). 'On the interplay of the universal and the particular: Case study of Edo', *Proceedings of CLS 35: The Panels*, 265–89.

Baker, Mark (2001). *The Atoms of Language*. New York: Basic Books.

Baker, Mark (2003). *Lexical Categories*. Cambridge: Cambridge University Press.

Baker, Mark (2005). 'The innate endowment for language: Underspecified or overspecified?', in P. Carruthers, S. Laurence, & S. Stich, *The Innate Mind*. Oxford: Oxford University Press, 156–74.

Baker, Mark (2008a). *The Syntax of Agreement and Concord*. Cambridge: Cambridge University Press.

Baker, Mark (2008b). 'The Macroparameter in a Microparametric World', in T. Biberauer (ed.), *The Limits of Syntactic Variation*. Amsterdam: John Benjamins, 351–74.

Baker, Mark (2010). 'Formal generative typology', in Bernd Heine and Heiko Narrog (eds), *Oxford Handbook of Linguistic Analysis*. New York: Oxford University Press.

Baker, Mark (2013). 'On agreement and its relationship to case: Some generative ideas and results', *Lingua* 130: 14–32.

Baker, Mark (In progress). *Case: Its Principles and its Parameters*. Cambridge: Cambridge University Press.

Baker, Mark & C. Collins (2006). 'Linkers and the Internal Structure of vP', *Natural Language & Linguistic Theory* 24: 307–54.

Baker, Mark & J. McCloskey (2007). 'On the relationship of typology to theoretical syntax', *Linguistic Typology* 11: 285–96.

Baker, Mark & Nadezhda Vinokurova (2009). 'On agentive nominalizations and how they differ from event nominalizations', *Language* 85: 517–56.

Baker, Mark & Nadezhda Vinokurova (2010). 'Two modalities of case assignment in Sakha', *Natural Language and Linguistic Theory* 28: 593–642.

Barbiers, Sjef (1995). 'The Syntax of Interpretation', dissertation, Leiden University, The Hague: HAG.

Barbiers, Sjef (2003). 'Generalized focus particle doubling', paper presented at CGSW 18, Durham.

Barbiers, Sjef (2005). 'Verb clusters and the division of labour between generative linguistics and sociolinguistics', in L. Cornips & K. Corrigan (eds), *Syntax and Variation. Reconciling the Biological and the Social. Current Issues in Linguistic Theory* 265. Amsterdam/Philadelphia: John Benjamins, 233–64.

Barbiers, Sjef (2007). 'Indefinite numerals one and many and the cause of ordinal suppletion', *Lingua* 117 (5): 859–80.

Barbiers, Sjef (2008). 'Microvariation in Syntactic Doubling: An Introduction', in S. Barbiers, O. Koeneman, M. Lekakou, & M. van der Ham (eds), *Microvariation in Syntactic Doubling*. Bingely: Emerald, 1–31.

Barbiers, Sjef (2009). 'Locus and limits of syntactic microvariation', *Lingua* 119 (11): 1607–23.

Barbiers, Sjef (2010). 'Focus particle doubling', in M. de Vries and J.-W. Zwart (eds), *Structure Preserved*. Amsterdam/Philadelphia: John Benjamins, 21–9.

Barbiers, Sjef & H. Bennis (2007). 'The Syntactic Atlas of the Dutch Dialects: A discussion of choices in the SAND-project', *Nordlyd* 34 (1) available at <http://www.ub.uit.no/baser/septentrio/index.php/nordlyd/issue/view/11>.

Barbiers, Sjef, H. Bennis, G. De Vogelaer, M. Devos, & M. van der Ham (2005). *Syntactic Atlas of the Dutch Dialects, Vol. 1*. Amsterdam: Amsterdam University Press.

Barbiers, Sjef, L. Cornips, & J. P. Kunst (2007). 'The Syntactic Atlas of the Dutch Dialects (SAND). A Corpus of Elicited Speech as an On-line Dynamic Atlas', in J. Beal, K. Corrigan, & H. Moisl (eds), *Creating and Digitizing Language Corpora. Vol. 1: Synchronic Databases*. Basingstoke/New York: Palgrave Macmillan, 54–90.

Barbiers, Sjef, O. Koeneman, & M. Lekakou (2009). 'Syntactic doubling and the structure of Wh chains', *Journal of Linguistics* 45, 1–46.

Barbiers, Sjef, O. Koeneman, M. Lekakou, & M. van der Ham (eds) (2008). *Microvariation in Syntactic Doubling*. Bingley: Emerald.

Barbiers, Sjef, J. van der Auwera, H. Bennis, G. De Vogelaer, & M. Devos (2008). *Syntactic Atlas of the Dutch Dialects*, Vol. 2. Amsterdam: Amsterdam University Press.

Barbosa, Pilar (1997). 'Subject positions in the null subject languages', *Seminarios de Linguística* 1: 39–63.

Barbosa, Pilar (2001). 'On inversion in Wh-questions in Romance', in A. Hulk & J.-Y. Pollock (eds), *Subject Positions in Romance and the Theory of Universal Grammar*. Oxford: Oxford University Press, 20–59.

Barwise, Jon & Robin Cooper (1981). 'Generalised Quantifiers and Natural Language', *Linguistics and Philosophy* 4: 159–219. [Reprinted in P. Portner & B. Partee (2002) *Formal Semantics*. Oxford: Blackwell, 75–126].

Bayer, J. (1996). *Directionality and Logical Form: On the Scope of Focusing Particles and WH in Situ*. Dordrecht: Kluwer.

Belletti, Adriana (2001). 'Agreement projections', in M. Baltin & C. Collins (eds), *The Handbook of Contemporary Syntactic Theory*. Oxford: Blackwell, 483–510.

Belletti, Adriana (2004a). 'Aspects of the Low IP Area', in L. Rizzi (ed). *The Structure of CP and IP—The Cartography of Syntactic Structures, Vol. 2*. Oxford: Oxford University Press, 16–51.

Belletti, Adriana (ed.) (2004b). *Structures and Beyond: The Cartography of Syntactic Structures, Vol. 3*. New York: Oxford University Press.

Belletti, Adriana (2005). 'Extended doubling and the VP periphery' *Probus* 17: 1–35.

Belletti, Adriana (2009). *Structures and Strategies*. London: Routledge.

Belletti, Adriana & Luigi Rizzi (1988). 'Psych verbs and θ-theory', *Natural Language and Linguistic Theory* 6: 291–352.

Benítez-Burraco, A. (2009). *Genes y lenguaje. Aspectos ontogenéticos, filogenéticos y cognitivos*. Barcelona: Reverté.

Bernstein, Judy & Raffaella Zanuttini (2010). 'What is verbal -s in English?', MS, Yale.

Berwick, Robert (1995). *The Acquisition of Syntactic Knowledge*. Cambridge, MA: MIT Press.

Berwick, Robert & Noam Chomsky (2008). 'The biolinguistics program: The current state of its development', MS, MIT.

Berwick, Robert & Noam Chomsky (2011). 'The biolinguistic program: The current state of its evolution and development', in A. M. Di Sciullo & C. Boeckx (eds), *The Biolinguistic Enterprise: New Perspectives on the Evolution and Nature of the Human Language Faculty*. Oxford: Oxford University Press, 19–41.

Berwick Robert C., Angela D. Friederici, Noam Chomsky, & Johan J. Bolhuis (2013). 'Evolution, brain and the nature of language'. *Trends in Cognitive Sciences* 17: 8998.

Besten, Hans den (1976). 'Surface lexicalisation and trace theory', in H. van Riemsdijk (ed.), *Green Ideas Blown Up. Papers from the Amsterdam Colloquium on Trace Theory*. Amsterdam: University of Amsterdam, 4–28.

Besten, Hans den (1983). 'On the Interaction of Root Transformations and Lexical Deletive Rules', in W. Abraham (ed.), *On the Formal Syntax of Westgermania*. Amsterdam: John Benjamins, 47–131.

Bianchi, Valentina (2006). 'On the syntax of personal arguments', *Lingua* 116: 2023–67.

Bianchi, Valentina & M. Frascarelli (2010). 'Is Topic a Root Phenomenon?' *Iberia* 2(1): 43–88.

Biberauer, Theresa (ed.) (2008). *The Limits of Syntactic Variation*. Amsterdam: John Benjamins.

Biberauer, Theresa (2011). 'In defence of lexico-centric parametric variation: two 3rd factor-constrained case studies', paper presented at the Workshop on Formal Grammar and Syntactic Variation: Rethinking Parameters (Madrid).

Biberauer, Theresa (2012). 'Constructing parametric hierarchies: Theoretical and empirical considerations (including what The Mafia has to do with it)', talk given at ReCoS Seminar, University of Cambridge.

Biberauer, Theresa & Philip Branigan (2012/in progress). 'Microparametric expression of a macroparameter: Afrikaans verb clusters and Algonquian grammars,' Abstract: Universities of Cambridge/Stellenbosch and Memorial University, Newfoundland.

Biberauer, Theresa, Anders Holmberg, & Ian Roberts (2008). 'Disharmonic Word Orders and the Final-over-Final Constraint (FOFC)', in A. Bisetto & F. Barbieri (eds), *Proceedings of the XXXIII Incontro di Grammatica Generativa*. Available at <http://amsacta. unibo.it/2397/1/PROCEEDINGS_IGG33.pdf>.

Biberauer, Theresa, Anders Holmberg, & Ian Roberts (in press). 'A syntactic universal and its consequences', to appear in *Linguistic Inquiry*.

Biberauer, Theresa, Anders Holmberg, Ian Roberts, & Michelle Sheehan (2010a). *Parametric Syntax: Nullsubjects in Minimalist Theory*. Cambridge: Cambridge University Press.

Biberauer, Theresa, Anders Holmberg, Ian Roberts, & Michelle Sheehan (2010b). 'Reconciling formalism and functionalism, a minimalist perspective', paper presented at the Annual Meeting of the Linguistics Association of Great Britain, University of Leeds.

Biberauer, Theresa, Anders Holmberg, Ian Roberts, & Michelle Sheehan (2013). 'Complexity in Comparative Syntax: The View from Modern Parametric Theory', unpublished MS. Available at <http://ling.auf.net/lingbuzz/001827>.

Biberauer, Theresa & Marc Richards (2006). 'True Optionality: When the grammar doesn't mind', in C. Boeckx (ed.), *Minimalist Theorizing*. Amsterdam: John Benjamins.

Biberauer, Theresa & Ian Roberts (2009). 'The Return of the Subset Principle', in P. Crisma & G. Longobardi (eds), *Historical Linguistics and Linguistic Theory*. Oxford: Oxford University Press.

Biberauer, Theresa & Ian Roberts (2010). 'Subjects, Tense and verb-movement', in T. Biberauer, A. Holmberg, I. Roberts, & M. Sheehan (eds), *Parametric Variation: Null Subjects in Minimalist Theory*. Cambridge: Cambridge University Press, 263–302.

Biberauer, Theresa, Ian Roberts, & Michelle Sheehan (2013a). 'No-choice Parameters and the Limits of Syntactic Variation', to appear in *Proceedings of WCCFL 31*. Sommerville, MA, Cascadilla Proceedings Project. Available at <http://ling.auf.net/lingbuzz/001828>.

Biberauer, Theresa, Ian Roberts, & Michelle Sheehan (2013b). 'Mafioso parameters and the limits of syntactic variation', paper presented at the 31st West Coast Conference on Formal Linguistics, State University of Arizona, Tempe.

Bittner, Maria & Ken Hale (1996). 'The Structural Determination of Case and Agreement'. *Linguistic Inquiry* 27: 1–68.

Blake, Barry (1994). *Case*. Cambridge: Cambridge University Press.

Blevins, Juliette (2004). *Evolutionary Phonology: The Emergence of Sound Patterns*. Cambridge: Cambridge University Press.

Bloom, Paul (ed) (1993). *Language Acquisition: Core Readings*. Cambridge, MA: MIT Press.

Bobaljik, J. (2002). 'A-chains at the PF-interface: Copies and "covert" movement', *Natural Language and Linguistic Theory* 20.2: 197–267.

Boeckx, Cedric (2001). 'French complex inversion in the light of a minimalist program', in J. Camps & C. R. Wiltshire (eds), *Romance Syntax, Semantics and L2 Acquisition*. Amsterdam: Benjamins, 43–56.

Boeckx, Cedric (2006). *Linguistic Minimalism. Origins, Concepts, Methods and Aims*. Oxford: Oxford University Press.

Boeckx, Cedric (2008a). *Bare Syntax*. Oxford: Oxford University Press.

Boeckx, Cedric (2008b). 'Did we really solve Plato's Problem (abstractly)?', in Y. Otsu (ed.), *Proceedings of the 9th Annual Tokyo Conference on Psycholinguistics*. Tokyo: Hituzi Syobo.

Boeckx, Cedric (2009a). *Language in Cognition: Uncovering Mental Structures and the Rules behind Them*. Malden: Wiley–Blackwell.

Boeckx, Cedric (2009b). 'The locus of asymmetry in UG', *Catalan Journal of Linguistics* 8: 41–53.

Boeckx, Cedric (2010a). 'Defeating lexicocentrism (Part A. Elementary Syntactic Structures)', unpublished MS. Available at <http://ling.auf.net/lingbuzz/001130>.

Boeckx, Cedric (2010b). 'Linguistic minimalism', in B. Heine & H. Narrog (eds), *Oxford Handbook of Linguistic Analysis*. Oxford: Oxford University Press, 485–505.

Boeckx, Cedric (2011a). 'Approaching parameters from below', in A. M. Di Sciullo & C. Boeckx (eds), *The Biolinguistic Enterprise: New Perspectives on the Evolution and Nature of the Human Language Faculty*. Oxford: Oxford University Press, 205–21.

Boeckx, Cedric (2011b). 'The emergence of the language faculty, from a biolinguistic point of view', in M. Tallerman & K. Gibson (eds), *The Oxford Handbook of Language Evolution*. Oxford: Oxford University Press, 492–501.

Boeckx, Cedric (2011c). 'Some Reflections on Darwin's Problem in the Context of Cartesian Biolinguistics', in A. M. Di Sciullo & C. Boeckx (eds), *The Biolinguistic Enterprise: New Perspectives on the Evolution and Nature of the Human Language Faculty*. Oxford: Oxford University Press, 42–64.

Boeckx, Cedric (2012a). 'A missing design perspective in I-linguistics', in S. Ojima, Y. Otsu, J. F. Connolly, & G. Thierry, *Future Trends in the Biology of Language*. Tokyo: Keio University Press, 95–116.

Boeckx, Cedric (2012b). 'Phases beyond explanatory adequacy', in Á. Gallego (ed.), *Phase Theory: Developing the Framework*. Berlin: Mouton de Gruyter, 45–66.

Boeckx, Cedric (2012c). 'The I-language mosaic', in C. Boeckx, M. Horno, & J.-L. Mendivil (eds), *Language from a Biological Point of View: Current Issues in Biolinguistics*. Newcastle upon Tyne: Cambridge Scholars Publishing, 23–51.

Boeckx, Cedric (this volume). 'What Principles and Parameters got wrong'.

Boeckx, Cedric (to appear a). 'Considerations pertaining to the nature of logodiversity, or how to construct a parametric space without parameters', in L. Eguren et al. (eds), *Rethinking Parameters*, Oxford: Oxford University Press.

Boeckx, Cedric (to appear b). *Elementary Syntactic Structures*. Cambridge: Cambridge University Press.

Boeckx, Cedric, Janet D. Fodor, Leila Gleitman, & Luigi Rizzi (2009). 'Language Universals: Yesterday, Today, and Tomorrow', in M. Piattelli-Palmarini, P. Salaburu, & J. Uriagereka (eds), *Of Minds and Language: A Basque Encounter with Noam Chomsky*. Oxford: Oxford University Press, 194–220.

Boeckx, Cedric, Norbert Hornstein, & Jairo Nunes (2010). *Control as Movement*. Cambridge: Cambridge University Press.

Boeckx, Cedric & Massimo Piattelli-Palmarini (2005). 'Language as a natural object; linguistics as a natural science', *The Linguistic Review* 22: 467–71.

Boef, E. (2013). 'Doubling in relative clauses. Aspects of morphosyntactic microvariation in Dutch', PhD dissertation, Utrecht University. LOT Dissertations 317.

Bok-Bennema, Reineke (1991). *Case and Agreement in Inuit*. Berlin: Foris.

Borer, Hagit (1984). *Parametric Syntax. Case Studies in Semitic and Romance Languages*. Dordrecht: Foris.

Borer, Hagit (2003). 'Exo-skeletal vs. endo-skeletal explanations: Syntactic projections and the lexicon', in J. Moore & M. Polinsky (eds.), *The Nature of Explanation in Linguistic Theory*. Stanford, CA: CSLI Publications, 31–67.

Borer, Hagit (2005). *In Name Only: Structuring Sense*. Oxford: Oxford University Press.

Bošković, Željko (2002). 'On multiple wh-fronting', *Linguistic Inquiry* 33: 351–83.

Bošković, Željko (2004). 'PF Merger in Stylistic Fronting and Object Shift', in A. Stepanov, G. Fanselow, & R. Vogel (eds), *Minimality Effects in Syntax*. Berlin: Mouton, 37–71.

Bošković, Željko (2008a). 'The NP/DP analysis and Slovenian', *Novi Sad Generative Syntax Workshop*, 53–73. University of Novi Sad.

Bošković, Željko (2008b). 'What will you have, DP or NP?', in *Proceedings of NELS* 37. GLSA.

Bošković, Željko (2009). 'On NP's and Clauses', talk presented at the International Conference on Sentence Types: Ten Years After, University of Frankfurt, Germany.

Bošković, Željko (2010). 'NPs and clauses', MS, University of Connecticut.

Bouchard, D. (2003). 'The origins of language variation', *Linguistic Variation Yearbook* 3, 1–42.

Bouma, G., P. Hendriks, & J. Hoeksema (2007). 'Focus Particles Inside Prepositional Phrases: A Comparison of Dutch, English and German', *JCGL* 10 (1): 1–24.

Brandi, Luciana & Patrizia Cordin (1989). 'Two Italian Dialects and the Null Subject Parameter', in O. A. Jaeggli & K. J. Safir (eds.), *The Null Subject Parameter*. Dordrecht: Kluwer, 111–42.

Bresnan, Joan, Anna Cueni, Tatiana Nikitina, & Harald Baayen (2007). 'Predicting the Dative Alternation', in G. Boume, I. Kraemer, & J. Zwarts (eds), *Cognitive Foundations of Interpretation*. Amsterdam: Royal Netherlands Academy of Science, 69–94.

Bresnan, Joan & Joni Kanerva (1989). 'Locative inversion in Chichewa: A case study of factorization in grammar', *Linguistic Inquiry* 20: 1–50.

Brody, Michael (1995). *Lexico-logical Form: A Radically Minimalist Theory*. Cambridge, MA: MIT Press.

Brody, Michael (2000). 'Mirror theory: Syntactic representation in perfect syntax', *Linguistic Inquiry* 31: 29–56.

Büring, D. & K. Hartmann (2001). 'The Syntax and Semantics of Focus-sensitive particles in German', *Natural Language & Linguistic Theory* 19: 229–81.

Bybee, Joan (2006). 'From usage to grammar: The mind's response to repetition', *Language* 82.4: 711–33.

Bye, Patrick & Peter Svenonius (2012). 'Non-concatenative morphology as an epiphenomenon', in J. Trommer (ed.), *The Morphology and Phonology of Exponence*. Oxford: Oxford University Press.

Caha, Pavel (2009). 'The nanosyntax of case', PhD dissertation, University of Tromsø.

Cardaillac, Kelly Reine (1976). 'A descriptive analysis of Gascon', *Zeitschrift für Französische Sprache und Literatur*, 86 (1): 88–93.

Cardinaletti, Anna (1990). 'Subject/object asymmetries in German null-topic constructions and the status of specCP', in J. Mascaró & M. Nespor (eds), *Grammar in Progress: Glow Essays for Henk van Riemsdijk*. Dordrecht: Foris, 75–84.

Cardinaletti, Anna (1997a). 'Subjects and Clause Structure', in L. Haegeman (ed.), *The New Comparative Syntax*. London: Longman, 33–63.

Cardinaletti, Anna (1997b). 'Agreement and Control in Expletive Constructions', *Linguistic Inquiry* 28 (3): 521–33.

Cardinaletti, Anna (2004). 'Toward a Cartography of Subject Positions', in L. Rizzi (ed.), *The Structure of CP and IP: The Cartography of Syntactic Structures, Vol. 2*. Oxford: Oxford University Press, 115–65.

Cardinaletti, Anna (2007). 'Subjects and *wh*-questions. Some new generalizations', in J. Camacho, N. Flores-Ferrán, L. Sánchez, V. Déprez, & M. J. Cabrera (eds), *The Best Romance: Selected Papers from the 36th Linguistic Symposium on Romance Languages (LSRL)*. Amsterdam: John Benjamins, 57–68.

Cardinaletti, Anna (2008). 'On different types of clitic clusters', in C. De Cat & K. Demuth (eds), *The Bantu-Romance Connection: A Comparative Investigation of Verbal Agreement, DPs, and Information Structure*. Amsterdam: John Benjamins, 41–82.

Cardinaletti, Anna (2009). 'On a (wh-)moved Topic in Italian, compared to Germanic', in A. Alexiadou, J. Hankamer, T. McFadden, J. Nuger, & F. Schaefer (eds), *Advances in Comparative Germanic Syntax*. Amsterdam: John Benjamins, 3–40.

Cardinaletti, Anna (2011). 'German and Italian Modal Particles and Clause Structure', *The Linguistic Review* 28: 493–531.

Cardinaletti, Anna & Lori Repetti (2008). 'The Phonology and Syntax of Preverbal and Postverbal Subject Clitics in Northern Italian Dialects', *Linguistic Inquiry* 39 (4): 523–63.

Cardinaletti, Anna & Lori Repetti (2010a). 'Proclitic vs enclitic pronouns in northern Italian dialects and the null-subject parameter', in R. D'Alessandro, A. Ledgeway, & I. Roberts (eds), *Syntactic Variation: The Dialects of Italy*. Cambridge: Cambridge University Press, 119–34.

Cardinaletti, Anna & Lori Repetti (2010b). 'Functional vowels in main questions in Northern Italian dialects', in R. Bok-Bennema, B. Kampers-Manhe, & B. Hollebrandse (eds), *Romance Languages and Linguistic Theory 2008. Selected papers from 'Going Romance'. Groningen 2008*. Amsterdam: John Benjamins, 37–58.

Cardinaletti, Anna & Michael Starke (1993). 'The Typology of Structural Deficiency: On the Three Grammatical Classes'. Paper presented at the 16th Glow Colloquium, Lund, University of Venice/University of Geneva, ms.

Cardinaletti, Anna & Michal Starke (1999). 'The Typology of Structural Deficiency: A Case-study of the Three Classes of Pronouns', in H. van Riemsdijk (ed.), *Clitics in the Languages of Europe. EALT/EUROTYP 20–5*. Berlin: Mouton de Gruyter, 145–233.

Carstens, Vicky (2005). 'Agree and EPP in Bantu', *Natural Language and Linguistic Theory* 23: 219–79.

Cheshire, Jenny, David Adger, & Sue Fox (2013). 'Relative who and the actuation problem', *Lingua* 126: 51–77.

Chierchia, Gennaro, Maria Teresa Guasti, & Andrea Gualmini (2000). 'Nouns and Articles in Child Grammar and the Syntax/Semantic Map', MS, University of Milano-Bicocca.

Chinellato, Paolo (2003). 'The Recovery of Subject Clitics in Mild agrammatism: A Generative Approach to Treatment', *Rivista di Grammatica Generativa* 28: 31–44.

Chomsky, Noam (1964). 'Current Issues in Linguistic Theory', in J. Fodor & J. Katz (eds), *The Structure of Language*. Englewood Cliffs, NJ: Prentice Hall.

Chomsky, Noam (1973). 'Conditions on Transformations', in S. Anderson & P. Kiparsky (eds), *A Festschrift for Morris Halle*. New York: Holt, Rinehart, and Winston, 232–86.

Chomsky, Noam (1976). 'Conditions on Rules of Grammar', *Linguistic Analysis* 2: 303–51.

Chomsky, Noam (1977). *Essays on Form and Interpretation*. New York/Amsterdam/London: North Holland.

Chomsky, Noam (1980). *Rules and Representations*. New York: Columbia University Press.

Chomsky, Noam (1981). *Lectures on Government and Binding*. Dordrecht: Foris.

Chomsky, Noam (1986a). *Knowledge of Language: Its Nature, Origins and Use*. New York: Praeger.

Chomsky, Noam (1986b). *Barriers*. Cambridge, MA: MIT Press.

Chomsky, Noam (1988). *Language and Problems of Knowledge: The Managua Lectures*. Cambridge, MA: MIT Press.

Chomsky, Noam (1993a). *Language and Thought*. Wakefield, RI: Moyer Bell.

Chomsky, Noam (1993b). 'A Minimalist program for linguistic theory', in K. Hale & S. J. Keyser (eds), *The View from Building 20. Essays in Linguistics in Honor of Sylvain Bromberger*. Cambridge, Cambridge, MA: MIT Press, 1–52.

Chomsky, Noam (1995). *The Minimalist Program*. Cambridge, MA: MIT Press.

Chomsky, Noam (2000). 'Minimalist inquiries: the framework', in R. Martin, D. Michaels, & J. Uriagereka (eds), *Step by Step: Essays on Minimalist Syntax in Honor of Howard Lasnik*. Cambridge, MA: MIT Press, 89–155.

Chomsky, Noam (2001). 'Derivation by phase', in M. Kenstowicz (ed.), *Ken Hale: A Life in Language*. Cambridge, MA: MIT Press, 1–52.

Chomsky, Noam (2002). *On Nature and Language*. Cambridge: Cambridge University Press.

Chomsky, Noam (2004). 'Beyond Explanatory Adequacy', in A. Belletti (ed.), *Structures and Beyond*. New York: Oxford University Press, 104–31.

Chomsky, Noam (2005). 'Three factors in the language design', *Linguistic Inquiry* 36: 1–22.

Chomsky, Noam (2007). 'Approaching UG from below', in H.-M. Gärtner & U. Sauerland (eds), *Interfaces + Recursion = Language?* Berlin: Mouton de Gruyter, 1–29.

Chomsky, Noam (2008). 'On phases', in R. Freidin, C. Otero, & M. L. Zubizarreta (eds), *Foundational Issues in Linguistic Theory: Essays in Honor of Jean-Roger Vergnaud*. Cambridge, MA: MIT Press, 133–66.

Chomsky, Noam & M. Halle. (1968). *The Sound Pattern of English*. New York: Harper Row.

Christophe, A., M. Nespor, M. T. Guasti, & B. Van Ooyen (2003). Prosodic structure and syntactic acquisition: The case of the head-direction parameter, *Developmental Science*, 6(2), 211–20.

Cinque, Guglielmo (1999). *Adverbs and Functional Heads: A Cross-Linguistic Perspective*. Oxford: Oxford University Press.

Cinque, Guglielmo (ed.) (2002). The Structure of CP and DP: The Cartography of Syntactic Structures, Vol. 1. Oxford: Oxford University Press.

Cinque, Guglielmo (2005). 'Deriving Greenberg's Universal 20 and its Exceptions', *Linguistic Inquiry* 36: 315–32.

Cinque, Guglielmo (2013). 'Cognition, typological generalizations, and Universal Grammar', *Lingua* 130, special issue *Core Ideas and Results in Syntax*.

Cinque, Guglielmo & R. Kayne (eds) (2005). *The Oxford Handbook of Comparative Syntax.* Oxford: Oxford University Press.

Cinque, Guglielmo & Luigi Rizzi (2008). 'The cartography of syntactic structures', in V. Moscati (ed.), CISL *Working Papers on Language and Cognition* 2: 43–59.

Cinque, Guglielmo & Luigi Rizzi (2010). 'The Cartography of Syntactic Structures', in *Handbook of Syntactic Theories.* Oxford: Oxford University Press.

Clark, Robin & Ian Roberts (1993). 'A computational approach to language, learnability and language change', *Linguistic Inquiry* 24: 299–345.

Cole, Peter (1985). *Imbabura Quechua.* London: Croom Helm.

Collins, Chris (1997). *Local Economy.* Cambridge, MA: MIT Press.

Collins, Chris (2002). 'Eliminating labels', in S. D. Epstein & T. D. Seely (eds), *Derivation and Explanation in the Minimalist Program.* Oxford: Blackwell, 42–64.

Collins, Chris & Edward P. Stabler (2011). 'A formalization of minimalist syntax' available at <http://ling.auf.net/lingbuzz/001691>.

Comrie, Bernard (2005). 'Alignment of case marking of full noun phrases', in M. Haspelmath, M. Dryer, D. Gil, & B. Comrie (eds), *The World Atlas of Language Structures.* Oxford: Oxford University Press, 398–403.

Coniglio, Marco (2006). 'German modal particles in the functional structure of IP', *University of Venice Working Papers in Linguistics* 16: 57–95.

Coniglio, Marco (2009). '*Die Syntax der deutschen Modalpartikeln: ihre Distribution und Lizensierung in Haupt- und Nebensätzen*', PhD dissertation, Università Ca' Foscari Venezia.

Coniglio, Marco (2011). *Die Syntax der deutschen Modalpartikeln.* Berlin: Akademie Verlag.

Contreras, Heles (1991). 'On the position of subjects', in S. Rothstein (ed.), *Perspectives on Phrase Structure: Heads and Licensing*, Syntax and Semantics 25. San Diego: Academic Press, 63–79.

Cornilescu, Alexandra (1997). 'The double subject construction in Romanian: Notes on the syntax of the subject', *Revue Roumaine de Linguistique* XLII, 3–4: 101–47.

Costa, João & Inês Duarte (2002). 'Preverbal subjects in null subject languages are not necessarily dislocated', *Journal of Portuguese Linguistics* 1: 159–76.

Craenenbroeck, J. van & M. van Koppen (2008). 'Pronominal Doubling in Dutch Dialects: Big DPs and Coordinations', in S. Barbiers, O. Koeneman, M. Lekakou, & M. van der Ham (eds), *Microvariation in Syntactic Doubling.* Bingley: Emerald, 207–50.

Cruschina, S. (2006). 'Informational focus in Sicilian and the left periphery', in M. Frascarelli (ed.), *Phases of Interpretation.* Berlin: Mouton de Gruyter, 363–85.

Cuervo, Maria Cristina (2003). 'Datives at large', PhD dissertation, MIT.

Culicover, P. (1999). *Syntactic Nuts: Hard Cases, Syntactic Theory, and Language Acquisition.* Oxford: Oxford University Press.

D'Alessandro, Roberta & Ian Roberts (2010). 'Past participle agreement in Abruzzese: Split auxiliary selection and the null-subject parameter', *Natural Language and Linguistic Theory* 28: 41–72.

Dankaert, L. (2012). *Latin Embedded Clauses.* Amsterdam: John Benjamins.

Déchaine, R. & M. Wiltschko (2002). 'Decomposing pronouns', *Linguistic Inquiry* 33, 409–42.

De Crousaz, Isabelle & Ur Shlonsky (2003). 'The distribution of a Subject Clitic Pronoun in a Franco-Provençal Dialect and the Licensing of Pro', *Linguistic Inquiry* 34 (3): 413–42.

Diesing, Molly (1992). *Indefinites.* Cambridge, MA: MIT Press.

Dixon, R. M. W. (1994). *Ergativity*. Cambridge: Cambridge University Press.

Dobrovie-Sorin, Carmen (1994). *The Syntax of Romanian: Comparative Studies in Romance*. Berlin: Mouton de Gruyter.

Dryer, Matthew S. (1998). 'Why Statistical Universals are Better than Absolute Universals', in K. Singer, R. Eggert, & G. Anderson (eds), *Proceedings of the 33rd Regional Meeting of the Chicago Linguistics Society. Papers from the panels on linguistic ideologies in contact, Universal Grammar, parameters and typology, the perception of speech and other acoustic signals*. CLS 33: 123–45.

Dryer, Matthew S. (2005). 'Order of subject, object, and verb', in M. Haspelmath, M. Dryer, D. Gil, & B. Comrie (eds), *The World Atlas of Language Structures*. New York: Oxford University Press, 386–9.

Dunn, John Asher (1995). *Smʼalgyax: A Reference Dictionary and Grammar for Coast Tsimshian*. Seattle: University of Washington Press.

Eguzkitza, Andolin (1998). 'Postposizioak euskal gramatikan', in I. Turrez, A. Arejita, & C. Isasi (eds), *Studia Philologica in Honorem Alfonso Irigoien*. Bilbao: University of Deusto, 83–8.

É. Kiss, Katalin (1996). 'Focussing as predication', in V. Molnar & S. Winkler (eds), *The Architecture of Focus*. Berlin: Mouton de Gruyter, 169–96.

É. Kiss, Katalin (2006). 'Focussing as predication', in V. Molnar & S. Winkler (eds.), *The Architecture of Focus*. Berlin: Mouton de Gruyter.

Ellegard, Alvar (1953). *The Auxiliary 'Do': The Establishment and Regulation of its Use in English*. Stockholm: Almqvist & Wiksell.

Elordieta, Arantzazu (2001). *Verb Movement and Constituent Permutation in Basque*. Leiden: LOT Dissertation Series.

Emonds, J. (1978). 'The verbal complex V-V in French', *Linguistic Inquiry* 9: 151–75.

Epstein, S. D. & T. D. Seely (2006). *Derivations in Minimalism*. Cambridge: Cambridge University Press.

Erker, Daniel & Gregory Guy (2012). 'The role of frequency in syntactic variability: Variable subject personal pronoun expression in Spanish', *Language* 88: 526–57.

Etcheberry, Jean-Baptiste (1966). *Frantziako Erregina*. Bayonne: Imprimerie Cordeliers.

Etcheberry, Jean-Baptiste (1969). *Obrak Mintzo*. Bayonne: Imprimerie Cordeliers.

Etcheberry, Jean-Baptiste (1978). *Han-Hemenka*. Bayonne: Imprimerie Cordeliers.

Etcheberry, Jean-Baptiste (1980). *Berriz Ere Beretarik*. Bayonne: Imprimerie Cordeliers.

Etcheberry, Jean-Baptiste (1981). *Hazparneko misionestak*. Bayonne: Imprimerie Cordeliers.

Etchepare, Jean (1958). *Iturraldea*. Amorebieta: Erroteta. Hiru hego.

Etxepare, Ricardo (2003). 'Valency and Argument Structure in the Basque Verb', in J. I. Hualde & J. Ortiz de Urbina (eds), *A Grammar of Basque*. Mouton Grammar Library 26. Berlin: Mouton, 363–425.

Etxepare, Ricardo (2006). 'Number Long Distance Agreement in Substandard Basque', *Studies in Basque and Historical Linguistics in Memory of R. L. Trask. The International Journal of Basque Linguistics and Philology*. Gipuzkoako Foru Aldundia Euskal Herriko Unibertsitatea / Diputación Foral de Gipuzkoa. Universidad del País Vasco(1–2), 303–50.

Etxepare, Ricardo (2012). 'Agreement configurations in Basque: A view from distance', habilitation thesis, IKER (UMR5478), Université Michel de Montaigne-Bordeaux.

Etxepare, Ricardo & Bernard Oyharçabal (2009). 'Hautazko datibo komunztadura ifarekialdeko euskalkietan', *Lapurdum* 13: 145–58.

Etxepare, Ricardo & Bernard Oyharçabal (2013). 'Datives and adpositions in northeastern Basque', in B. Fernandez & R. Etxepare (eds), *Syntactic Microvariation in Datives*. Oxford: Oxford University Press, 50–95.

Evans, N. & S. C. Levinson (2009). 'The myth of language universals: Language diversity and its importance for cognitive science', *Behavioral and Brain Sciences* 32: 429–92.

Fasanella-Seligrat, A. (2011). 'Els problemes de Plató, de Darwin i de Greenberg', *Els Marges* 94.

Fassi Fehri, Abdelkader (1993). *Issues in the Structure of Arabic Clauses and Words*. Dordrecht: Kluwer.

Felser, C. (2004). 'Wh-copying, phases and successive cyclicity', *Lingua* 114: 543–74.

Fernández, Beatriz (1997). 'Egiturazko Kasuaren Erkaketa Euskaraz', PhD dissertation, University of the Basque Country.

Fernández, Beatriz & Jon Ortiz de Urbina (2008). 'Datibo komunztadura ekialdeko hizkeretan', MS, University of the Basque Country and University of Deusto.

Fernández, Beatriz & Jon Ortiz de Urbina (2009). *Datiboa Hiztegian*, MS, University of the Basque Country and University of Deusto.

Fernández, Beatriz & Jon Ortiz de Urbina (2010). *Datiboa hiztegian*. Bilbao: EHU-UPV.

Fodor, J. A. & M. Piattelli-Palmarini (2010). *What Darwin Got Wrong*. New York: Farrar, Straus, and Giroux.

Fortuny, J. (2008). *The Emergence of Order in Syntax*. Amsterdam: John Benjamins.

Fox, Danny & David Pesetsky (2004). 'Cyclic linearization of syntactic structure', *Theoretical Linguistics* 31: 1–46.

Frampton, J. & S. Gutmann (2002). 'Crash-proof syntax', in S. D. Epstein & T. D. Seely (eds), *Derivation and Explanation in the Minimalist Program*. Oxford: Blackwell, 90–105.

Franck, J. & R. Lassotta (2012). 'Revisiting evidence for lexicalized word order in young children', *Lingua*, 122 (1): 92–106.

Franck, J., S. Millotte, & R. Lassotta (2011). 'Early word order representations: Novel arguments against old contradictions', *Language Acquisition* 18: 121–35.

Franck, J., S. Millotte, A. Posada, & L. Rizzi (2013). 'Abstract knowledge of word order by 19 months: An eye-tracking study', *Applied Psycholinguistics* 34: 323–36.

Frank, Paul (1990). *Ika Syntax*. Arlington, Texas: SIL and University of Texas-Arlington.

Frege, G. (1892). 'Über Sinn und Bedeutung', *Zeitschrift für Philosophie und Philosophische Kritik* NF 100, 25–50.

Freidin, Robert & A. Carlos Quicoli (1989). 'Zero-stimulation for parameter setting', *Behavioral and Brain Sciences*, 12 (2): 338–9.

Frisch, S. (1999). 'Review of Thomas Berg (ed.), *Linguistic Structure and Change: An Explanation from Language Processing*', Oxford: Clarendon Press (1998). *Journal of Linguistics* 35: 579–655.

Fukui, N. (2006). *Theoretical Comparative Syntax*. London: Routledge.

Gallego, Á. (2011). 'Parameters', in C. Boeckx (ed.), *Oxford Handbook of Linguistic Minimalism*. Oxford: Oxford University Press, 523–550.

Gallistel, Charles R. (2009). 'The Foundational Abstractions', in M. Piattelli-Palmarini, J. Uriagereka, & P. Salaburu (eds), *On Minds and Language*. Oxford: Oxford University Press, 58–73.

George, Leland & Jaklin Kornfilt (1981). 'Finiteness and boundedness in Turkish', in Frank Heny (ed.), *Binding and Filtering*. Cambridge, MA: MIT Press, 105–29.

Gertner, Y., C. Fisher, & J. Eisengart (2006). 'Learning words and rules', *Psychological Science* 17 (8): 684–91.

Gervain, Judith & Jacques Mehler (2010). 'Speech Perception and Language Acquisition in the First Year of Life', *Annual Review of Psychology* 61: 191–218.

Gervain, Judith, M. Nespor , R. Mazuka, R. Horie, & J. Mehler (2008). 'Bootstrapping word order in prelexical infants: A Japanese–Italian cross-linguistic study', *Cognitive Psychology* 57 (1): 56–74.

Gibson, E. & K. Wexler (1994). 'Triggers', *Linguistic Inquiry* 25 (3): 407–54.

Giles, Howard (1994). 'Accommodation in communication', in R. E. Asher (ed.), *Encyclopedia of Language and Linguistics*. Oxford: Pergamon Press.

Gilligan, Gary (1987). '*A Cross-Linguistic Approach to the Pro-drop Parameter*', PhD dissertation, University of Southern California.

Giorgi, Alessandra (2010). *About the Speaker: Toward a Syntax of Indexicality*. Oxford: Oxford University Press.

Giusti, Giuliana (2012). 'Acquisition at the interface. A caveat for syntactic search', in S. Ferré, Ph. Prévost, L. Tuller, & R. Zebib (eds), *Selected Proceedings of the Romance Turn IV. Workshop on the Acquisition of Romance Languages*, Newcastle upon Tyne: Cambridge Scholars Publishing, 104–123.

Goldberg, Adele E. (2003). 'Constructions: A new theoretical approach to language', *Trends in Cognitive Sciences* 7: 219–24.

Goldberg, Adele E. (2013). 'Explanation and constructions', *Mind and Language*, to appear.

Goldberg, Lotus (2005). '*Verb-stranding VP Ellipsis: A Cross-linguistic Study*', PhD thesis, McGill University. <http://www.lotusgoldberg.net/dissertation/Goldberg-PHD-1st-half.pdf>.

Gould, S. J. (1977). *Ontogeny and Phylogeny*. Cambridge, MA: Harvard University Press.

Greenberg, Joseph H. (1963). 'Some universals of grammar with particular reference to the order of meaningful elements', in J. Greenberg (ed.), *Universals of Language*. Cambridge, MA: MIT Press, 73–113.

Grewendorf, Günter (2012). 'Wh-Movement as Topic Movement', in L. Brugè, A. Cardinaletti, G. Giusti, N. Munaro, & C. Poletto (eds), *Functional Heads: The Cartography of Syntactic Structures*. Oxford: Oxford University Press, 55–68.

Grewendorf, Günter & W. Sternefeld (eds) (1991). *Scrambling and Barriers*. Amsterdam/New York: John Benjamins.

Grimshaw, Jane (1979). 'Complement Selection and the Lexicon', *Linguistic Inquiry* 10: 270–326.

Grimshaw, Jane (1986). 'Subjacency and the S/S$'$ Parameter', *Linguistic Inquiry* 17: 364–9.

Grimshaw, Jane (1991). 'Extended projections', MS, Brandeis University.

Groat, Eric & John O'Neil (1996). 'Spellout at the LF interface', in W. Abrahams, D. Epstein, & H. Thrainsson (eds), *Minimal Ideas: Syntactic Studies in the Minimalist Framework*. Amsterdam: John Benjamins, 113–39.

Grohmann, K. (2003). *Prolific Domains: On the Anti-locality of Movement Dependencies*. Amsterdam: John Benjamins.

Gropen, Jess, Steven Pinker, Michelle Hollander, Richard Goldberg, & Ronald Wilson (1989). 'The Learnability and Acquisition of the Dative Alternation in English', *Language* 65: 203–57.

Guasti, Maria Teresa (2002). *Language Acquisition: The Growth of Grammar*. Cambridge, MA: MIT Press.

Guimarães, Maximillian (2000). 'In Defense of Vacuous Projections in Bare Phrase Structure,' in M. Guimarães, L. Meroni, C. Rodrigues, & I. San Martin (eds), *University of Maryland Working Papers in Linguistics* 9: 90–115.

Gulya, János (1966). *Eastern Ostyak cherstomathy*. Bloomington, Ind.: University of Indiana Press.

Haase, Martin (1992). *Sprachkontakt und Sprachwandel im Baskenland: Die Einflüsse des Gaskognischen und Franžischen auf das Baskische*. Hamburg: Buske.

Haddican, Bill (2008). 'Euskal perpausaren oinarrizko *espez-buru-osagarri* hurrenkeraren aldeko argudio batzuk', in I. Arteatx, X. Artiagoitia, & A. Elordieta (eds), *Antisimetriaren hipotesia vs. buru parametroa: auskararen oinarrizko hitz hurrenkera ezbaian*. Bilbao: EHU-UPV.

Haegeman, L. (1990). 'The Syntax of Motional *goan* in West-Flemish', in R. Bok-Bennema & P. Coopmans (eds), *Linguistics in the Netherlands*. Dordrecht: Foris, 81–90.

Haegeman, L. (1992). *Theory and Description in Generative Syntax—A Case Study in West Flemish*. Cambridge: Cambridge University Press.

Haegeman, L. (1995). *The Syntax of Negation*. Cambridge: Cambridge University Press.

Haegeman, L. (2012). *Adverbial Clauses, Main Clause Phenomena, and Composition of the Left Periphery: The Cartography of Syntactic Structures, Vol. 8*. New York: Oxford University Press.

Haegeman, L. (2013). 'The syntax of registers: Diary subject omission and the privilege of the root', *Lingua* 130, special issue *Core Ideas and Results in Syntax*.

Hale, Ken (1983). 'Warlpiri and the grammar of non-configurational languages', *Natural Language and Linguistic Theory* 1: 5–47.

Hale, Ken & S. Jay Keyser (1993). 'On argument structure and the lexical expression of grammatical relations', in K. Hale & S. J. Keyser, *The View from Building 20: Essays in Linguistics in honor of Sylvain Bromberger*. Cambridge, MA: MIT Press, 53–110.

Hale, Ken & S. Jay Keyser (2002). *Prolegomenon to a Theory of Argument Structure*. Cambridge, MA: MIT Press.

Hale, Mark & Charles Reiss (2008). *The Phonological Enterprise*. Oxford: Oxford University Press.

Halle, Morris (1997). 'Distributed Morphology: Impoverishment and Fission', *MIT Working Papers in Linguistics* 30: 425–49.

Halle, Morris & Alec Marantz (1993). 'Distributed Morphology and the Pieces of Inflection', in K. Hale and S. J. Keyser (eds), *The View from Building 20*, Cambridge, MA: MIT Press.

Halle, Morris & Alec Marantz (1994). 'Some key features of Distributed Morphology', in A. Carnie, H. Harley, & T. Bures (eds), *Papers on Phonology and Morphology*, MITWPL 21, 275–88.

Hamblin, Charles (1958). 'Questions', *Australasian Journal of Philosophy* 36: 159–68.

Harbour, Daniel. (2004). 'On the unity of "number" in semantics and morphology', available at <http://ling.auf.net/lingbuzz/000089>.

Harley, Heidi (2003). 'Possession and the double object construction', MS, University of Arizona.

Harley, Heidi (2011). 'A Minimalist Approach to Argument Structure', in C. Boeckx (ed.), *The Oxford Handbook of Linguistic Minimalism*. Oxford/New York: Oxford University Press.

Harley, Heidi & Elizabeth Ritter (2002). 'Person and number in pronouns: A feature-geometric analysis', *Language* 78: 482–526.

Haspelmath, Martin (1993). *A Grammar of Lezgian*. Berlin: Mouton de Gruyter.

Haspelmath, Martin (2008). 'Parametric versus functional explanations of syntactic universals', in T. Biberauer (ed.), *The Limits of Syntactic Variation*. Amsterdam: John Benjamins, 75–107.

Hauser, Mark, Noam Chomsky, & William T. Fitch (2002). 'The Faculty of Language: What is it, who has it and how did it evolve?', *Science* 298: 1569–79.

Heine, B. & T. Kuteva (2002). *World Lexicon of Grammaticalization*. Cambridge: Cambridge University Press.

Henry, Alison (1995). *Belfast English and Standard English: Dialectal Variation and Parameter Setting*. New York/Oxford: Oxford University Press.

Hinzen, Wolfram (2006). *Mind Design and Minimal Syntax*. Oxford: Oxford University Press.

Hinzen, Wolfram (2009). 'Hierarchy, Merge, and Truth', in M. Piattelli-Palmarini, J. Uriagereka, & P. Salaburu (eds), *On Minds and Language*. Oxford: Oxford University Press, 123–41.

Hirsh-Pasek, K. R. & R. M. Golinkoff (1996). *The Origins of Grammar*. Cambridge, MA: MIT Press.

Holmberg, Anders. (2001). 'The syntax of yes and no in Finnish', *Studia Linguistica* 55: 140–74.

Holmberg, Anders (2005). 'Is There a Little Pro? Evidence from Finnish', *Linguistic Inquiry* 35: 533–64.

Holmberg, Anders (2007). 'Null subjects and polarity focus', *Studia Linguistica* 61: 212–36.

Holmberg, Anders (2010a). 'Parameters in minimalist theory: The case of Scandinavian', *Theoretical Linguistics* 36:1–48.

Holmberg, Anders (2010b). 'Null subject parameters', in T. Biberauer, A. Holmberg, I. Roberts, & M. Sheehan (eds.), *Parametric Variation: Null Subjects in Minimalist Theory*. Cambridge: Cambridge University Press, 88–124.

Holmberg, Anders & Urpo Nikanne (2002). 'Expletives, subjects and topics in Finnish', in P. Svenonius (ed.), *Subjects, Expletives, and the EPP*. New York: Oxford University Press, 71–105.

Holmberg, Anders & C. Platzack (1995). *The Role of Inflection in Scandinavian Syntax*. Oxford/New York: Oxford University Press.

Holmberg, Anders & I. Roberts (2013). 'The syntax-morphology relation', *Lingua* 130, special issue *Core Ideas and Results in Syntax*.

Hopper, Paul & Sandra Thompson (1980). 'Transitivity in grammar and discourse', *Language* 56: 251–99.

Hornstein, Norbert (1999). 'Movement and control', *Linguistic Inquiry* 30: 69–96.

Hornstein, Norbert (2009). *A Theory of Syntax*. Cambridge: Cambridge University Press.

Hornstein, Norbert, J. Nunes, & K. K. Grohmann (2006). *Understanding Minimalism*. Cambridge: Cambridge University Press.

Hourcade, André (1986). *Grammaire Béarnaise*. Pau: Association Los Caminaires.

Hualde, José Ignacio (2002). 'Regarding Basque postpositions and related matters', in X. Arti-agoitia, P. Goenaga, & J. A. Lakarra (eds), *Erramu Boneta. Festschrift for Rudolf P.G. de Rijk. ASJU Supplements 44*. Bilbao: University of the Basque Country, 325–40.

Hualde, José Ignacio & Jon Ortiz de Urbina (eds) (2003). *A Grammar of Basque*. Berlin: Mouton de Gruyter.

Huang, C. T. James (1982). '*Logical Relations in Chinese and the Theory of Grammar*', PhD dissertation, MIT.

Huang, C. T. James (1984). 'On the distribution and reference of empty pronouns', *Linguistic Inquiry* 15: 531–74.

Huang, C. T. James (2005). 'Analyticity', class lectures, MIT/Harvard LSA Summer Institute.

Hulk, A. & J.-Y. Pollock (eds) (2001). *Subject Positions in Romance and the Theory of Universal Grammar*. Oxford: Oxford University Press.

Hutchison, John (1981). *A Reference Grammar of the Kanuri Language*. Madison, Wisc: African studies program, University of Wisconsin.

Hyams, N. (1986). *Language Acquisition and the Theory of Parameters*. Dordrecht: Reidel.

Hymes, Dell (1971). *On Communicative Competence*. Philadelphia: University of Pennsylvania Press.

Inkelas, S. & C. Zoll (2005). *Reduplication: Doubling in Morphology. Cambridge Studies in Linguistics* 106. Cambridge: Cambridge University Press.

Jackendoff, Ray (1983). *Semantics and Cognition*. Cambridge, MA: MIT Press.

Jackendoff, Ray (1990). *Semantic Structures*. Cambridge, MA: MIT Press.

Jackendoff, Ray (1996). 'The architecture of the linguistic-spatial interface', in P. Bloom, M. A. Peterson, L. Nadel, & M. F.Garrett (eds), *Language and Space*. Cambridge, MA: MIT Press, 1–30.

Jackendoff, Ray (1997). *The Architecture of the Language Faculty*. Cambridge, MA: MIT Press.

Jackendoff, Ray (2005). 'Alternative minimalist visions of language', *Proceedings from the 41st Annual Meeting of the Chicago Linguistic Society*, 2, 189–226.

Jackendoff, Ray (2010). *Meaning and the Lexicon: The Parallel Architecture 1975–2010*. Oxford: Oxford University Press.

Jaeggli, Osvaldo A. & Ken J. Safir (1989). 'The null subject parameter and parametric theory', in O. A Jaeggli & K. J. Safir (eds), *The Null Subject Parameter*. Dordrecht: Kluwer, 1–44.

Jelinek, Eloise (1984). 'Empty Categories, Case and Configurationality', *Natural Language and Linguistic Theory* 2: 39–76.

Jelinek, Eloise (2006). 'The pronominal argument parameter', in P. Ackema (ed.), *Arguments and Agreement*. Oxford: Oxford University Press, 261–88.

Jeong, Youngmi (2007). *Applicatives: Structure and Interpretation from a Minimalist Perspective*. Amsterdam: John Benjamins.

Jespersen, O. (1917). *Negation in English and Other Languages*. Copenhagen: A. F. Høst.

Jones, Bob Morris (1999). *The Welsh Answering System*. Berlin: Mouton de Gruyter.

Joos, M. (1957). *Readings in Linguistics*. American Council of Learned Societies. Washington.

Karttunen, Lauri (1976). 'Discourse referents', in J. McCawley (ed.), *Syntax and Semantics 7: Notes from the Linguistic Underground*. New York: Academic Press. 363–85.

Kayne, Richard (1975). *French Syntax*. Cambridge, MA: MIT Press.

Kayne, Richard (1983a). *Connectedness and Binary Branching*. Dordrecht: Foris.

Kayne, Richard (1983b). 'Chains, Categories External to S, and French Complex Inversion', *Natural Language and Linguistic Theory* 1: 107–39.

Kayne, Richard (1994). *The Antisymmetry of Syntax*. Cambridge, MA: MIT Press.

Kayne, Richard (2000a). *Parameters and Universals*. New York: Oxford University Press.

Kayne, Richard (2000b). 'Overt versus Covert Movement', in R. Kayne, *Parameters and Universals*. New York: Oxford University Press.

Kayne, Richard (2002). 'Pronouns and their antecedents', in S. D. Epstein & T. D. Seely (eds), *Derivation and Explanation in the Minimalist Program*. Oxford: Blackwell, 133–66.

Kayne, Richard (2005a). 'Some Notes on Comparative Syntax, with Special Reference to English and French', in G. Cinque & R. Kayne (eds), *Handbook of Comparative Syntax*. New York: Oxford University Press, 3–69. [Reprinted in Kayne 2005b, 277–333].

Kayne, Richard (2005b). *Movement and Silence*. New York: Oxford University Press.

Kayne, Richard (2008). 'Antisymmetry and the Lexicon', *Linguistic Variation Yearbook* 8: 1–31.

Kayne, Richard (2010). 'Antisymmetry and the Lexicon', in A. M. Di Sciullo & C. Boeckx (eds), *The Biolinguistic Enterprise*. Oxford: Oxford University Press, 329–353.

Kayne, Richard (2011). 'Why Are There No Directionality Parameters?', in M Byram Washburn, K McKinney-Bock, E. Varis, A. Sawyer, & B. Tomaszewicz (eds), *Proceedings of the 28th West Coast Conference on Formal Linguistics*, Cascadilla Proceedings Project, Sommerville, MA, 1–23.

Kayne, Richard (2013). 'Comparative Syntax', *Lingua* 130: 132–51.

Kemp, C., A. Perfors, & J. B. Tenenbaum. (2007). 'Learning overhypotheses with hierarchical Bayesian models', *Developmental Science* 10: 307–21.

Kenstowicz, Michael (1989). 'The null subject parameter in modern Arabic dialects', in O. A Jaeggli & K. J. Safir (eds), *The Null Subject Parameter*. Dordrecht: Kluwer, 263–75.

Kiparsky, P. (1973). 'Elsewhere in Phonology', in S. Anderson & P. Kiparsky (eds), *A Festschrift for Morris Halle*. New York: Holt, Rinehart, and Winston, 93–106.

Kochovska, Slavica (2006). 'Intervention effects in Macedonian wh-questions', paper presented at *The 42nd Annual Meeting of the Chicago Linguistic Society*, April 6–8, 2006, Chicago.

Koopman, H. (2000). *The Syntax of Specifiers and Heads*. New York: Routledge.

Koopman, H. & D. Sportiche (1991). 'The Position of Subjects', *Lingua* 85: 211–58.

Koster, J. (2010). 'Language and tools', MS, Universiteit Groningen.

Kracht, Marcus (2002). 'On the semantics of locatives', *Linguistics and Philosophy* 25: 157–232.

Krifka, M. (1992). 'A Framework for Focus-Sensitive Quantification', in C. Barker & D. Dowty (eds), *Proceedings of SALT* 2. Columbus, Ohio State University, 215–36.

Kroch, Anthony (1994). 'Morphosyntactic variation', in K. Beals, J. Denton, R. Knippen, L. Melnar, H. Suzuki, & E. Zeinfeld (eds), *Papers from the 30th Regional Meeting of the Chicago Linguistic Society, vol. 2: The Parasession on Variation in Linguistic Theory*. Chicago: Chicago Linguistic Society, 180–201.

Kuryłowicz, Jerzy (1964). *The Inflectional Categories of Indo-European*. Heidelberg: Carl Winter Universitätsverlag.

Labov, William (1969). 'Contraction, deletion, and inherent variability of the English Copula', *Language* 45: 715–62.

Labov, William (1972). *Language in the Inner City*. Philadelphia: University of Pennsylvania Press.

Labov, William (1994). *Principles of Linguistic Change. Vol. 1: Internal Factors.* Oxford: Blackwell.

Labov, William (2001). *Principles of Linguistic Change. Vol. 2: Social Factors.* Oxford: Blackwell.

Laenzlinger, Christopher & Julien Musolino (1995). '(Complex) Inversion and triggers', *GenGenP* 3.1: 77–96.

Lafitte, Pierre (1979). *Grammaire Basque.* Baiona: Elkar.

Lafon, René (1980). *Le Système du verbe basque au XVIe siècle.* Baiona: Elkar.

Laka, Itziar (1990). 'Negation in Syntax: On the Nature of Functional Categories and Projections', PhD dissertation, MIT.

Landau, Idan (2000). *Elements of Control: Structure and Meaning in Infinitival Constructions.* Dordrecht : Kluwer.

Lapointe, S. (1980). *A Theory of Grammatical Agreement: Outstanding Dissertations in Linguistics.* New York: Garland.

Lasnik, H. (2002). 'All I ever wanted to be was a teacher!', an interview conducted by L. Cheng and R. Sybesma. *Glot International* 6: 320–28.

Lefebvre, Claire & Pieter Muysken (1988). *Mixed Categories: Nominalizations in Quechua.* Dordrecht: Kluwer.

Legate, J. (2002). '*Warlpiri: Theoretical Implications*' PhD dissertation, MIT.

Legate, J. (2008). 'Warlpiri and the second position clitics', *Natural Language and Linguistic Theory* 26 (1): 3–60.

Levin, Beth (2008). 'Dative Verbs: A Crosslinguistic Perspective', handout, Stanford University.

Levin, Beth & Malka Rappaport-Hovav (2008). 'The English dative alternation: The case for verb sensitivity', *Journal of Linguistics* 44: 129–67.

Li, Peggy, Yarrow Dunham, & Susan Carey (2009). 'Of Substance: The Nature of Language Effects on Entity Construal', *Cognitive Psychology* 58: 487–524.

Lidz, Jeff & Alexander Williams (2009). 'Constructions on holiday', *Cognitive Linguistics* 20: 177–89.

Lieberman, Erez, Jean B. Michel, Joe Jackson, Tina Tang, & Martin A. Novak (2007). 'Quantifying evolutionary dynamics of language', *Nature* 449: 713–16.

Lightfoot, David (1979). *Principles of Diachronic Syntax.* Cambridge: Cambridge University Press.

Lightfoot, David (1991). *How to Set Parameters: Arguments from Language Change.* Cambridge, MA: MIT Press.

Lohndal, Terje & Juan Uriagereka (2010). 'The logic of parametric theories', *Theoretical Linguistics* 36: 69–76.

Longa, V. M. & G. Lorenzo. (2008). 'What about a (really) minimalist theory of language acquisition?', *Linguistics* 46: 541–70.

Longobardi, Giuseppe (2003). 'Methods in parametric linguistics and cognitive history', *Linguistic Variation Yearbook* 3: 101–38.

Longobardi, Giuseppe (2005). 'A minimalist program for parametric linguistics?', in H. Broekhuis, N. Corver, R. Huybregts, U. Kleinhenz, & J. Koster (eds), *Organizing Grammar.* Berlin: Mouton de Gruyter, 407–14.

Longobardi, Giuseppe & Ian Roberts (2010). 'Universals, diversity and change in the science of language. Reaction to: "The myth of language universals and cognitive science"', *Lingua* 120: 2699–703.

Lorenzo, G. (2007). 'Lo que no hace falta aprender y lo que no se necesita conocer. Nota crítica: Linguistic Minimalism: Origins, Concepts, Methods, and Aims, de Cedric Boeckx', *Teorema* 26: 141–8.

Lorenzo, G. & V. M. Longa (2003). 'Minimizing the genes for grammar: The minimalist program as a biological framework for the study of language', *Lingua* 113: 643–57.

Lorenzo, G. & V. M. Longa (2009). 'Beyond generative geneticism: Rethinking language acquisition from a developmentalist point of view', *Lingua* 119: 1300–15.

Lorimer, D. L. R. (1935). *The Burushaski Language 1: Introduction and Grammar*, Vol. 1. Cambridge, MA: Harvard University Press.

McDaniel, Dana (1989). 'Partial and multiple wh-movement', *Natural Language and Linguistic Theory* 7: 565–605.

McGinnis, Martha (2001). 'Variation in the phase structure of applicatives', *Linguistic Variation Yearbook* 1: 105–46.

McGinnis, Martha (2002). 'Object Assimmetries in a Phase Theory of Syntax', in J. T. Jensen and G. van Herk (eds), *Proceedings of the 2001 CLA Annual Conference. Cahiers Linguistiques d'Ottawa*: 133–44.

Manninen, Satu & Diane Nelson (2004). 'What is a Passive? The Case of Finnish', *Studia Linguistica* 58: 212–51.

Manzini, Maria Rita & Leonardo M. Savoia (2002). 'Parameters of subject inflection in Italian dialects', in P. Svenonius (ed.), *Subjects, Expletives, and the EPP*. Oxford: Oxford University Press, 157–99.

Manzini, Maria Rita & Leonardo M. Savoia (2005). *I dialetti italiani e romanci. Morfosintassi generativa*. Alessandria: Edizioni dell'Orso.

Manzini, Maria Rita & K. Wexler (1987). 'Parameters, binding, and learning theory', *Linguistic Inquiry* 18: 413–44.

Marantz, Alec (1991). 'Case and licensing', paper presented at *The 8th Eastern States Conference on Linguistics*, University of Maryland, Baltimore.

Marantz, Alec (1993). 'Implications of Asymmetries in Double Object Constructions', in S. A. Mchombo (ed.), *Theoretical Aspects of Bantu Grammar*. Stanford: CSLI Publications, 113–50.

Marantz, Alec (2013). 'Verbal Argument Structure: Events and Participants', *Lingua* 130: 152–68.

Marr, D. (1982). *Vision*. San Francisco: Freeman.

Matthews, D., E. Lieven, A. Theakston, & M. Tomasello (2005). 'The role of frequency in the acquisition of English word order', *Cognitive Development* 20: 121–36.

Matthews, D., E. Lieven, A. Theakston, & M. Tomasello (2007). 'French children's use and correction of weird word orders: A constructivist account', *Journal of Child Language* 32(2): 381–409.

May, R. (1985). *Logical Form: Its Structure and Derivation*. Cambridge MA: MIT Press.

Merchant, Jason (2001). The Syntax of Silence: Sluicing, Islands, and the Theory of Ellipsis. Oxford/New York: Oxford University Press.

Merchant, Jason (2004). 'Fragments and ellipsis', *Linguistics and Philosophy* 27: 661–738.

Michel, Jean B., Yuan K. Shen, Aviva P. Aiden, Adrian Veres, Matthew K. Gray, Joseph P. Pickett, Dale Hoiberg, Dan Clancy, Peter Norvig, Jon Orwant, Steven Pinker, Martin A. Nowak, & Erez L. Aiden (2011). 'Quantitative Analysis of Culture Using Millions of Digitized Books', *Science* 331: 176–82.

Miyagawa, Shigeru (2010). *Why Agree? Why Move? Unifying Agreement-based and Discourse Configurational Languages*. Cambridge, MA: MIT Press.

Miyagawa, Shigeru & Takae Tsujioka (2004). 'Argument structure and ditransitive verbs in Japanese', *Journal of East Asian Linguistics* 13: 1–38.

Mobbs, I. (2008). '"Functionalism", the design of the language faculty, and (disharmonic) typology', MPhil, University of Cambridge.

Mohanan, Tara (1995). 'Wordhood and lexicality: Noun incorporation in Hindi', *Natural Language and Linguistic Theory* 13: 75–134.

Moore, John (1998). 'Turkish copy-raising and A-chain locality', *Natural Language and Linguistic Theory* 16: 149–89.

Moscati, E. (2007). '*The Scope of Negation*', PhD dissertation, University of Siena.

Mounole, Celine (2011). 'Evolution of the transitive verbs in Basque and appearance of datively marked patients', in G. Authier (ed.), *Ergativity, Transitivity and Voice*. Berlin: Mouton.

Mulder, Jean Gail (1994). *Ergativity in Coast Tsimshian*. Berkeley: University of California Press.

Naigles, L. (1990). 'Children use syntax to learn verb meanings', *Journal of Child Language* 17: 357–74.

Narita, H. (2010). 'The Tension between Explanatory and Biological Adequacy. A Review of *Theoretical Comparative Syntax: Studies in Macroparameters*, Naoki Fukui, Routledge, London and New York (2006)', *Lingua* 120: 1313–23.

Neeleman, A. & H. van de Koot (2006). 'Syntactic Haplology', in M. Everaert & H. van Riemsdijk (eds), *The Blackwell Companion to Syntax, vol. IV*. Oxford: Blackwell, 684–710.

Nevins, Andrew (2007). 'The representation of third person and its consequences for person-case effects', *Natural Language and Linguistic Theory* 25: 273–313.

Nevins, Andrew & Jeffrey K. Parrott (2010). 'Variable rules meet impoverishment theory', *Lingua* 120: 1135–59.

Newmeyer, Frederick (2004). 'Against a parameter-setting approach to language variation', in *Language Variation Yearbook*, Vol. 4. Amsterdam: Benjamins, 181–234.

Newmeyer, Frederick (2005). *Possible and Probable Languages: A Generative Perspective on Linguistic Typology*. Oxford/New York: Oxford University Press.

Newmeyer, Frederick (2006). 'A rejoinder to "on the role of parameters in Universal Grammar: A reply to Newmeyer" by Ian Roberts and Anders Holmberg', MS, University of Washington, Seattle.

Newmeyer, Frederick (2008). 'Linguistic minimalism: Origins, concepts, methods, and aims (review)', *Language* 84: 387–95.

Nicolis, M. (2008). 'The Null Subject parameter and correlating properties: The case of Creole languages', in T. Biberauer (ed.), *The Limits of Syntactic Variation*. Amsterdam: John Benjamins, 271–94.

Niyogi, Partha & R. C. Berwick (1996). 'A Language Learning Model for Finite Parameter Spaces', *Cognition* 61: 161–93.

Noyer, Rolf (1992). 'Features, positions and affixes in autonomous morphological structure', PhD thesis, MIT.

Nunes, J. (2004). *Linearization of Chains and Sideward Movement*. Cambridge, MA: MIT Press.

Odden, D. (1988). 'Antigemination and the OCP', *Linguistic Inquiry* 19: 451–75.

Oehrle, Richard T. (1978). 'The Grammatical Status of the English Dative Alternation', PhD dissertation, MIT.

Ordóñez, Francisco & Antxon Olarrea (2006). 'Microvariation in Caribbean/non-Caribbean Spanish interrogatives', *Probus* 18 (1): 59–96.

Ormazabal, Javier & Juan Romero (1998). 'On the syntactic nature of the *me-lui* and the Person-Case Constraint' *Anuario del Seminario Julio de Urquijo* 32: 415–34.

Ormazabal, Javier & Juan Romero (2001). 'A brief description of some agreement restrictions', in B. Fernández and P. Albizu (eds.), *Kasu eta Komunztaduraren Gainean-On Case and Agreement*. Bilbao: University of the Basque Country, 215–41.

Ormazabal, Javier & Juan Romero (2007). 'The object Agreement Constraint'. *Natural Language and Linguistic Theory* 25: 315–47.

Ormazabal, Javier & Juan Romero (2010). 'The derivation of dative alternations', in M. Duguine, S. Huidobro, & N. Madariaga (eds), *Argument Structure and Syntactic Relations from a Crosslinguistic Perspective*. Amsterdam: John Benjamins.

Ortiz de Urbina, Jon (1994). 'Datibo komunztaduraren gainean', in R. Gómez & J. Lakarra (eds), *Euskal Dialektologiako Kongresua*. Donostia: Gipuzkoako Foru Aldundia, 579–88.

Otero, Carlos (1976). 'The dictionary in Generative Grammar', unpublished MS, UCLA.

Ott, D. (2009). 'Stylistic Fronting as Remnant Movement', *Working Papers in Scandinavian Syntax* 83: 141–78.

Ouhalla, J. (1991). *Functional Categories and Parametric Variation*. London: Routledge.

Oyharçabal, Bernard (1992). 'Elizanburu kondairalariaren euskara' [Le basque de J.-B. Elissamburu conteur], *Actes du Congrès consacré à J.-B. Elissamburu*, Sare (Pyrénées Atlantiques) 20–21 décembre 1991, URA 1055 et Académie de la langue basque, Euskera, 1992,1, Bilbao, 231–46.

Oyharçabal, Bernard (2010). 'Argument Structure Building: Dative Applicative Heads in Basque', in M. Duguine, S. Huidobro, & N. Madariaga (eds), *Argument Structure and Syntactic Relations from a Crosslinguistic Perspective*. Amsterdam: John Benjamins.

Palay, Simin (1980). *Dictionnaire du béarnais et du gascon modernes*. Paris: CNRS.

Pearl, L. S. (2007). 'Necessary bias in natural language learning', PhD dissertation, University of Maryland.

Perlmutter, David (1971). *Deep and Surface Constraints in Syntax*. New York: Holt, Rinehart, and Winston.

Pertsova, Katya (2007). 'Learning form-meaning mappings in the presence of homonymy', PhD thesis, UCLA.

Pesetsky, D. (1982). '*Paths and Categories*', PhD dissertation, MIT.

Peterson, David A. (2007). *Applicative Constructions*. Oxford: Oxford University Press.

Piattelli-Palmarini, Massimo (1989). 'Evolution, selection and cognition: From "learning" to parameter setting in biology and in the study of language', *Cognition* 31: 1–44.

Piattelli-Palmarini, Massimo (2010). 'What is language that it may have evolved, and what is evolution that it may apply to language', in R. K. Larson, V. Déprez, & H. Yamakido (eds), *The Evolution of Human Language: Biolinguistic Perspectives*. Cambridge: Cambridge University Press, 148–162.

Picallo, M. Carme (1998). 'On the extended projection principle and null expletive subjects', *Probus* 19: 219–41.

Pietsch, Lukas (2005). *Variable Grammars: Verbal Agreement in Northern Dialects of English*. Tübingen: Max Niemeyer Verlag.

Pigliucci, M. & G. Müller (eds) (2010). *Evolution—The Extended Synthesis*. Cambridge, MA: MIT Press.

Pikabea, Josu (1998). *Lapurtera idatzia (XVII–XIX). Bilakaera baten urratsak*. Bilbao: University of the Basque Country.

Pinker, Stephen (1984). *Language Learnability and Language Development*. Cambridge, MA: Harvard University Press.

Pinker, Stephen (2011). *The Better Angels of our Nature*. London: Allen Lane.

Poletto, Cecilia (1993). 'Subject Clitic/Verb Inversion in North Eastern Italian Dialects', in A. Belletti (ed.), *Syntactic Theory and the Dialects of Italy*. Turin: Rosenberg & Sellier, 204–51.

Poletto, Cecilia (2000). *The Higher Functional Field: Evidence from Northern Italian Dialects*. Oxford: Oxford University Press.

Poletto, Cecilia & Jean-Yves Pollock (2004). 'On the Left Periphery of Some Romance Wh-Questions', in Rizzi (ed.), *The Structure of CP and IP: The Cartography of Syntactic Structures, Vol. 3*. New York: Oxford University Press, 251–96.

Pollock, Jean-Yves (1989). 'Verb Movement, Universal Grammar, and the Structure of IP', *Linguistic Inquiry* 20: 365–424.

Pollock, Jean-Yves (1998). 'On the Syntax of Subnominal Clitics: Cliticization and Ellipsis', *Syntax* 1.3: 300–30.

Poplack, Shana & Sali A. Tagliamonte (1989). 'There's no tense like the present: Verbal s inflection in early Black English', *Language Variation and Change* 1: 47–84.

Postal, P. (1974). *On Raising*. Cambridge, MA: MIT Press.

Preminger, Omer (2009). 'Breaking Agreements: Distinguishing Agreement and Clitic-Doubling by Their Failures'. *Linguistic Inquiry* 40: 619–66.

Pylkkanen, Liina (2002). 'Introducing Arguments', PhD dissertation, MIT.

Ramchand, Gillian (2008). *Verb Meaning and the Lexicon*. Cambridge: Cambridge University Press.

Raposo, E. (2002). 'Nominal gaps with prepositional modifiers in Portuguese and Spanish: A case for Quick Spell-Out', *Cuadernos de Lingüística del I. U. Ortega y Gasset* 9: 127–44.

Rebuschi, Georges (1982). 'La structure de l'énoncé en basque', PhD dissertation, Paris (Coll. ERA-642), Laboratoire de Linguistique Formelle et Département de Recherches Linguistiques. Paris VII.

Reiss, C. (2003). 'Quantification in structural descriptions: Attested and unattested patterns', *The Linguistic Review* 20: 305–38.

Renzi, Lorenzo & Laura Vanelli (1983). 'I pronomi soggetto in alcune varietà romanze', in P. Beninca, M. Cortelazzo, A. L. Prosdocimi, L. Vanelli, & A. Zamboni (eds), *Scritti linguistici in onore di Giovan Battista Pellegrini*. Pisa: Pacini, 121–45.

Reuland, Eric (2011). *Anaphora and Language Design*. Cambridge, MA: MIT Press.

Rezac, Milan (2006). *Basque Morphosyntax*. MS, University of Nantes/CNRS.

Rezac, Milan (2009). 'On the unfiability of repairs for the Person Case Constraint: French, Basque, Georgian and Chinook', in R. Etxepare, R. Gomez, & J. A. Lakarra (eds.), *Beñat Oihartzabali gorazarre [Festschrift for Bernard Oyharçabal]*. Supplements of the International Journal of Basque Linguistics and Philology *(ASJU)*, XLIII: 1–2. University of the Basque Country, 769–90.

Richards, M. (2008). 'Two kinds of variation in a minimalist system', *Linguistische Arbeits Berichte* 87 (Universität Leipzig) 87: 133–62.

Richards, M. (2009). 'Stabilizing syntax: On instability, optionality, and other indeterminacies', presented at the Syntax workshop, Universität Stuttgart, March 2010.

Riemsdijk, Henk van (2002). 'The unbearable lightness of Going', *The Journal of Comparative Germanic Linguistics* 5 (1–3): 143–96.

Riemsdijk, Henk van (2008). 'Identity Avoidance: OCP-Effects in Swiss Relatives', in R. Freidin, C. Otero, & M. L. Zubizarreta, *Foundational Issues in Linguistics*. Cambridge, MA: MIT Press, 227–50.

Rijk, Rudolf de (1990). 'Location nouns in standard Basque', *ASJU* 24: 3–20.

Rijk, Rudolf de (2008). *Standard Basque*. Cambridge, MA: MIT Press.

Rizzi, Luigi (1978). 'Violations of the Wh Island Constraint in Italian and the Subjacency Condition', *Montreal Working Papers in Linguistics*, 11. [Reprinted in Rizzi (1982). Issues in Italian Syntax. Dordrecht: Foris, 49–76].

Rizzi, Luigi (1982). *Issues in Italian Syntax*. Dordrecht: Foris.

Rizzi, Luigi (1986). 'Null Objects in Italian and the Theory of pro', *Linguistic Inquiry*, 17(3): 501–57.

Rizzi, Luigi (1990). *Relativized Minimality*. Cambridge, MA: MIT Press.

Rizzi, Luigi (1991). 'Residual verb second and the Wh criterion', *Technical Reports in Formal and Computational Linguistics* 2. University of Geneva.

Rizzi, Luigi (1996). 'Residual Verb-second and the Wh-criterion', in A. Belletti & L. Rizzi (eds.), *Parameters and Functional Heads: Essays in Comparative Syntax*. Oxford: Oxford University Press, 63–90.

Rizzi, Luigi (1997). 'The Fine Structure of the Left Periphery', in L. Haegeman (ed.), *Elements of Grammar*. Dordrecht: Kluwer, 281–337.

Rizzi, Luigi (2000). *Comparative Syntax and Language Acquisition*. London: Routledge.

Rizzi, Luigi (2001). 'On the position "Int(errogative)" in the left periphery of the clause', in G. Cinque and G. Salvi (eds), *Current Studies in Italian Syntax: Essays Offered to Lorenzo Renzi*. Amsterdam: Elsevier, 287–96.

Rizzi, Luigi (ed.) (2004a). *The Structure of CP and IP: The Cartography of Syntactic Structures*, Vol. 2. New York: Oxford University Press.

Rizzi, Luigi (2004b). 'Locality and Left Periphery', in A. Belletti (ed.), *Structures and Beyond: The Cartography of Syntactic Structures, Vol. 3*. New York: Oxford University Press.

Rizzi, Luigi (2005). 'On some properties of subjects and topics', in L. Brugè, G. Giusti, N. Munaro, W. Schweikert, & G. Turano (eds), *Contributions to the Thirtieth 'Incontro di Grammatica Generativa'*. Venezia: Libreria Editrice Cafoscarina, 203–24.

Rizzi, Luigi (2006a). 'Grammatically-Based Target-Inconsistencies in Child Language', in K. U. Deen, J. Nomura, B. Schulz, & B. D. Schwartz (eds), *The Proceedings of the Inaugural Conference on Generative Approaches to Language Acquisition—North America, Honolulu, University of Connecticut Occasional Papers in Linguistics* 4: 19–49.

Rizzi, Luigi (2006b). 'On the Form of Chains: Criterial Positions and ECP Effects', in L. Cheng & N. Corver (eds), *On Wh Movement*. Cambridge MA: MIT Press, 97–133.

Rizzi, Luigi (2009a). 'Language Invariance and Variation', in M. Piattelli-Palmarini, J. Uriagereka, P. Salaburu (eds), *Of Minds and Language: The Basque Country Encounter with Noam Chomsky*. Oxford/New York: Oxford University Press, 211–20.

Rizzi, Luigi (2009b). 'Some elements of syntactic computation', in D. Bickerton & E. Sza-thmáry (eds), *Biological Foundations and Origin of Syntax*. Cambridge, MA: MIT Press, 63–88.

Rizzi, Luigi (2010). 'Language variation and universals: Some notes on N. Evans & S. C. Levinson (2009) "The myth of language universals: Language diversity and its importance for cognitive science"', in P. Cotticelli Kurras & A. Tomaselli (eds), *La grammatical tra storia e teoria—Studi in onore di Giorgio Graffi*. Alessandria: Edizioni Dall'Orso, 155–62.

Rizzi, Luigi (2013a). 'Notes on cartography and further explanation', *Probus* 25: 197–226.

Rizzi, Luigi (ed.) (2013b). 'Core Ideas and Results in Syntax', *Lingua* 130 special issue.

Rizzi, Luigi & Ian Roberts (1989). 'Complex inversion in French', *Probus* 1: 1–30.

Rizzi, Luigi & Ur Shlonsky (2006). 'Satisfying the Subject Criterion by a non subject: English Locative Inversion and Heavy NP Shift', in M. Frascarelli (ed.), *Phases of Interpretation*, Berlin: Mouton, 341–61.

Rizzi, Luigi & Ur Shlonsky (2007). 'Strategies of Subject Extraction', in H.-M. Gärtner & U. Sauerland (eds), *Interfaces + Recursion = Language? Chomsky's Minimalism and the View from Syntax-Semantics*. Berlin: Mouton de Gruyter, 115–60.

Roberts, Ian (1993). *Verbs and Diachronic Syntax: A Comparative History of English and French*. Dordrecht: Kluwer.

Roberts, Ian (2007). *Diachronic Syntax*. Oxford: Oxford University Press.

Roberts, Ian (2010a). 'A Deletion Analysis of Null Subjects', in T. Biberauer, A. Holmberg, I. Roberts, & M. Sheenan (eds.), *Parametric Variation: Null Subjects in Minimalist Theory*. Cambridge: Cambridge University Press, 58–87.

Roberts, Ian (2010b). *Agreement and Head Movement: Clitics, Incorporation, and Defective Goals*. Cambridge, MA: MIT Press.

Roberts, Ian (2010c). 'On the nature of syntactic parameters: A programme for research', presented at the 2010 Mayfest on 'Bridging Typology and Acquisition'.

Roberts, Ian (2012). 'Macroparameters and minimalism: A programme for comparative research', in C. Galves, S. Cyrino, R. Lopes, F. Sandalo, & J. Avelar (eds), *Parameter Theory and Linguistic Change*. Oxford: Oxford University Press, 320–35.

Roberts, Ian & Anders Holmberg (2005). 'On the role of parameters in Universal Grammar: A reply to Newmeyer', in Broekhuis et al. (eds), *Organizing Grammar*. Berlin/New York: Mouton de Gruyter, 538–53.

Roberts, Ian & Anders Holmberg (2010). 'Introduction: Parameters in a minimalist theory', in T. Biberauer, A. Holmberg, I. Roberts, & M. Sheehan (eds), *Parametric Variation: Null Subjects in Minimalist Theory*. Cambridge: Cambridge University Press, 1–57.

Roberts, Ian & Anna Roussou (2003). *Syntactic Change: A Minimalist Approach to Grammaticalization*. Cambridge: Cambridge University Press.

Rohlfs, Gerhard (1968). *Grammatica storica della lingua italiana e dei suoi dialetti. Vol. II: Morfologia*. Torino: Einaudi.

Rooth, M. (1985). 'Association with focus', PhD thesis, GLSA, University of Massachusetts, Amherst.

Rooth, M. (1992). 'A Theory of Focus Interpretation', *Natural Language Semantics* 1: 75–116.

Ross, J. R. (1967). '*Constraints on Variables in Syntax*', PhD thesis, MIT.

Rothstein, Susan (2004). *Structuring Events: A Study in the Semantics of Lexical Aspect.* Oxford: Blackwell.

Rude, Noel (1986). 'Topicality, transitivity, and the direct object in Nez Perce', *International Journal of American Linguistics* 52: 124–53.

Rude, Noel (1988). 'Ergative, passive, and antipassive in Nez Perce', in M. Shibatani (ed.), *Passive and Voice.* Amsterdam: John Benjamins, 547–60.

Rudin, Catherine (1988). 'On multiple questions and multiple WH fronting', *Natural Language and Linguistic Theory* 6: 445–502.

Ruwet, Nicolas (1982). *Grammaire des insultes et autres études.* Paris: Editions du Seuil.

Sakas, William G. & Janet D. Fodor (2001). 'The structural triggers learner', in S. Bertolo (ed.), *Language Acquisition and Learnability.* Cambridge: Cambridge University Press, 172–233.

Sallaberry, Etienne (1978). *Ene sinestea.* Itxaropena: Zarautz.

Salvi, G. (2005). 'Some firm points on Latin word order: The left periphery', in K. É. Kiss (ed.), *Universal Grammar in the Reconstruction of Ancient Languages.* The Hague: Mouton de Gruyter, 429–56.

Samuels, B. (2009). 'The structure of phonological theory', PhD dissertation, Harvard University.

Samuels, B. (2011). *Phonological Architecture: A Biolinguistic Perspective.* Oxford: Oxford University Press.

SAND I. See Barbiers et al. 2005.

SAND II. See Barbiers, Sjef, J. van der Auwera, H. Bennis, G. De Vogelaer, & M. Devos (2008).

Shlonsky, Ur (2009). 'Hebrew as a partial null-subject language', *Studia Linguistica* 63: 133–57.

Sigurðsson, Halldór Á. (2003). 'The Silence Principle', in L.-O. Delsing, C. Falk, G. Josefsson, & H. Sigurðsson (eds), *Grammar in Focus, Festschrift for Christer Platzack 18 November 2003, Vol. 2.* Lund: Wallin & Dalholm, 325–34.

Sigurðsson, Halldór Á. (2004). 'The Syntax of Person, tense, and speech features', *Rivista di Linguistica/Italian Journal of Linguistics* 16: 219–51.

Sigurðsson, Halldór Á. (2009). 'Remarks on features', in K. Grohman (ed.), *Explorations of Phase Theory: Features and Arguments.* Berlin: Mouton de Gruyter, 21–52.

Sigurðsson, Halldór Á. (2011a). 'On UG and materialization', *Linguistic Analysis* 37: 367–88.

Sigurðsson, Halldór Á. (2011b). 'Uniformity and diversity: A minimalist perspective', *Linguistic Variation* 11: 189–222.

Smith, Jennifer (2000). 'Synchrony and diachrony in the evolution of English: Evidence from Scotland', PhD thesis, University of York.

Smith, Jennifer, Mercedes Durham, & Liane Fortune (2007). '"Mam, my trousers is fa'in doon!": Community, caregiver, and child in the acquisition of variation in a Scottish dialect', *Language Variation and Change,* 19: 63–99.

Smith, N. & A. Law (2009). *On Parametric (and Non-Parametric) Variation, Biolinguistics* 3: 332–43.

Snyder, W. (1995). 'Language acquisition and language variation: The role of morphology', PhD dissertation, MIT.

Snyder, W. (2001). 'On the nature of syntactic variation: Evidence from complex predicates and complex word-formation', *Language* 77: 324–42.

Snyder, W. (2002). 'Parameters: The View from Child Language', in Y. Otsu (ed.) *Proceedings of the Third Tokyo Conference on Psycholinguistics*. Tokyo: Hituzi Shobo, 27–44.

Sobin, N. (2002). 'The Comp-trace effect, the adverb effect and minimal CP', *Journal of Linguistics* 38: 527–60.

Son, M. (2006). 'Directed Motion and Non-Predicative Path P', *Working Papers on Language and Linguistics*, Nordlyd: Tromsø, 176–99.

Speas, Margaret (2006). 'Economy, agreement, and the representation of null arguments', in P. Ackema, P. Brandt, M. Schoorlemmer, & F. Weerman (eds), *Arguments and Agreement*. Oxford: Oxford University Press, 35–75.

Sportiche, D. (1981). 'Bounding Nodes in French', *The Linguistic Review* 1: 219–46.

Sportiche, D. (2013). 'Binding Theory: Structure sensitivity of referential dependencies', *Lingua* 130: 187–208.

Starke, Michal (2001). '*Move Dissolves into Merge. A Theory of Locality*', PhD dissertation, University of Geneva.

Starke, Michal (2002). 'The day syntax ate morphology', class taught at the EGG summer school, Novi Sad.

Starke, Michal (2006). Nanoseminar, class taught at the University of Tromsø.

Starke, Michal (2009). 'Nanosyntax: A short primer to a new approach to language', in P. Svenonius, G. Ramchand, M. Starke, & K. T Taraldsen (eds): *Nordlyd* 36.1, and available at <http://ling.auf.net/lingbuzz/001230>.

Stechow, A. von (1991). 'Focussing and backgrounding operators', in W. Abraham (ed.), *Discourse Particles*. Amsterdam/Philadelphia: John Benjamins, 37–84.

Sudhoff, S. (2010). *Focus Particles in German*. Amsterdam/Philadelphia: John Benjamins.

Suñer Margarita (2003). 'The Lexical Preverbal Subject in a Romance Null Subject Language: Where Art Thou?', in R. Nunez-Cedeño, L. López, & R. Cameron (eds), *A Romance Perspective in Language Knowledge and Use: Selected Papers from the 31st Linguistic Symposium on Romance Languages* (LSRL). Amsterdam: Benjamins, 341–57.

Svenonius, Peter (2006). 'The emergence of axial parts', in P. Svenonius & M. Pantcheva (eds), *Working Papers in Linguistics*, 33–1. Special issue on adpositions, Nordlyd: Tromsø, 49–77.

Svenonius, Peter (2008a). 'Spatial P in English', MS, CASTL, University of Tromsø.

Svenonius, Peter (2008b). 'The position of adjectives and other phrasal modifiers in the decomposition of DP', in L. McNally & C. Kennedy (eds), *Adjectives and Adverbs: Syntax, Semantics, and Discourse*. Oxford: Oxford University Press, 16–42.

Svenonius, Peter (2012). 'Spanning', available at <http://ling.auf.net/lingbuzz/001501>.

Szabolcsi, A. (2005). 'Strong vs. Weak Islands', in M. Everaert & H. van Riemsdijk (eds), *The Blackwell Companion to Syntax*, Vol. IV. Oxford/New York: Wiley-Blackwell.

Tai, J. H.- Y. (1984). 'Verbs and Times in Chinese: Vendler's Four Categories' in D. Testen, V. Mishra, & J. Drogo (eds), *Papers from the Parasession on Lexical Semantics*. Chicago Linguistic Society, 289–96.

Taraldsen, Knut T. (1978). 'On the NIC, Vacuous Application and the That-Trace Filter', Bloomington, Indiana University Linguistics Club.

Taraldsen, Knut T. (1986). 'Som and the Binding Theory' in L. Hellan & K. K. Christensen (eds), *Topics in Scandinavian Syntax*. Dordrecht: Reidel.

Tomasello, M. (2000). 'Do young children have adult syntactic competence?' *Cognition 74*: 209–53.

Tomasello, M. (2003). *Constructing a language: A Usage-based Theory of Language Acquisition.* Cambridge, MA: Harvard University Press.

Tomasello, M., N. Akhtar, K. Dodson, & L. Rekau (1997). 'Differential productivity in young children's use of nouns and verbs', *Journal of Child Language 24*: 373–87.

Torrego, Esther (1984). 'On Inversion in Spanish and Some of its Effects', *Linguistic Inquiry 15*: 103–53.

Torrego, Esther (2002). 'Aspect in the Prepositional System of Romance', in D. Cresti, T. Satterfield, & C. Tortora (eds), *Current Issues in Linguistic Theory. Selected Papers from the XXIX Linguistic Symposium of Romance Languages.* Amsterdam: John Benjamins, 326–46.

Tortora, Christina & Marcel den Dikken (2010). 'Subject agreement variation. Support for the configurational approach', *Lingua 120*: 1089–1108.

Trask, R. Lawrence (1995). 'On the history of the non-finite verb-forms in Basque', in J. I. Hualde, J. A. Lakarra, & R. L. Trask (eds), *Towards a History of the Basque language.* Amsterdam: John Benjamins, 207–34.

Troberg, Michelle (2008). 'Dynamic Two-place Indirect Verbs in French: A Synchronic and Diachronic Study in Variation and Change of Valence', PhD dissertation, University of Toronto.

Uriagereka, Juan (1999). 'Minimal restrictions on Basque movements', *Natural Language and Linguistic Theory 17* (2): 403–44.

Uriagereka, Juan (2008). *Syntactic Anchors.* Cambridge: Cambridge University Press.

Valian, Virginia (1991). 'Syntactic subjects in the early speech of American and Italian children', *Cognition 40*: 21–81.

Vandeloise, Claude (1986). *L'espace en français.* Paris: Éditions du Seuil.

Vanelli, Laura (1984). 'Pronomi e fenomeni di prostesi vocalica nei dialetti italiani settentrionali', *Revue de linguistique romane 48*: 281–95.

Vanelli, Laura (1987). 'I pronomi soggetto nei dialetti italiani settentrionali dal Medio Evo ad oggi', *Medioevo Romanzo 12*: 173-211.

Vecchiato, Sara (2000). 'The *ti/tu* interrogative morpheme in Québec French', *GG@G—Generative Grammar in Geneva 1*:141–64.

Vicente, Luis (2007). *The Syntax of Heads and Phrases: A Study of Verb (Phrase) Fronting.* LOT PhD Dissertation 154, Leiden University.

Vilkuna, Maria. (1995). 'Discourse configurationality in Finnish', in K. É. Kiss (ed.), *Discourse Configurational Languages.* Oxford: Oxford University Press, 244–68.

Vinokurova, Nadezhda (2005). 'Lexical categories and argument structure: A study with reference to Sakha', PhD dissertation, University of Utrecht.

Wang, Q., D. Lillo-Martin, C. Best, & A. Levitt (1992). 'Null subject vs. null object: Some evidence from the acquisition of Chinese and English', *Language Acquisition 2*: 221–54.

Webelhuth, G. (1992). *Principles and Parameters of Syntactic Saturation.* Oxford: Oxford University Press.

Weiß, H. (2008). 'The Possessor that Appears Twice: Variation, Structure and Function of Possessive Doubling in German', in S. Barbiers, O. Koeneman, M. Lekakou, & M. van der Ham (eds), *Microvariation in Syntactic Doubling.* Bingley: Emerald, 353–402.

West-Eberhard, M. J. (2003). *Developmental Plasticity and Evolution*. Oxford: Oxford University Press.

Wexler, K. (1998). 'Very early parameter setting and the Unique Checking Constraint: A new explanation of the optional infinitive stage', *Lingua* 106: 23–79.

Williams, Edwin (2003). *Representation Theory*. Cambridge, MA: MIT Press.

Willson, Stephen (1996). 'Verb agreement and case marking in Burushaski', *Work Papers of the Summer Institute of Linguistics North Dakota* 40: 1–71.

Woolford, Ellen (2006). 'Lexical case, inherent Case, and argument structure', *Linguistic Inquiry* 37: 111–30.

Xu, Fei (2010). 'Count nouns, sortal concepts, and the nature of early words', in J. Pelletier (ed.), *Kinds, Things, and Stuff: New Directions in Cognitive Science, Vol. 13*. Oxford: Oxford University Press, 191–206.

Yang, C. (2002). *Knowledge and Learning in Natural Language*. Oxford: Oxford University Press.

Yang, C. (2004). 'Universal Grammar, statistics or both?', *Trends in Cognitive Sciences* 8: 451–6.

Yang, C. (2010). 'Three factors in language acquisition', *Lingua* 120: 1160–77.

Yang, C. & T. Roeper (2011). 'Minimalism and language acquisition', in C. Boeckx (ed.), *Oxford Handbook of Linguistic Minimalism*. Oxford: Oxford University Press, 551–73.

Yu-Ying Su, Julia (2009). Inner Aspect in Mandarin Chinese, available at <http://ling.auf.net/lingbuzz/000895>.

Zamparelli, Roberto (2000). *Layers in the Determiner Phrase*. New York: Garland.

Zanuttini, R. (1997). *Negation and Clausal Structure: A Comparative Study of Romance Languages*. New York/Oxford: Oxford University Press.

Zimmermann, Malte (2004a). 'Zum wohl: Diskurspartikeln als Satztypmodifikatoren', *Linguistische Berichte* 199: 1–35.

Zimmermann, Malte (2004b). 'Discourse particles in the Left Periphery', *ZAS Papers in Linguistics* 35(2): 543–66.

Zubizarreta, Maria Luisa (2001). 'The Constraint on Preverbal Subjects in Romance Interrogatives', in A. Hulk & J.-Y.Pollock (eds), *Subject Positions in Romance and the Theory of Universal Grammar*. Oxford: Oxford University Press, 183–204.

Zwarts, Joost (2005). 'Prepositional Aspect and the Algebra of Paths', *Linguistics and Philosophy* 28: 739–79.

Index of languages and dialects

Index of subjects